INTERVIEWS

Gerald Matt

INTERVIEWS

Gerald Matt

KUNSTHALLE wien

Verlag der Buchhandlung Walther König, Köln

for Sebastian von Mayreck

Content

Vorwort

*Linear texts have played only a passing role in the existence of mankind,
"history" was only an interlude, and we are presently in the process of a
return to "normal" forms of life, such as two-dimensionality, the imaginary,
the magical and the mythical.*

Vilém Flusser, Ins Universum der technischen Bilder, Göttingen 1989, p. 9

The following interviews are selected from a larger number of conversations with artists in the course of my recent curatorial and art publishing activities. Over several years, I was able, in most cases, to observe these artists' work through repeated personal encounters and as they passed through the international exhibition circuits. Some of the artists went on to participate in different exhibitions that I curated.

"The artist is the primordial cell of the exhibitions-, communications- and distribution-structures of the model that is art – but it is ultimately carried by other persons, who hitch themselves up in front of, or parallel to, this system", writes Christoph Tannert, co-editor of the *Men in Black: Handbook of Curatorial Practice*. Here, he refers to the "know-it-all curator and exhibitions organiser … who is in a position to either overload the art objects with an intellectual patina or to sink them at will." Besides us, evermore frenzied curators, may, as we wildly chase after recognitions and distinctions, on occasion no longer see the forest for the trees; the artists themselves must be given a public square or dialogue platform to oppose hermeneutical and institutional constraints. In my opinion, the interview is an especially suitable form of balanced communication between originator and distributor, because the artist directly provides information. "The right to tell a story is more than a mere linguistic act", states the philosopher Homi K. Babha. In this sense, we, as trustees, should let the originators of art do more of the talking, as opposed to forcing the art to fit in with our own narratives' framework.

In the conversations assembled here, the artists, in a manner that is at once involved and eloquent, ironical and critical, whimsical and arch, refute the cliché of the speechless visual artist, whose language finds an outlet solely in the work itself. The conversations also demonstrate that artistic articulation and the artist's medium cannot be separated. To add another voice in this context, the dedicated Hamburg collector, Harald Falckenberg, has noted in his book, *Ziviler Ungehorsam. Kunst im Klartext*: "The task must be to protect and, where it is necessary, to recover, the specific quality, the stubbornness of art. Young art must not close its eyes to new techniques and new media, to social problems and questions of economic theory. But it should accomplish its forays into new realms by the means of art."

Just how such boundaries are overstepped by artful means is illustrated very clearly in the following conversations. Even if I did not intend to propagate particular artists or artistic directions in this selection, the question remains if there is a common denominator joining their work and guiding my decisions. I would like to answer in a twofold way, incorporating my own personal views on the one hand and generally recognisable common features, on the other hand.

For me there is, first of all, the fascination emanating from the visual power of images that is strong enough to prevail against the tide of visual signs in our "pictorial society", a power, which does not merely command our attention for a short term, but is capable of inscribing images into our minds.

Beyond that, there is the power to unsettle current conventions of the present day, a power that causes other ways of seeing or even new perspectives to be set free in the viewer. Both these aspects are joined together, as I see it, in numerous works of the artists speaking to us here. It may be as different as the language of their images and the concepts or intentions embedded in their work.

What generally recognisable sympathies can be detected in the works of these fourteen artists, all of whom, incidentally, belong to the generation, as I do myself, of today's 30 to 50-year-olds?

Some of the general tendencies of art production in the "Age of Digitalisation" can be seen here, such as the use of different media with an emphasis on film and video. Digitalisation refers to a repatriation of all production into computerised operations, with a levelling of the differences of material texture through the computer as equaliser. Vilém Flusser wrote in 1989:

> The telematised people will deny their bodies; ... they will all be swept away by the gravitational pull of telematisation, by a gambling frenzy. The objective world, by being denied, will dissolve on the horizon of the telematic person. He or she will be, in a sense of the word as yet unsuspected by us, 'unconditional', and thus free in the sense that we employ when we say that the spirit is free to wander wherever it pleases. It is a matter of a freedom as granted by drugs, a freedom of denying the objective world, the world of conditions, of things. A psychedelic freedom. Technical pictures are psychedelic ones (*Ins Universum der technischen Bilder,* p. 118).

To what extent, then, have we come closer, in our time, to this vision? The artists interviewed here have few traces left of the direct relationship to, or fixation with, the materials, which marked earlier generations. They are characterised by the fugitive, evanescent elements, which exemplify the appearance and disappearance of technical pictures on the screen. They switch their media, using, according to their needs, the photograph and the video, then the panel and installation, then the sculpture or performance. The so-called "signature", which was so often demanded of the artist, has now been dispersed across a number of different media. The hand of the artist no longer articulates itself in a certain brush-stroke or a distinct form of the lighting, but in a subjective assemblage/bricolage. Personality is seen as a wandering, nomad-like spirit, which attempts to operate with the media and through the media, a self-expression within its own dissemination.

Nevertheless, in terms of a dialectical reversal occurring parallel to the dematerialisation process, a new trend towards object-like wholes can be discerned – albeit filtered through the experience of digital fleetingness.

Many younger artists have tired of volatile parades of pixelated images and have become enraptured by textures and material surfaces and the multifarious shapes of natural phenomena and civilisational residue. Thus, Aidas Bareikis enjoys operating as a chaos practitioner, who transforms inferior materials such as household trash and defective children's toys into assemblages of rubbish

presented in clinically clean gallery spaces, creating virtual favelas, secular voo-
doo altars, and installations on the verge of self-dissolution.

Tony Matelli, an all-purpose provocateur on various levels of art production,
caused hyper-real looking weeds, as part of one of his exhibitions, to sprout all
over the corners of Kunsthalle Wien's project space. The point here was not so
much to encourage a "return to nature", as to highlight the erosion of the civi-
lised and domesticated worlds we inhabit, undermined, as they are, by uncontrollable vegetative proliferations.

Michael Lin, in turn, creates extraordinary spatial atmospherics with the help of
floral patterns, intense colour saturations and discrete intermediate shades. His
intention, says the artist, is to create "provisional locations" rather than "further
remarkable zones", where the emptiness of the exhibition space is linked ideologically and in terms of practical living with the idea of a social space – a space
open to discourse, participation, as well chilling in a temporary party zone.

Another tendency, which is reflected in this volume of interviews, is the inclusion of the narrative element, of the small, and frequently also rather personal
story. The telling and inventing of stories – for a long time suspected of being
the disease carrier for ideologies – has become de rigueur again. In the construction of one's own stories or one's own histories, there can be found a moment of
self-assurance, aimed at counter-balancing the loss of major social utopianism.
These histories possess both local and global colour. They frequently originate
within one's own cultural and geographical area, yet become processed through
the channels of global communications where they are subjected to variations,
enrichments and embellishments in the course of their journey through the networks and permutations of an artistic consciousness, which draws its intensities
from a physical and likewise virtual nomadic existence. These are the stories of
our contemporaries who are witness to our time, and who are subjected to existential ordeals as they get caught up in the tensions between global experience
through worldwide communications and a reflexive recollection of regionalism,
between the dialectic of physical limitations and virtual infinity. Stories and histories become a kind of material at one's disposal; something that can be re-
adjusted to artistic consciousness ever anew, like garments at a fitting, or body
extensions for the completion of fluctuating personalities.
    Private mythologies employed as a fabric can receive nourishment from the
artists' own lives. In the case of Tracey Moffatt, for example, the myths of the
Aboriginal Nations and the experience of their own social position balanced
against the sociology of white Australia, has given her work its ideological departure point; while for both Shirin Neshat and Kimsooja it was the experience of
two separate cultures. Matthew Barney's individual mythologies derive their
power from the American dream, from cinematic history and classic mythology
as much as from the iconography of popular culture. Travelling, too, offers mate-

rial for private mythologies, as gliding in and out of different milieus and cultures becomes a major theme. Travel and the nomadic life style are understood as an attempt to bracket the world together, as a measure against the loss of a "real" world, by shifting the artistic world into the digital sphere.

Here again we encounter the principles of assemblage and bricolage, whose first conscious appearance we witnessed in the area of music production. But this "technique" begins to manifest itself in the realm of art, following the successful "struggle of the sixties against the normative pressure of ultra-modernism" (Huyssen/Scherpe), as early as the 1970s. "The situation in the seventies was … marked by a wide-ranging dissemination of artistic processes, which all cannibalised the remains of the avant-garde and modernism, plundering its vocabulary while plugging it with pictures and motives from pre-modernism or simply non-modern cultures." (Huyssen/Scherpe, (Eds.) *Postmoderne – Zeichen eines kulturellen Wandels*, Hamburg 1986, p. 24.)

In the intervening years that debate has subsided, as contemporary artists have learned to switch – metaphorically speaking – with elegance and transparent ease between the ivory towers and the inner cities, creating the grammars of their expressive desires from ephemeral found pieces, biographical memory fragments and highly individualised archival research. "Heating up" artefacts, which have been decomposing in the lofts of oblivion, is a favourite strategy of subverting the dictates of innovation.

The artists presented here belong – like myself – to a generation that was socialised through films, television and popular music. The clarification of history and cultural signs resulted in a re-energising process of archival spirits, particularly the archives of popular culture. Media transmitted the ideology, as well as the ideological critiques, of ultra-modernist codification. We were able, from this position, to launch questions, but had no answers to give. Ellen Cantor speaks of the possibility that today everyone can set up their own personal cosmology – that after the collapse of the ideological framework of religion and morality, a kind of ideal utopian freedom can now be obtained; while at the same time the sense of security, of a clear identity, has faded.

What has emerged, however, is a new awareness of politics. After a long time of being blamed for its lacklustre attitude towards the political sphere, contemporary art is now once again expressing opinions and seeking confrontations – sometimes explicitly, as seen in the work of provocative artists like Santiago Sierra and Teresa Margolles or Anri Sala, who keeps investigating the relationship between the individual and society in an ever-changing series of laboratory situations.

But it is no longer the art of Agitprop. There are no ideological camps, just a probing of the uncharted spaces of new attitudes of resistance. This may often give a pre-verbal expression to existential possibilities within a world that would seem to find its ultimate rationale in the identification of target markets and in the formatting of product lines. Such political works devote their energies to cultural comparisons, to the conditions of workers in the Third World, to the anti-globalisation movements....

Beyond that, groups such as assume vivid astro focus are also indicators of a newfound love for collective production. The old ideals of the 1960s, hoping to multiply creativity by pooling artistic energies and to bury the concept of the master artist by encouraging the democratic participation of the many in the process of design and configuration, fell fallow in the 1980s and 90s during the era of solipsism and aesthetic navel gazing. Now, under the conditions of globalisation and the intercontinental networks, collectivism has once again appeared on the agenda. This is equally true of open-ended systems such as those of assume vivid astro focus, who have always invited local activists to participate in their installative works, or the artistic partnerships following the principles of Platonic dialogues as in the case of Deutschbauer/Spring or a creative agency like Chicks on Speed. Apart from the musical nucleus of Chicks on Speed, the four women members of this electronic pop band are also active as filmmakers, organiser-producers of happenings and curators of pop compilations that celebrate female creativity. In addition, the women act as networking nodules, as points of energy, where the most diverse creative currents, ranging from fabric design to poster art, converge.

The interviews gathered together in this volume, therefore, attempt to provide a panoramic overview of contemporary artistic production modes without demystifying the aesthetic puzzle with hasty answers. The point here is not to exhibit shut and dried views of the world but to sketch open systems that admit some space for continuing discourse. Allow yourself to be carried forward by the flow of words without expecting exhaustive help for your life. Entirely in keeping with the motto that Raymond Pettibon wrote on one of his drawings: "Whatever you are looking for, you won't find it here."

Gerald Matt
Director Kunsthalle Wien

Dank

My thanks go out to all the artists for the openness and directness of their participation in these conversations as well as their willingness to be involved in the preparation of the interviews for publication. They invested often lengthy portions of time and energy into this project. My thanks also go to Angela Stief, project manager, who was of invaluable assistance to me personally in researching and preparing the interviews. I am also grateful to Lucas Gehrmann, Thomas Miessgang, Sigrid Mittersteiner and again Angela Stief, with whom I jointly carried out some of the interviews and who assisted me in editing the final copy. And our joint thanks are due, once again, to our graphic designer, Dieter Auracher, for all his work and the felicitous and appealing book design.

Eduardo Aparicio

If you know Cuba, you know the 20th century.

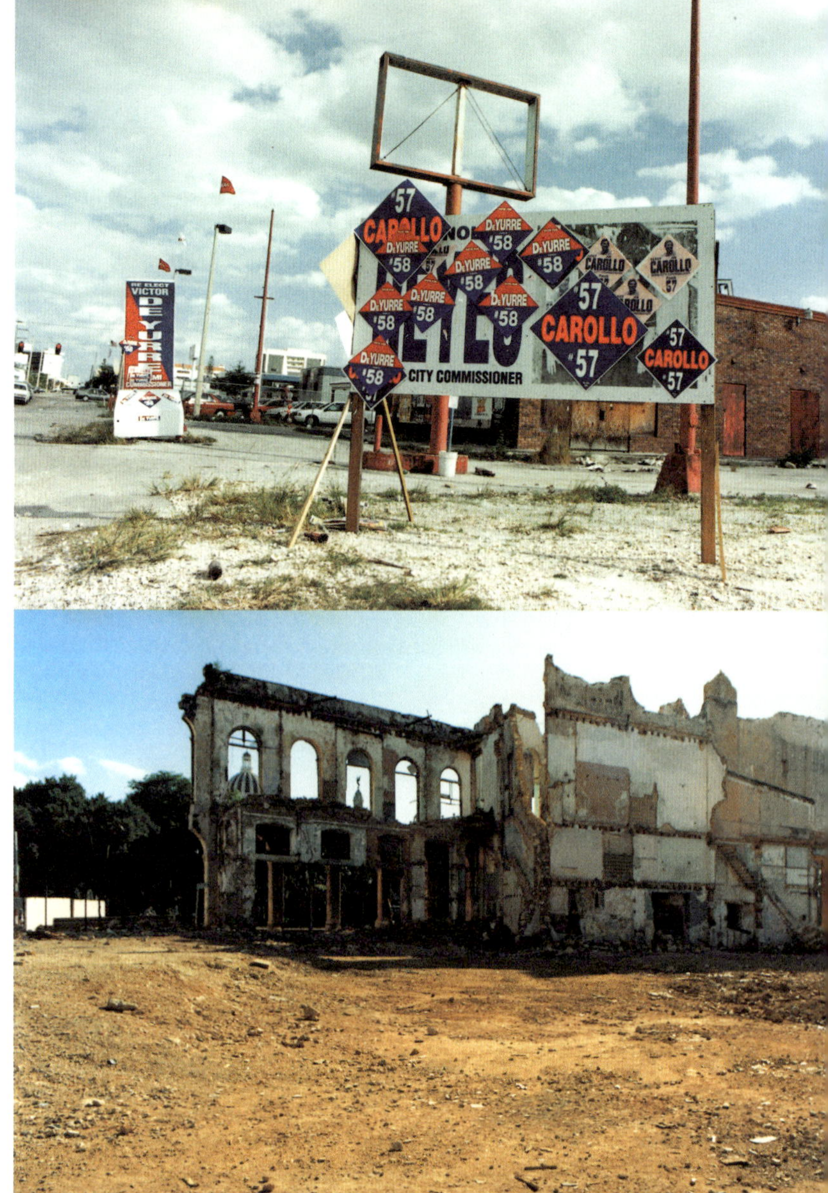

Eduardo Aparicio,
Elecciónes, 1994

In your portfolio *Fragmentos de narraciones cubanas* (Fragments from Cuban Narratives), a series of portraits – photographs and statements – of Cubans living in the US, which you made in 1994, the year you settled down in Miami, you say: "A camera is … a tool for observation and investigation." In your series *Entre Miami y La Habana* (Between Miami and Havana), which is presented in the Vienna exhibition, you combine pictures from Cuba with pictures from the Miami/Florida area. In both places you investigated national Cuban signs and symbols, such as the Cuban flag, the picture of Che, the map of Cuba … It is not easy to ascertain the place where the photographs were taken at first glance – was it Havana or was it Miami?

If "observation and investigation" are linked with documentation and documentation with reality, you apparently intend to show at least two possible realities. What is your definition of documentation in connection with photography and "reality"?

There are numerous photographers, mostly European, and a few from the US, that have been documenting Cuba over the last few years, both its cities and its landscape. Their luscious photographs fill the pages of book after book, all beautifully laid out and printed in large format, intended for anyone's coffee-table. That's what I understand to be the current trend in documentary photography about Cuba.

My approach is not documentation but intervention. I am not a documentary photographer, but an interventionist. There is an official, dominant discourse about Cuban reality both in Cuba and in the US and my work aims at challenging this official discourse through a visual intervention. My work offers an alternative vision of what the dominant discourse makes us believe.

Though the official discourse about Cuba in Cuba might seem to be the exact opposite of the dominant discourse about Cuba in the US, these two discourses do have much in common, they are really two sides of the same coin. Echoing each other, they constitute one single dominant discourse that makes us believe that Cuba and Miami are irreconcilable realities, with the good guys on one side and the bad guys on the other, with happiness on one side and unhappiness on the other, with success on one side and failure on the other. My work seeks to contradict that version by offering a corrective to the polarized vision that dominates the debate about Cuba.

In order to counter that official version, I resort to the strategies that would seem most convincing to the viewer, such as using the conventions of documentary photography. I am not interested in documentary photography as such. I approach a photographic project as a kind of essay, not a photo-essay in the tradition of US news magazines, but in the older, literary sense of the term: a simple composition, raising issues about a single topic from a personal point of view without pretending to offer complete answers. In that sense, my photographic projects present a thesis, they raise a question, not offering an answer but an alternative way of seeing, and the images are my selected evidence.

Such was the case with *Fragmentos de narraciones cubanas*, a series which presents a multiplicity of voices as an alternative to the dominant discourse in order to undermine it. This also holds true for *Entre Miami y La Habana* most people would expect a series of diptychs about Cuba and Miami that present contrasts between two irreconcilable realities. I show equivalent realities instead. It is a reality of eroded, tired-out national fetishes and a misplaced cult of maleness as power. While Cuban culture is alive and thriving in the visual arts, in music, literature and multidisciplinary research, the project of a Cuban nation, which originated in the 19th century, is a big failure. In order to hide that failure, Cubans both in Cuba and in the US have invented a triumphalist discourse that is repeated ad nauseam. I think my diptych *Triunfos* (Triumphs) makes this evident. "Triunfo" is nothing more than a pawn shop in Miami where you can bring your jewellery to exchange for a small amount of quick cash. And 'Triunfo – Sabor Coco' ('Triumph – Coconut Flavor') is nothing more than a candy bar that might momentarily sweeten your palate at a government-owned dollar store in Cuba, a candy bar you may find next to various items with the image of Che Guevara that are nothing more than pathetic trinkets for sale.

You do want to create an image, then, which is more adequate to reality, more truthful, by confronting distorted self-images or projections with the other reality. Therefore, it isn't actually you but rather the onlooker that produces the corrected, more adequate image. This is why your "interventions" call for someone with detailed knowledge of the cultural and historical background on an issue. If you present your works now outside the world they originated in, for example in Central Europe, in Vienna, the people there will certainly produce their own "intermediate images" which frustrate the enlightening aspect that is certainly important to you – and all the more important to you because you, as the author and editor of a periodical, fight for certain interests and rights, for those of homosexual people, for example.
I would like to ask whether it is more important for you that your works come up to your sociopolitical intentions or that they evoke something new, some other reality in the eyes of the people that look at them.

The evocative and the sociopolitical are not mutually exclusive. In fact, I think good art will always be both, like Goya's *Desastres de la guerra* or Picasso's *Guernica*. If nothing else, art must, at the very least, be reflective.

The diptychs of Havana and Miami are connected with my experience of migration and exile, with living a life in two places at the same time: here and there. They are about the invention of a personal space that defies conventional mapping methods. They are about weaving in and out of familiar and unfamiliar territory, of taming the unknown by transferring or projecting onto it what's familiar. These diptychs point to a kind of ambivalent space, a space that's neither here nor there – and that is precisely the space I inhabit.

In a larger sense, my experience of exile and rupture is related to that of millions of people. These diptychs of Havana and Miami are not just about those two specific places. They are also related to the forces that determine such ruptures, the forces of ideology. Obviously, the reading of any photograph will depend on the viewer's prior knowledge. But I don't think a European viewer looking at the diptych of José Martí for instance needs to know who Martí was to understand it as a reflection on ideology. In fact, I actually think that such reading would most likely be the most immediate approach for a European viewer. The man carrying that big placard of Martí down a street in Miami cannot even see where he's going. The history that he is supposedly so proud to carry becomes a burden and an obstacle. Meanwhile, at the small Martí memorial in Cuba, one of those small memorials made of concrete which are ubiquitous there, the words on the book have been eroded by time. Cult is thus being made of a man whose words are neglected. Ideology is an elusive topic. The Martí diptych offers an ambivalent play, reflecting no doubt the value of Martí's legacy, but also a certain anxiety about the cult of ideologues.

What about the narrative element in your series? Don't the symbols and written signs in many of your pictures and the common subject tell a story, or also tell one? Is the concept of narration important in regard to your conviction that we should create our reality ourselves?

Photography is a language. So is visual culture. The symbols and the written signs are like parts of a puzzle, like sentences with blanks the viewer has to fill in. The symbols need to be deciphered, decoded. They don't really have a meaning of their own. They only have meaning within the context they originate in and within the context of the viewer's reading. Some diptychs offer two sets of incomplete analogies, like this is to A what X is to B. Others offer two sets of analogies with a question mark: Is this to A what that is to B? Looking at *En nosotros está* which means "It's in us" or "It's with us", the key words are "victoria" (victory) in Cuba and "libre" (free) in Miami. These two key words have become fetishes within their original contexts in the Marxist sense of the term. Victory and freedom have been enshrined as concepts to be revered, far from their practical meaning in daily life. I also consider them fetishized in the Freudian sense, since the true pleasure that could be derived from a genuine victory or a genuine sense of freedom has been transformed into a kind of neurotic, obsessive repetition of those words which provides no real satisfaction. The overuse of "victoria" is clearly a cover-up for failure. The overuse of "libre" is clearly a cover-up for not feeling free at all. In fact, Miami is a city where even a newspaper stand has to be chained down to a post, where we cover the doors and windows of our homes with all sorts of iron grids to protect ourselves against theft, which means that we end up making ourselves live behind bars all the time, and in constant fear. There is not much sense of real freedom in our daily lives, yet the local media are constantly bombarding us with claims of freedom: "libre" is the most overused word in Cuban Miami; so is "victoria" in Cuba. The area surrounding that sign in Havana and the look on the faces of the people walking on the street do not spell victory. "Victoria" and "libre" are two different masks for a common failure.

These diptychs attempt to mark the point where the dominant discourse, the so-called master script, and the personal narrative contradicting it intersect. Why is personal narrative important? The dominant discourse suppresses personal narrative. In the series *Fragmentos de narraciones cubanas* the idea was to give voice to personal narrative. I firmly believe that breaking one's silence is a most effective way of chipping away at the distortions imposed by dominant discourses, an effective strategy for undermining their power.

What are the differences and parallels between the way you work and the film medium, especially regarding the constitution of reality and the aspect of staging things – some of your works, above all those combined to make a diptych, seem to be based on some form of mise-en-scène. What about this?

It is funny you should ask. I started studying film in Chicago at the same time as photography. I felt a stronger call from photography. Before that, my background was in linguistics and literature. At one point I thought I wanted to be a screenwriter. My first film project was an adaptation of William Saroyan's *The Daring Young Man on the Flying Trapeze*.

And yes, I absolutely love setting things up in a studio or, better yet, creating tableaux with same-gender couples in ordinary domestic settings in their homes. The idea of using a real place to create a fiction, which is, at the same time, rooted in the reality of that place fills me with enthusiasm, gets my creative juices flowing. The last set of photographs I showed at the Espacio Aglutinador consisted of triptychs of Cuban gay couples in Miami in the most ordinary situations at home: doing the dishes, vacuuming the floor, fixing dinner – all in patriotic red, white and blue.

Again, a constant concern of mine is to say: wait a minute, there are other stories happening here, other stories that we never hear about, here they are. And of course they are presented as evidence, using the generally accepted strategies of documentary photography, but yes, they are set up.

Now, I should say they are not set up in a rigid way, instead I try to work in the same way filmmakers do if they use improvisation: you create a situation, there is no script, except for a general description of a theme, and you let your people do the rest. I am a big, big fan of Italian neo-realism.

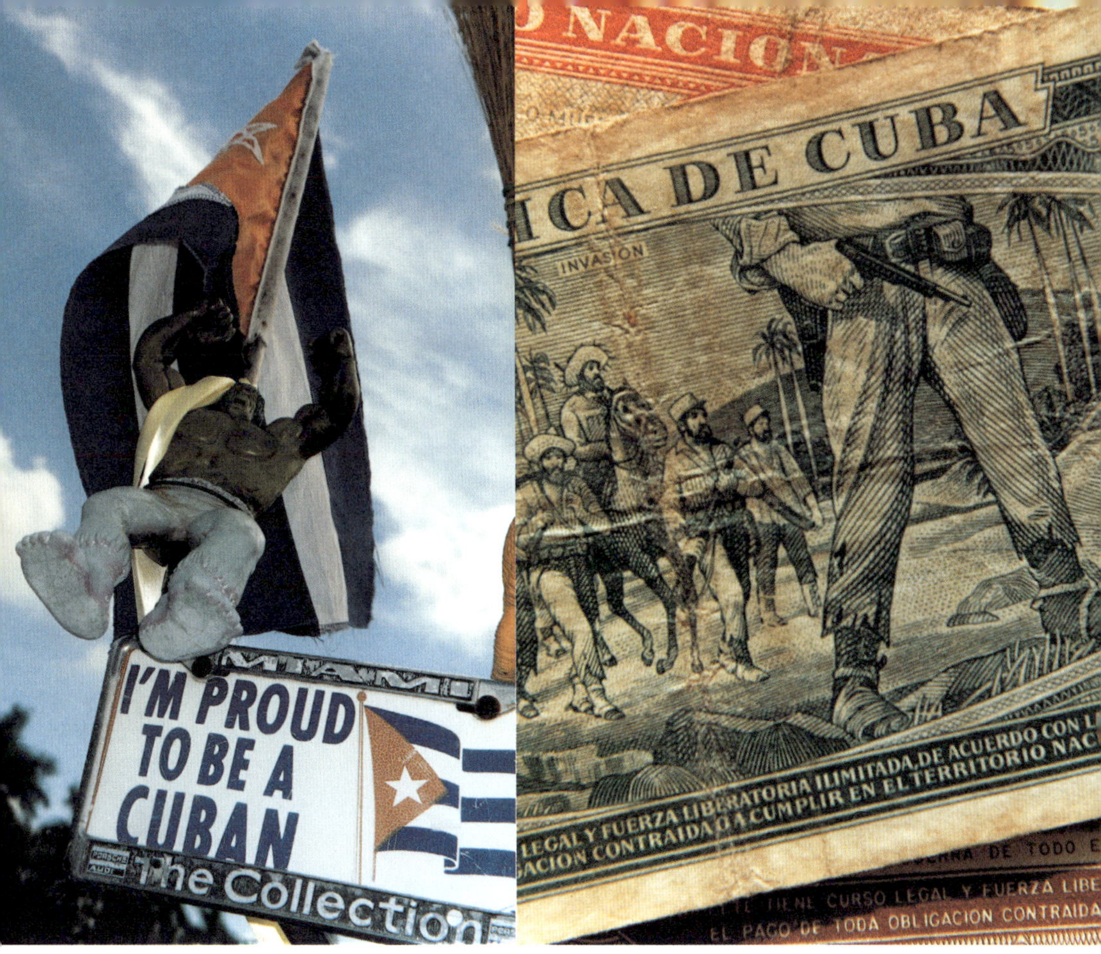

Eduardo Aparicio,
Masculinidad y Nación,
1995

And I love melodrama! So it should be no surprise that I am a big admirer of Fassbinder's work. Now, that may all sound like a very odd mixture of tastes. However, I think something very important that Fassbinder did was to intertwine or rather show the interconnectedness between national identity, sexual identity and personal drama, which I call personal narrative. My photographic work aspires to do that: mixing the macropolitical and the micropolitical. That is what I want my photographs to do – but not just mix them, but show their interconnectedness, and yes, challenge the top from the bottom.

The same way that Fassbinder's Germany could serve as a metaphor for a whole cluster of contemporary social and political issues, my work about Cuba can be a metaphor, I think. Though Cuba may be perceived as a marginal reality by many, what's happened to us in the last hundred years is at the very core of the twentieth century. Doctors used to say that if you knew tuberculosis, you knew medicine. Today they say that if you know AIDS, you know medicine. I'd say, if you know Cuba, you know the 20th century.

You left Cuba in 1969. In an interview with Coco Fusco you mentioned that you frequently meet with Cuban artists of the so-called eighties-generation, who left the island in the early nineties escaping a wave of censorship and a debilitated economy. While you sometimes come to Cuba to show your work there, they don't. What about the reactions regarding your work in Cuba, in the US and on the part of the artists who emigrated – are there any remarkable differences?

I have been very well received in Cuba both by fellow artists and by the public. I find people and other artists very eager to know what it is like to be a Cuban living in the US. I shun the label Cuban-American. I have a long list of Cuban writers, musicians, painters who have produced core works about Cuban identity from a position of exile. *Cecilia Valdés*, the quintessential nineteenth century Cuban novel of manners, was published by Cirilio Villaverde while in exile in New York. Martí himself lived most of his life outside of Cuba. His *Versos libres*, much influenced by Walt Whitman and used as lyrics in the song *Guantanamera*, were written during his fourteen years' stay in New York City. Wifredo Lam produced most of his work in France. Many of the musicians who have made Cuban music popular around the world throughout the 20th century have done it from outside Cuba (Pérez Prado with his mambo in Mexico, Ernesto Lecuona in New York in the forties and fifties, and Celia Cruz since 1959). I have never heard anyone refer to Wifredo Lam as a Franco-Cuban artist. So why should anyone call me a Cuban-American artist?

One of my greatest moments of joy was to welcome a group of Cuban artists who came to the US on a three months' fellowship last year. Sandra Ceballos, the director of the Espacio Aglutinador, was among them. The project was organized with Ernesto Pujol as advisor. As you know, Ernesto is a Cuban artist based in New York, and Sandra lives in Cuba.

I feel a great bond of love, friendship and professional respect for Sandra and for Ernesto. I am thrilled whenever we get to work together or exhibit together. I believe each touches the same nerve in his own way. I think that our work is connected beyond any differences.

Eduardo Aparicio in conversation with Gerald Matt in 1999 on the occasion of the exhibition *Kuba – Landkarten der Sehnsucht* at Kunsthalle Wien.
Eduardo Aparicio was born in Guanabacoa, Cuba in 1956. He lives and works in Miami, Florida.

assume vivid astro focus

To some extent, collectiveness and anonymity are also ways of questioning notions, such as, biography, intention, inspiration, responsibility, and copyright.

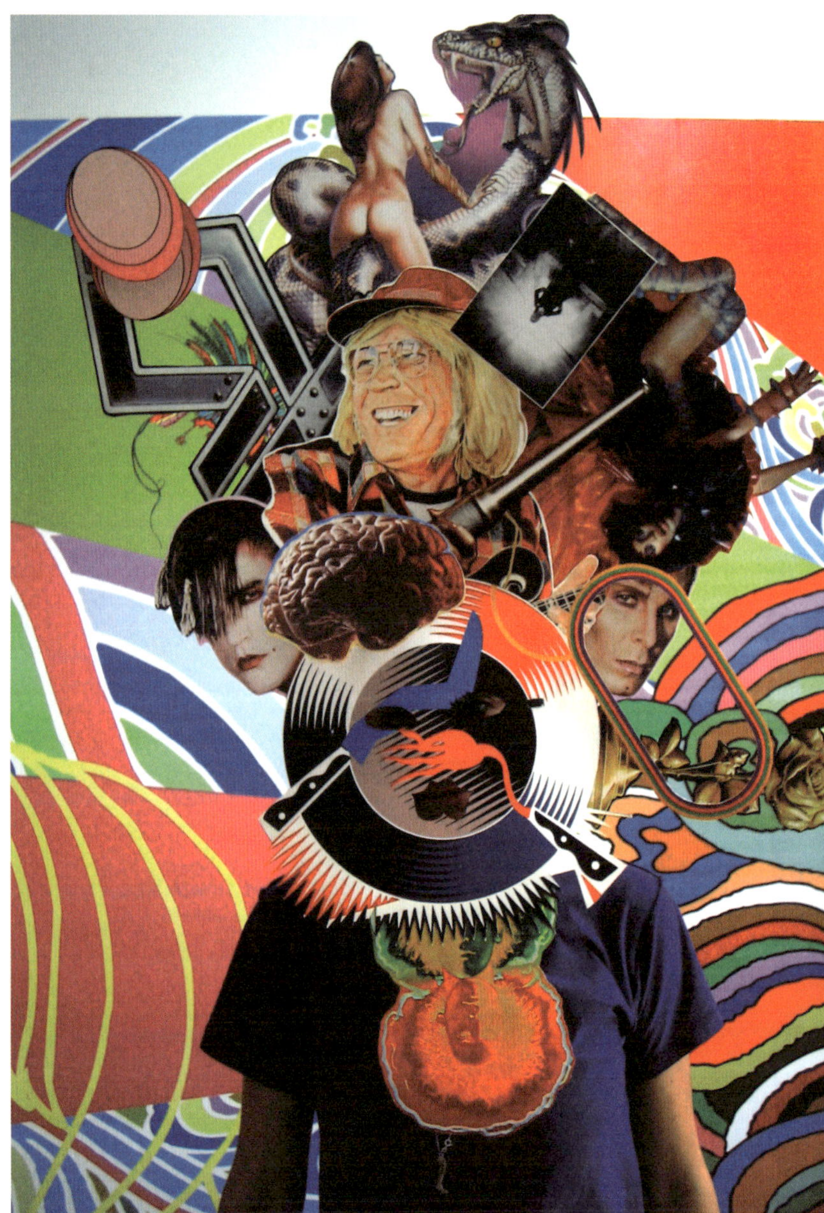

avaf self portrait

I assume that it is most correct to address you in the plural (instead of the singular). Will the answers to my questions be joint answers, or will you take turns speaking? Does one of you speak for everyone?

We will all bring in our insights to form one written voice. It may be that just one of us talk, or it may be a combination of our voices, depending on the question.

How does decision-making work in a collective? Can everything actually be discussed and always resolved with consensus?

It's less about consensus, than about trust and admiration. We trust one another and admire one another's visions. Sometimes, one of us brings up an idea that is contrary to what the others were thinking, but it is accepted out of admiration anyway. That presents us with new roads and ways of seeing the work. We are not control freaks and, in fact, we like change and challenges. There is no mastermind who tells the others what we will go for. So, whenever we are faced with a decision, we either go for the most reasonable option, or for the change—what we haven't done yet. As the work is composed of so many different layers, there is room for various decisions.

Particularly in the 20th century, the role of the author was heavily discussed. Post-structuralists, such as Michel Foucault or Roland Barthes, even announced the death of the author, and thereby – as it were – generated the birth of the reader. With a multiple authorship, does the accent shift from an over-powerful author in favor of the recipient?

We truly wish that was true. We think that this shift is a bit more complicated than just questioning authorship. It is also related to the way the institutions usually work. Our projects are particularly affected by this relationship, because whatever we bring to a space, we make specifically for it. There is a lot of self-censorship and paranoia concerning lawsuits from the institution nowadays, which end up shaping artists' projects in many ways. In fact, the biggest challenge for us is always the institution, which constantly poses obstacles whenever we want to shift the power to the recipient. We are frequently asked to rearrange/change our ideas. It's not that we put a finished and self-contained painting in the space and just hang it up.

What we do is closely related to the relationship with the institution and its space. We see its best and its worse sides. And what is interesting about this is that there is some sort of history that is never talked about. There is no outlet for these raw ideas reshaped by the institution. We also feel disconnected from the press, which is another big challenge for us. The press always refers to you through comparison to a recent past, and it can never neutralize itself from history. It's as if the past is always necessary to understand the present.

We would like to challenge writers and critics to refrain from relating an artist to any past, and to talk about the work from a present point of view. We feel that these relations to the past are easy and create a biased approach to your work. For this reason, the new is never seen. And this oppressive relation, to both the institution and the press, ends up shaping the way the viewer experiences your work.

But to stress your point, our *butch queen realness with a twist in pastel colors* video program is, indeed, closely related to empowering the viewer. Probably, the main reason for creating *bqrwtpc* is to share knowledge. Knowledge is power, power for creating and directing your own life. *bqrwtpc* offers a comment on the inaccessibility of these video pieces. TV programs, like *Soul Train*, or music videos by people like Klaus Nomi were never released on video, or have been out of print for many years. A good section of this program is based on our ongoing Internet-based research to find bootleg copies of these materials through ebay, yahoo groups, and on-line community and discussion groups. So, we are presenting our own research, a research that is, in fact, available to all viewers. You just need Internet access. In this way, we expect to bring knowledge to the public and entice them to do their own research on the material they feel most connected with.

To some extent, collectiveness and anonymity are also ways of questioning notions, such as, biography, intention, inspiration, responsibility, and copyright.

Where does the name assume vivid astro focus come from? What is assume vivid astro focus's history? How long have you existed?

avaf should always be referred to in lower case. One of our members was once taken aback by a guy named ASTRO, a make-up artist who lives in New York. At first, we were fascinated by the broad range of usage and mass media connections to the name ASTRO: astroboy, astrology, astroturf, astronaut, astroflight, astromovers. We were already looking for a new pseudonym at the time, and thought ASTRO would be a good project name for us. Then, another early incarnation was *superastrolab*, but that was too much like the band Stereolab, and it was too hip. We wanted something that would be harder to remember and definitely something long, a name like *Exploding Plastic Inevitable*. We also wanted a name that didn't have any cutesy meaning when abbreviated.

Around that same time, there was this record cover show at Exit Art in New York called *Cover Me*, which we had all visited and loved. It was more than just the cover designs and images: we were also intrigued by the words, the band names, and the album titles. We decided to go back to the show and write down every single word that would appeal to us with no reference to where it came from, so we could completely disconnect the word from its origin. That's when avaf was born, sometime around mid-2001. A few years later, a friend gave us a book on Throbbing Gristle (TG) and we were able to track down the possible roots of two of the words we chose to use.

TG's collection of rare tracks was entitled Assume Power Focus. Music is, indeed, a symbol for our activities. avaf then became NOT an entity, NOT a character, but a project name. We wanted to use a pseudonym (which we all had used before in different ways and places), so people could focus on the work and not on our personalities. We are not interested in the whole star fuckers scene. We want to live a simple life and hang out with simple people like us. We want to be contaminated by other people. We want to have friends. We believe in generosity and equality, in sharing and inclusiveness.

How many people are in the collective varies according to the projects we are involved with. For that reason, there is no sense in showing our faces, and that's why we always wear masks. And, by the way, we want to have different pseudonyms for each different project we produce. We recently started doing this with *absorb viral attack fantasy*. The next one will be: *a very anxious feeling* and *alucinete vadia arregaça o foco*.

How do you decide on your selection of motifs for your wallpaper?

The decision-making process varies. The wallpapers are a compilation of elements we call "decals", elements we work with at a specific time. First, a few words on the "decals". Our idea is that whoever purchases them would ultimately be able to create their own wallpaper by combining different elements. These people can also print these "decals" on whatever substrate or in whatever size they want to. The "decals" can be applied to Plexiglas, foam, Xerox, paper mask, a t-shirt, a puzzle, a print, or simply a sticker. We believe that no one is better than the collector to decide on the substrate they should be printed. In this way, the collector also has some power over the work, as he can manufacture it according to the dialogs he/she would like to establish with other pieces in his/her collection. If the display of his collection is based on, let's say sculptures, he/she can produce the "decal" in a more sculptural manner. That's his/her choice.

But, to come back to your question. Regarding the *Tom Cruising* wallpaper series, for instance, we wanted to develop a wallpaper to wrap the interior of our installation at the MOCA L.A. for this show called *Ecstasy*, curated by Paul Schimmel. We spent two months living in L.A. One of our concerns for this show was to bring gay politics into the work. We were disgusted by recent news of a teenage gay couple hung in Iran, and by the extreme right-wing promotion for rallies against gay marriage and "sodomy" in the States. We wanted to talk about freedom and repression. In L.A., we were also constantly bombarded by news on Tom Cruise, his fundamentalist Scientology faith, and the assumptions he is a closeted gay man. We also wanted to pay a tribute to groups like the Cockettes – a performance group from late '60s, early '70s based in San Francisco – composed mostly of bearded gay guys who would cross-dress and live in a community. Based on this, we decided to create this iconic figure, *Tom Cruising*, a Tom Cruise gone drag as the centerpiece of the wallpaper and environment. At the same time, this installation was a homage to the history of clubs and dance music and their close relationship to the birth of gays rights, at least in America.

Clubs were not simply hedonistic heavens, but spaces for unity within that community. We were also fascinated by pictures of contortionists and the weird sexuality that they emanate. Then we decided to compile images of contortionists from the Internet and make drawings of them in different positions, and we made them all bearded and hairy.

We created this one figure, The Hair Cutter, a symbol, for us, for the repression of hair within gay culture – mostly American – usually spread through gay porn where models are shaved head to toe. Based on this, we made drawings of all these hairy guys with sections of their bodies shaved, as if a result of a confrontation with the Hair Cutter. We added a noose to the design of *Tom Cruising I* (the wallpaper title) to relate to the two Iranian guys that were beaten and hung in public. We started compiling images of protest graffiti against Bush that we found on the street and made drawings of them as well. Bush was also added to the wallpaper with canned beans being poured on his head to show the state of his brain.

We are usually interested in the local graffiti of the cities we go to, and always take tons of pix of them. L.A. has a very interesting street wall drawings/graffiti scene. Some of these graffiti and wall drawing were incorporated in *Tom Cruising I*. We are very interested in artists, like Antonio Lopez and General Idea, and images related to their works also became part of *TC I*. But at the same time, the wallpaper is not created just as a piece in itself, but as a comment on a given space. Its design and proportions are determined by the dimensions of the first wall it was ever exhibited on, by the way the viewer comes into the space we are working with, by the other elements that are part of the installation, and by existing architectural elements, such as, doorways and columns. So, its conception and choice of elements is also determined by architecture.

Technically, how are the wallpapers made?

Most wallpapers we make start with drawings on acetate that are scanned, cleaned up, and sharpened in Photoshop. These elements are then turned into vectors, and we color them in Illustrator, where we also work on compositing the wallpaper piece. As a vector file, the wallpaper is free from the constraints of pixel-based works. Once turned into vector, a work can be blown up to whatever size without losing resolution. Some other wallpapers

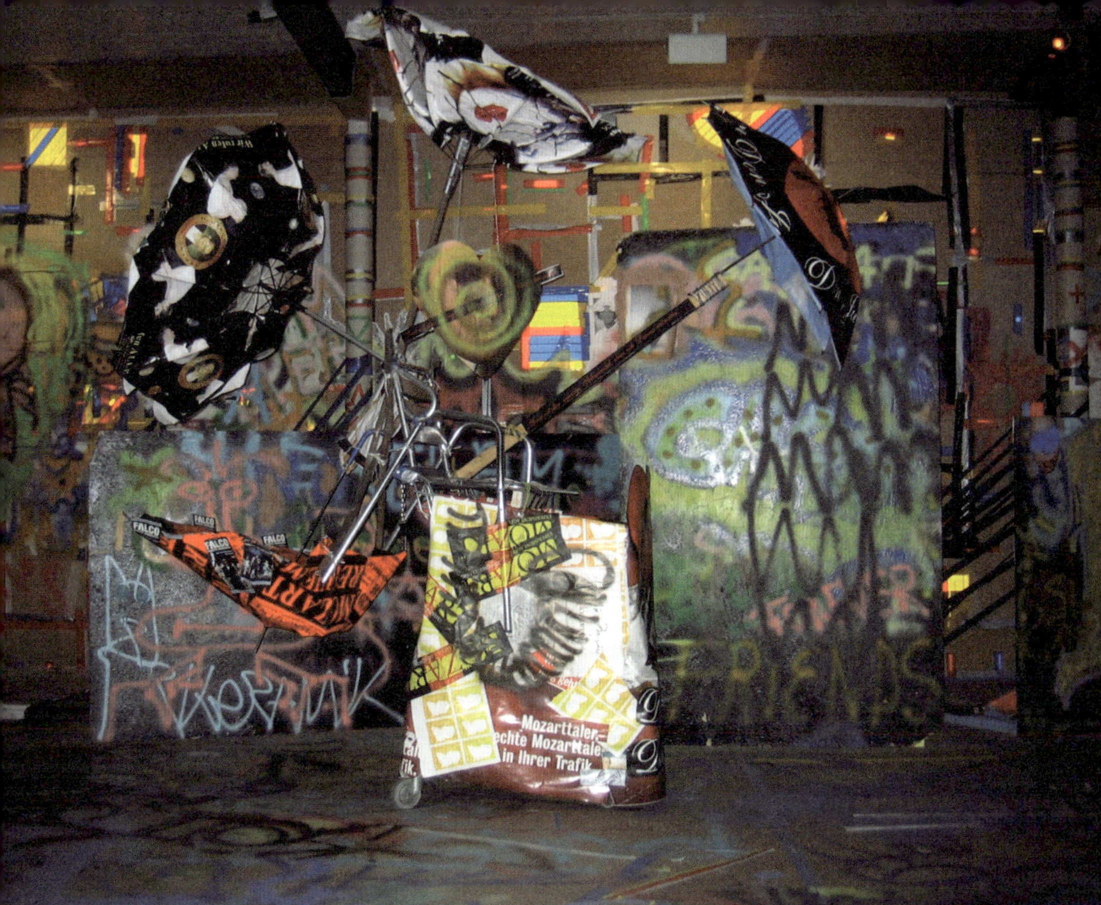

Installation view, Kunsthalle Wien 2006: assume vivid astro focus, *OPEN CALL*

are Photoshop files, and are a mixture of appropriated and original imagery mixed with vector elements. Once ready, the wallpaper file is sent to an office that produces billboards or giant digital prints.

We call them wallpapers, but they are in fact vinyl prints, they are not paper strictu sensu. We started making what we call "wallpapers," because of Felix Gonzales-Torres billboard pieces, and in fact we see them more as landscapes rather than as actual wallpaper. There is no repeated motif (with the exception of the first wallpaper we ever produced), and it's not sold in rolls.

Could you please explain your artistic concept for the project space of the Kunsthalle Wien? The barricading of the space or the windows is a practice that you already realized in a similar way in your last exhibition in Japan.

Well, first we had to deal with the budget limitations your institution presented us, and the huge space we were given. That is a dichotomy we usually face when dealing with institutions. They have little money, but big spaces and want something that is popular and that will please and attract their public. Generally our projects are expensive, because we deal with existing spaces and their given dimensions. There are also so many different layers in our installations. One important characteristic of avaf projects, though, is that they are not entirely high-tech. We like to have a rough edge to the installations we produce. We like to deal with technology, but don't want to be sleek at all. We want to show how technology is accessible in the western world we live in, and how it can be used as tool of expression and creativity.

Through dealing with smaller budgets, we realized it was a great opportunity to make this rough edge even more evident in the work and to juxtapose it to the faux sleekness of our wallpapers. In this way, we can somehow bring our wallpapers back to the origin of the real media they come from (billboard prints).

At the same time, a great source of inspiration, as we said before, is graffiti street culture. There is some sort of empowerment in this activity that relates to the way we see our work. Also, a city like New York has been in a serious process of gentrification, and many neighborhoods are completely changing; whole blocks of older buildings are being torn down to make room for yuppie high rises and hotels. In this transitional moment of change, barricades of cheap/reused/trashed plywood panels are put up to conceal these construction sites—they should, in fact, be called destruction sites. The local community usually reacts to them with graffiti and plastering them with posters and slogans. At the same time, these reused plywood panels are reminiscences of other destruction sites and the reaction of other communities. We felt that having such a central space in the city of Vienna, we somehow needed to offer it back to the public and transform the Kunsthalle into a raw space that could be overtaken by local artists, musicians, performers, and students. Just as if we were squatting the Kunsthalle, or as if it had been sacked. That's when we proposed the space to work on an open-call basis for the local community to transform it either into a space of performance or protest. We expect people to graffiti on top of our works, put up announcements of their own events, bring their friends to play music together, or just have a beer and watch the *bqrwtpc* video program.

You create all-encompassing art works. In your shows, alongside architectonic interventions and wallpapers, there are often music and film/video programs. How did this situation arise?

The wallpapers are one of the tools we use to involve the viewer in a conceptual/sensorial experience. For us, one important element in our projects is to create a space, through installation, in which many layers of ideas and actions are possible. We see the installation as a space of diversity and multiplicity. Our wallpapers were always conceived according to the space given to us, and since the very beginning, there has been some degree of public participation. Because the wallpapers were (are) always related to a specific space, architecture gradually became more and more present in the work.

From that moment on, it was only natural to provide a space and/or performance that would envelop and activate the viewer. It is a process whereby the viewer – artwork relationship is altered or even reversed in some way: instead of the viewer looking at a wall, we wanted a wall to literally absorb the viewer – and the most obvious way to achieve this was for the picture to acquire its missing third dimension, i.e. to evolve from a two-dimension piece to a three-dimension entity: by either "giving birth" to free-standing sculptures or by becoming a sculpture itself. A fourth dimension, time, is rendered, for instance, through inflated balloons that expire within a few days, through one-shot performances on the day of the opening, and, of course, through the fact that some pieces are destroyed after each show.

Thoughts about architecture bring us closer to the viewer. The public needs to be the master of architecture and to mold it according to their needs and dreams. Our growing relationship to architecture has made avaf projects even more ephemeral. A lot of our installations are simply destroyed after the show comes down. We are also really interested in this reminiscence, in this memory of space.

Femininity plays a major role in your work; there is Carla, the reference figure and muse, then there are repeated allusions to and portrayals of female genitalia, porn queens, and naked women...

We would rather call it "hyper femininity". In reality, most of the feminine images we use in our projects are, in fact, transgender images. We are interested in the concept of hyper realness and the legendary, intrinsic to vogue communities in the States (in fact the *bqrwtpc* video program's name is a combination of different categories from vogue ball competitions and are a homage to them. The video program is punctuated by scenes of vogue ball competitions). These communities mostly consist of non-privileged gay African-Americans and Latinos. As Guy Trebay expressed well in his article *Legends of the Ball: Paris is Still Burning*: "Among the ball children, there is no greater honorific than 'legendary' a status for which no fixed standard exists. A legend might be a man or a woman or a transgendered person or a butch dyke or a femme queen. A legend might be a brilliant voguer or somebody whose cross-sex impersonations inspire awe. Once attained, legendary status is never revocable. That legends are invisible to the eyes of the larger world causes no great concern at the balls, where they not only live on but are forged anew." (*The Village Voice*, January 12–18 2000).

We are interested in the creation of this legendary muse, some sort of a contemporary archetype of Hyper Femininity, an explosion of sexuality that transgender people impersonate so well. At the same time, transgendered persons are on the edges of society and are subject to many cultural taboos and criminalization. So, the symbols of Hyper Feminism we use in our works are also symbols of transgression for us.

You issue long *to do lists*. Your works include references to pop and high culture. In a certain way, you are also collectors. Your works demand a great deal of research. Are there archives where you file your knowledge and document your ideas?

Our *to do lists* are one example of these files. We make *to do lists* everyday, lists of production we need to follow for a certain show, lists of people we need to thank for helping us and gifts to be sent to them, friends we need to call, things somebody else told us we should look at or listen to, etc. We used to release *to do lists* statements related to shows we were working on. These lists/statements were a compilation of different daily *to do lists* from previous months. We are obsessed with information and we want to share this information. The *TDLs* also serve as a guide for things we examine and research and, in a way, they offer that knowledge to the viewer and work in a similar way to that of the *bqrwtpc* video program. We are indeed avid collectors, but our collections grow inside a certain project we are working on.

At times, we can collect images of home improvement, for instance, but then move on to collect picture discs, heavy metal magazines, or homemade DVDs documenting different vogue balls in America. These collections are always according to a specific project we are working on. For instance, in 2004, we were developing a series of collaborations with L.A. band/artist duo Los Super Elegantes. We collaborated on a song and wanted to release a picture disc with it. Then, we decided to start collecting picture discs and bidding on them on ebay. In a few months, we had a nice small archive of old picture discs that served us as database of what people had done with that media in the past.

Nevertheless, the idea of making a picture disc with LSE was never realized, so we ended up transforming the picture discs into paper masks that we wore at the opening of another avaf project for Miami collector Rosa de la Cruz. Since we wanted to keep our anonymity in such a heavy-handed art world event, we decided to distribute the masks to conceal people's faces and our own at the party.

Intentions inside our projects (like the collection urge) mutate according to situations and opportunities and turn into other ideas. That is closely related to the way we approach knowledge. For us, the thread of knowledge is infinite, and our necessity for it is never completely fulfilled. And we want to share that with the public, to somehow spread our obsession to the viewer.

I know your sources of inspiration are very diverse. Are there any artists you are particularly interested in at the moment?

This is a tough question. Our interest in other people's work varies a lot over time, and it also varies according to the projects we are working with.

In the past, our interest has shifted from Öyvind Fahlström to Ed Ruscha, Ettore Sottsass to Kenny Scharf, Urs Fischer to Vaginal Davis. General Idea seems to be the one inspiration that has accompanied us for the longest time. We still, in fact, want to work with them in the near future (or at least with AA Bronson, who is the only surviving member). We started doing that for our project for Rosa de la Cruz, when avaf were art advisors to her and made her buy GI's AIDS wallpaper piece from the 80s. The wallpaper was used as part of our installation for Rosa de la Cruz.

Vaginal is another artist we are still waiting for the perfect opportunity to work together with. We tried in the past, but the institution we were dealing with blocked it. Vaginal is very controversial on her own, and we think the museum was already filled with controversies surrounding our own project.

You counter the easy digestibility and user-friendliness of, one could almost say, an aesthetics that makes use of the surface with a thoroughly political approach, which precisely ventilates the lack of hierarchy in the production and reception of art. In your installation in MOCA, Bush and Pope Benedict XVI crop up...

We feel like this question was answered previously...

What are your projects and plans for the future?

We would like to keep on working on the *bqrwtpc* video program, to incorporate more and more materials from different sources, countries and eras, and make it at least one hundred hours long. We would like to concentrate on making music and just do that for a while and release a White Label (anonymous) picture disc album. We would like to work with dancers, AIDS activists, local communities, and protesters. Soon we will release the first avaf book for which we will be appropriating Maurizio Cattelan's *Permanent Food* magazine style and concept. Maybe we should also release a book of our proposals before they were edited/censored by the institutions.

avaf in conversation with Gerald Matt in the summer of 2006 on the occasion of the exhibition *assume vivid astro focus: OPEN CALL* at Kunsthalle Wien project space.
The members of assume vivid astro focus live and work at the most different places around the globe.

Aidas Bareikis

Painting is always on the surface, it is always a stretcher, it always hangs elevated in a particular spot, it is always a commodity, it is always self-important, and you are not allowed to deviate.

Aidas Bareikis

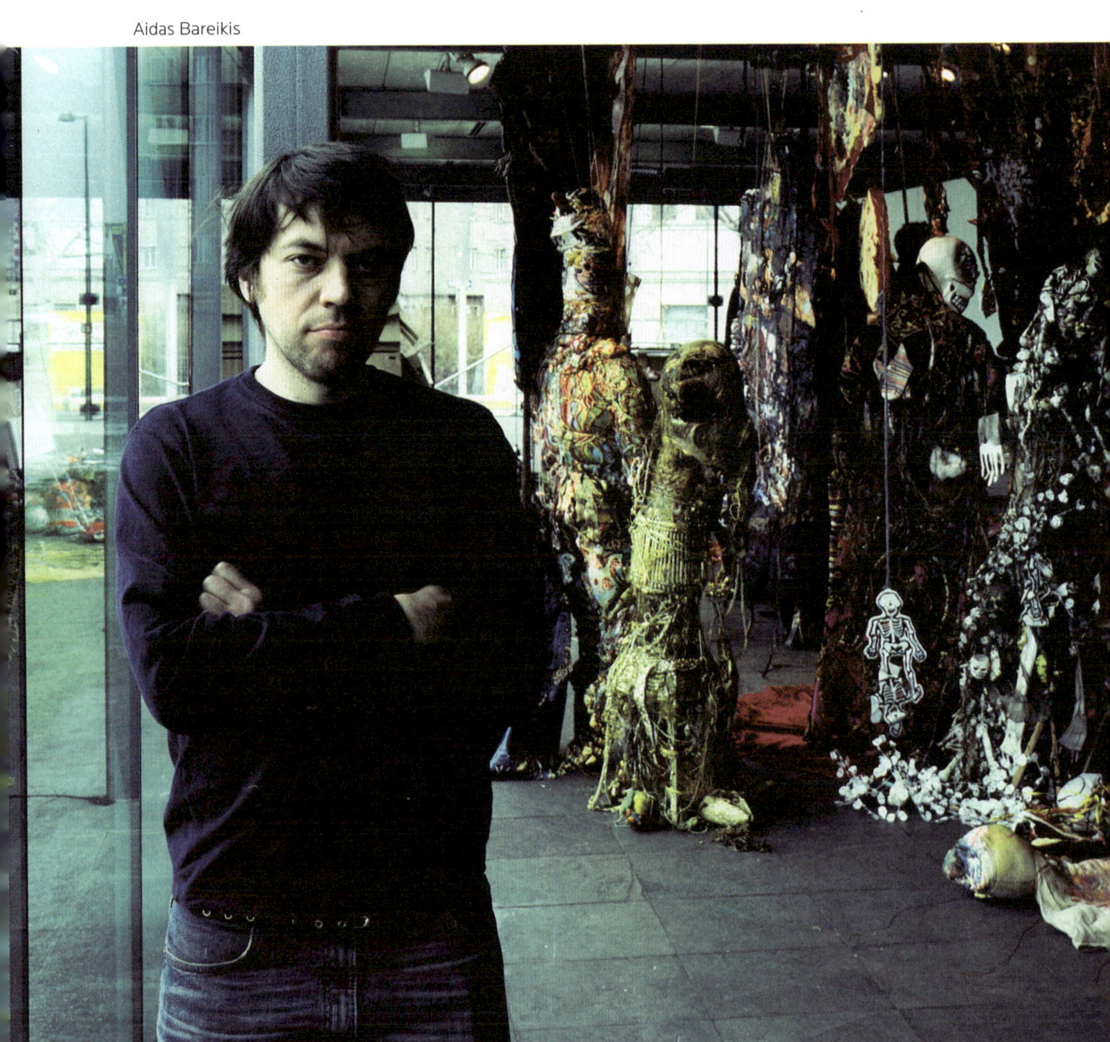

You were born in Vilnius in 1967 and spent your childhood and youth in the Soviet Union – in a state that collapsed when you were 23. Today, Lithuania is part of the European Union – and you live in New York. Where is home for you?

I come from an empire which supposedly "lost" the confrontation with another empire which supposedly "won" that confrontation. So many things to identify with (Europe, Eastern Europe, the United Force of International Immigrants, the Lithuanian Émigrés, the Post-Soviets, the Green Card American Wannabees)! This sounds incredibly cinematic, but the fact is that Vilnius is a blast and I live in Brooklyn at the moment.

Why did you leave Lithuania? Because New York was so interesting as an art place?

I actually wanted (and still want) to explore ideas.

And you thought you could not do this in Lithuania?

Not really, not at that time. Lithuania was slipping into this post-revolution stand-still vacuum. There was a point when I said to myself, "What's next? Look at yourself now, it is time to go … And where am I going? I am going to New York."

But you did not leave for economic reasons, you left because you thought New York was a more interesting place for your artistic career?

Well, I left – you know – for greed. And also because I had the possibility. I came with a Fulbright scholarship. I was busy burning bridges, coping with the cultural shock, taking English-classes 14 hours a day, getting lost in subways, going to college, and so on. So it was an unlucky situation which turned out to be a very good experience.

Did you work when you had the Fulbright scholarship?

Yes, I did construction and demolition jobs.

Demolition? This goes well with some of your later artworks. Did you work as an artist at that time?

Yes, these were the heydays of deconstructivism. I sort of tried to push just a little step further, towards absolute destruction, which turned out to have been a prophetic approach. What is going on now with cultural and ideological affairs and events is exactly that. Pure violence, rich, mysterious, and beautiful, under layers of hypocrisy and pretension.

That history continues to seethe beneath the surface seems to be a general aspect of your work. You collect set pieces and transform them into tableaux of orchestrated chaos. A child's bicycle, rubber boots, color pails, hoses, a leg prosthesis, scattered shoes, bloody rags, garbage – these are the essential ingredients of your work *Tomb of the Unknown Soldier* (2000). It is not the myth of the hero but the anonymous, filthy suffering that is left.

In its "badness," this was the most far-out piece I ever did. It turned out to be on the brink of "complete destruction." It was anti-art. Anyway, the *Tomb of the Unknown Soldier* with its intense symbolism and poetics of infinity and everything reminds me of things like the *axis mundi* or 3000 years of war or some kind of absolute statement which badly provokes such a fuck-up. My personal understanding that the celebration of a foot soldier's true heroism would be something like "everybody is in deep shit" certainly mattered too. So I thought of making a piece that looked like something in between a splash orgy and the aftermath of a suicide bomber … his is how history continues to seethe beneath the surface for me.

Ed Kienholz, who, taking a special pleasure in the bizarre and monstrous, relied on waste products for his tableaux (which you do too in a certain way) and loved to collect things, to roam flea markets searching for items which radiated some magic. Where do you get your material?

In terms of material, I try to be truthful to my geopolitical situation. Two examples: Nine years ago, I was evicted from my apartment by a police marshal. I was homeless. The same day, I won the Green Card Lottery. This scenario gave me the idea for a piece I called *You have 15 minutes to leave*, which I was going to realize as part of the Skowhegan Residency Program. (I was accepted soon after my eviction.) My prime interest in Skowhegan was to have a home and get a free lunch. So I went there with nothing, frankly, and started a massive shoplifting campaign, mainly at Wal-Mart, in order to get the things to produce the piece. The day for which the "Famous Visiting Artist Studio Visit" was scheduled, I got arrested by the county sheriff for shoplifting, and the whole thing resulted in a complete fiasco. Or, here is another: as a Fulbright student, I went to Hunter College and got into the Robert Morris class. With only little English, I worked for a demolition company on the side at that time; the crew was entirely Spanish speaking, and I got five bucks an hour. Based on my demolition experience, I made a piece called *Be Right Back*, the main part of which consisted of tiles I scraped from my studio floor. Because of my lack of English at that time, I understood almost nothing that Robert Morris had to say about the piece, but I think he was talking a lot about Hegel. So in terms of material, I

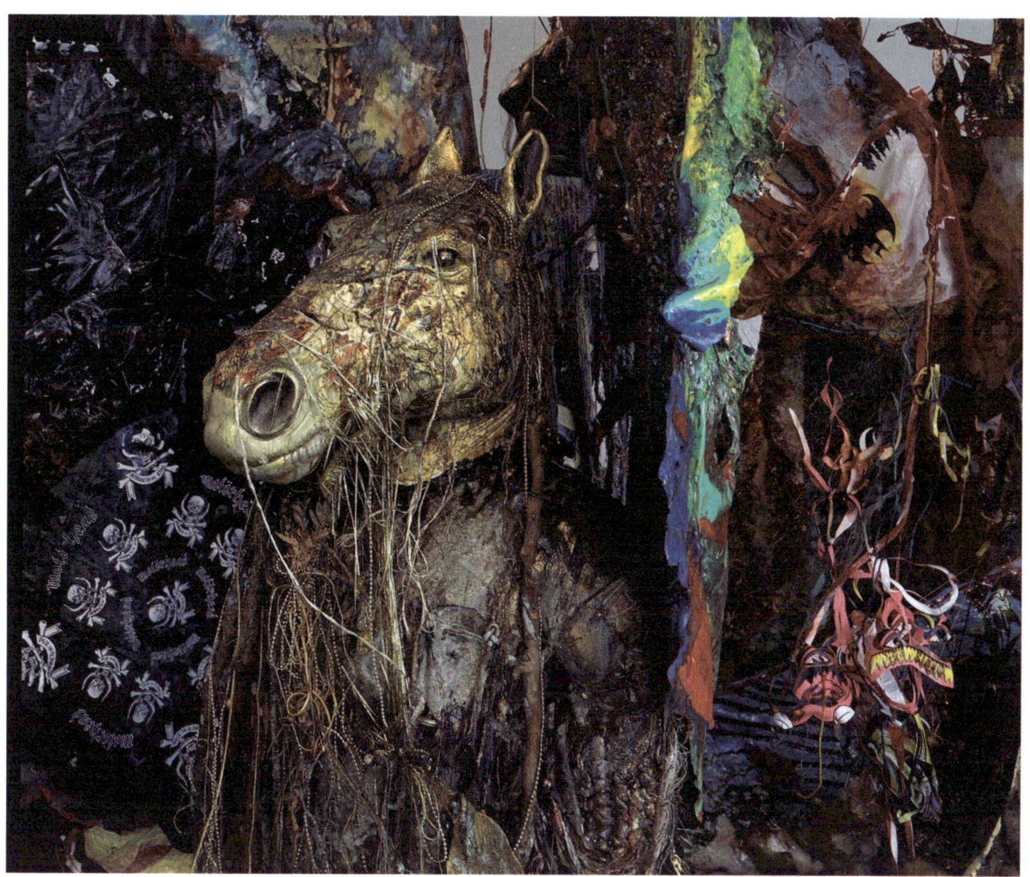

hunt for bargains like everybody else in the slightly faulty, slightly delusional world around me.

Your constructs consist of nothing but *objet trouvé* materials: potentially poisonous techno waste, motor cycle parts, science fiction masks made of plastic, emulsion paint, salt, acid, sprayed foam, molten wax, mostly in morbid colors. You seem to choose your trash elements for their bizarre effects – though their use or production is surrounded by an aura of cruelty. Displaying a certain degree of alchemistic obsession, you subject these materials to the effects of fire, pressure, light, chemicals, and organic substances. What is your relation to the materials you use?

With the spreading of high-end production, high-expense high-tech, one-hundred-hour movie ambitions, and so on, and, as a result, installation practices growing increasingly elitist and claustrophobic, I attempted to break out by means of raw experimentation. In other words, the philosophy was that raw physics is still a true philosophy. I dedicated myself to all kinds of peculiar laws of new forms of impoverished alchemy, obsessively extending the list of "amazing tricks" and immersing myself in a subversive universe of processes, in comparison with which the pivotal "virtual reality" was simply crap, in my view. My prime intuition was "low-tech science" strategies and their idiosyncratic, anachronistic procedures, the idea that nothing, not even waste, must be excluded from this self-sustained, self-reflective recycling cycle, as it were.

You started as a painter, attended an academy.

Yes, I attended an academy, and I painted for many years.

Do you still identify with this work, or has there been some kind of big clash that made you think that it is time to do something new?

I never give up anything completely, I guess because of greed. I wanted to be on top of everything. But the thing with painting is that it subjects you to a particular routine or discipline that I do not like. It is always on the surface, it is always a stretcher, it always hangs elevated in a particular spot, it is always a commodity, it is always self-important, and you are not allowed to deviate. It still bothers me.

So you would not exclude that you will paint again one day?

No, I would not.

When did you stop painting? Did it have to do with your move to the United States?

Well, yes. I stumbled upon this New York School of painting right away and had expected much more freedom in New York. And it was no good time for me personally, and I simply could not afford painting.

What about the paintings you did before? Were they abstract?

I tried a lot of things from figural to abstract to objects.

Which artists and traditions were important for you? What was your education like in Lithuania that was still part of the Soviet Union at that time? Was it very traditional? Was it mainly socialist realism you were educated in?

In Lithuania, there was a tradition of quiet subversion. We had absolutely no information. People had to rely on intuition. At the university, you attended the traditional academic courses such as anatomical drawing. But afterwards, we would gather in what we understood as avant-garde groups that dedicated themselves to an approach that ran completely contrary to the main courses, something we understood as Land Art. That was great. You see, I was also lucky to live in Lithuania at that time.

You analyze the consumer society's waste, the decomposition of philosophical and emotional values. Your assemblages and installations are agglomerations of disgusting things – which have moreover been deformed, warped, maltreated. Yet, the overall impression is a cheerful aesthetics that is downright disturbing. Your works do not radiate a morbid beauty but a colored, sparkling vitality.

I like the interpretation of reality as some kind of choreography with an almost schizo-disorderly quality. It is not necessarily nihilistic, and I think it has not got much to do with a decline or decomposition of values but rather with a subjective projection of intricate layouts of complex signifiers aimed at cracking the façade of preconceived "normality." Sometimes, it has the illusion of spectacle, an exaggerated theatricality or, at least, an insistent frontality. Going all the way from the selection of objects that would communicate the idea of a potential energy and then releasing that energy by gesture, grotesque treatment, or some kind of subversive process eventually leads to an overall impact of perverse grandeur on the level of "total" art which triggers the viewer's imagination to release more of that energy in the form of tripping or something like that. This is the way to achieve the chaotic distinctness of this schizo-choreography – where fantasy rubs out the borderline with reality in an aggressive manner.

You show three works in our project space. *Glad to Hear from You* (2002) relates to 9/11. After hearing about the attacks on the World Trade Center, relatives, friends, and acquaintances from Lithuania called to make sure you are alright. Most conversations ended with the phrase "glad to hear from you." This is what you chose as the title for your work which you, coming from Brooklyn, made for an exhibition in Vilnius.

I actually show one big piece which encompasses three separate works. *Straight to the Top, I'll Take…* is a retrospective remix of *Glad to Hear from You*, *La Charme de la Vie*, and *Rise up Solitude*. *Glad to Hear from You* was commissioned right after 9/11 for a specific occasion, the 10 year anniversary of the Contemporary Art Centre in Vilnius. It was supposed to be my comeback piece after 10 years abroad. Glad to hear from you, so to say. What strange coincidence! This polite phrase just kept popping up in communications with Vilnius on entirely different occasions: 9/11 and planning this comeback show.

Analyzing your works, art critics frequently refer to the more recent history of art from Lynda Benglis and her latex carpets, Jason Rhoades, and Franz West to

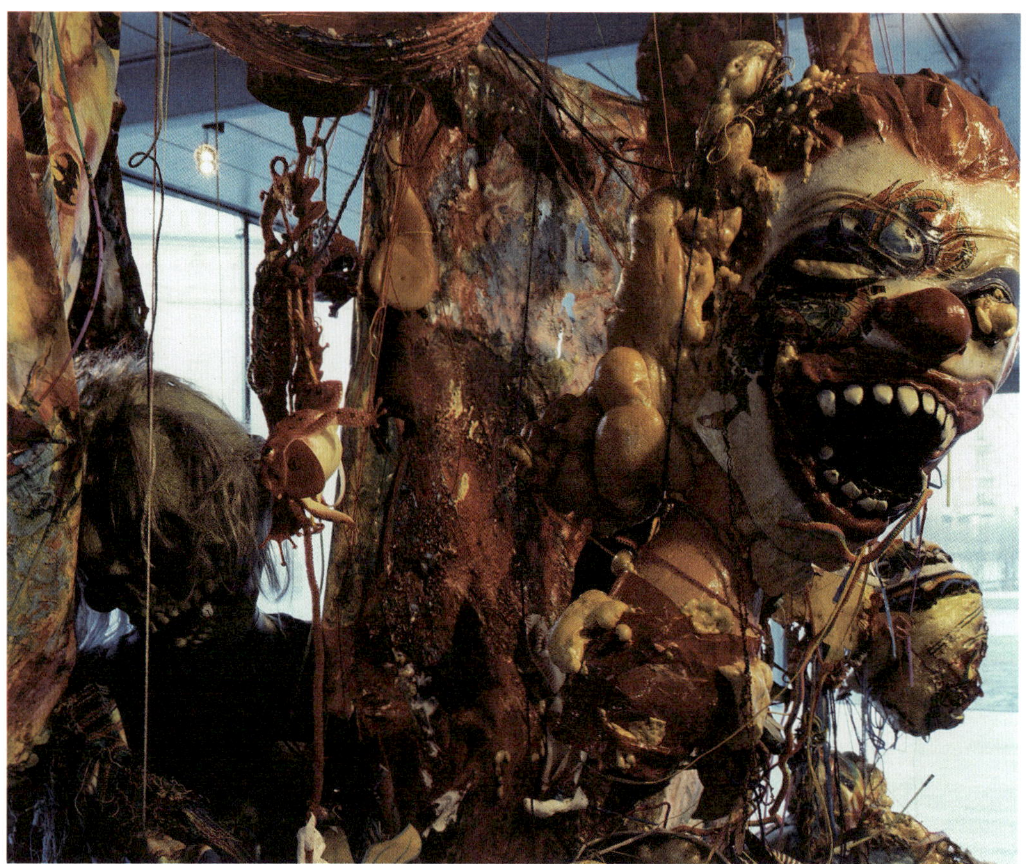

Piero Manzoni who has thrown the traditional aesthetics of subject and meaning overboard and, relying on a wide range of materials such as cotton, feces, kaolin, glass wool, fiberglass, and the human body, created a very original alchemistic and anarchistic art beyond all trends and labels.

Yes, I am very greedy, I never really quit anything. I always wanted it to be everything. Painting: yes, sculpture: yes, installation: yes, of course! And at the same time, everything is completely open, nothing is fixed, or subject to deliberate control.

Your *Embarkation for Cythera*, which was presented on the occasion of the opening of Leo Koenig's Brooklyn gallery in 1999, quotes the famous painting by Jean-Antoine Watteau in the Louvre. Breathing a self-sufficient sensuousness, Watteau's figures stand for the gallant attitude towards life characteristic for French Rococo and present themselves as an allegory of freedom triumphing over moral constraints. Where Watteau has putti hovering in the air, you prefer garbage and replace his flags shimmering hazily behind veils of mist with cheap plastic nets of a very similar orange tone, which you hang from the walls. There are no couples embarking for a pleasure trip to Lovers' Island. The only thing left are traces from today's consumer society, junk.

Watteaus's work also represented the retreat of the class, said farewell to the French aristocracy graciously embarking to an imaginary island in face of the upcoming revolution (no ass-kicking there). I was intrigued by the parallels of that allegory to the highly promised virtual reality of our times (the year was 1999). And, as an ironic parallel to that allegory, I wanted to make a piece which looked like some kind of abstract virtual island – intensely Rococo but a wasteland actually.

In the same year, you participated in the exhibition *Generation Z* in the P.S.1 Contemporary Art Center, showing your work *Yellow Peril – Friendly Fire* (1996), a piece related to the story of your life. You did your military service in the Soviet army from 1985 to 1987 and were put into action in the War in Afghanistan.

There is no story about me in action in Afghanistan by the way, there is only a story of how I got out of it. There is another story though about artists and writers in China long ago who refused to go to war, a war engulfing the whole country at the time, and who turned into yellow cranes for ever. There is also a saying referring to memories as "yellow dust" – I am not sure where this comes from. But anyway, *Yellow Peril – Friendly Fire* originated from the notion that memories or rather a film of memoirs literally flow into a field of yellow color. Since yellow is such a stubborn abstraction in these cases, the result of the clash is this fall-out of something neither abstract/yellow nor some concrete memory but after-images following the flash of bliss, as it were, something that still contains the mood of cinematographic sequences of something sad or serious, yet doubtlessly distantly abstract, pictures emerging and vanishing or slowly collapsing.

When did you start the kind of work you do now?

In the beginning, I was very involved in this scattered installation thing. I used to do scattered pieces. Amnesia was good for a certain romanticism and poetics of entropic, non-specific pieces or spaces governed by gravity, congestion, interruption. I was fascinated by the idea that everything can be changed, that everything is variable, but, at a later stage, I began to sober down and to realize that this approach does not produce the impact I wanted.

What was the problem? Why did it not produce the impact you wanted?

I wanted to develop something more personal, something implying the chance for a direct stand-off, something big and spectacular.

Sculptural?

Sculptural. Very physical, but without any involvement in terms of performance. A visual spectacle without the promise of entertainment, so to speak. Something like that. Something squinting at this darker side, this monstrous world of demiurges and demons.

What did you change?

I started to make these free-standing sculptures I call Mug Pullers.

Mug Pullers?

Mug Pullers, yes. When we were kids, we competed against each other by making the most scary faces we could. The winner was the one who made the most impact. It is an archetypical competition that was also used as a Dada strategy. I thought that this might be interesting because it is an allegory of imperfection. It is based on the reality of fantasy. Fantasy is reality. Which is also a good exercise to address political issues.

What is the political impact? Are there political issues you deal with in your works?

Yes, in some abstract way. The main point is a provocation in terms of values. Take the destructive dimension of a work, for example – you just have to exercise a little bit of that to achieve the opposite goal. By destruction, it becomes almost indestructible. The shipment of a work is no problem; it can take a beating, it cannot be destroyed. The greater the destruction, the better it looks.

So there will always be some interactive side to your work? Would it worry you if a work suffers changes by being transported or maybe even by people who do something with it?

No, this happened a number of times. Some works I had in Lithuania, for example, could not be presented as works of art at customs because a paper was missing. So they did not pack them at all. I am not talking about boxes or plastic, there was nothing. They just shuffled everything into a truck. And when the truck arrived at the museum, they opened the back door and everything just fell out.

The museum people must have been shocked!

Yes.

This is exactly what museum people do not understand.

> You are right. And I had to explain. I said, "Don't worry! You know, this is expected, and it's actually productive." I think this is a thing that is still shocking people, is still experienced as a provocation in terms of values.

Is it some form of re-evaluating the artwork in its relationship to society? Nowadays, artwork is worshipped to such a degree that it is better transported than people, it is more protected, it is treated like a religious item in a way. This is why your attitude is quite provocative for museum people and the artworld. To treat a work of art like some piece of garbage.

> Yes, but art is also looted, such as in Baghdad, and destroyed every day. My point of view is more existential, I would say. The truth is that everything is crumbling into dust while we speak.

Vita brevis, ars longa. But maybe even art will crumble into dust one day…

> No, I am pretty sure that it will vanish in a very beautiful way. But the important thing is that some mythology survives. It is hard to gamble – time will show, as we say. There are no guarantees, but I do believe that, in terms of the creative process, you will sometimes produce better art from garbage than if you buy a very, very expensive machine and produce garbage instead of art.

Would you call the things you work on at the moment sculptures? Which word would express your approach best?

> We are coming back to my greed. I could call them paintings…

Because you still paint on them?

> Yes, of course, I will never give up painting. I could also call them sculptures.

Do you want to try other media? Did you ever think of using video or film as a means to express yourself?

> Yes, I thought about that. About machines, about computers. But I do not like these things in principle. This has to do with my father who was very involved in semi-conductor technology. In our conversations, we came to the conclusion that we both hate computers.

We got something in common here. Is an artwork or the process of making art a physical undertaking for you?

Yes, I prefer the physical approach.

So, you like to do things yourself, use your own hands?

Yes.

What is your next project? Or what would you like to do if there were no restrictions? Is there anything you would like to do if you had all the possibilities?

I think I would do what I do now…

Aidas Bareikis in conversation with Gerald Matt in November 2004 on the occasion of the exhibition *Aidas Bareikis: Straight to the Top, I'll Take…* at Kunsthalle Wien project space.
Aidas Bareikis was born in Vilnius, Lithuania in 1967. He lives and works in New York.

Matthew Barney

Self-discipline and resistance are probably the main coordinates for making a narrative about creating art.

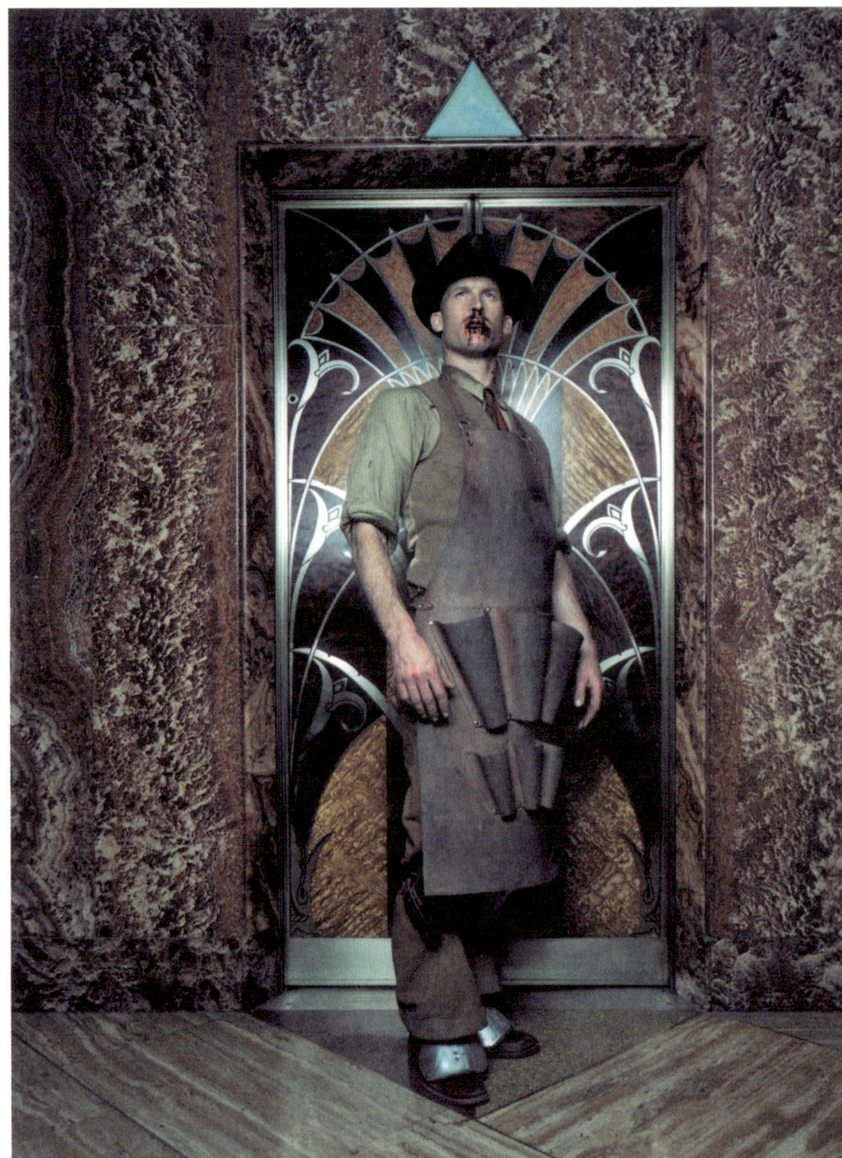

Production still:
Matthew Barney,
CREMASTER 3, 2002

Many of your works appear to deal with you and your body. A critic once said that your works are a choreography of the body's limits. In *CREMASTER 1*, which we showed at the Kunsthalle Vienna in 1997, you do not appear yourself. Why?

I couldn't have been a convincing Goodyear. I wanted *CREMASTER 1* to exist inside a genre in a more significant way than *CREMASTER 4* had, and to be more free from hybridity. I also wanted it to have a simplicity and purity that wouldn't depend on relationships in any way, but would rather have to do with the isolation of this character. In that way, I felt that my presence would complicate things.

You have always used the muscle as a central metaphor for your work. A muscle needs resistance in order for a certain form to be produced. Are self-discipline and resistance your main coordinates for creating art?

They are probably the main coordinates for making a narrative about creating art.

You once described the *CREMASTER* project as a creeping virus, and you used the concept of a virus as if you were speaking about a living organism and the changes that it goes through. You have now completed the *CREMASTER* film series with the opening at the Musée National d'Art Moderne in Paris. What holds the films together and what are the distinctions between them?

My feeling is that the exhibition finally brings together what the *CREMAS-TER* cycle is, which is a sculpture that is made up of moving images, object systems, and still images.

Would it be true to say that you extend sculpture through film and that you endow it with the possibilities and variables of time and space that film provides, adding a dynamic component that is not inherent in it?

I'm not able to answer that question.

What role do the photographs and objects shown at your exhibitions play? Are they archive objects or artistic works independent of the film?

I'm most interested in believing that they are all part of the same form; that the objects are distillations from the narrative text, but that they are insepa-rable as a larger narrative sculpture.

I would like to speak about two characters in your work, Jim Otto, the American football player, and Harry Houdini, the escape artist. These characters appear

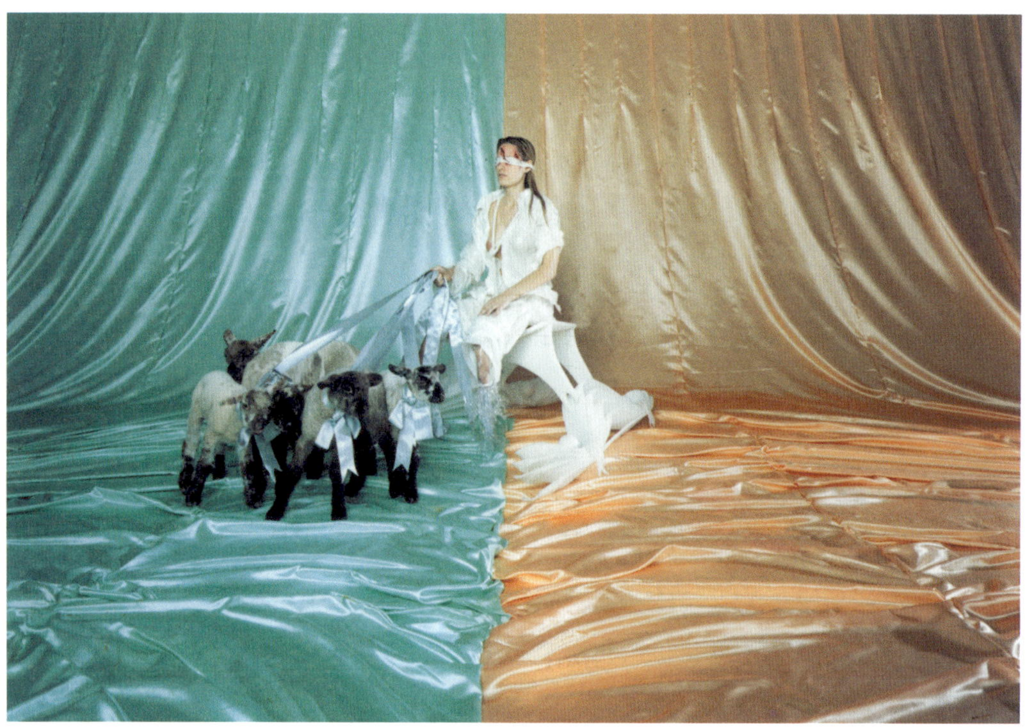

Production still:
Matthew Barney,
CREMASTER 3, 2002

repeatedly in your works, almost like ciphers. Could you tell us the significance of these characters for you personally and for your work?

I grew up idolizing the Oakland Raiders. The Raiders were, in the 1970's, a team of renegades and misfits who were unbeatable. Jim Otto was their center. He was considered an ironman and fiercely competitive in the way that he never missed a game due to injury in his career. I started putting together this narrative that dealt with the preservation of potential energy within a system. I was thinking that characters could be developed to occupy different poles within this system. I started with Harry Houdini as the representative for a hermetic position, one where potential energy was conserved through an extremely internalised practice. I needed a character who could form an opposition to Houdini, an extremely external character. Otto felt right in that he was the center of the offense. He put the ball into play and started the competition. In this scenario, Houdini became a reluctant quarterback, unwilling to accept the ball.

When I think of Jim Otto, who is a football star, I also think of the football stadium in *CREMASTER 1*. I associate American football with fixed rules, a system to which Otto belongs. Is that why you make Otto into such a strong-willed figure in your artistic repertoire? Are there biographical reasons for referring to Otto and football?

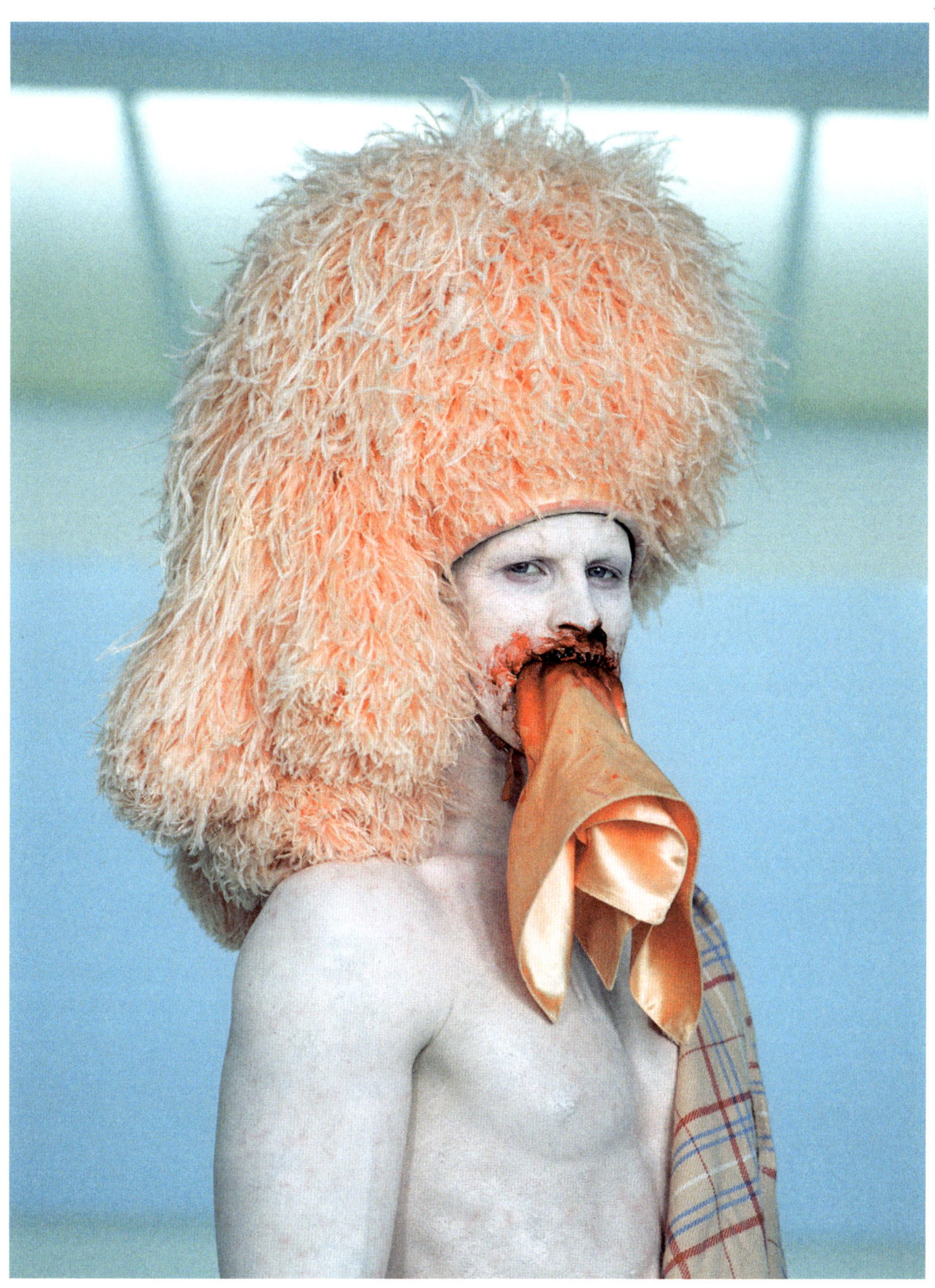

Production still:
Matthew Barney,
CREMASTER 3, 2002

I believe I first understood abstraction, on a basic level, on the football field. We would spend hours studying ourselves, from an overhead perspective, on film and in chalkboard drawings. You begin to experience yourself from that perspective, even as you move through the network of 22 players as you look for holes in the system.

On first analysis, there seems to be practically nothing improvised, accidental or spontaneous in your work. For the *CREMASTER* projects in particular there is a dense structural organization and a maximum of form and discipline, which reminds me of Peter Greenaway. Do you prefer the clarity of Apollo to the chaos of Marsyas?

One of the functions of the episodes growing in scale with each instalment is that they continue to be slightly out of control in their production. I'm addicted to this.

Regarding this idea of clarity, organization, what already exists, the evident structure, discipline, including the discipline required to carry out a clear idea, what does this mean in terms of production?

These are the ingredients to the rules of the game. As a team, we all understand these things well. As much as anything, they are the adhesive to the project. As a collective, these things become even more dominant than the conceptual framework.

Do you like working with so many people or is it simply the fact that film as a medium requires this type of planning?

I do like working with a team of people. It feels natural to me.

Robert Bresson once said of his films that the combination of lines and space leaves the narration behind and overtakes it. Is your work based on this type of abstract narration?

I think it probably begins and ends in abstraction, passing temporarily through narration.

What role does symmetry play in your work? Is it a condition that is always strived for but never achieved?

Yes.

In *CREMASTER 1* Goodyear draws diagrams in an airship that are used as models for the choreographic patterns danced by a chorus line in the stadium below.

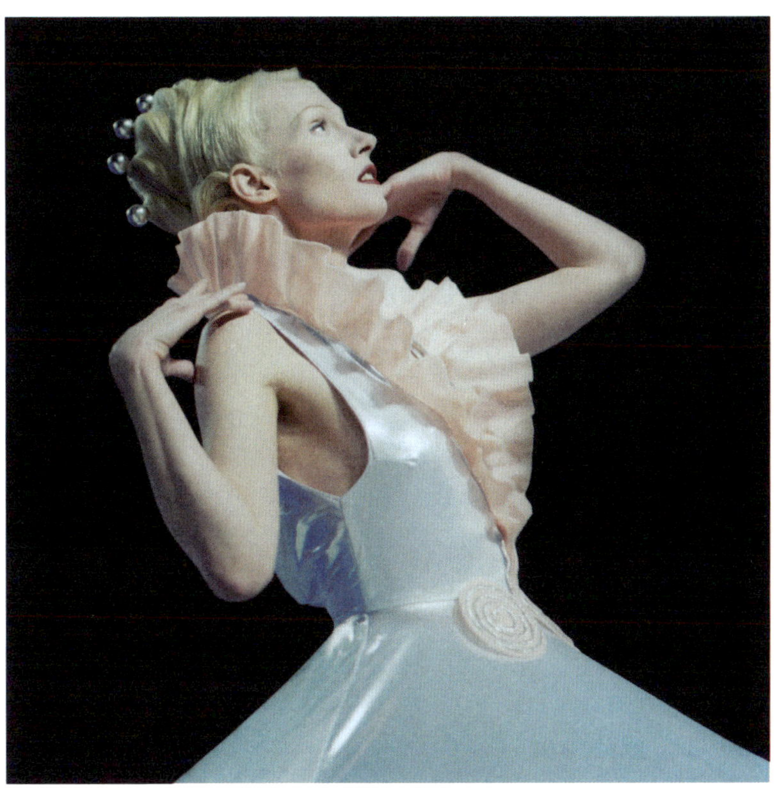

People are organized in space by Goodyear and you. The strict symmetry of the dancers in the film is reminiscent of Busby Berkeley and Leni Riefenstahl. What is your attitude to these artists? Do you take a special interest in the relationship between will and power, the subject of Siegfried Kracauer's *Mass Ornament*, for example, and hence in the way human organization functions?

The field formations in the Berkeley and Riefenstahl films have that same kind of problem you brought up before. They are attempting to achieve a perfect symmetry and fail to do so. The smiling chorines are begging you to believe it has been achieved, but it just isn't true. I'm very attracted to this problem as a condition of sculpture making.

At first glance *CREMASTER 1* appears glamorous but the more one watches the film, the more one senses a strange tension and the irritating timelessness and absence of space. There are the peculiarly undefined figures and grotesquely distorted fauns, satyrs and hybrid characters, the stadium in *CREMASTER 1*, which you place in a nocturnal vacuum, and much more. It is sometimes like a horror film or nightmare. Can you tell us something about your interest in the structures of horror films and their relation to your films?

Horror films have been useful for me as models of a narrative system where the emotional weight in the story can be shared by the architecture and the landscape, and in that way, the emotional burden can be removed from the characters.

What is your relationship to the outside world, to society? You create a very strict, hermetic system in your art. Would you define yourself as an artist with political ambitions?

I chose art as a way to communicate. Constructing a visual language continues to be the most natural way for me to communicate.

What do you find so fascinating about stars like Ursula Andress and Richard Serra, who appear in *CREMASTER 5* and *CREMASTER 3*?

I believe they are able to exist within the piece as abstractions in spite of their specificity as cultural icons. Their essence is of a kind of extreme physicality, almost violence. They, in their own practice, transform that into form. The *CREMASTER* project needs to continue to prove to itself that violence can be sublimated into lightness.

In *CREMASTER 2* you play Gary Gilmore, a central character in the film. What is your connection with Gilmore?

I was raised in the Mormon Basin of southern Idaho, that boarders on Utah. Gilmore's story was a way of dealing with that landscape, and to try to capture the psychological tone of that part of the country.

In *CREMASTER 3* the Chrysler Building is the main character. Everything happens around the building. Is this a symbol for the beginning and end of the American dream?

I was asking the Chrysler building to convey a quality that I believe isn't exclusively American, although I think it flourished in America in the 1920's and 30's. I think this kind of problematic ambition will always exist.

CREMASTER 5 takes place in Budapest and at the opera house there. What made you choose the opera? Were the grand passions of opera a source of inspiration for your film?

The primary location for *CREMASTER 5* was the bathhouse. I looked first at the Ottoman baths, then began to feel more drawn to aspects of the city that were built at the end of the 19th century, and had a nearly artificial feeling. I abandoned the Ottoman baths and started drawing a connection between the Gellért Bath, the Lanchid Bridge, and the State Opera House, and writing a story that could eventually function like an opera.

The *CREMASTER* cycle, which you worked on for eight years, is now complete. Does this give you a feeling of emptiness or a readiness to embark on new projects?

I'm very ready to begin a new project. I need a strong feeling of closure to move on, and the *CREMASTER* cycle exhibition is giving me this feeling.

Matthew Barney in conversation with Gerald Matt in the autumn of 2002. Kunsthalle Wien presented the exhibition *Matthew Barney: CREMASTER 1*, 1997. Matthew Barney participated in the exhibition *Superstars – Das Prinzip Prominenz: Von Warhol bis Madonna* (2005) at Kunsthalle Wien and BA-CA Kunstforum.
Matthew Barney was born in San Francisco, California in 1967. He lives and works in New York City.

Vanessa Beecroft

> *The power of a homogeneous group in comparison with a heterogeneous mass of people. And this group contradicts a position of power because they are bare, stripped, exposed, controlled.*

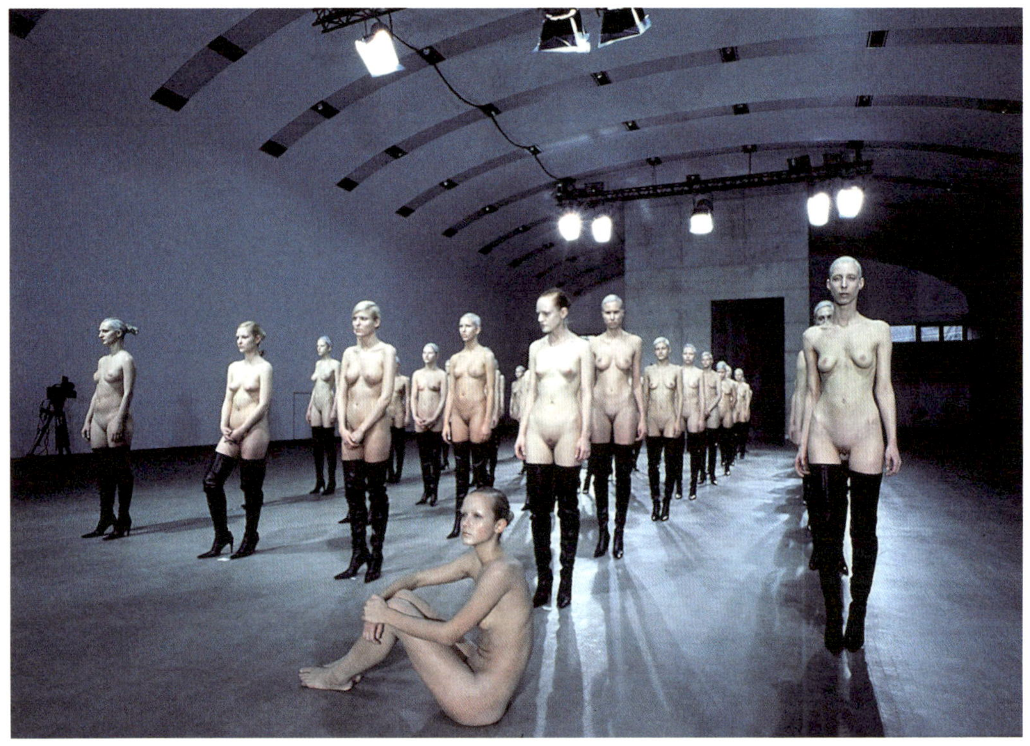

Installation view,
Kunsthalle Wien 2001:
Vanessa Beecroft,
VB 45

The fetishist arrangement of the body as an object of desire in your choreographies of bodies in space reflects important elements of the fashion world. You have in fact collaborated with renowned fashion designers such as Tom Ford/Gucci in your performance at the Guggenheim Museum in New York. At the same time, you contrast the frivolity, spontaneity and ephemeral nature of the world of fashion with the slow pace of your performances and the physical effort made by your models, to the point of exhaustion. Your performances give the impression of a lack of freedom and of the instrumentalization of persons and their image. What is the connection between your work, the world of fashion and the manipulation of images?

> The scope of my work is different from that of fashion. I like what you say above but I am unsure of the connection.

In connection with the previous question, your work also hints at the monotony and standardization of the contemporary idea of beauty, particularly when one bears in mind the developments in gene technology, genetic mutations and cloning. How do you see your work in relation to these phenomena?

> I have an aspiration to minimalism that never gets satisfied when I realize a performance, but it doesn't have anything to do with cloning. I usually pick each girl for her looks and her portraiture. I can still identify each of them in the mass portrait that a performance is. When I think of a performance I think of a monochrome. I try to realize the monochrome with a group of girls, but always end up disappointed by their realism and the arrogance of their physical presence.

In your performances, you arrange people into homogeneous, uniform components of a "mass ornament", as Siegfried Kracauer described it. Do you see these arrangements as the expression of the powerlessness of the individual in a crowd, or the power of a homogeneous group in comparison with a heterogeneous mass of people?

> The power of a homogeneous group in comparison with a heterogeneous mass of people. And this group contradicts a position of power because they are bare, stripped, exposed, controlled.

What is the role played by the photographs and video documentation of your performances that are shown at your exhibitions? Are they historical records or works of art in their own right?

> They are historical records realized with an aesthetic means that upgrades some of them to the class of artworks. I am very bad at tolerating objects and I have a difficult time admitting that photographs from the perform-

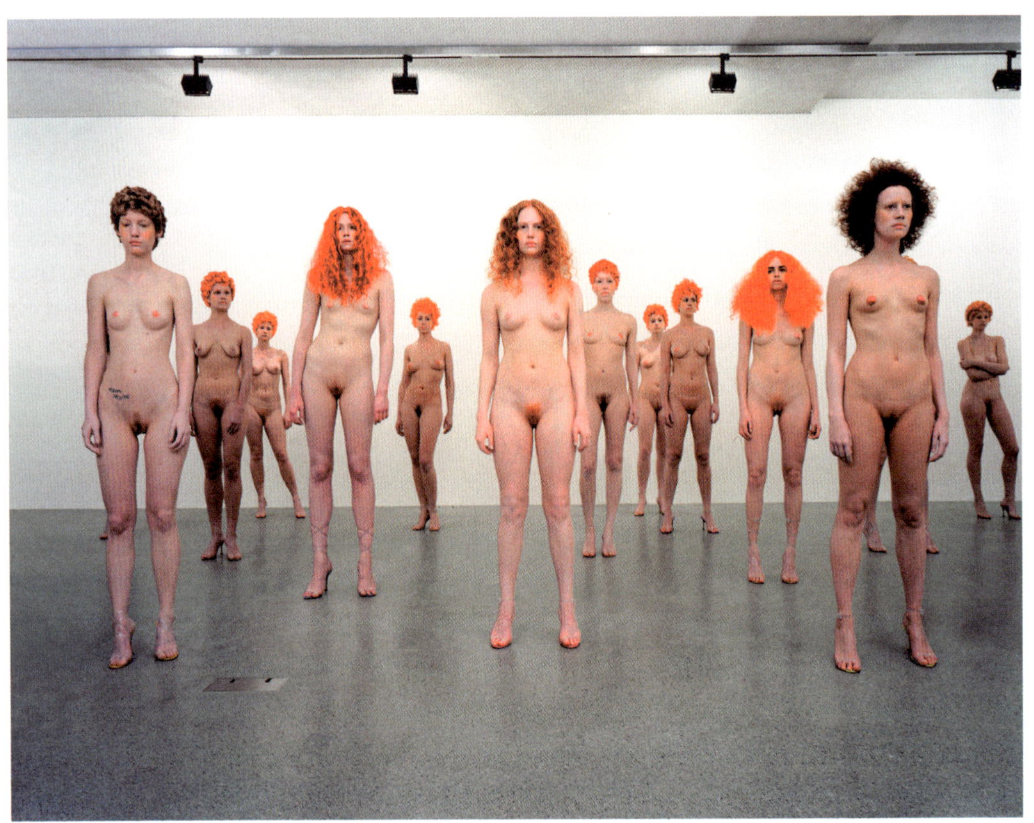

Vanessa Beecroft,
VB 43, 2000

ances can reproduce the event. The event cannot be reproduced. Some photographs or videos give an idea of it but they are not it.

Many of your performances are, as you say yourself, inspired by classical painting. They continue a long tradition of nude painting associated with great names
like Titian, Manet or Modigliani. At the same time, your static arrangements are
also reminiscent of classical sculptures. How do your performances relate to
tableaux vivants and classical art as the "consummate mastery of life through
the discipline of form" (Arnold Hauser)?

I was raised in Italy where paintings in museums and churches were my first
art reference. In the middle, between real people and gods there were the
people in paintings, usually Madonnas, children and strange beings.

The reference to classical painting also brings to mind the traditional relationship
between the painter and the model. How do you work with your models? How do
you select them and to what extent do you give them instructions as to how and
where they should stand?

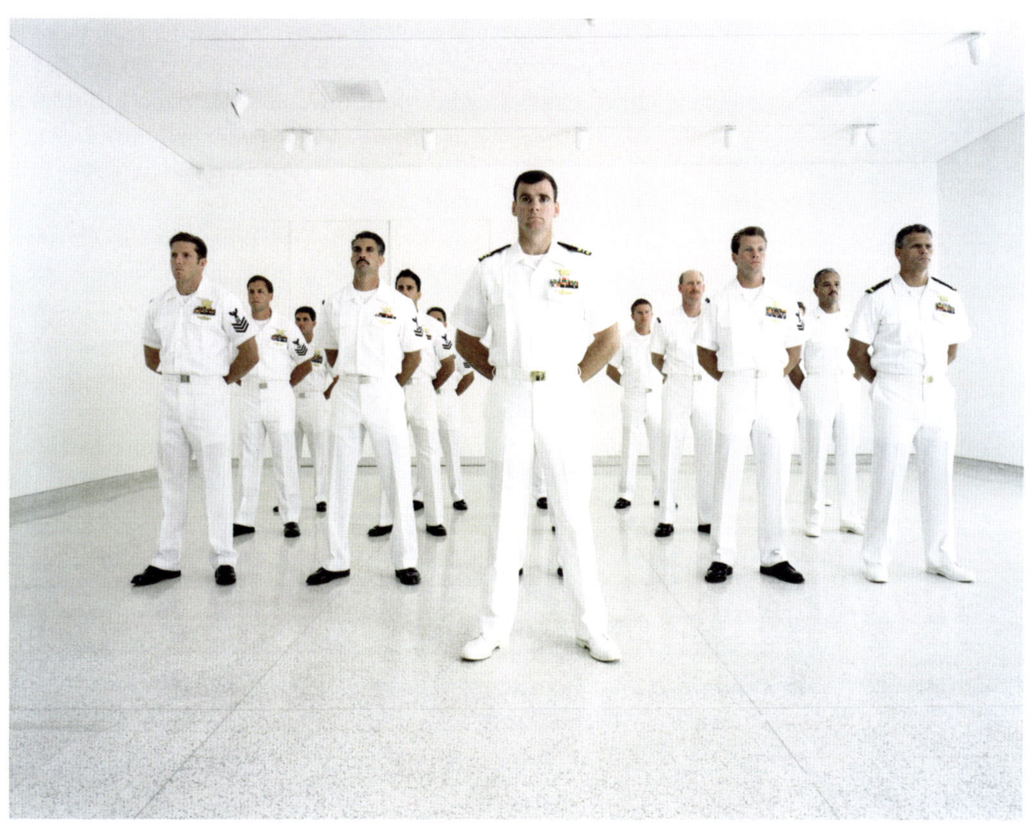

There is a typical face that reoccurs in my work: it is British looking, Vanessa Redgrave, Twiggy, the Madonna by Pollaiolo. When I look at photographs from my father's side of the family, I realize that is the portrait of his mother, his sister and now his younger daughter Jennifer. The selection of the models depends on the site in which the performance takes place and my idea for the piece. Usually models and street-cast women have standard features. I relate more to tall and pale women. Rules are given to the girls prior to a performance; the most important one is "do not speak". Other rules help them to keep distance from the audience, to isolate themselves from the outside and to feel like a picture.

Your synthetic arrangements appear to negate the basic elements of body art, such as individuality and the expressiveness of the body. How do your performances relate to body art?

Individuality and the expressiveness of the body are expressed in my work and that is probably what relates the performances to body art. The difference is that individuality and expressiveness of the body only interest me visually, if at all.

You trained as a stage designer and your arrangements could therefore be seen as a type of "living theatre set". Your models are instructed to stand still, not to act and not to interact with the public. These instructions are similar to ones that might be given by a theatre director. Some of your earlier performances also make reference to plays (e.g. Samuel Beckett in *Play*). How do you relate to the theatre?

I chose to study scenography in Milan to avoid the sadness of students making art at school. I still do not work unless I have commitments. I become stressed in art studios, art schools or sites for creativity as a science. Stage design has been an excuse to observe a virtual space, a perspective space in which to compress a scene, like in the Renaissance paintings of Bramante and Raffaello, a way still to have a relationship with Architecture. I went to the theatre in Milan and watched Brecht, Carmelo Bene, or experimental foreign groups, but never felt it was interesting for today.

Can you tell us something about the development of your early performances? Your first exhibitions had a strong and intimate autobiographical character, e.g. in the presentation of your diary for the previous eight years at Galleria Massimo De Carlo in Milan (1994). How did you design these performances? What was the underlying context? What role is played by your own life in your performances today?

My first performance happened by accident. Giacinto di Pietrantonio, a teacher at my school, asked me to show my watercolours in a Gallery for the final year. I'd never shown a work before. I had just kept an obsessive food diary to control my diet during several years. Another element was the fact that I used to look at girls in the street and felt disturbed by them. I presented a typewritten copy of the diary and invited these beautiful girls to come and wear my personal wardrobe for the duration of the opening in the Gallery. The girls had a relationship with the diary, they were invited as a "special public" but they became the strongest visual material that I decided to use from then on.

The performances replaced my drawings. I do not design them, they just come to my mind when I am asked to a show, in terms of composition, numbers, colours, reaction to the institution, city or country in which they take place.

The title of your performances has tended to consist of your initials followed by a serial number. How has the nature of your work changed over the years? In your most recent performances (e.g. Vinsebeck/Bielefeld) is there not a greater emphasis on the representation of a heterogeneous, all-embracing "female cosmos"?

I have a tendency to obsession that takes two forms: one is the one of repeating the same thing over and over, the other is the fact that I never feel anything is accomplished and I need to try again and again to get it perfect. The work has changed because it has adapted to personal and external factors, but still I feel it has not fulfilled its purpose. At the end I would like to have brought a realistic subject to abstraction, but I am not sure how.

The latest project includes older women, my mother, my mother-in-law, my half sister, etc. I am getting old and I wanted to see if you could feel any difference in a group of different ages. A source of inspiration has been *Grey Gardens*, a documentary on two women (an aunt and cousin of Jackie K. Onassis) who are still beautiful but have lost contact with reality, sanity and men in a rotten house in Long Island.

Vanessa Beecroft in conversation with Gerald Matt in the autumn of 2002. The artist presented her performance *VB 45* at the opening of Kunsthalle Wien at Museumsplatz. She also took part in the exhibition *Get Together–Kunst als Teamwork* (1999) at Kunsthalle Wien.
Vanessa Beecroft was born in Genova, Italy in 1969. She lives and works in New York.

German to English translation by Nick Somers.

Candice Breitz

Much of my work deals with the question of how we become who we are, and to what extent this process is influenced by our absorption of the values sold to us by the mainstream media.

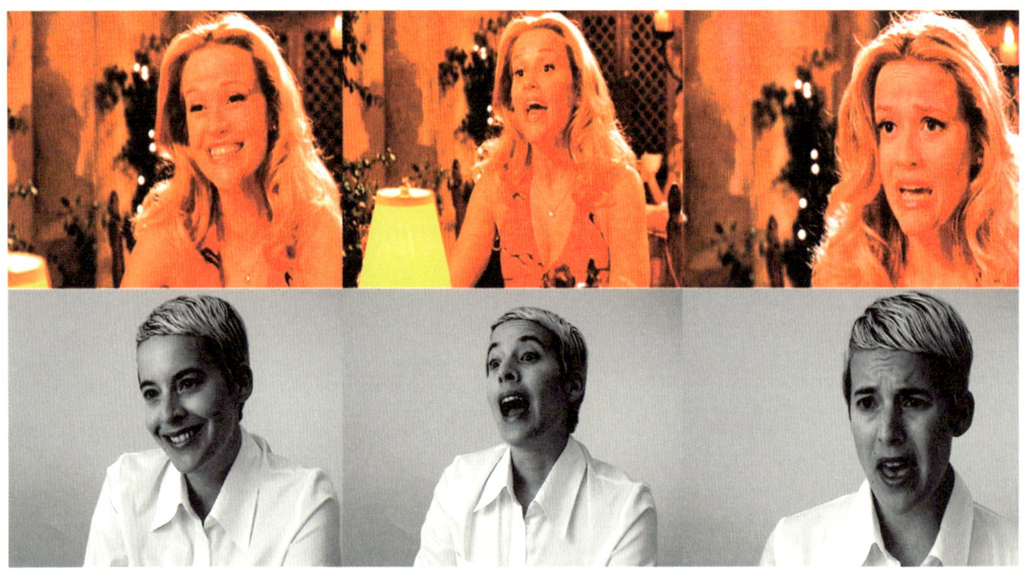

Candice Breitz, Stills from
Becoming Reese, 2003

In Kunsthalle Wien, we included your work, *Becoming*, in our exhibition *Superstars*. To be honest, the space required for this installation has been a challenge for our house. How do you accommodate the diverse facilities in exhibition halls?

Larger installations always pose a challenge to art institutions. The primary challenge is an economic one - not every museum has the funding necessary to install a large multi-channel installation. This is a limitation that one has to accept as an artist - the fact that an institution that might very much want to show your work, may simply not be able to afford to. Then there's always the question of space, the question of whether an institution has the space to dedicate to larger works. These are practical issues. If my work can't be shown for either of these reasons (or both), I certainly don't take it personally. In the case of some works, the spatial requirements are somewhat flexible, but if a work doesn't fit into the available space, there's no point in forcing it. Every artist encounters certain limitations regarding where and when their work can be shown, whether these are practical or political… but in the end, it's neither important nor necessary for the work to be shown at *every* art institution. What *is* important is that the work is shown well each time it is shown. I've found that there are more than enough art institutions out there that enjoy the challenge of stretching to show an ambitious installation. And when this doesn't work out, there are a number of creative ways to deal with the situation: some institutions would see the problem of limited space, for example, as an opportunity to invite the artist to make a new work that could fit into the existing space.

How important is the installative element in your work?

The spatialization of the moving image is central to my installations. I very seldom make single-channel work. I'm interested in creating a space in which the viewer encounters a number of different channels of information. I try to avoid giving the viewer the easy satisfaction of a single point of view or perspective, because I believe that the viewer is the one who ultimately decides on the relation between different elements of a work of art. In my multi-channel installations, each channel or element is treated as an instrument or a layer; which, when combined, produce a kind of random composition. The compositions are random because I am not interested in controlling or strictly determining the relationship of one channel to the next. Rather, I am interested in presenting them as a series of possibilities. The final remix is given over to the viewer, who choreographs the work in a sense, according to how s/he moves through the space of the installation and experiences each channel relative to the other channels and within the space. I have the prerogative of deciding which elements and what kinds of elements are thrown into the mix, but in the end the viewer is invited to navigate through the selected elements independently to some extent.

With found footage technique and with re-use of image and sound-materials, you refer to the images themselves as products of an increasingly dominant media industry. You isolate Hollywood-clichés out of their original contexts, interlace them in a new composition and condense them to an absurd extreme. Are you a moralist?

I like the fact that the answer to that question is not clear. Interestingly enough, when my work is shown in the United States, critics tend to read the work as embracing and affirming the culture that it remixes. In contrast, European writers more often than not insist that the work is a critical attack on the global entertainment industry. Viewers should be given credit for being able to make up their minds for themselves about what is good and bad. It is more interesting for a work of art to ask questions than to offer answers. The raw material that I use is re-presented in such a way that a number of different conclusions are possible, in contrast to mainstream entertainment, in which the goodies and baddies are clearly delineated as such from the outset. The viewer is asked to read and translate the work rather than to simply be the passive receiver of a prepackaged message.

You deal a lot with questions of personal identity – identity with the background of globalized dream-machine of MTV, Superstar and fun-society.

Much of my work, including *Becoming* – which you are currently showing at the Kunsthalle - deals with the question of how we become who we are, and to what extent this process is influenced by our absorption of the values sold to us by the mainstream media. More and more, we learn who we are not only from our parents and from our immediate social contexts, but also from the culture industry. In that sense, the media has gradually come to share (and in certain instances to take over) the complex job of raising us. It's uncanny how efficiently the star-fan relationship maps itself onto the parent–child relationship. The star/parent offers itself to the fan/child as a prototype to be emulated and duplicated, not only in terms of what to wear and how to talk, but also in terms of what to think and how to behave. The endless and anxious debate over precisely what effect television and the mass media are having on 'our' children ("Are high-school shootings the inevitable result of listening to too much Marilyn Manson?"); or, even on adults ("Does violent porn invariably lead to rape?"), is really just the banal way that conservative critics have found to ask questions that have far more profound implications: "Why aren't our children reproducing our values? Why can't we control them? Why aren't they becoming who we want them to become?" This is a fundamentally uninteresting approach to the problem, since it invariably leads to censorship, which in turn leads to illiteracy. Rather than trying to control what or who 'our' children watch and/or emulate, we should be teaching them how to read and watch more discerningly, how to actively cut and paste meaning from the media rather than feeling obliged to sit back passively and swallow it all whole.

Your style of working is very precise and technically laborious. For the work *Mother + Father* that you introduced at the Venice Biennale 2005, you have isolated the figures from original film-context and set them in front of a black background.

I wanted to see to what extent it might be possible to divorce my sampled *Mothers* and *Fathers* from their original movies — to what extent I could truly make them mine. I've always been fascinated by how completely a sample can be absorbed by hip-hop, or other cannibalistic forms of music. It seems to me that musicians are a lot further along than visual artists in this respect. *Mother + Father* is an aggressive attempt to hack a cast of actors out of several existing movies, an attempt to re-channel labor originally invested in the economy of Hollywood into my alternative economy. The actors have been quite literally cut out of their movies, freed from their original settings frame-by-excruciating-frame. I refer to their participation in my work as 'involuntary acting.' I like to believe that as somebody who buys movie tickets, reads magazines, and watches television, I am a minor but significant shareholder in the *Meryl Streep Corporation* or in *Julia Roberts Inc.* As an economic supporter of this culture, I (and you) contribute to the inflation of labor that makes Hollywood what it is. Having paid my fair share towards financing this inflated industry, I feel perfectly entitled to step in and get the actors to work for me every now and again. That said, grabbing the strings and playing puppet-master is not as simple as it may sound. As the sampled actors perform for me, their digital twitches and jerks can be read as symptomatic of their dilemma as hostages, reluctantly dancing to a tune they have not chosen. Although I set out to kidnap the actors and get them to do my bidding as completely as possible, I would say that in the end, the whole experience of making the work felt less like working with marionettes than like a tug of war between myself and my involuntary cast. This was an interesting result because it confirms my suspicion that in the end meaning always resides somewhere between the sample and the sampler, rather than simply belonging to one or the other.

You often use movie-clippings as material. How do you handle the problem of copyrights?

If we live in large urban centers, we have no choice but to consume the cultural produce of global capitalism. But consumption is necessarily followed

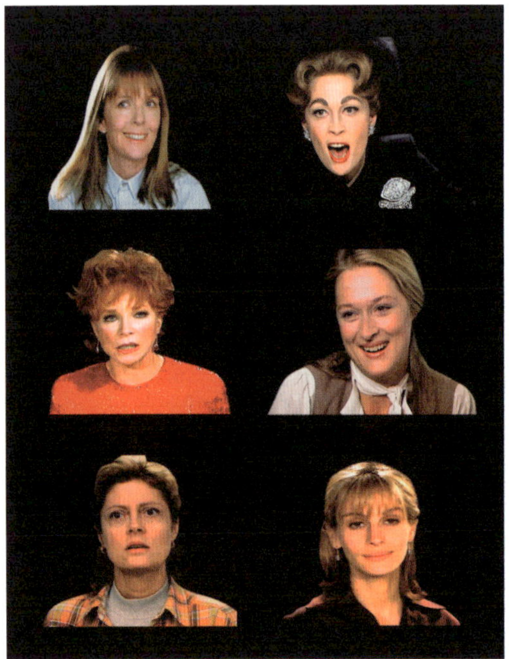

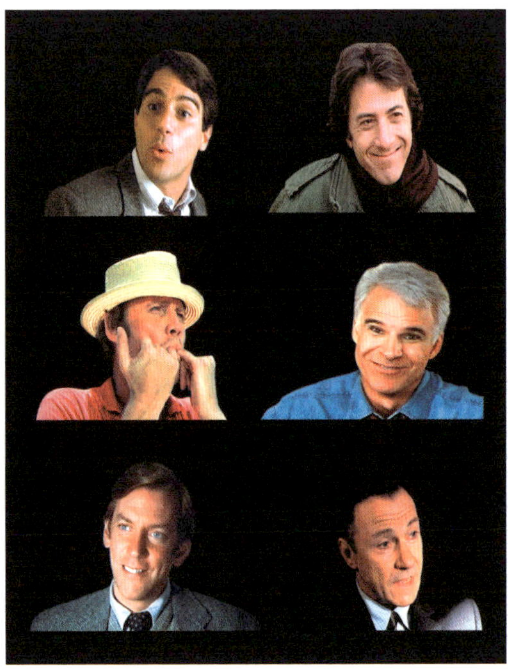

Candice Breitz, Stills from *Mother*, 2005

Candice Breitz, Stills from *Father*, 2005

by digestion, and digestion inevitably results in excretion. This is a polite way of saying that if we have no choice but to consume what the mass media feeds us, then we must insist on completing the digestive cycle – we must insist on the right to chew up, process and regurgitate mass media forms, to translate them as we see fit. I see this as a basic right, for which we should not have to ask permission or pay a fee.

At the beginning of your artistic career, you felt invited to the biennale more as a South African than as an artist. How do you see your position as an artist coming from a country outside the mainstream of art world? Did – and does – your place of birth influence your work?

The tendency of certain biennales to insist on the ethnicity or nationality of artists is a problem experienced by many artists who have had their first opportunities to exhibit in contexts such as biennales. In fact, it seems that there is an almost inevitable chronology: as a country gains global acceptability in economic and/or political terms, artists from that country are increasingly likely to be invited to show their work internationally and may enjoy a moment of being fashionable within the art world for a season or two (take, for example, the unprecedented fashionability of South African artists in the post-Apartheid moment or the fresh respectability of Russian artists after the dissipation of the Cold War). While Austrian artists are not expected to make work about *apfelstrudel* and Canadian artists are not expected to make art about ice-hockey, there is often a silent expectation when it comes to the inclusion of artists from less mainstream art countries: "make art about where you're from, and about what makes you different… or stay at home." It's a double-bind for many artists because some were making perfectly sincere work that was specific to their experience before being 'discovered,' but once the work gets thrown into the global machine, any reference to cultural specificity or ethnicity or nationality starts to serve very different purposes. I saw this happening in the critical response to my work quite early on – people would spend more time discussing where I was from than looking at the work. Since this kind of socio-biographical reading of works of art has never interested me, I realized that if I wanted to continue exploring the ideas that were important to me, I had to find a way to do so that might avoid such responses. Around 1996, I decided to avoid using visual elements that referred too literally or directly to the South African context. One can never escape where one is from. Nor should one want to or have to. But one's place of birth or gender or religion cannot transparently yield all the answers to the meaning of one's work. I like to be invited to exhibit my work because the work is regarded as compelling, not because of the passport I hold… or because I am a woman… or because I'm half-Jewish….

Taking part in the big events of art scene, the art fairs, the biennales and triennales, is part of the job for artists. Do all the cities become interchangeable with time? Has geographic origin lost impact?

As capital leaks across borders, creating a generic cityscape furnished by Ikea and nourished by Starbucks, cities certainly have to fight harder for their idiosyncrasy. But that tends to make the particularities of a given city all the more memorable and – from a marketing point of view – all the more sellable. This takes me back to the last question you asked about whether the geographical origin of artists should play a role in how we read their work. Both of these questions point to the dilemma that is at the heart of global capitalism…. As things become more and more the same in big cities around the world (global capitalism seems to ask), is it more lucrative to fetishize the remaining cultural differences (mining third world cultures for new and exotic trends), or to aggressively undermine cultural specificity to the ends of creating a universe of 'global citizens' whose affiliation to international consumer culture exceeds any specific sense of national or cultural belonging? In other words, should difference be turned into fashion or should fashion insist that there is no longer any difference? What are we to do with linguistic and ethnic differences, the shifts in beliefs, life-styles and budgets that mark the transition from one consumer market to the next? The marketing and public relations divisions of global companies have time and time again used photomontage to articulate this quandary. The attention-grabbing *United Colors of Benetton* campaign, for example, has relied almost entirely on a cut-and-paste aesthetic, producing saturated images of a young Jew with a young Arab, a black woman breast-feeding a white baby, an American child with a Russian child, etc. Here the shiny hyper-visualization of difference is employed to the ends of promoting consumption and sameness, thus bringing the contradiction full circle. The ingenuity of such ads lies in their ability to spectacularize and commodify the social and cultural differences that they appropriate as their consumer platform, while in the same stroke camouflaging the extent to which global capital works at erasing such differences.

To produce art is a lot of work. You have to research, to prepare, to technically execute, and to do, or at least to supervise, the installation in shows; you are involved in permanent communication. What are the limits of your personal productivity?

I work in fits and starts. There is an intense period of production for six to eight months, during which I get very little sleep and push myself to the point of physical exhaustion. But this is always followed by a slightly slower period of gestation, during which I travel, read, watch movies, write down ideas and process what's going on in my head, until I reach the point of being able to jump into the next period of production. So far, this rhythm has worked pretty well for me. I try to delegate as much as possible of the day-to-day running of the studio to my assistants, and work very closely with a small team of excellent technicians, which takes some of the heat off me, and allows me to focus more on the content of the work.

What project are you currently working on?

I'm working on a number of new projects parallel to each other. They're all pretty labor-intensive and could change dramatically before I'm ready to exhibit them… so I'm keeping them under wraps for now! Depending on when the new works are ready, I hope to show them at the Baltic Centre for Contemporary Art in Gateshead or at MUSAC in León sometime later this year….

Candice Breitz in conversation with Gerald Matt and Sigrid Mittersteiner in January 2001. The artist took part in the exhibition *Superstars – Das Prinzip Prominenz: Von Warhol bis Madonna* (2005) at Kunsthalle Wien and BA-CA Kunstforum.
Candice Breitz was born in Johannesburg, South Africa, in 1972. She lives and works in Berlin.

Tania Bruguera

*I like the idea of living in a space between two ideologies, two systems. This
gives me the illusion that I can have some distance, detachment from a place
in order to understand it, the illusion that, in this way, I will have as few
blind spots as possible.*

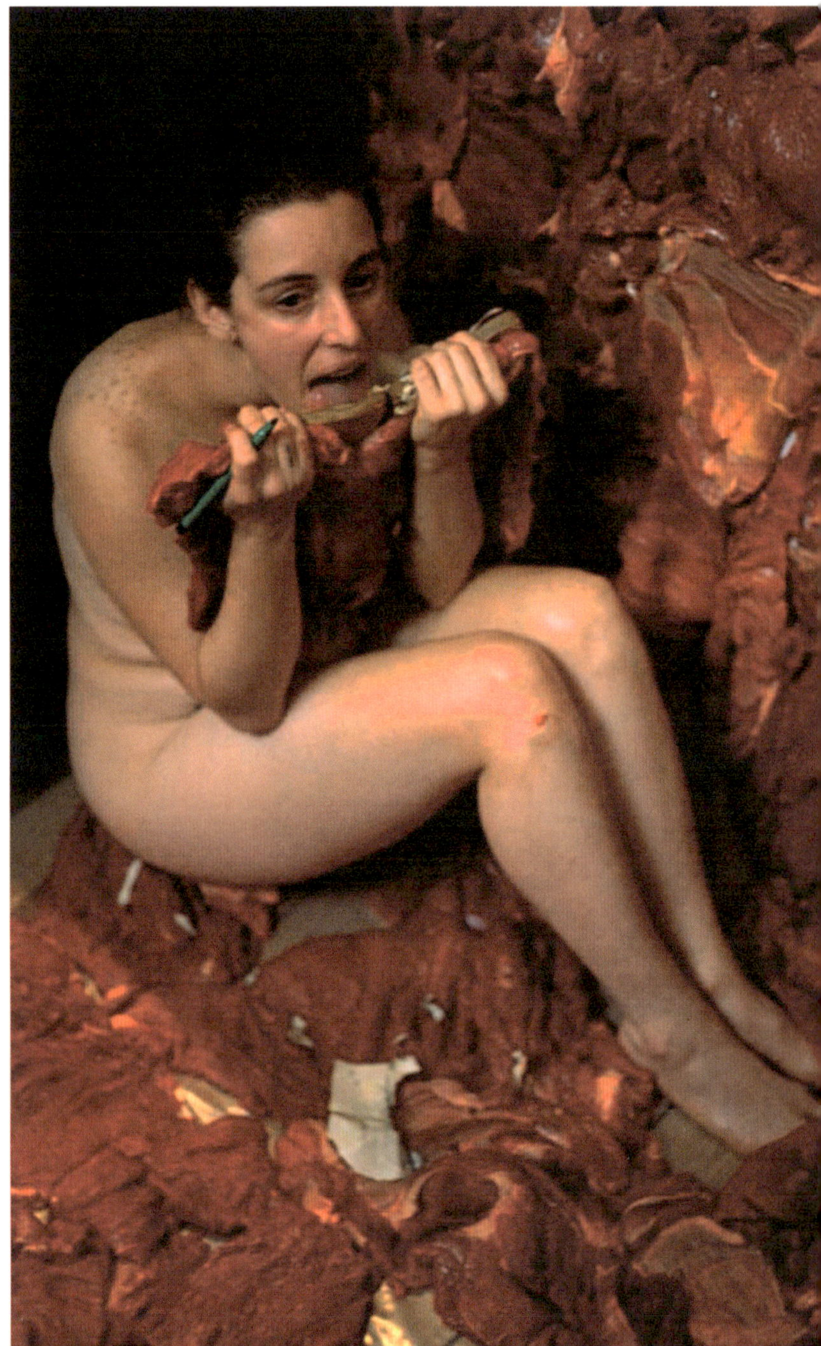

Tania Bruguera,
El cuerpo de silencio,
1997-1999

One might say that the performative, the inclusion of one's own person, a syncretic approach encompassing Catholic religion and African myths, as well as existential themes prevail in your earlier work.

In my earlier work, the performative was definitively an important aspect. It was not until later on, around 1996, that I began to create performances, and by that I mean pieces in which I had a direct physical presence and in which there was an educated audience. Lately, I have gone back to those first performative ideas. I think this may be because I am again interested in the value of behavior as an artistic and linguistic tool, as well as a social one; behavior being a set of codes widely understood, with only minor social differences from one place to another. This is important to me because I want to communicate ideas, and it is hard to do site-specific political work that is understood in a wider context without running the risk of it becoming propaganda. Another reason why I have returned to the performative is because I find it more closely connected with the idea of art as a gesture with symbolic implications, a gesture that is the piece; by which I mean, its structure, its implications, its consequences. When I was creating performances, I was bothered by the spectacle. I wanted to have a more "invisible" scenario, to do gestures, not actions; I wanted to disappear, to have a more flexible mode of operation. I had gotten tired of performance, it was not that exciting anymore. I get bored very quickly and I guess performance was no exception. I liked the idea of going back to an art in which the artistic nature was not that easy to define and which worked in the realm of life. Then came the day when someone who had invited me to perform asked how many chairs I wanted in the space. I said to myself: okay … something is wrong here.

It is interesting that you ask about African religions and the performative in the same question. There definitively is a relationship. It has been very hard for me to formulate my relationship with religion and to deal with my desire to be disengaged from it. I was raised both in the animist and atheist traditions … with an awareness of both Marx and healing plants … That is where the syncretism is, between Marxism and animism. Both philosophies – or should I call them ideologies? – are based on the principle of the tangible changeability of the course of life. Both are utilitarian tools, or at least both present themselves that way. Both start and end in reality; both assume very concrete consequences in the course of events. I have denied the way people have read my work as religious, especially some of my performances, because this usually has been the result of a very exotic approach; my being Cuban has allowed this very problematic situation to come about, which is the easiest road in terms of interpreting the work and invalidating any effort to propose anything a bit more complex. My work was never intended to illustrate religion nor talk about it. In this, Juan Francisco Elso, a former professor of mine, and a friend, was a big influence.

A *santeria* practitioner himself, he told me once that there were things that one could not see and that were frequently at work in the pieces. By that he was referring to energy. He called it *carga* (charge) and good pieces were *cargadas* (charged). This is the same term used in African religions to name something (object or action) that has been prepared for use in real life, for its journey to change destiny. In addition, in Cuba, African religions are not morbid, restrictive and penitent ways of viewing life but very practical ways to live and to acquire tactical knowledge. Animism is an applicable religion, not an iconographic reference. It is alive and current. Catholicism, by the way, I only quoted once, in *The Burden of Guilt*, and it was because I thought that sacrifice was universally understood through the image of a lamb. But I am not that interested in the way that religion creates symbols and associations, nor in the heavy historical readings of them. Since all religions are an archive of social conduct and its possible practical results or consequences, I just think that some may have created a more interesting set of relationships. I could, for example, at some point be more interested in Judaism or Buddhism than in Catholicism.

At the Istanbul Biennial in 2003, you presented your work *Poetic Justice*, which drew considerable attention internationally and which was later viewed at the Venice Biennial last year. What is this work about?

Well… this is the only time I have created a piece in which, political meanings aside, or precisely because of them (in this case, it was an exploration of contemporary post-colonialism through the media), I wanted to do something "beautiful." I was thinking of beauty in terms of the appreciation for the labor required to create artwork; also, of the meaning residing only in the material, where the operations and all their possible interpretations are exposed and available. I was also thinking of the possibility of mystifying the gap between high technology and used tea bags, both attractive and familiar; of beauty in terms of the "space" between the actual walk through the piece and the selection of one-second historical news reels. I wanted, for the first and only time in my work as artist, people to ask themselves how much money the production required … How long did it take to do? How many people participated? Who did the labor? Who drank the tea? How was it transported? Who produced the original newsreels? Where were the newsreels filmed? What was happening in them? These are all questions relevant to an inquiry about specific acts of post-colonialism while, at the same time, the audience is distracted by the seductive and familiar smell of tea, something not threatening at all but very comfortable and subtle.

I was very interested in the idea of use and recycling, of being used and being recycled.

I think it is important to say that this piece was first conceived in India at the Khoj workshop, a three-week residency program. But it was completed in Berlin, where I went for a week directly afterward. In a way, this piece is my reaction to a CNN report I saw in my Berlin hotel room about Cuba. The reporter had totally misread events – or was it a problem of cultural translation involving postcolonial attitudes?

The sound installation you produced in Chicago is the centerpiece of your presentation in the project space of the Kunsthalle Wien. It schematizes the communication strategies of politicians and audience responses to these; yet, you forgo the use of graphic representation, more precisely, the non-verbal form of expression so characteristic of the mass media. The rejection of the image seems to be Ariadne's thread running through your project.

I have been interested before, in *Untitled* (Havana, 2000), in the means by which politicians communicate, expressing their ideas and decisions. *Portraits* is, as the title suggests, portraits of several political figures. Portraits not of the way they look but, rather, an attempt to portray them through the effects they had on people.

The series focuses on political figures that have had an impact on world events. Each speech is carefully selected, depending on the importance of the speech itself or (in the case of the historical figures) the accessibility of the recorded material. The selection covers a wide range – for example, there is Hitler's address to the Reichstag on May 4, 1941, in which he reviews his actions since 1937. Although he includes a lot of information by which he could have been ethically questioned and judged, he instead gained even more power. There is also Pope Paul VI's statement on the occasion of the 20th anniversary of the UN, the first recording of a pope speaking in such a venue and as a head of a state. After the speech, there was considerable applause, signifying a kind of approval of his double status. Even if visitors do not have access to the original speech, there is a reference available on the walls next to the speakers, just in case anyone wants to do additional research; this reference includes the name of the speaker, the name of the speech (or the name as it is known historically), as well as the date and place it was delivered.

The fact that I substitute the text, the message of the discourse, for the reaction to it, the emotional effect among the population present at such events, is a comment on the repetitiveness of political agendas, the formal use of such venues to inform, and the similar way in which such political resources have been used for the strategic manipulation of public opinion. Those emotional effects are the fuel that makes the machine of history work; it is the way by which people can express their spontaneous approval. It is a moment of direct dialogue between the leader and the people, one in which the people's "voice" is the clapping.

The original recorded sound – the words, rhythm, intensity, and speed of the speech – was carefully translated into musical notes with the help of Julia

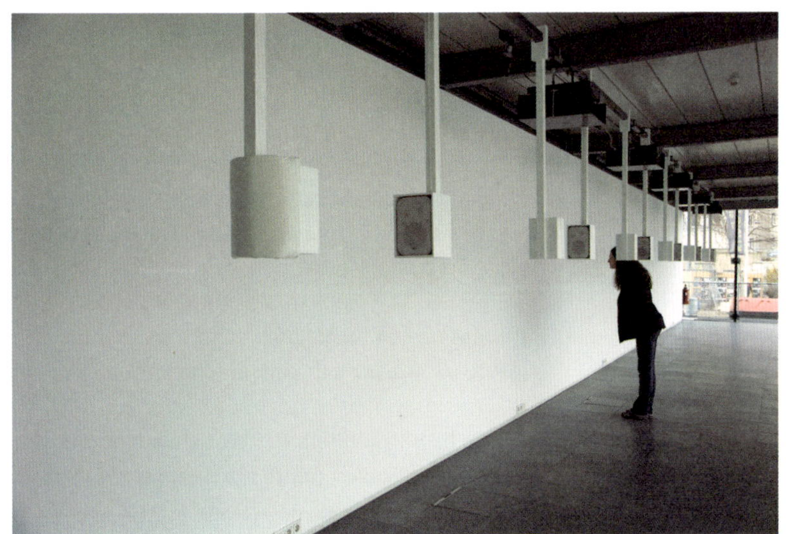

Installation view,
Kunsthalle Wien 2006:
Tania Bruguera,
Portraits

Miller, a composer and computer software designer. The resulting musical scores were performed by a professional (and classically trained) chorus that delivered it by clapping the notes, each in its own way, so they do not sound the same. There was no conductor, just the scores. Each political speech was recorded separately and is delivered via a separate pair of speakers. After you approach the overall confusing sound of the recorded pieces all being played at once, you are confronted with each one as a specific and detailed experience. I think it is very important that the speakers are all positioned one meter away from the wall so in order to best experience it you have to be facing the wall (where the information of the original speech is provided), almost as if experiencing some sort of punishment.

Concerning the relationship between speeches and music, I wanted to mention the antiphon, the name of which derives from the 479–411 BC Athenian orator who rarely spoke in public but wrote defenses for others to speak. An antiphon is a response usually sung in Gregorian chant to a psalm or some other part of a religious service and performed by two semi-independent choirs interacting with one another.

The reason I am not using any visual reference but only the speakers and the very subtle (white vinyl on white wall) reference text is because I want the audience to focus on themselves, to look at their own reactions. The space has other non-visible elements, such as sulfur mixed with the paint used on the wall. Sulfur has been a very special chemical because of its wide range of uses from gunpowder to medicine (in war and peace). We also experiment with a chemical used in tear gas to see if we can trigger a false and uncontrollable emotional reaction: people crying. It is a very important aspect of the piece that the audience sees itself crying. This creates a disruptive effect since they have a physical response related to an emotional response. But this is neither in relationship to nor a consequence of their political or psychological perception. It is the first time I use some sort of humor in my work, and that may have to do with my lack of faith in such political strategies. I want the audience to think about that.

Yes, the title of the piece is *The Dream of Reason*, a clear reference to Goya's plate # 43 from *Los Caprichos*. This is the second piece I have created as a result of living in the United States. I guess the increasingly dictatorial attitude of the U.S. government has had something to do with it … [smile]

I am really glad that this piece will be performed for at least one day, although ideally, it should happen everyday, for at least a week, on each occasion at a different time of day, so that it keeps its element of surprise. I am glad because it has been censored twice before, to my surprise. The first time was in Paris, where an artist had invited me to intervene in his solo show at a commercial gallery, and the second time was in Madrid, at a group show.

The Dream of Reason is the "invasion" of an area by a uniformed security guard (with no company label) who appears with a guard dog. The dog has a muzzle. Every ten minutes a new guard appears with a new dog. This happens continuously until there are 15 guards on the premises at the same time (the number of guards depends on the size of the area, so this could change in future presentations). The guards do not address the audience, not even if the audience approaches them. They do not have eye contact with them. The guards circulate slowly around the compound, surveying something that which we cannot determine.

The piece was first conceived for an indoor space but the public space will work much better in relationship to its hyperrealism. The audience is not aware or notified of the piece being as a performance. The piece will always be shown at the same time as the exhibition but in another space, speaking to the sometimes apparent disconnection between repression and public speeches, showing how repression is always in the background. As you said, the piece signals a heightened sense of potential danger, one that is never revealed but sensed.

The print *The Dream of Reason Produces Monsters* and the series it was part of were first published on 6 February 1799 in the newspaper *Diario de Madrid*. The newspaper had an editorial to introduce this work by Goya. It says, and I quote: "[the author] has exposed to the human eyes forms and attitudes that have only existed, until now, in the human mind" (*Els Caprichos de Goya*, Ed. Sa Nostra, Caixa de Balears, Barcelona 1996). In my piece, this also happens but through the materialization of a concept we see an experience through the media or just hear about it most of the time: and that is repression.

Repression and fear are important strategies used by governments and power in general. The levels of intensity in which they are used vary from self-censorship to torture but I find the best politicians are those who know how to work with metaphors and who are good at assigning symbolically shared implications to their repressive gestures.

How would you define your own relation to power and politics?

Power is something I do not completely understand yet, that may be why I work with it. But politics is something I have grown up with. Both (mostly politics) were all that was talked about at my house when I was growing up. It even separated my parents. Politics is something I have lived and I am involved in while in Cuba, even if I do not want to be, because it is inescapable, a permanent presence. Politics in Cuba has a very narrow meaning; it is mostly used in reference to the government and to ideology. In the United States, it is more often used with regard to interpersonal relations. In each case, I find what is not addressed at all to be very interesting. Power, on the other hand, is something people are very aware of in the United States. Although politics can be more like the practical language of society while power is its implementation, both are a very good example of the simultaneity and indissoluble connectivity of idea and action – maybe that is why I am so intrigued.

You live some of the time in Cuba and the rest in Chicago. Leaving aside for the moment the issue of political polarization between Cuba and the USA, what has been your experience of the emotional, cultural and aesthetic relations between the two worlds?

I share my time between these two places. I like the idea of living in a space between two ideologies, two systems. This gives me the illusion that I can have some distance, detachment from a place in order to understand it, the illusion that, in this way, I will have as few blind spots as possible. But who knows …? Maybe I have just become completely blinded by the wind outside the airplanes …

Nevertheless, this life has been very interesting and intense, especially since, so far, I have chosen not to live in New York – which some people say is not really the United States: a unique place where, for an artist, the art world has such a strong presence. Coming to the United States has been a good exercise in contrasting what I had previously learned about the place with what I have since lived and experienced. Some of these things are specifically related to the United States, others to capitalism. Having to relearn so many basic things has been very good because at this age you learn while questioning what you learn. It almost seems like, while in Cuba, the government wants people to focus on it, but they do not allow you any access. In the United States, the government does not want you to focus on it but you do have access, or at least something that feels like it.

I have been really interested in what is missing, unspoken, in both places. It has been fascinating to look at the US system of control, the ideological one, economic censorship, and ideas of modern slavery, the heroic status of celebrities, and their positions in the political game.

I have been particularly interested in the importance given in the United States to narrative, frequently spoken narrative, while in Cuba the narrative is mostly broken (maybe that is why Fidel, who mastered oratory, is so successful), and we speak through actions instead. The power of media in the United States is something that has no parallel in Cuba. In Cuba, mass media are very clearly a propaganda tool, so, in a way, their impact is lost and they resemble an informational checkbox rather. In the United States, they are also a propaganda tool but they are used differently, through them your brain gets filled with narratives, with many of them, so many that it seems as if you do not have any space left to create your own. I sometimes feel as if I am in a computer game set in the United States and I have to walk through a forest full of traps and distractions, some of them really pleasing. In Cuba, the game would be taking place in a desert (and probably with no oasis in sight) but at least you would be able to see the horizon, or maybe I should rephrase this and say: in a desert where all you can see is the horizon.

I have to say that it has been very healthy to have direct access to information without mystification, as happens in Cuba. By this I mean that you do not have to depend on travelers to bring you books and information or may keep a book for just one week because so many people want to read it. Yet, I have to say that the feeling of preciousness, of the human chain of knowledge, of subversion, has a certain charm. The fact that you can access things firsthand is a different challenge because you have to believe in yourself very strongly. In Cuba, all knowledge is mediated by a previous screening. But I have to be honest and say that in terms of art, this was amazing, because my generation read all the literary classics and saw a lot of good films. Of course, the problem was that it was already deemed safe, already canonized, but nevertheless it was a great cultural foundation. In the United States, you are your own screener, you have to determine what is and what is not, you frequently see things as they happen, and that makes things look more natural, more human, and more doable. – I suppose this was some stream of consciousness rather than a clear description of my life between Havana and Chicago …

Lately, I have been very attracted to the idea of moving to Europe, to experience that system, which, at least from afar, seems to be dealing with interesting struggles.

Political themes form the point of departure for much of your work. Would you say that it is possible for art to trigger social change?

It may sound silly but I completely believe in this, and there are many examples of it in art history.

This is a very complex subject, and I do not think I am completely ready for this conversation, but I may share some of my ideas, which are, quite frankly, still in flux. This is actually the theme of one of my new pieces. I will read you a section of what I have written by way of description:

"For some time, I have been questioning the idea of the creation and existence of artwork as a representational act. I have been thinking about art's practical implications and the need for the artist to act as a responsible agent creating useful artwork. Artwork should not only be useful but should exist in the realm of reality; otherwise, it automatically becomes a representation again, one that exists only in the realm of possibility.

When I talk about the realm of reality, I assume reality not as something representative or mimetic regarding the artwork's construction but in relation to its information, circulation and consumption. 'Realism' is the artistic strategy while at the same time its public realization/actualization. Rather than creating a sample, art is then something of real consequence."

I find it very interesting that some artists dealing with this have decided at some point "not to do art," or at least that is the way it has been perceived by others. Maybe it is not that art has an end but that those artists and their practice have entered another dimension of production and circulation for their art and, as in physics, we cannot see it although it can be explained, formulated, and even controlled. This is my approach to the ideas I call "Arte de Conducta."

Tania Bruguera in conversation with Gerald Matt in the spring of 2006 on the occasion of the exhibition *Tania Bruguera: Portraits* at Kunsthalle Wien project space. The artist took part in the exhibition *Kuba – Landkarten der Sehnsucht* (1999) at Kunsthalle Wien.
Tania Bruguera was born in Havana, Cuba, in 1968. She lives and works in Havana and in Chicago, Illinois.

Cai Guo-Qiang

Nowadays, I am travelling a lot physically, but my core philosophies seem to move closer to my roots.

Cai Guo-Qiang

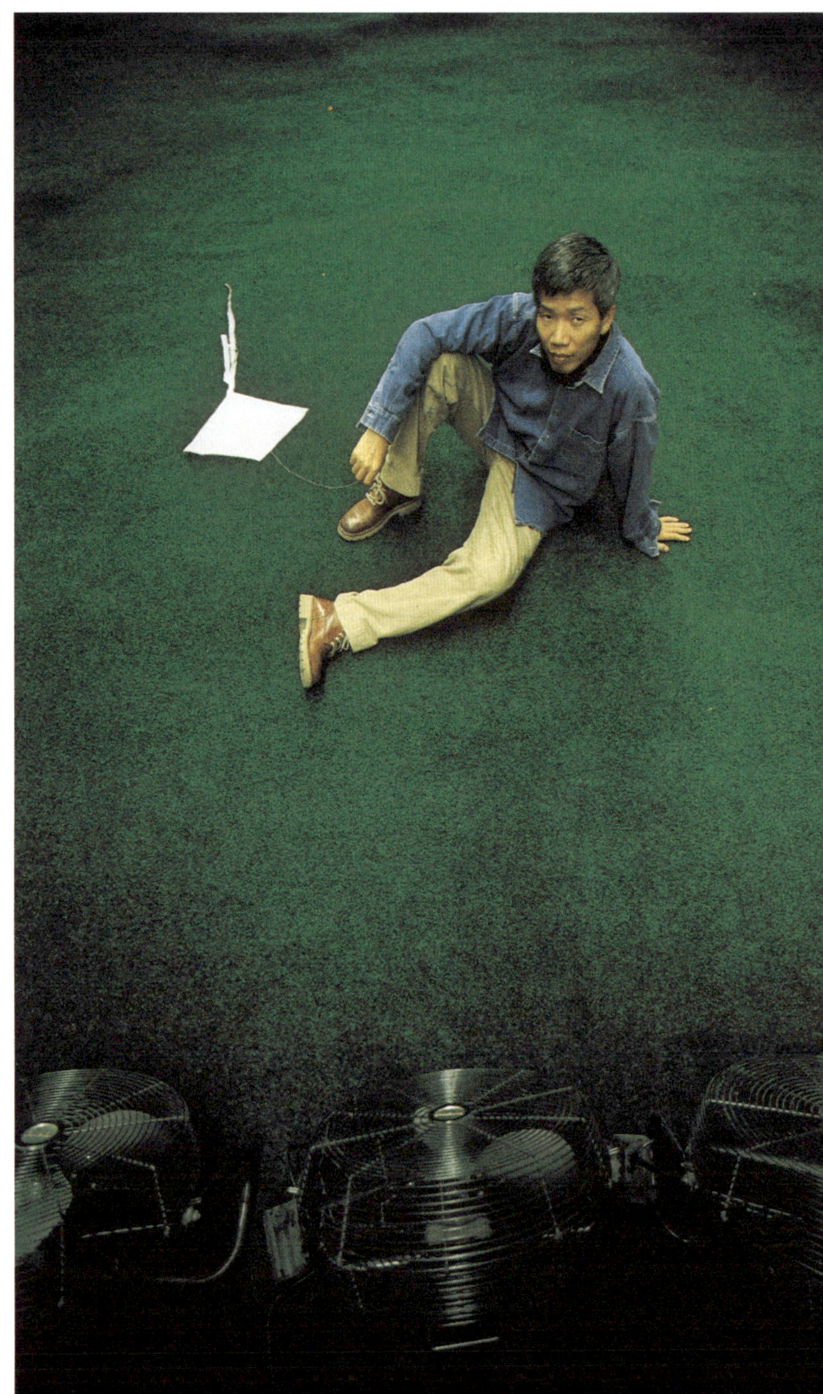

Kunsthalle Wien 1999:
Cai Guo-Qiang

When you were a kid, you were completely stuck on going to the moon. Have you been able to fulfill your childhoof dream? Have you made it to the moon?

> At some point in my life, I realized that the chance of going to the moon is very slim, so I started thinking about projects of going to the moon in different ways and going even further than the moon. But I think everybody will get there eventually.

Planets or satellites are possible observation stations for extraterrestrials, for whom you have continuosly made projects over the past ten years. One of the most impressive ones was the extension of the Great Wall of China by a fire line that might have been seen from somewhere up there. The project *Dragon Sight Sees Vienna* is number 32, the latest of your *Projects for Extraterrestrials*. Did these projects follow a general idea from the very beginning up to the project for Vienna?

> When I did the Great Wall piece, I was living in Japan and was really focused on the universe and the end of the universe, and I used the idea of another pair of eyes looking at us and looking at the earth. So my work from that period often refers to this aspect. At that time I wasn't very concerned with people seeing my work because I knew there would be other eyes looking down. It's different now: I do want people to see the project in Vienna. This shows that I have changed in some ways after my arrival in the USA, in the West. Now, I not only think about the universe but also about cultural exchange and political and socioeconomic conflicts. As we know, the dragon is a symbol of the East, a symbol of power from the heavens, from the universe; it is a bridge between man and the universe and supernatural powers. This is why it's something positive to call the Chinese "children of the dragon". Yet, in the West, the dragon is often seen as a monstrous force; and when the western media talk about the new economical powers of the East, they often use the dragon for illustration. Well, this dragon is not content to stay in one corner of the world. When he gets some pocket money, he starts travelling around. And the pouring of Asian tourists into Vienna is inevitable, since the city is such a famous attraction, especially for Asian eyes. The visitors will also bring the dialogue and conflicts of different cultures with them.

When you left China for Japan and New York, you took traditional Chinese materials, ideas, symbols and signs with you in your suitcase. Which influence did your travels and the different situations have on you baggage?

And, as for living in a foreign country, travelling a lot and keeping one´s world at the same time: Do you consider yourself to be in a process of emigration or rather on a long continuing journey?

I feel that it is a journey without destination, without a clear destination. In China, one´s spirit and ideas often travel but it is sometimes difficult to travel physically. Nowadays, I am travelling a lot physically, but my core philosophies seem to move closer to my roots. That our environment is in constant change and development is so rapid makes us realize what is not changing in ourselves, makes us look for the unchangeable.

The Chinese references in your work strike me as rather significant. Could you comment on that aspect of your projects?

I think that these references are only natural. All people in the world use what is passed down to them. The question is how well you employ your traditions and your cultural heritage. To us Eastern artists, the Western artists also draw on their own culture and traditions. When we see their humanitarian concerns achieving a universal level and find their works impressive from the creative point of view, we are equally moved. The point is whether we can use our stories and signs, relate them to today´s fundamental human concerns and introduce new approaches and forms of artistic expression. Even though issues like the Y2K bug and mushroom clouds are considered global signs, like dragons and herbal medicine, which are derived from a very specific cultural background, they are without much value if they do not fulfill their role within the artistic manifestation.

You are interested in the theory of evolution, in the Big Bang as well as in smaller bangs, in explosions and their visual signs. Has this anything to do with the old Chinese notion of energy and its flow?

According to Lao-tzu, there was nothing before the birth of the universe. It began as a big fireball. This is a notion that is quite similar to modern theories of the universe and the chaos theory. But I am not an expert on it, I just pick up a ball here and kick it there, so it's all mixed up – inside of me as well.

Well, to me the explosions on your projects seem to emphasize that there is always a "before" and an "after". Your show here, as a contribution to be the millennium, has the title *I am the Y2K Bug*: it both marks an intersection in time and hints at some "fault" within the order of the digital calendar.

We will soon witness a fleeting moment that will mark a change of eras. The project *I am the Y2K Bug* was made specifically for Vienna. The Kunsthalle is also at a turning point from the old to the new. Something new will emerge at the site where the Museumsquartier is being built. The opportunity was there to do something on this occasion.

My work is often related to the issue of change, especially when there

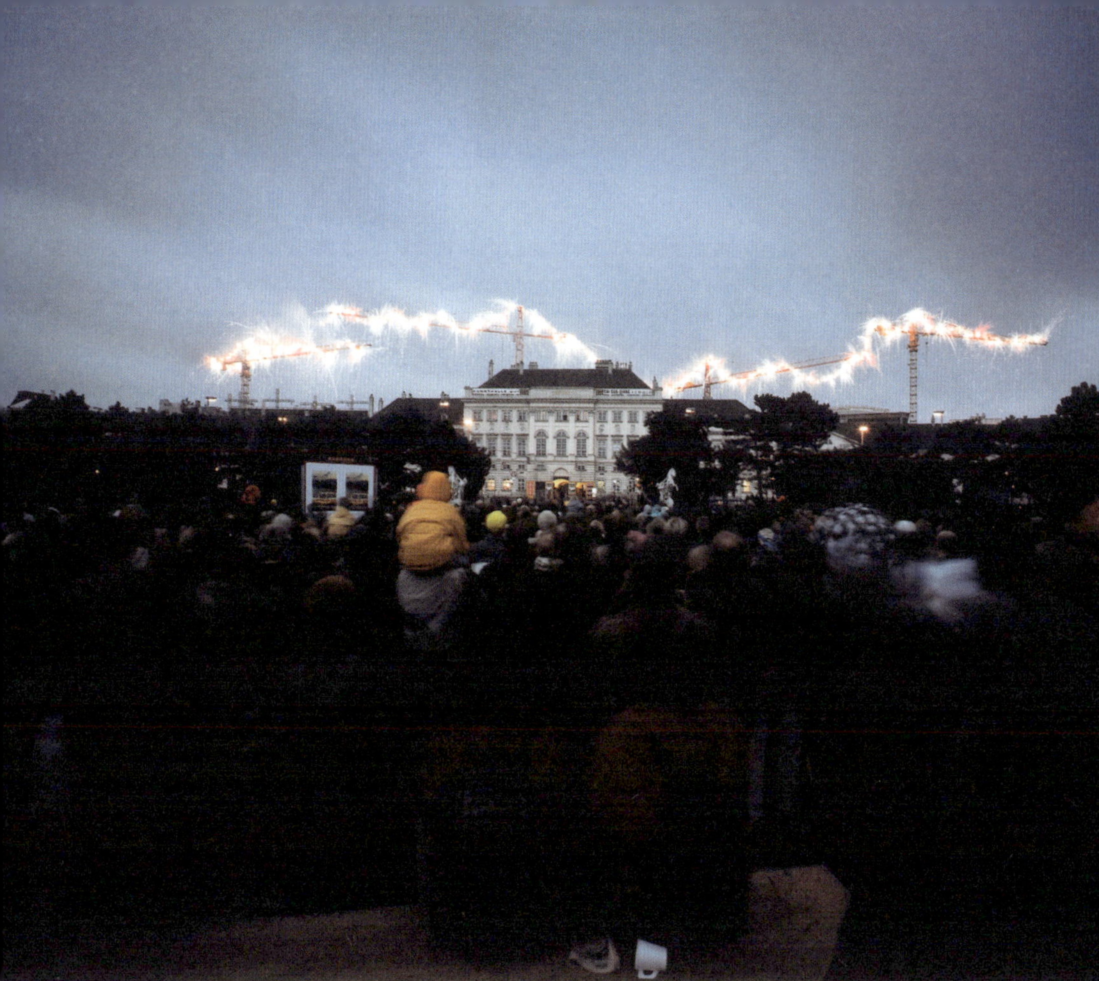

are oppositions and conflicts. In the East, people recognize contradictions, accept and absorb them; they have a collective and holistic way of looking at things. This is my basic attitude towards my work. But the Western ability to analyze a situation and grasp the problem as well as its approaches of confronting and solving it have also deeply influenced me, as I grew up in socialist China and was educated according to Marxist lines.

Is there a difference between working outside and inside?

Working outside and working inside is quite different. Outdoors is public. You have to obtain a permission if you want to have a big explosion. it's a bit like participating in a parade and marching down the middle of the street, not caring for traffic lights and shouting out slogans. It's a very unusual experience.

This sounds like a demonstration, a political action. Would you regard the explosions you staged in prominent places of the world – in front of the Statue of Liberty, within the prohibited area of the atomic test site in the desert of Nevada, in

Hiroshima and at the Great Wall of China – as political statements as well? What about China where you had worked as an artist before?

My work does have political aspects. I would not do anything just for the fun of it, without any perspectives or background. In the mid-eighties, when I started out, repression was strong in China. Explosions were an outlet for me, something that could free me from the social pressure back then. Facing the pressure, one can either become active and do something, or withdraw, or emigrate. That´s what I did: I left for some place where I could do what I wanted to do.

Leaving China meant entering a different cultural and artistic tradition, which you may have got to know before. What about the land art of the sixties, what about Robert Smithson or Walter De Maria? Did they influence your work, or did you just become aware of these approaches when you already worked on these kinds of issues?

When I was in China, there was a lot of information on art that came in through Hong Kong – environmental art, pop art, conceptual art, etc. What this news told me was: "What the hell, you can do anything you want." I believe this was extremely important, it gave me freedom.

What about the conditions and difficulties that confront an artist from the East working in the West?

Just like Western artists sway between humanitarian concerns in art and the pure art for art´s sake formalism, I follow my reflections. Like a pendulum, I am constantly oscillating. As we face new concerns and challenges, it is our impulse to extend our cultural tradition and to establish new approaches and manifestations. But having worked and lived within the Western system for so long, its concerns also become ours. Though these two ways of looking at things may overlap in some areas, they are very distant from each other at times. I guess that this context is very characteristic for the thinking of an artist like me.

What do you want the audience to experience through the installation in the Kunsthalle?

This exhibition is essentially "empty". Without people there is no work. The work happens when the audience interacts with the space. If someone walks in and around the room, the computer will send a signal to set off the mushroom clouds. The first room is vertically oriented: the clouds rise towards the arched ceiling. The last room in the exhibition hall echoes the openness of the space: the work only exists when someone is in the room and flies the kite. The space extends out horizontally with the line of the kite.

The other crucial concept for the exhibition is time. This is a "fluid installation" – time is more important than space. Asian traditions have a very special understanding of material and time. In Japan, for example, Shinto temples are pulled down and reconstructed with new material in exactly the same way every few decades. But when you point at the building and ask how old it is, the answer may be that it is one thousand years old. And you wonder and ask yourself, "How can this be? It looks brand new." Both points of view are right: the material structure of the temple is new, but formally and in its essence the temple is one thousand years old. And the same holds true for the smoke clouds here in the exhibition in the Kunsthalle: whether hundreds, thousands or hundreds of thousands of mushroom clouds may appear in the space – it is in fact one and the same thing.

Cai Guo-Qiang in conversation with Gerald Matt in 1999 on the occasion of the exhibition *Cai Guo-Qiang: I am the Y2K Bug* at Kunsthalle Wien.
Cai-Guo Qiang was born in Quanzhou, Province Fujian, China in 1957. He lives and works in New York.

Chinese to English translation by Jennifer Wen Ma.

Ellen Cantor

In these volatile times, I am concerned with expressing what is possibly permanent in my life.

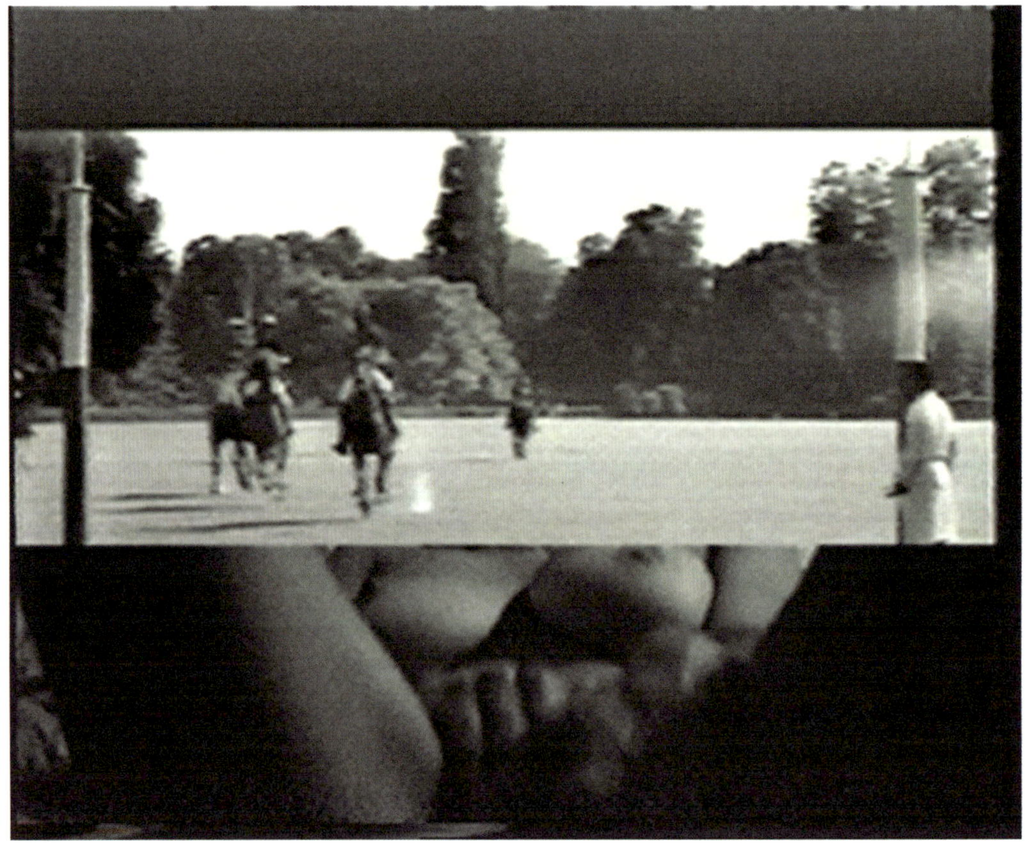

Video still: Ellen Cantor,
*Madame Bovary's
Revenge*, 1995

Your most recent video piece, *Evokation of My Demon Sister* reminds me in some ways of *Within Heaven and Hell* where you intercut scenes of extreme innocence with extreme violence. In *Evokation of My Demon Sister*, however, there seems to be only relentless disaster – you could even call it *Within Hell and Hell*. What inspired you to make this work?

Although there are catastrophes all the time in the world, I usually function in a state of relative oblivion. However, the destruction of the World Trade Center was completely shocking to me and affected me far more personally. I left America over five years ago. But, last year I returned to New York to buy an apartment and ended up spending the entire summer there. I came back to London on 10th September. When I saw the attack on 11th September, my first thought (when I had one) was that my real estate value would go down (typical New York "sentiment") … and then, of course,

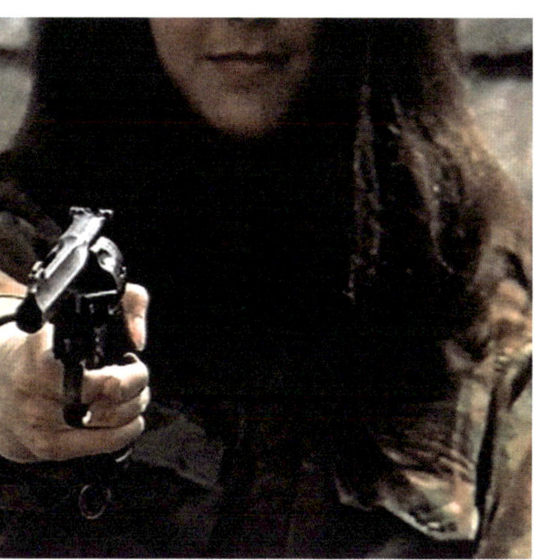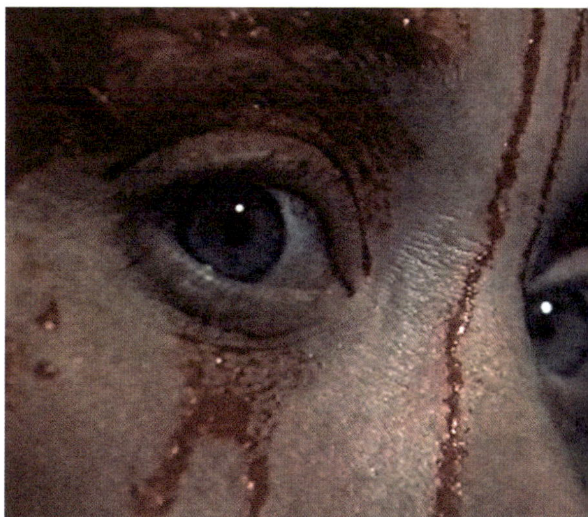

Video stills:
Ellen Cantor, *Evokation of My Demon Sister*, 2002

overwhelming sorrow, and concern for my family and friends. And I felt very isolated. My friends in London experienced this calamity much more casually, even light-heartedly. Needless to say, my friends in New York were utterly traumatised and could not relate to me and my life here anymore.

Also, my intimate life seemed to interface exactly with this disaster. Basically I felt internally "blown away" – and this feeling increased over time. Grappling with and trying to comprehend this catastrophe led me to make *Evokation of My Demon Sister* 2002. Intentionally, like a prayer for a brighter future, I finished this on New Year's day. My idea was to redramatise through contemporary imagery the ancient myth of Kali. Kali had destroyed the world to revenge herself against Krishna for abandoning and betraying her. My video stars Carrie – 20th century's original telekinetic avenger.

Over the past year I have met you several times in both New York City and London. How has living simultaneously in America and Europe affected you and your artmaking?

Well for one, I received going away parties and was welcomed home every other month on two continents, which made me feel … well, loved. I needed to be in New York. I had to mourn with the city and feel what had happened. And I observed the changes – basically the "resurrection" the city underwent over the following year. Every time I arrived in New York, it seemed like the mood and the way people interacted had evolved. The city seemed completely different each trip. So I felt I would lose touch with the essence of my home if I did not continually return. On the other hand, in London I could distance myself from American politics, get on with my work and live "normally".

The sense of being in two places felt like a dream - I loved flying. Like Russian roulette … the airplane felt like a comforting zone … the responsibility for my life was out of my hands … I would either wake up alive or dead.

I tried to express this sense of floating through time and space in the slide piece *My Best Friend* which was shown in Bregenz at Magazin 4 this past summer. The first half of the slide piece documents my friend in my New York City apartment, ending with a close-up of me asleep on my bed. Next, the camera moves further away to show the larger picture – I am in the same clothes, same position, but strangely the white blanket has turned into a white carpet. I have awakened in my studio in London.

I go to answer the door and suddenly, in place of my best friend is her *near*-identical sister … In *My Best Friend*, I tried to show the schizophrenic fluidity that had become my day-to-day life. Also, I made this piece with my friend because I wanted to express our incredible closeness, even though we live so far apart. By imagining each other's lives when we are separated, through friendship and love we *can* travel in spirit.

What are you working on now? How do you see your work evolving since I first saw your wall drawing installation in New York and presented your wall drawings and videos in the Voralberger Kunstverein in 1997?

Through my wall drawings I was striving to express the fragile transitory nature of existence - the struggle to believe in eternal love, which is constantly being eradicated by life's experiences and shifting memory. I spent an obsessive amount of hours creating the wall drawings even though I knew they would be painted over – my representation of impermanence. For the show in Austria, I also made a series of drawings *Remember the 14 days and nights*, where I collaged roses into each drawing—they blew off, dried up and broke as I was working. Keeping this work intact was ridiculously difficult.

In these volatile times, I am concerned with expressing what is possibly permanent in my life. I think of the mysterious bond of love I feel for my partner, my friends, my family … an inner reality which seems indestructible and unfathomable. My intention is to express this essence which, exists despite bad feelings and utter chaos. After spending time looking at some early paintings I made, I have begun a re-exploration of oil painting to see if I can develop my ideas through this more permanent enduring medium. Right now I am painting the story of Barbie and Allah.

Stupid, inept and frustrated. I wish I could reach a greater awareness and capacity to express myself so that I could truly affect and guide people. On a television documentary I heard that Mozart was secretly expressing the Rosicrucians' ideals through *The Magic Flute*. In further reading I found out that the Rosicrucians were a group of men in the Middle Ages that anonymously travelled throughout Europe with the sole purpose of healing people and the ills of their time. They had been taught how to communicate with nature and the inner spirits and understood how to move through time and space. They could pass on their knowledge to whoever they thought was capable and ready to be initiated. Apparently, Sir Francis Bacon (who was possibly Shakespeare) was a Rosicrucian. I suppose at this time in my life I would like someone to come around and let me in on what the fuck is going on.

In his interpretation of dreams, Freud interprets the dream of flying and fear of falling as a repetition of childhood experiences. Falling is connected with affection: "Most children fall at one time or another and are picked up and cuddled." Dreams of falling are linked with the surrender by women to temptations, and flying dreams with the male erection. In your video *Be My Baby* you combine love scenes with scenes of astronauts in space. Is this a reference to Freud's theories?

I find Freud curious in an autobiographical and historical sense. The ideas he expresses seem to me idiosyncratic to his own experience and fantasy and to the culture and time he was from. But I have difficulty relating them to my own life experiences.

One of my main sources of inspiration for *Be My Baby* was a series of lectures by Rudolf Steiner titled "The Manifestations of Karma" (Hamburg 1910). He speaks about accidents, death, illness, and synchronistic encounters in relationship to individual and collective evolution into higher consciousness.

In this video I was concerned with how to transcend tragic experience and heal painful memory. In some way, like in Hitchcock's film *Vertigo*, grave memory is a centrifuge (blindly) cycling/leading us back into our wounds. Often after fucked-up experiences, people try to approach life in a new way, experience it with new people, but find themselves again and again in similar situations. It seems unfathomable how this occurs or how to extricate oneself from this servitude of past sorrows impeding on one's present possibilities.

In the latter part of the video I try to invoke a fresh psychic direction. By imaging a "gravity-less" world – an astronaut floating in space for the first time, a couple laughing, doing front flips down a hill, another astronaut doing somersaults in his space ship – I tried to externalise inner metaphors for innocence and freedom from constrained confusion. As an artist, I often question myself whether an imagined hope, a wish, can forge a path into reality.

Another source of inspiration for *Be My Baby* was a dirty joke on the internet: A man asked his wife for a blow job. She said, "I'll give you one the day our next door neighbour's son lands on the moon!" Their neighbour's son was Neil Armstrong.

You make drawings, photographs and videos. What is the relationship between these media in your work and how do you link them?

Mainly my art is based on narrative structures that are, in part, privately encoded personal dialogues. More or less, I find working in each media comparable. For example drawing for me is similar to video editing in that I am expressing emotions through creating acute relationships with the images and sound. Finding the order of the pictures, cutting them, replacing them … is very much like erasing, pencilling and collaging images.

When I put together an exhibition I try to discover ways to integrate the various components to create a complete narrative. For example, when I make a wall drawing and have a video playing in the next room, not only do the two narratives link together, but the sound from the video piece animates the drawings.

More and more I have been trying to integrate the various aspects of my work into one integral piece. In my most recent video *Barbie London* I combine images from film, drawing and text, as well as performance from Barbie dolls, puppets and myself, to create a complex romantic story. Also, at each given moment, I try to assimilate simultaneous levels of emotional experience: humour, pain, pleasure, anger, love, etc. I've been thinking about how the lyrics in soul music are often deeply sad, yet the beat is sexy and up and the overall impact is joyful.

You collect Barbie dolls and love sentimental films like *The Sound of Music*. You draw fairy princesses talking of sex and love. You mix *The Sound of Music* with

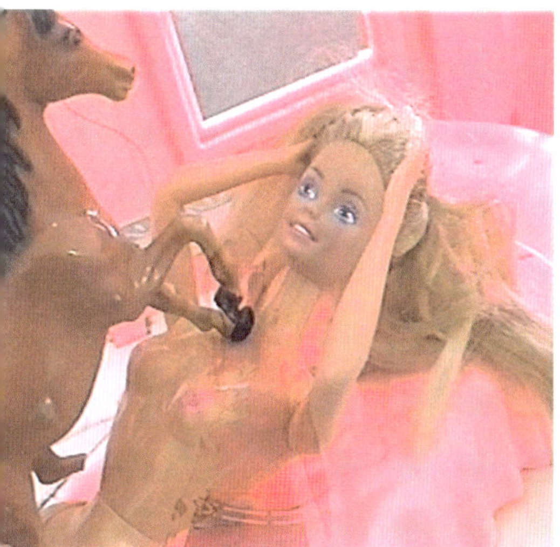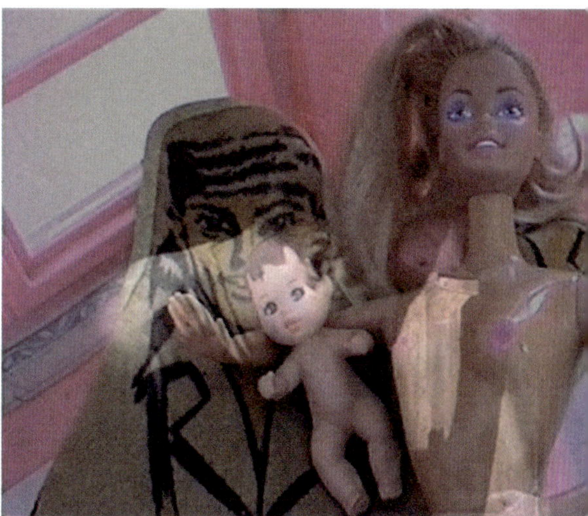

images from *The Texas Chainsaw Massacre* to create a horror scenario of frenzy and disfigurement. What is the role of the childhood/adult dichotomy in your work?

Like a Renaissance Madonna, Barbie has become a popular icon for artists, children, adults … My mom didn't allow me to play with Barbie because she thought, as a feminist, that Barbie was a poor role model for women and would stunt my creativity. Secretly I played with dolls beyond the age children are really supposed to and now I find artmaking for me in some way is like a continual doll game. Ironically, as a girl, dolls were a way to empower and express myself – create "reality". Still, when I look at these dolls that partially formed my female identity, I wonder how much of my individual self is real? Beauty, sexiness, self-abnegation, kindness …

As an adult, I like to look at, live through, fairy tales and figure out in which ways these mythologies represent truths and wisdoms about living and on the other hand in which ways they propagate stereotypes and superstitions. Then I imbue my characters, Snow White, Barbie, Cinderella, Prince, Bambi, … with psychological, spiritual, emotional, and physical reality as I experience it – hopes, dreams, desires and the hardcore actuality of being me. In this way I am able to gauge and separate myself from cultural expectations.

Sometime ago my friend and I discussed *The Little Mermaid*. Strangely enough, like Barbie, she has no pussy. She falls in love with a human prince, but in order to shed her tail and pursue him, she has to give up her ability to speak and she has no feet. She has to follow him on bloody bones and goes to great extents to disguise her physical and mental anguish. In the end she loses him, but is made into an angel as a consolation. On the one hand, I recognize this feeling of self sacrifice and unrequited desire. Still I wonder what the objective of this story is: to teach girls not to lose their virginity before they procure marriage? Moreover, as in many fairy tales, nothing is told about the prince's emotions or inner conflicts – he is one dimensional – the steadfast object of desire. In any case, through my work I am searching to reinvest images of women, as well as men, with their full human complexity and capacity.

Often in my work, I am looking at human corruption and trying to find symbols and transformative powers back into/forward towards what I believe is the essential purity of spirit. Often in shamanistic myths, animals, like bears and deers, represent an individual's supernatural power and divinity. And, in fairy tales, there are characters, like the blue fairy in *Pinocchio*, that represent holy guidance. In *Barbie London*, Barbie and double Ken (Dr. Jeckyl and Mr. Hyde) are in the end transformed into two bear cubs playing in the woods together. Ultimately, my work forms a personal cosmology I have developed to represent and extend my faith.

The title of your catalogue we produced is *My Perversion is the Belief in True Love*. Is this a paradox?

My experience with "true love" is that it is true. Yet, like in the film *Vertigo* even if there is real chemistry between people it is tenuous and can easily be destroyed by psychological illness, fear, catastrophe, confusion and miscommunication. Moreover, retaining personal faith and devotion in the midst of a pervasively pessimistic/sceptical culture is not so easy.

In the end, it becomes a question for me as to how to actually live with "love" in contemporary society. The role of men and women has already changed. Both have the possibility of active positions in financial determination, and greater possibility in how to enact their gender and sexuality. There are so many choices, one can have multiple lovers, one can have careers and interests outside the family unit, and one can live and travel anywhere in the world. Formerly, stereotypes created structures for people to live within, and religion once created a prescribed lifestyle and morality. Without these formats, we have much more freedom to be our "selves", but it is not clear how to live in relationship to another or even how to be ourselves. In some ways now, we live within ideal utopian freedom.

Although people still identify with how they were brought up, actually there is no defined role model or stability anymore. We more or less are forging a new path. However, when this "new way" becomes further determined, like in the course of most revolutions, again our possibilities will be calcified. But it is precarious to live with no security and no fixed identity. I find vertigo (spinning, dizzy, spiralling) more and more relevant to our times because we live with such an implosion of mental, physical and spiritual stimuli without any directed route as to how to live multidimensionally. I try not to panic.

I don't think this aspect of my work is particularly capricious or even personal, this is how I see the world. The complexity and vastness of modern society alone is beyond all learning and preconditioning. We live in a global society that is controlled by commerce, yet for the most part we lack knowledge as to how the world is controlled. It clearly affects us and yet we don't know how we are effected. There is greed, evil as well as magnanimity, good. Communication and technological advances are made very rapidly, before one can learn what has been achieved. There is an incredible amount of information as well as misinformation coming through the media, the internet, etc. – too much to actually comprehend. At present, there are unpredictable utopian possibilities. For instance with hacking, it seems to me that this form of pirating offers an alternative autonomy – liberation from gender, age, financial hierarchy, and totalitarianism. Inadvertently, it contributes to the democratic process.

In any case, reality is destabilised and there are not very many distinguishing borders (physically/morally). For better or worse, it is impossible to distinguish a clear overall value system and even international borders are an illusion in this context.

I suppose there are differences *and* parallels. In *Be My Baby,* a filmclip from John Cassavetes' *Faces,* in which a man tries to wake up an unconscious woman who has attempted suicide, by slapping her, is repeated again and again. Each time the soundtrack and the surrounding images shift, this seemingly violent sequence takes on a different meaning.

I am interested in the various manifestations of violence. There are diverse meanings extending from erotic pleasure and fetishism to physical and emotional violation. There are personal forms of violence in which one harms oneself inwardly with self doubt and hatred and contrarily there are positive forms of aggression in which, through psychic determination, one can grow through obstacles. It is a completely vast subject, which I often explore through my work. And of course, there is always the overriding question as to how to exist harmoniously within oneself in a society which is built on historic precedence of human violation and is constantly in states of war and human degradation.

You love Proust and have read his work several times. The subject of Proust's work, like Hitchcock's *Vertigo*, is time. The second half of the film is taken up with Scottie's attempt to recreate the past. Are you remembering things past?

In my artwork/life, memory is a constant concern and struggle. Firstly, I was brought up to remember the Holocaust in order to prevent history from repeating itself. These personal memoirs hurt and frighten me, and I carry this deep pain in myself. Also, as I discussed in *Be My Baby,* woundful memories are unconsciously reenacted. Part of my artwork is the memory of childhood and adult experiences. But naturally within this memory, I would like to be free of fear, loss, panic – to be free to experience and explore the present joyfully.

Ellen Cantor in conversation with Gerald Matt in 2001 and in December 2002. The artist presented films at Kunsthalle Wien project space and took part in the exhibition *Don Juan alias Don Giovanni oder "zwei und zwei sind vier" oder "Lust ist der einzige Schwindel, dem ich Dauer wünsche"* (2006) at Kunsthalle Wien and Ursula Blickle Foundation, Kraichtal.
Ellen Cantor was born in Detroit, Michigan in 1961. She lives and works in London.

Chicks on Speed

We love working too much on an explosive mess of activity; we forget to make a product.

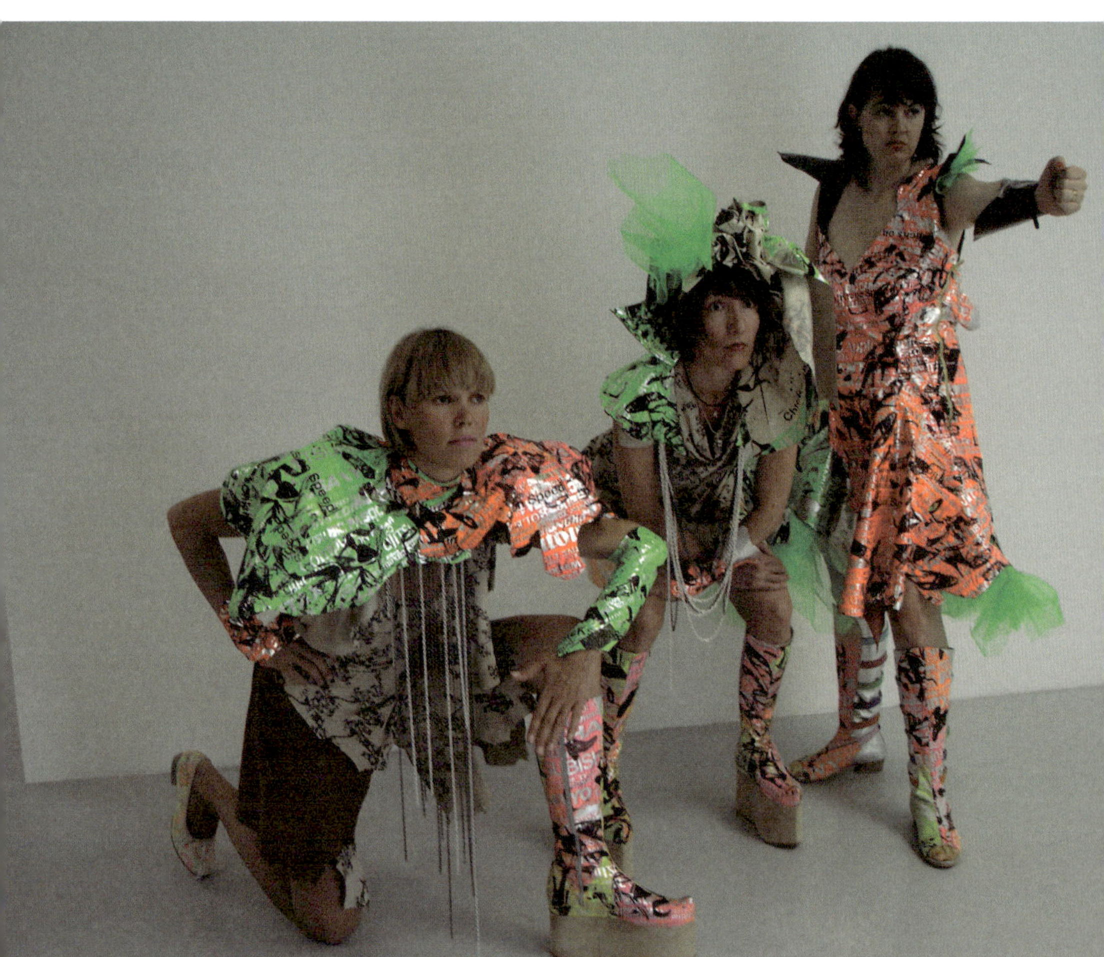

Chicks on Speed, 2005

Chicks on Speed (CoS) are, just now, very much in the public eye within the art and gallery scene. However, you also write on your website that, "CoS will save us all from pretentious art snobs who don't understand it if it is not in a museum." So what exactly is your relationship to the visual arts?

Love/Hate. We love working too much on an explosive mess of activity; we forget to make a product. Unlike the Situationists where part of the concept was to leave out the product, we love products but we produce things like a short film, a happening, etc. from which it is difficult for gallery owners to make money.

The dark side is the incestuous nature of the business and in Germany there are loads of sexist wankers. Some of them are actually friends of ours; alone they are fine, but when one goes out with them and they meet their buddies, they remind us why there are so many women sick of men.

CoS is not, after all, just a music enterprise, but rather a multi-tasking operation. You create videos, art installations, graphic work, fashion design, and so forth. So where do you see your own position within the contemporary entertainment culture?

We used to be seen as freaks, but after a few years we were taken seriously.

We were advised by our professors to focus on one thing and do it well. However, we really wanted to do everything and thus focused on quantity. More is more; we know that for sure.

During the Art Basel exhibition in Miami, you staged a performance in South Beach (not far from the Container from Art Positions). What is your relationship to galleries and the art market? Who buys your work?

The art market has not discovered us yet. We have a large archive; perhaps in 20 years they will develop a taste for our work. The market does not yet appreciate the kind of work women are doing. The market is still based on weight: big sculptures and paintings, etc. We are still waiting for that to change.

CoS wants to save the world from old bores who cannot understand bands that don't feature guitars. One of your best-known songs is called, "We don't play guitars." What do you have against guitars?

There are so many guitar-playing wankers out there who only want to play something between their legs. We have our machines; in fact, we have some pretty loud guitar samples, we have watched guitar-yanking wankers go pale at sound checks because we were way harder then they were. The popularity of electronica has changed things in the last 5 years since we wrote that song.

Two of your members are from English-speaking countries, yet your music is often referred to as "Eurotrash". How do you view old Europe and what artistic challenges does it offer you?

Our group would not exist in either the US or Australia. We are a collective. In America, people think hierarchically. Furthermore, our roots are European: COBRA, Dada, Lettrismus.

Munich, your home base, has long been a disco stronghold, certainly since the days of Donna Summer. Now this once-derided type of music has become hip once again, thanks to the attentions lavished on it by people such as DJ Hell, Jason Forrest, and others. What significance does disco music, trace elements of which can be detected in your own music as well, have for your aesthetics?

Hmmm …

In your *Program to Save the World* you also proclaim a wish to abolish The Boring DJ. The record spinner was certainly a cult figure of the nineties, being enthroned as the eclectic saviour of a pop music gone stale. How do you, as an electronic ensemble, view this entire DJ culture today?

It was so boring for a while; however, now some people have livened it up.

You have staged performances in institutions housing people receiving psychiatric treatment. Do you pursue a conscious scheme of employing your art as a means of social intervention?

From the beginning, we have always seen ourselves as social workers; from when we were doing *Seppi Bar* in Munich, creating a space, where we, the students and non-students, determined what went on, who got kicked out.

CoS is sometimes thought of as being something like Peaches with a feminist agenda. How does a feminism filtered through post-pop and trash aesthetics define itself today?

First, that is not at all correct: Peaches is on an emancipation mission using the language of sex & rock. We don't lecture our audiences on how they should be emancipated. We work with an aesthetic that has nothing to do with the main-stream definition of what makes a woman sexually attractive. That is also true with Peaches.

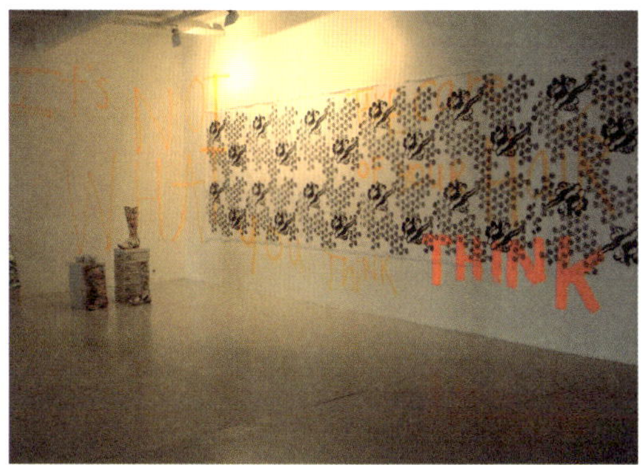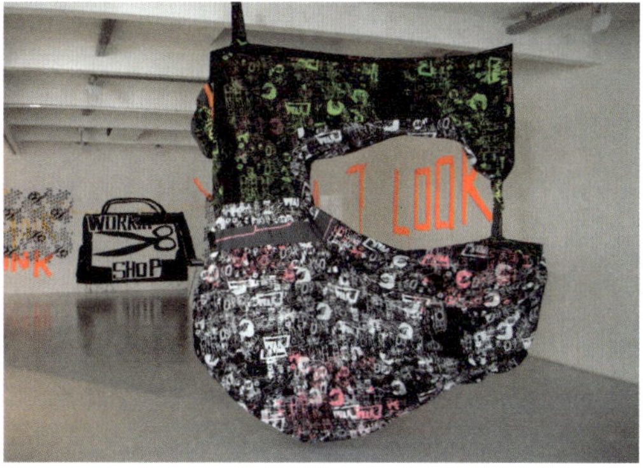

Installation views, Kunstraum Innsbruck: Chicks on Speed, *It's not what you think, it's the way you look*, 2005

After the spectacular rise of the Riot Grrrls at the start of the nineties, things quieted down around feminine rock and pop. How do you see the future of women's bands in an industry still dominated by males?

We think that Pop is short lived. Our last record was barely bought, but we are still being booked a lot. There seem to be a lot of festivals and clubs who really want to book female acts that do something unusual and are entertaining; that is, after all, what it's about.

In your album graphics and other visual elements you work with collages and cut-ups. Which artistic currents of the present do you feel a particular affinity to and, conversely, which artists to you detest? Where will your artistic journey take you? And what are your upcoming projects?

We work with a lot of other artists, A. L. Steiner, a photographer from New York, Deborah Schamoni; a camerawoman and director; Kathi Glas, textile designer, and with Anat Ben–David, who frequently steps in for me at live shows because I have a six-month-old baby … we hope the group grows bigger and stronger and develops into an international movement active in many more disciplines. We are working on a musical for fall 2006. In March 2006 in Barcelona, Alex made a female compilation and festival called *Girl Monster*, the CD will be released on Chicks on Speed records. We toured the USA in November 2005 and released a new CD/DVD, and I have, in what could be described as a side–project, written music for a production of *Antigone* at Thalia Theatre in Hamburg.

Chicks on Speed in conversation with Gerald Matt in the spring of 2006. The artists took part in the exhibition *Go Johnny Go! The E-Gitarre – Kunst und Mythos* (2003) at Kunsthalle Wien.
The Chicks on Speed are: Alex Murray-Leslie, born in Australia in 1970; Melissa Logan, born in the USA in 1970; and Kiki Moorse, born in Germany in 1967. They live and work in Munich, Germany.

Steven Cohen

I am not a well-intentioned 'political art' plumber. My art is about trying to articulate the results of an experiment while it happens.

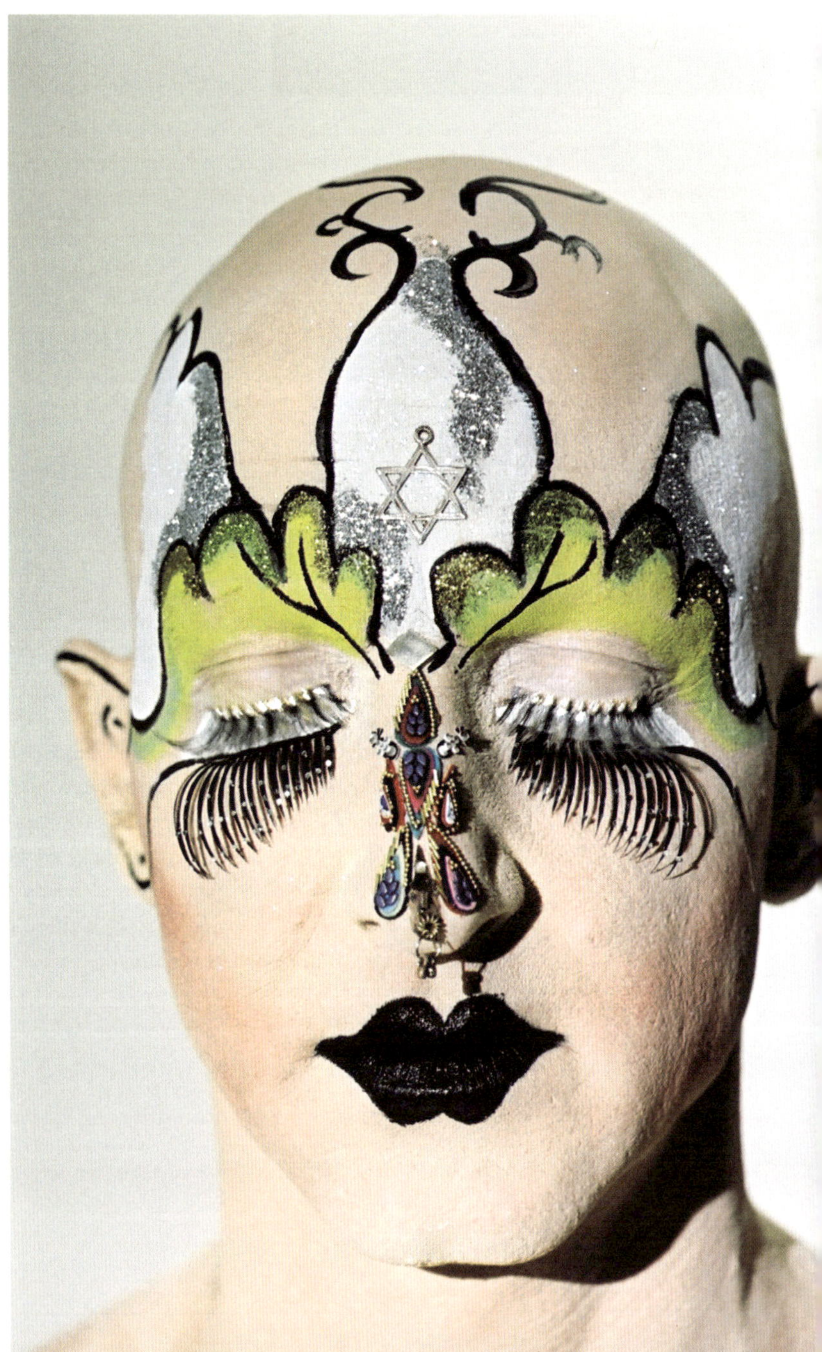

Steven Cohen

You have broken up the project space of Kunsthalle Wien into separate areas and will be presenting the performance *Dancing Inside Out* live on nine evenings after the opening ceremony. Could you enlarge on your exhibition concept?

I have divided the project space of KHW into two areas. The first area is a black box where I will project three existing video artworks – *Broken Bird* (2001), *Chandelier* (2002), *Maid In South Africa* (2005).

The second and larger area will be for the ten performances of *Dancing Inside Out*. This space will also include large photographic prints as well as three mannequins bearing the costumes from the performance. I have chosen *Dancing Inside Out* as the overall title of the exhibition as each work deals with the outward manifestation of an inward state as expressed through movement of the (costumed) body in space, private and public.

Through these un-dance live art actions, I aim to function as a speculum, not as a suture. It is difficult for me to speak but more difficult still to be silent … and to make my secrets public is always to enter into a dangerous confidence with you, the public.

Taking dance to its extreme, the performance of *Dancing Inside Out* has at its heart, the contradictions inherent between reality and imagination, intimate and public zones, pride and shame, genocide and survival, the macabre and the ordinary, to be proudly Jewish yet anti-Zionist. *Dancing Inside Out* is about the pain of being human and the joy of being alive, and, like our own lives, it is an incomplete experiment.

In your artistic pursuits, you have given intense attention to issues relating to Jewishness, the persecution of Jews, and homosexuality. Does this represent an autobiographical approach?

Identity issues have always been the basis of my artistic production … since I was six years old I have had an enormous awareness of myself as queer, Jewish, white and male - and how that positions me in relation to the outside world. So it's not just me! me! me!, but me, you, and what happens between us. For me, persecution of any one kind always carries with it resonances of related discrimination.

In your radical performances, entitled *Queer*, you breach political as well as social taboos. Do you consider the medium of art to be suitable as a means of achieving political resistance? Could it, in your opinion, trigger processes of social change?

Art is a suitable but insufficient means of achieving political resistance. Although I do believe that art triggers processes of social change within individuals, violence and militant protest work much better on a grand scale. I don't know how to use a gun or build a bomb … and so my only weapons are artistic innovation, beauty and revelation through creative deconstruction.

You originate from South Africa (Johannesburg) – to what extent do you get involved with the political situation in your home country?

In South Africa, the social is political – and I get involved in every way in which art has the possibility to be there, or to become there. I have radically intervened in a range of zones and situations, from a neo-Nazi rally to a dog show and a bridal show, a township, a rugby match, gay pride marches, a squatter camp, the National General elections. What I do is always question – going to a squatter camp in a chandelier is asking the question, "what will happen when I wear an illuminated chandelier-tutu into lightless squatter territory?" with no intention of resolving anything – it's not like, "I'm going to wear a chandelier and go to a squatter camp and fix things" – I am not a well-intentioned 'political art' plumber. My art is about trying to articulate the results of an experiment while it happens.

Is there, in your opinion, such a thing as a common South African culture that unites both the black and the white population groups?

There is a common South African culture between black and white population groups at a point where difference meets discourse … art and tolerance are catalysts for that. We have a tragic shared history full of courage, conflict and sacrifice, which is balanced by a shared future with the hope for negotiated acceptance.

You work very strongly in a manner that transcends boundaries. Theatrical production aspects and the very pointed use of music prevail, playing as important a role in your works as specifically dance-related elements. What directorial intentions stand behind all this?

The video artworks, although existing in their own right, are really the residues of the uninvited and unexpected (and often unwelcome) public interventions. I have none of the supports (such as music) during the actions themselves.

In fabricating the video artworks, I am interested in combining camp old Hollywood glamour with hard-core reality, and elements of Yiddish theatre with mundane life and actual histories … "there's no business like Shoah business, like no business I know". As far as dance goes, I consider all movement to be dance, from staggering around in high heels to peristalsis.

In your performances and happenings you never appear as your own self, but as an actor with a mask-like, somewhat bizarre facial make-up, frequently naked but wearing some grotesque costume or carrying a symbolic object. Are these disguises to be viewed as deliberate artistic means and what is their precise significance?

I would say I only ever appear as my own self, exaggerated and manipulated. Sometimes, in the doing of the work, I have a sense of being beside myself (in a cabbalistic sense) – of being there with you watching me, also amazed and amused and scared and insulted. The costumes are disguises, which reveal, they are the sculptural elements of the work … and once they are placed on my living body and situated in a specific location, and func-

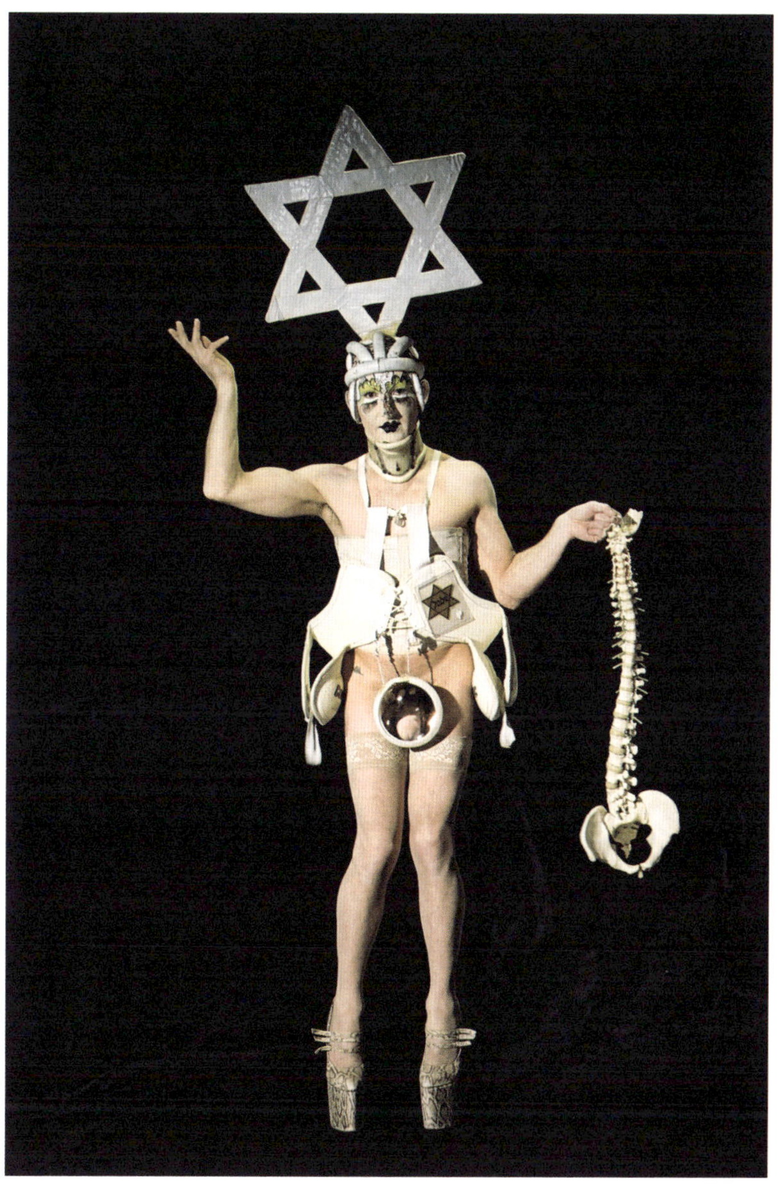

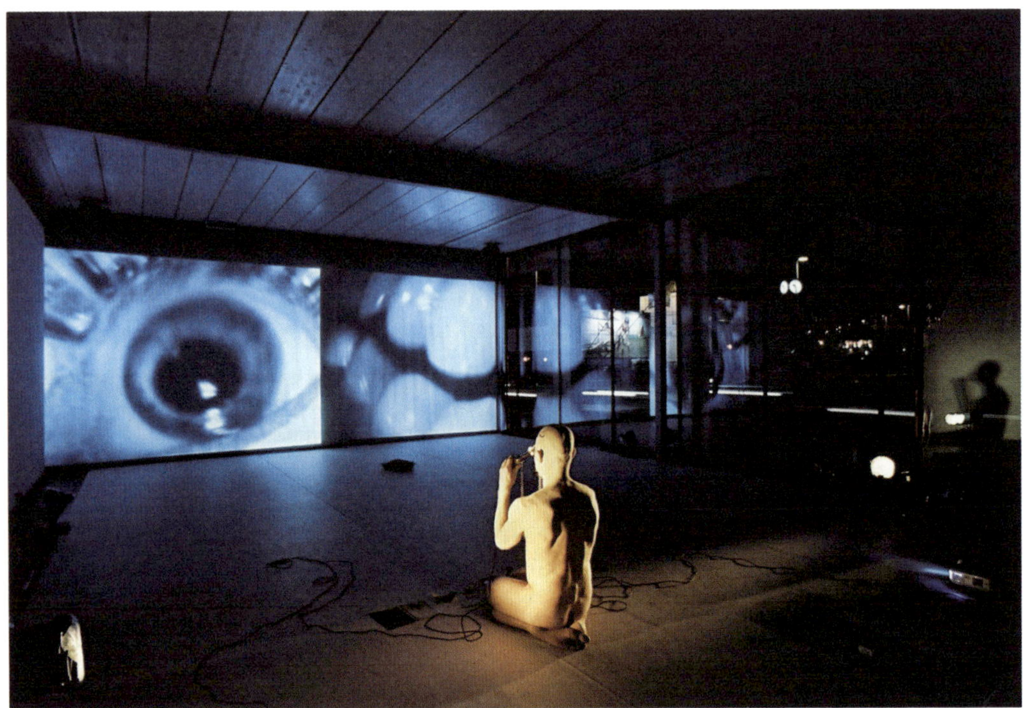

tion in public – the combination of that is the art. Every element used in transforming myself into a visual spectacle is significant and deliberate … it is all constructed … up until the point at which I go out and have to let go, and collaborate with the way of the universe, with what happens, which is always uncontrolled and deliciously unexpected.

What significance do you ascribe to the provocation inherent in your covering your genitals with a so-called "Jews' Star" or Jewish Star of David of the sort forced on Jews in Nazi Germany – as you did in *Dancing Inside Out*?

In the performance of *Dancing Inside Out*, I wear as a 'cache-sex' a yellow star which is a decoration from a Jewish prayer–shawl bag. For me, it is not a provocation, but an aesthetic and discreet way of asking if my circum–cised and genetically Jewish persecuted cock is a sacred object. One of the elements within the work *Dancing Inside Out* is a video record of a public intervention I did in Lyon, France. Then I did wear an authentic yellow star (of the sort you describe) to the Centre of Resistance and Deportation, together with a giant Star of David headgear and a large magnifying glass dangling in front of my penis to make super-evident my circumcision … while I performed a lament dance at what was previously the local Gestapo headquarters.

Is there, in your opinion, such a thing as a separate homosexual aesthetic? If so – how would you define it?

I think the homosexual aesthetic is like the heterosexual aesthetic but with extra elements and a twist … sort of like haemorrhoids plus glitter.

Do you view the "homoerotic perspective" as possessing a specific subversive context?

Somehow, when it's put like that, 'homoerotic perspective' sounds like advertising used in the commodification of gay culture, something to profit from alternative lifestyles. There's a lot of sell-out in the rainbow flag of contemporary gay culture that has forgotten the pink triangle … and that's not subversive at all. But the basic butt-fuckers perspective will always have a scary and subversive context.

According to Sartre we are condemned to live in freedom and therefore must newly reconstruct ourselves from day to day. This is probably true in an even stronger measure for homosexuals, even though a gay culture and gay movement do exist. Would you agree?

Yes … sometimes I have to reconstruct myself several times in a single day … and that is when I am making art and I am most free.

You studied psychology, among other things – how did your artistic career develop?

I made my first performance work at six years old. My development as an artist was informed by my intellectual pursuits, studying diverse subjects ranging from psychology to genetics to film criticism and social anthropology … but also by mundane experiences like walking to the shops, having sex, doing housework, being beaten up, losing friends to AIDS—all research for productivity. I actively became an artist when I was forcibly conscripted into the racist whites-only South African Defence Force (1985-1987). I spent three months in an army mental asylum when I refused to bear arms – I was just a little too sane to function in a psychotic military system. For the remaining 21 months in the army, I secretly studied photographic silkscreen techniques (Ruth Prowse School of Art, Cape Town South Africa) at night, and obsessively printed and painted delicately brutal textiles with images of violence, racism, discrimination and sexuality … my source imagery ranged from photographs stolen from the Defence Force archives to my own original photographs. Subsequently, I did this for ten years.

When I was 33 years old, a decade of being hungry and angry and constantly working, led me to contract a range of diseases simultaneously, and

I spent several months hospitalised and bed-ridden, watching the calendar go by as if it was a clock. Seeing my body change shape and size, my piss go black and my eyes go yellow, opened up to me the unexplored palette of possibilities that my own body could be the primary source of my art, and I became a performance artist working in live art. I chose to represent through actual presence, to paint my face not canvas, to reveal things about other people through my own nakedness, to deconstruct social functioning via my uninvited public interventions. So it took me several leaps off the edge and much fingering through my scar tissue to find my G-spot for creative development. Since 1998, I have been making, flying, falling, crawling, daring and dancing … on my own, but never alone, always with the support of my co-creator and life-partner Elu. Through loving each other, we have survived ourselves.

At present you are living in France (in La Rochelle) – do you want to stay on in Europe or are you planning a return to South Africa? Is it easier to position yourself as an international artist being based in Europe than it is from your home country?

Well, you (Gerald Matt) became aware of my work on your visit to South Africa where I physically wasn't but where my work abounds, so I trust that it's ultimately the quality of the work, which will determine my position. Of course, it's easier to sell things when your shop is on the main road, but I despise the supermarket aspect of art in Europe - I'm more interested in forcing unwanted gifts onto stangers than selling at a profit to big-name clients. I intend to return home to South Africa as soon as I stop finding new meaning from being in foreign places, when the smells become familiar and my tail stops wagging.

Which project of yours would you like to see completed next?

I have three projects swirling around in my head like jewels in the lavatory, so the first project is to not flush … but to organise perfect settings for these artistic gems.

Steven Cohen in conversation with Gerald Matt in the beginning of 2006 on the occasion of the exhibition *Steven Cohen: Dancing Inside Out* at Kunsthalle Wien project space.
Steven Cohen was born in Johannesburg, South Africa, in 1962. He lives and works in La Rochelle, France.

Julius Deutschbauer und Gerhard Spring

We would like to describe ourselves as political air violinists, who cover political melodies but who offer up no political performances for the plain and simple reason that we carry them out in the air.

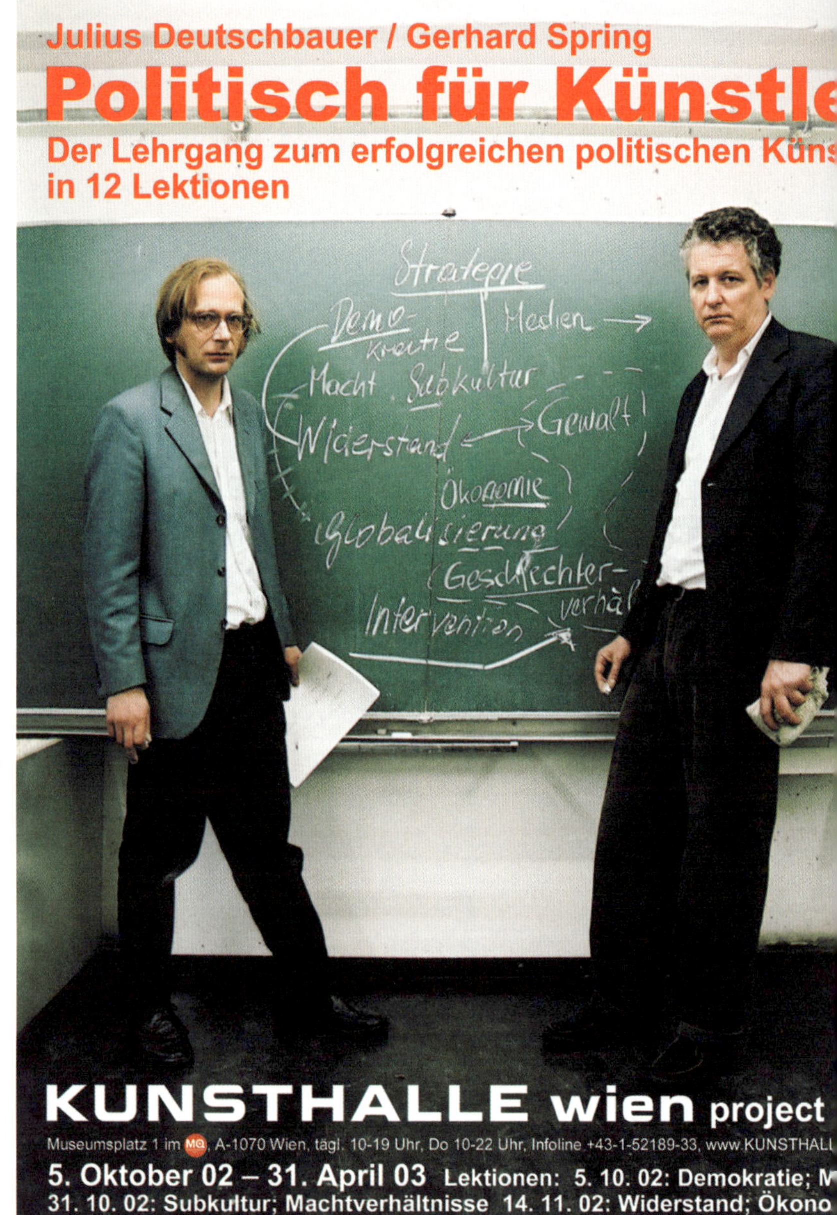

Deutschbauer/Spring,
Politisch für Künstler,
2003

For most of the past six years, you've been performing as the Deutschbauer/ Spring duo and the frequency of your actions, lectures, theatrical performances, exhibitions, karaoke evenings, etc. etc., has been increasing dramatically. One could almost say: let not an evening pass without inviting Deutschbauer and Spring. Is this activist omnipresence part of your artistic and political platform or has it developed simply as a result of rising demand? When will we see a poster announcing, "Deutschbauer/Spring to Open Artists' Agency for Deutschbauer/ Spring"?

Well, would that even be desirable? Up until now we've preferred to represent others rather than ourselves. It is also a tricky business, standing up for yourself. Pretty soon you might not have a leg to stand on. Self-administration sounds quite enticing, but it soon turns you into a barkeeper serving his own beer from one hand to the other. No, honestly, that is one poster you just won't ever see.

And no opening poster either, introducing you as an institution?

That one already exists.

Oh, I guess I must have overlooked it, then, in among the overwhelming abundance

Donations account *Poor Poet,* P.S.K., account number 7459 6368.

Bingo. The Post Office Bank account we opened five years ago was an institution serving ourselves as "poor poets."

Two artists, starving to death on a single fat bank account?

Yes. Unfortunately, there is no such thing as 'artists dying of thirst.'

The 'morning shakes' as a world career.

Art critics and audiences seem to be split into two opposing factions with regard to Deutschbauer/Spring. There are those who are your loyal fans, who presumably turn up not just at all of your premieres, but also collect all of your books and posters—which is, incidentally, by no means an easy feat, given that you produce a dozen of them each year. The other faction thinks of you as charlatans, negating any serious intent on your part, and considering you personally, yourselves, and your products, as "facile" and "frivolous". There are well-known representatives of the cultural scene with illustrious names to be found in both camps. Some of your opponents may have conceivably been victims of one or another of your sendups, such as the series of dialogues called "Morak and many others". In other words, you've created your own enemies, at least in part. Was that an artistic and political strategy, or just a cunning device?

> We would love to have enemies, but seem to be having for the most part just enmities. Of course we profit from the economics of having enmities, but a real circle of enemies would naturally be much more profitable. As even Nietzsche was wont to say — or, perhaps Carl Schmitt, himself a masterful enemy — it is a decent enemy that turns mere fiends into political foes. So a genuine enemy could still help to turn us into serious political artists. The friend of my enemy is my own best opponent, against whom I will spar even by political means.

Or War …

> … the Mother of all Political Artists [laughter].

One of your principles — possibly unknown to, or unrecognised by, some people or even most people — is that you will only reproduce what others have already said or done before. Which is to say that you will sample, do bricolage…

> … handicrafts, …

… mixing selected quotations, fragments, elements taken from world literature, art, science, politics and so forth in what is, in my opinion, a highly virtuoso manner, and in vessels that you have previously labelled according to some theme or title. At the same time, however, you go by, in your own words, the motto stating, "subtraction undoes addition." Now do you really only take bits away, or don't you also put lots of things together, such as, for example, the "horrid paintings" of your posters, or the entirely raw statements of your invited authors on individual lessons in *Political Jargon for Artists*?

> The things we find are held together by paste we produce ourselves, just like the dung beetle rolling his giant pills from all the shit he finds scattered about his habitat.

Doesn't the dung beetle also add his own shit to the pill he rolls up?

> Well, naturally, we mix in a good deal of our own shit into the pills that we put on offer.

Deutschbauer/Spring as art therapists?

> Art doctors, yes, prescribing a sprinkling of hilarity to anyone who fails to see the humour in art. Professional blunders and suits of malpractice

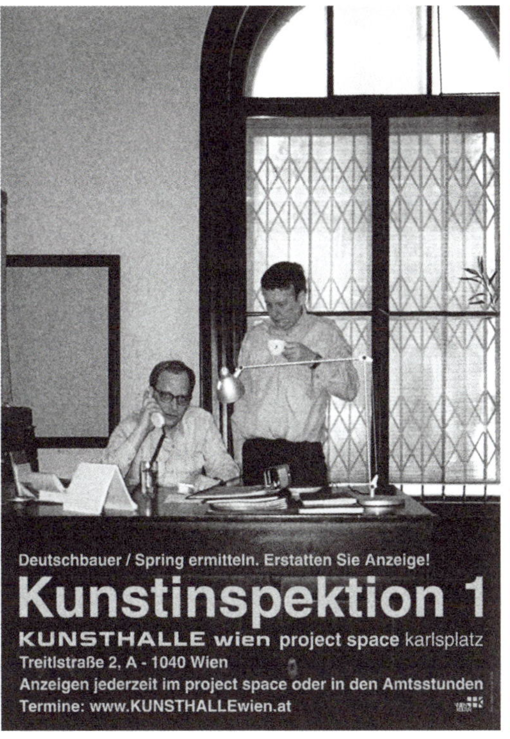

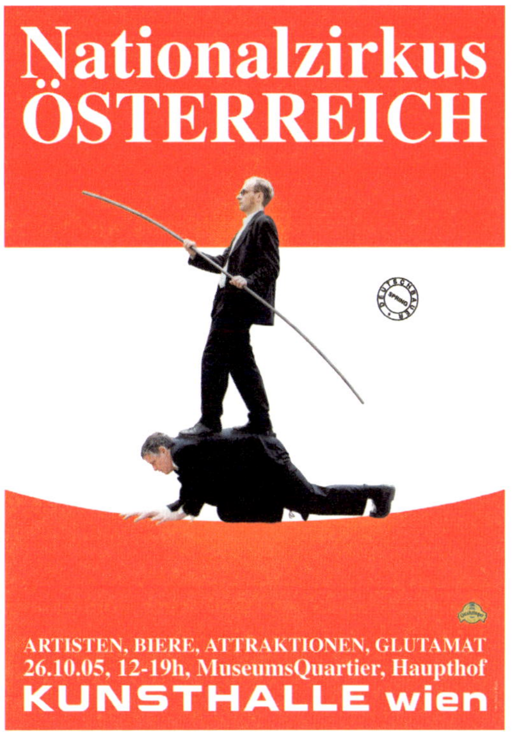

Deutschbauer/Spring, *Kunstinspektion 1*, Kunsthalle Wien project space 2004

Deutschbauer/Spring, *Nationalzirkus Österreich*, Mariahilferstraße/Museumsplatz, Wien 2005

included. So, for example, when we did our introductory art appreciation course, *Inspecting the Arts 101*, audiences were most happy to join in.

When you did that art inspection at the project space of Kunsthalle Wien, pressing charges against various art offences, the audience actually became a part of your performance. Likewise in *Theatre Karaoke* and your *Anti-Fascist Amusement Park,* where audiences were intimately involved in the action. In all of these examples, however, you take charge of events, offering, as it were, clear operating instructions. Now, do you view the audience as a creative potential for the possible optimisation of your work or rather more as a means to an end in the implementation of concepts, which – if I can offer an advance interpretation – hold up a mirror to consumerist behaviour in general?

Consumer behaviour is not to be dismissed out of hand. We all take part in it, because we must. But also we make no distinction between the creative potential and the audience as a means to a specific end, which is art. The means, like the painter's brush, isn't merely passive—it just operates within a limited sphere of action. We happen to set up a framework for a participating audience, just as our principals do with us. It offers the immense advantage of not having to start from scratch. People coming to our shows don't face a blank sheet of paper, but, rather, for example, a form requesting proof of their anti-fascist attitude or they may be charged with artistic misconduct. What declarations or denouncements eventually fill up the page is up to the audience.

Shouldn't an evening with you be a more creative affair than a night at the police station?

No, we don't need to be any more creative than the police.

With projects such as *Terror in the Amusement Park* – with attractions that convey the impression of the audience actually taking part in the terror – or *The Language of Handicap* – featuring faked or closely imitative interviews with disabled persons from around the world – or the *Anti-Fascist Amusement Park* – one cannot help but be reminded of cynicism of a fairly foul kind. As Rainer Metzger once quoted Peter Sloterdijk in this context, "Cynicism is the enlightened false consciousness." How cynical are you guys, viewed from your own perspective, or how would you define your kind of cynicism?

Well, what would be the correct consciousness, then, and above all—who has it? Passing judgment on that question might be cynical—a fact that Sloterdijk and Metzger clearly overlooked. Also, cynicism represents a desperate attempt at insight – not enlightenment. As Hans Blumenberg has said, the cynic resolutely defends himself against the fact that he was once laughed out of court. Only someone who can bear to be laughed at, to be the object of ridicule, is immune to becoming a cynic. If you don't want to be a cynic, you'll have to be able to laugh at yourself. The projects you mentioned are exercises in laughing at ourselves, much more than cynicism. As Robert Musil nicely put it, cynicism equals irony minus love, or you could say that irony equals cynicism plus love. We're far too much attached to the things we laugh about, we love them like we love ourselves, so we can't be cynics.

Your work also reminds me of slapstick humour, hilarity, laughter, ridicule through repetition.

Yes, although with this exercise in ridicule, we also make fun of ourselves. Laughter is the political aspect of our work. Curiously enough there is hardly any art around today that declares itself to be political and is funny at the same time. Who declared that political art should be bereft of laughter? Politics has never been as funny as it is today. You don't need to be a cynic or a heretic to notice that. Remember Nestroy, who subjected politics to ridicule and succeeded in being reviled as a reactionary by revolutionaries and revolutionary artists; while, conversely, reactionaries called him a revolutionary. In his revolutionary play, *Freedom Comes to Krähwinkel*, we get this funny wedding at the end between the reactionary woman and the revolutionary man. By this ridiculous solution Nestroy was able to laugh at the revolution and the counter-revolution, the so-called Restoration, as well as himself. There is a kind of double laughter – as Baudelaire says, ironic laughter must be laughter about oneself, in the sense that one stumbles over one's own accident, and turns back, laughing about it as a disinterested spectator. Naturally, laughter always needs a kind of serious intent to provide a background for it, which in our case is the political dimension – something we simply have to laugh about, because it is always the accident we stumble over, politics being its very own accident.

Maybe so [laughter]. Or maybe we're just a couple of hecklers like the *Muppet Show's* Statler and Waldorf, the two old guys in the balcony, who can't watch an episode without throwing in their two cents' worth. Unlike those fellows, though, we don't announce our preferences. We just want to be observers, watching things as they unfold, so we can re-enact them ourselves, however faultily. The problem that some people may have with us as political artists is that this kind of imitation doesn't look critical enough. It is, as *frame* once put it, "semi-critical and not really funny." It hits the mark. To be really critical we would have to step between things, arrest them and keep them apart rather than playing alongside them and singing out of tune along with them, i.e., we'd have to parody them. On the other hand, what worries us about the social and political types of interventionist art is that, essentially, you can only be either for or against things.

Would you say that you act more like a mirror? There, too, there is no for or against, just a reflection.

But a mirror providing the kind of reflection would be like *Rameau's Nephew* by Diderot. This is a character that was viewed for a long time as an artist type, as infamous as he was loved, described by Hegel as a no-goodnik and know-nothing. So Rameau's nephew repeats the things that he himself is attached to with all his body and soul, literally in the air. We would like to describe ourselves as political air violinists, who cover political melodies but who offer up no political performances for the plain and simple reason that we carry them out in the air. That is to say, we place political statements up in the air, so that they can be subjected, off and on, to a bit of the hot blasts that they usually expel, themselves.

Does this also apply to the *Anti-Fascist Amusement Park* that you performed at the *Politics at the Free Theatre* festival in Berlin? It caused a fair bit of a ruckus.

That's one piece where we most clearly positioned ourselves in the "in-between", which a large section of the audience naturally couldn't handle very well. People want a clearly marked position where everything's been decided well in advance. In the time since we started performing *Park* we've become aware that we're providing a projection screen for a kind of negative identification. What we're offering audiences is a negative form they can distinguish themselves from, in both a positive and angry way.

Some of your actions like "People Watching", "Laughing Gas Chamber" and "Shooting Range with Resistance Fighters" seem to be deliberately conceived to provide a nuisance factor.

That precisely is the service we provide, a socially interventionist sadomasochistic public service culminating in a stamped Anti-Fascist Certificate along with a badge in gold. We are rapidly becoming the dominatrix couple of the anti-fascist imagination.

Is this true also of the "National Circus Austria" number you performed at the behest of the Kunsthalle Wien in Vienna?

This work, along with *National Tottering Day Austria* was simply a set piece for the National Year of Commemoration. We wanted to remind people that a year devoted to commemorating is immediately claimed for re-nationalisation, complete with all the martial gestures that go hand in hand with it. So you could have a National Day of Games but not a National Day of Shame.

Is your contribution to the Vienna Mozart Year 2006 just another compulsory exercise like that?

Yes. Our *Mozart Report 2056* sees us established as the two Major Administrative Officers of the ubiquitous "Spirit of Mozart." The same with our *Don Juan Flirting Machine*, which we are employing for the first time at the joint *Don Giovanni*-exhibition of Kunsthalle Wien and the Ursula Blickle Foundation. Fulfilling our jubilee commitments most painstakingly, duty bound, you might say, by the higher cause of flirtatiousness.

At the ARCO 2006 Art Fair you were being deployed, for example, as the *interviewing machine austria at arco,* asking questions in Spanish…

Without understanding a word of Spanish.

Which the Spanish people in attendance apparently didn't even notice. They were feeling splendidly entertained.

When we asked questions such as "Did you know the Republic of Austria

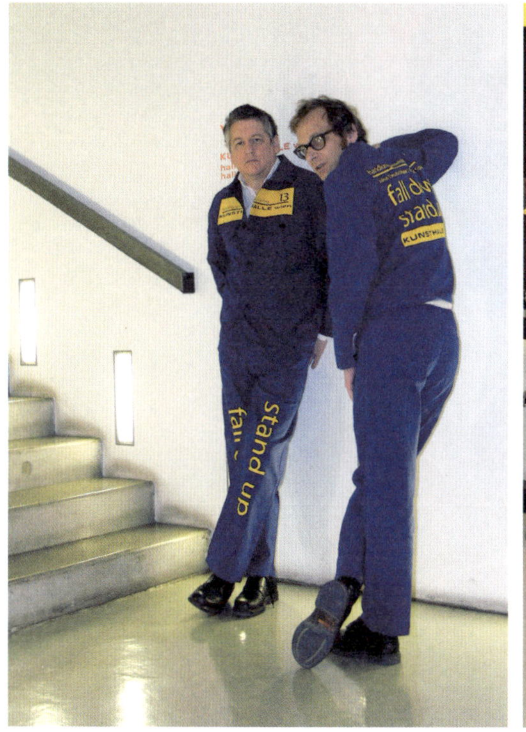

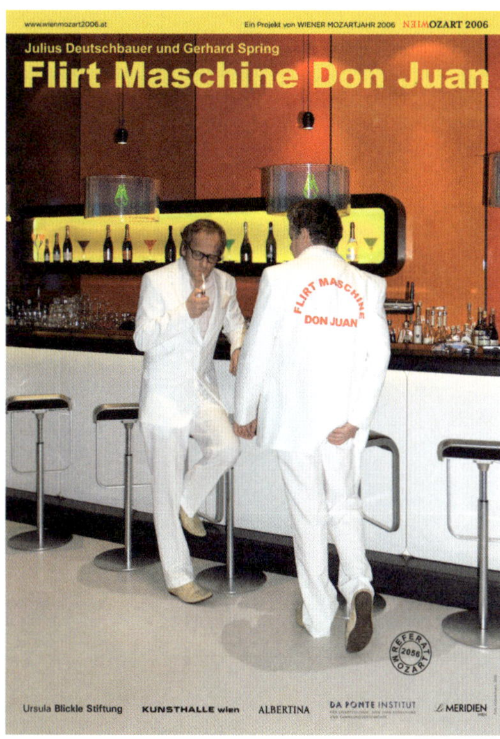

Deutschbauer/Spring, *Interview Machine, Austria at ARCO* 2006

Deutschbauer/Spring, *Flirt Maschine Don Juan,* 2006

doesn't even exist?" they even laughed. As for our stack of posters, they completely pillaged it.

You very much enjoy working with posters. Do you see the poster as a political medium?

Well, it's like a wall newspaper, with a lot of picture and a little bit of text. Like a tabloid picture paper reacting to the headlines of another picture paper. So it's semi-topical, just to add another one to our list of semis. Cheers! [laughter and drinking] We would even go so far as to say that the poster is bold and eye-catching and in that regard it also serves as an artistic role model for our work. We don't want to set loose any kind of complicated messages upon an unsuspecting world – We'd rather perform or imitate some bold and eye-catching attitudes, where imitation is still a kind of performance.

Aren't you contradicting yourselves, though, when your study course, *Political Jargon for Artists,* contains so much theory and is so complicated it's virtually impossible to read and decipher the texts? One theatrical journal[1] even referred to you, in this context, as "digger rats ferreting through the rubbish heap of political theory."

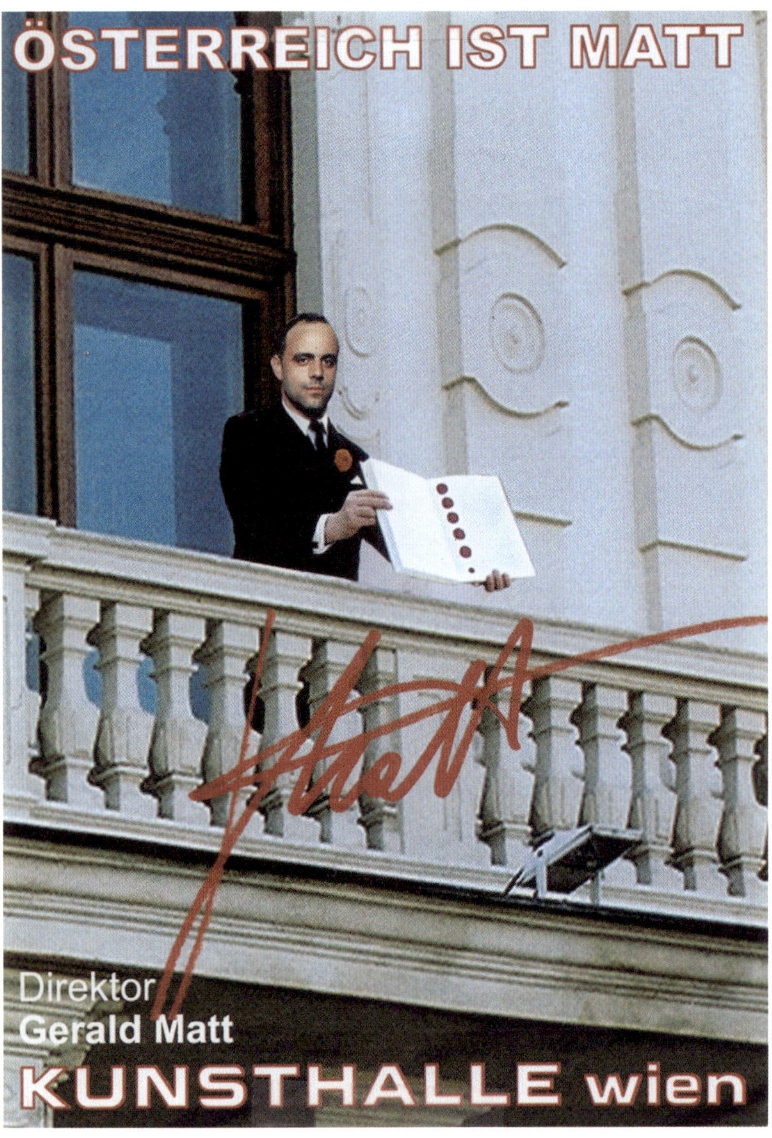

Deutschbauer/Spring,
Österreich ist Matt, 2005

It is precisely this degree of complication in the texts that mirrors the bold and eye-catching attitude, which we have stumbled across in art theory and which we simply mimic or recreate. It is part and parcel of the boldness of art theory, part of its easy recognisability that it likes to adorn itself with the plumage of others, with as many foreign and famous feathers as it can muster, which causes the texts to become, on the one hand, extremely complicated while, on the other hand, more and more people seem to be saying the same thing. We distinguish ourselves from this trend only by leaving off the learned annotations to the quotations that we like to rewrite. We don't just paraphrase the words outside the quotation marks, we also rewrite the text within quotations, which causes the plumage to get ruffled, and so it can be used also as a feather duster or a lavatory brush.

So irony serves as your artistic *leitmotif* in this respect, as well.

Always taking into account the duplication of irony and allegory, which is important to us. Allegory is the rhetorical counterpart that creates a kind of static, a stasis in the instincts that drive the emotional life of the ironist. It stays the flow of ironic verbiage and inserts a pattern, a stereotypical dual entity of picturesqueness and significance. Irony, on the other hand, never manages to come up with any pictures, because it destroys everything that is intended to be repeated. As Walter Benjamin once stated, the allegorist collects stereotypes as an augmentation of his own self. He recognises the seriousness of this positing, and its arbitrariness, upon which he himself depends down to the very language he uses. Its is for this reason, too, that Benjamin referred to the combination of irony and allegory as "serious fun."

So do you as an artist duo act similarly, in real life, to these two characters you portray? Is one of you serious, while the other is more fun-oriented? Or, to put this concluding question differently, could your art be characterised as the art of dissimulation or falseness – because you play two opposing roles at the same time?

Well, think of the Russian philosopher Mikhail Bakhtin, who, in art, pursues something like the carnivalesque element, which is also based on disguising oneself and imitating others. There, too, the false and the genuine can be found simultaneously, side by side, because the issue is one of playfully imitating role models and personalities of public life, who verifiably exist. We celebrate this kind of carnival all year round in the work that we do.

Julius Deutschbauer and Gerhard Spring in conversation with Gerald Matt and Lucas Gehrmann in the spring of 2006. The artists participated in the exhibition *Deutschbauer/Spring: Politisch für Künstler* at the Kunsthalle Wien project wall and took part in the exhibition *Don Juan alias Don Giovanni oder "zwei und zwei sind vier" oder "Lust ist der einzige Schwindel, dem ich Dauer wünsche"* (2006) at Kunsthalle Wien and Ursula Blickle Foundation, Kraichtal.
Julius Deutschbauer was born in 1961 in Klagenfurt, Austria. Gerhard Spring was born in 1962 in Scheibbs, Austria. Since 2000, they live and work as the duo "Deutschbauer/Spring" in Vienna.

German to English translation by Tom Appleton.

1   *Theater heute*, January 2004, p. 76

Uroš Djurić

From the beginning, my art had always been socially oriented; I was exploring conflicts and the relations between identity and society.

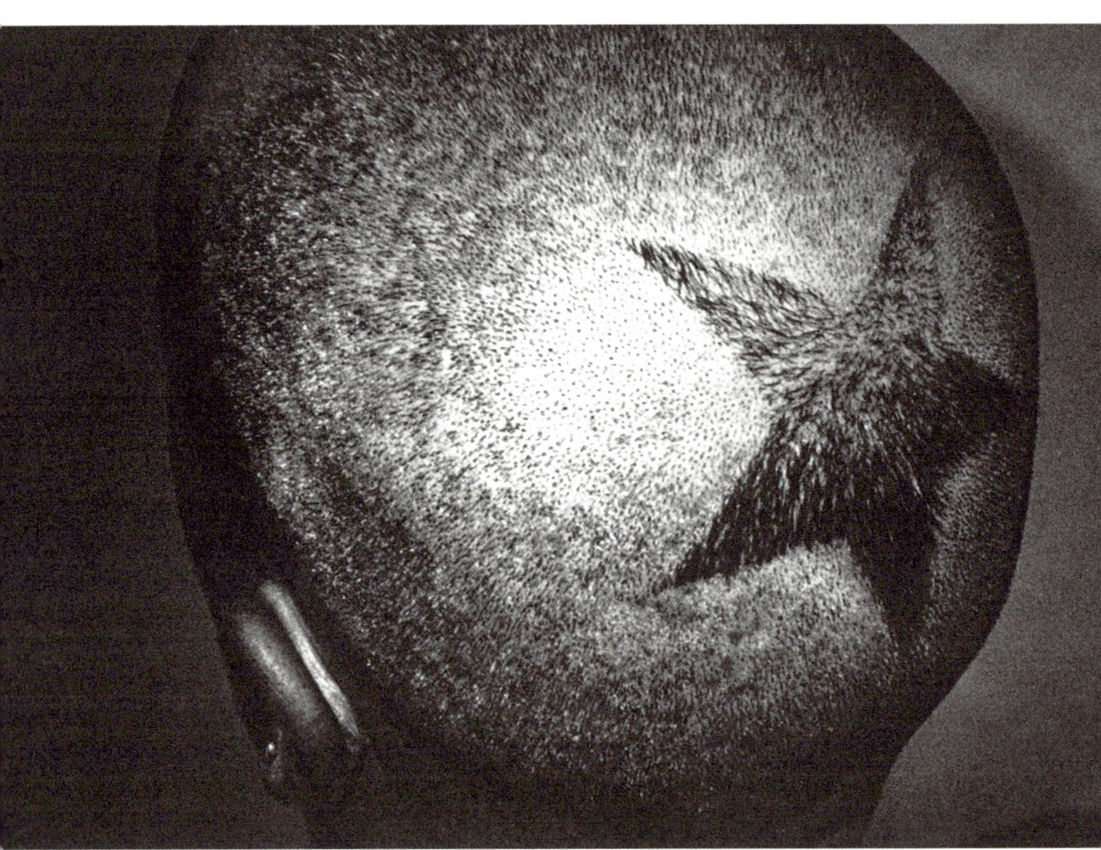

Uroš Djurić, *Untitled (Black Star)*, 1999

In most of your pictures, your own portrait is in the centre. In 1994, you and Stevan Markuš published the *Autonomism Manifesto*. On the basis that human beings are not rational, but seek rational explanations; the authors decided to make the self-portrait the main subject of their art.

The concept of Autonomism is based on the projection of personality as a mediator of ideas. The self-portrait creates its historically determined model with the specific feature that the author's image acts as a part of the content by being included in the representation. This image is not used as a simple mirror image of the painter or his appurtenances and affiliations, but as a tool for conceptual manoeuvres.

Since we started exhibiting, around 1990, the moguls of art criticism and theory have marked us as a "new figuration", presenting us as a new big thing, drastic, provocative, urban-oriented representatives of the "media generation" – the generation that acquired its knowledge of art history through reproductions and illustrations – comics, sci-fi and horror addicts, pop junkies… All nonsense. They built a pedestal for our monument: all we had to do was to jump on it and strike a pose. Surprisingly, we sat down and wrote a manifesto, which was an odd thing in the 90s, but the message was sharp and precise.

What were the reactions?

The Untouchables were in a state of shock… I mean you can't do that! No one ever does it, biting the hand that feeds you, no matter how wrong that hand might be! But it wasn't good enough for us…

We had been framed in a Hollywood cliché of "fugitives", but what they didn't notice was that we're both quite educated. Markuš… this guy was raised on the classical paradigm, while having problems with the law. He was an unpredictable dude, heavy street fighter, his parents were desperate. His parents are teachers of literature in grammar schools; they travelled abroad a lot in the 70s – as did my own family. I saw the Venice Biennale in 1978, when I was 14. I was constantly bumming 'round Europe during the 80s… So what if we were spending most of our lives as restless street punks? It was all our choice! We didn't want to feed any of those stereotypes.

Did you see the *Autonomism Manifesto* as a programme of artistic opposition?

The *Autonomism Manifesto* was written to reject all these limitations. As Markuš said in an interview: "It was created to reduce potentially shallow stories about our painting to a minimum. The Manifesto is not a programme and doesn't purport to change anything essential in art, because such attempts bring about aesthetic radicalisation, in other words, art products, which are the image of their own death. And so it is not avant-garde either, we consider ourselves to be classics." We defined our position through the term *autonomy*, which was interpreted to mean "obedience to its own laws" and established the personal principle as the major principle of all. According to specific social and political circumstances around us, we promoted subversion as an ability not to get caught up in a big process of development and contribution to some generalised progress, based on the marginalisation of human values and seemingly clear aims. Younger art theorists immediately recognized that attitude. Stevan Vuković recently wrote, concerning it, "*…the Autonomists' intention to produce histories of their own, stories that escape the constraints of theory-led production, interpretation dominated by art historians, and exhibited in the framework imposed by the curators…*" We wanted to create the context in which the work is being produced, viewed and exhibited. When we talk about autonomy, we're not talking from the position of some romantic, 19th century individual. Vuković also said that we (both Markuš and I) were always aware of the histories of the terms we were using and the very term 'Autonomism' refers mainly to left-wing social and political movements, which emerged in the 1960s from worker-based (operaismo) roots, fighting to force changes in the organization of the system independent of the state, trade unions or political parties. He said that our Manifesto was published about the time of the big revival of worker-based discourse, firstly in political and then cultural studies, which had its highest peak when the book, *Empire,* of Hardt and Negri went into print and became part of the library of every left-oriented intellectual. In that new context the term 'Autonomy' was linked not to 'individual autonomy' but to the 'autonomy of networks' and the power of productive synergies.

That was an important observation and a reason why this wasn't recognized by the previous generations of art theorists. Mainly because their leftist practice was something very different.

Your suprematist landscapes and self-portraits as well as works of *Non-Objective Autonomism* refer strongly to the formal code of the Russian Avant-garde of the 1920s.

After the Manifesto had been published and the big exhibition we had in '95, there was kind of a silence around us. No shows, no bids. I was broke, had neither money nor studio. Local wars followed with social crises reaching their climax… I got an offer to get back to the Academy for post-graduate studies, which I did. I spent three very important and fertile years there. I immediately started to research my own position, trying to understand where and how I got into this clash with the representatives of the art establishment. The main catch was their travesty of the idea of conceptual art according to some rigid norms of conceptual aesthetics. Suddenly I recalled one case. In 1983, I saw the exhibition of Russian avant-garde in the *Museum of Contemporary Art* in Belgrade, collected from Russian museums. Malevich, who's already glorified as an icon of radical modernism, was presented with works that were part of the so-called *Post-suprematist figuration* of the mid-20s. The organizers were a bit disappointed as this phase was still treated as a regression compared to his previous revolutionary *Suprematist* cycle. I stood in front of *The Athletes* or *Red Cavalry*, fascinated… Regression? What were they talking about? There was an interesting step, a big change in scope towards the interpretation of that period, which came in the mid/late 80s – early 90s. Anyway, it was an ideal platform from which to develop my own concept. I treated the whole History of Art as a dead object, a ready-made. I jumped into a formal element of Malevich's iconographic model and stripped it of all social and historical manipulation by putting it into a different context, filling it with unexpected contents. From the beginning, my art had always been socially oriented; I was explor-

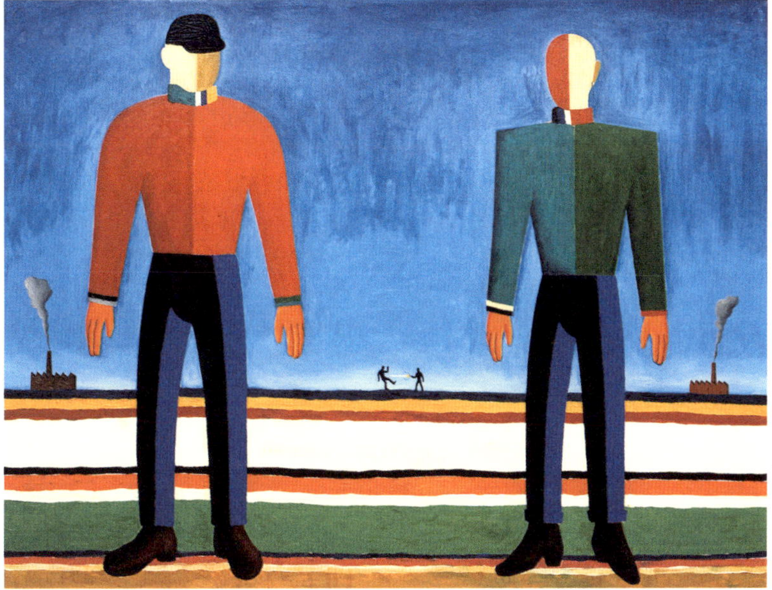

Uroš Djurić, *Non-objective Autonomism. Murder or 2 Greatest Serbian Painters Subdued by Their Own Greatness*, 1997

ing conflicts and the relations between identity and society. For example, Malevich was doing these "portraits" of different classes or social types like sportsmen, peasants, mystics and carpenters; dealing with the collectivist euphoria and class struggles of that historical period. Our civilization was experiencing other phenomena, the crisis of self that emerged from conformism, consumerism and global indifference. So I started to do portraits of real people, canonizing the friends and protagonists of the Belgrade arts scene. Frontal portraits were rendered in the iconographic pattern of Malevich's late period, which means that the identity of the portrayed person was not recognized, as is usual in portrait painting, by the facial features, the characterization of the image, but by given attributes such as gesture, or a personal affinity for the fetishism of clothes. We're all our own products and we project our visions of self as well as certain attitudes, which could be treated as iconographic models. According to Malevich's theory, namely, that the face is experienced only as a mask hiding the truth about our being. The project was presented in June 1998, as a solo show in the Salon of the Museum of Contemporary Art in Belgrade, under the title *Non-objective Autonomism*. The defenders of Conceptual aesthetics, to some extent comparable to Malevich's case, thought it was a flop, a step backward. A year after, they were published in *Flash Art*.

In your show *Go Johnny Go*, you have been represented with around a dozen drawings and paintings – all self-portraits with various electric guitars. You are not only a visual artist; you are a musician as well. Did you play all these instruments yourself?

No, I didn't. I'm not a musician. I play the guitar, but this is different, and an important aspect of my life. I have a big record collection; my hi-fi's constantly on while I'm working, almost like a ritual. I have spent half of my life in nightclubs. Most of my gang lived on the edge of social streams; we were marginalised. Lack of money was our reality. *Guitar Self-portraits* came from that sense of frustration; when you can't realize your desires due to objective circumstances. These works were the projection of fantasies. In *Autonomism Manifesto*, we're talking about that state, the desire to express a possible reality detached from the real world, as well as the art itself, the state where fantasy together with concrete events, real and made-up characters or objects, historical styles and art movements, ideas, signs, symbols and performances go on functioning undisturbed. Context is only the scenery where the symbolic constitution of a possible reality is happening, where the "personal principle" can be expressed to the full.

I earned a big sum of money in the year 2000. The very first thing I did was to go to the nearest guitar shop and buy myself the most expensive Fender Telecaster, with its natural wood body and rosewood neck. Then I started to work on self-portraits that included my new guitar, a realized fantasy; a kind of living experiment in the field of social and class emancipation.

You were part of the Belgrade punk-scene in the 1980s and then moved to Berlin. The beginning of the dissolution of Yugoslavia through war caught up with you in Brussels, when you were installing a show. You were not permitted to return to Germany. What were your feelings when you got back to your hometown?

I'll try to explain this more precisely as all these experiences were important in forming the Autonomism concept. I started in 1980, when I joined the incipient punk scene; I played with *Urban Guerrilla*, a short-lived but radical and influential band. The scene was hot and expansive but suddenly it expired in late '83 – '84, while I was in the army. I got back to a changed city. I started to study art history, I spent three strange years there, I lost interest after the first year, it was such a waste of time. The only good thing that was happening in the mid-80s was the rise of an alternative scene around the Academy night club, run by Fine Arts students as well as a whole bunch of losers, freaks, punks, chic chicks, gays and junkies, all mixed. I was travelling abroad a lot, and that's how I discovered Berlin. The city surrounded by The Wall looked like an established utopia of the kind we inhabited in the Belgrade nightclubs. I got in contact with people that were part of the Autonomist political movement, perhaps the most powerful social alternative in Europe at that time. The key thing was that I articulated my idea of art in such surroundings. I never moved to Berlin, but I travelled there quite often – thanks to the Eastern block the return ticket cost around 10 DM. I had already been enrolled at the Belgrade Academy of Fine Arts and I spent almost every summer from 1988 to 1992 in Germany. When I was in my final year, Milica Tomić invited me along with several other art-ists to take part in some exhibition in Brussels. It was our first show abroad. The civil war had already started, but we weren't really aware of the scale of its devastation. Then, on 1 June 1992, which was the day of our opening, the UN sanctions against Yugoslavia started. We were stuck there; our flight was cancelled. Milica went to Frankfurt; I went to Berlin. Serbs were already singled out as the bad guys; I didn't want to stay in that atmosphere, with the unseen mark on my head. The huge demonstrations against Milošević started right after the sanctions were implemented and soon after I decided to go back, to confront reality, I wanted to be part of that. I thought, "The Shithead would be politically dead by the end of the year." Milica came back to Belgrade in December. This was the time of our rise on the local scene.

At the end of the 1990s you started to work on the *Populist Project*. The main thesis is that populism as a hegemonic ideology has displaced social utopias; the main theme is the interaction of the star-system and identity. In *Celebrities*, you exhibit yourself, in various situations with famous people from different spheres, with politicians, artists, movie stars and musicians.

During the 90s, our society was passing through heavy political and social turbulence, the complete social and class structure was upside down, being permanently filled with populist contents. In comparison with the 80s and my conscious living on the margins of the public sphere, the 90s pushed me into centre-field; I became a star. I was suddenly recognized as one of the most prominent figures on the contemporary art scene as well as a character from feature films, having radio shows on the B92 station, participating in the publishing of adult comics, working as a graphic designer, a DJ… even though I was in the centre of the public and media interest, there was a huge disproportion between my class and my social position. My public success and activities weren't something one could materialize at that time. The closed society, with completely different parameters compared with the outside world, was a leading phenomenon of our way of life. The real stars in Serbia of the 90s were criminals, war heroes, politicians, folk singers, merchants, and bankers… This pseudo-elite formed a new class based on open material interest, monopolies and fast enrichment. The main criterion for entering the club was to be part of their game. The only space in which I might confirm my "star" position was in portrait shots with foreign celebrities. Even though all the photos were coming from the real situations; they looked more like a fantasy than a reality. It's connected to the spirit of the time.

Hometown-Boys, First Serbian Porn, Art and Society magazine, represent your artistic response to the war in Yugoslavia. A series of faked magazine covers, digitally mounted from your own photographs and downloads from the internet – lifestyle with a ribald dose of sex, glamour and bawling chauvinism. Are you sarcastic?

I wouldn't say so. We're witnessing something that looks like a programme, a new Bible or populism manifesto produced in the form of a lifestyle magazine. Basically, these magazines are opinion makers of the new age, the age of consumerism. They're called lifestyle magazines, but they don't sell style, they sell norms and ideological postulates of populist ideology. *Hometown Boys* sells a lifestyle of my own, and it's real. Maybe it's bad, but that's what I am, that's the whole spectrum of my interests, what I'm made of… I'm not selling an inaccessible ideal; I'm presenting reality, which any lifestyle should be. That's my self-portrait in the shape of a magazine cover. Many people told me they would like to read it…

God Loves the Dreams of Serbian Artists – Uroš Djurić in a group portrait with European football clubs: real photography, no montage. The world of art and the world of football both have their own and quite different moral justifications. Are you living as a cross-border commuter?

The role of both art and football in the emancipation of the lower classes in the late 19th and early 20th century was enormous. These were referential fields, meeting places of the classes that were in deep conflict. My grandfather, who was a tailor in Budapest, played for Ferencváros before The Great War. He was a social democrat, a worker who spoke three languages. His ideal was South America, as France was the only republic in Europe. He went to London via Berlin with two comrades, they wanted to take a ship and go to Lima. He changed his mind and went back to the royal-imperialist monarchy. In just two generations, one of his sons became a world-

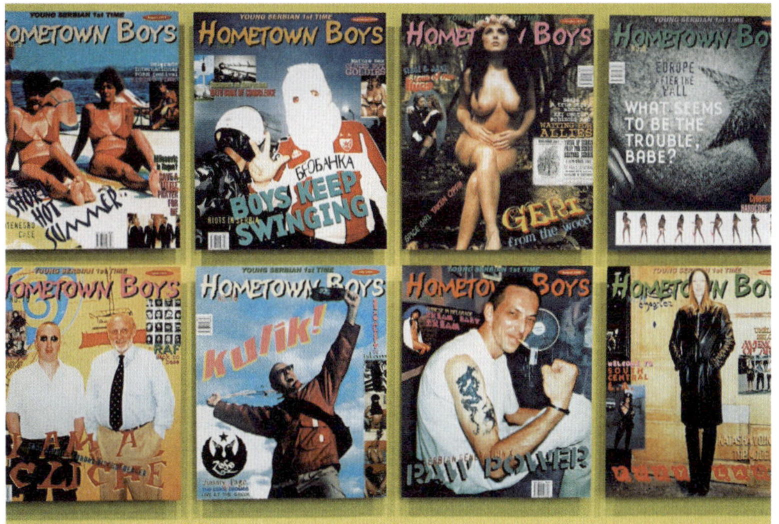

Installation view, Kunsthalle Wien 2003: Uroš Djurić, *Populist Project Hometown Boys*, 1999-2000

renowned byzantologist and vice-president of the Serbian Academy of Science and Arts, the other two became a machine engineer and a painter, one daughter had a diploma in archaeology, the grandchildren are a visual artist, a film editor, a musician, a costume designer, an art historian… a huge jump in social terms, like nothing that ever happened before in history. He was not alive to see all that, but he lived for it, he belonged to the generation that trusted in progress. I was following that line.

In the second half of the 90s, after the end of the UN sanctions, the only big international stars that appeared in Belgrade were football players that were playing international matches. Being a local star, I was invisible to them. So I started to appear in hotel lobbies, taking fan photos with all the major players like Gullit, Shearer or Matthaus… It was such a depression then, nobody was there, no one cared, I was the only freak waiting… From the moment I established myself on the international scene, my position changed, so I started to negotiate directly with clubs. I was photographed together with the team, dressed properly in a club kit, in a form that simulated the official club photo. That's a simple story about acceptability, about progress and models of society.

Pioneers. Artists of the former socialist countries, decorated with the red scarf that was yours when you were a boy and a member of the Red Pioneers. Socialism is dead – long live Socialism?

A decade after the demolition of the *Berlin Wall*, we had plenty of exhibitions and writings from the West that attempted to put Central/East European art into a kind of schema – *The West having 'discovered' Central/Easter European art in the late 90s!* – resulting in the creation of a highly artificial counterbalance. This dismissal prevented any understanding of the subtle dif-

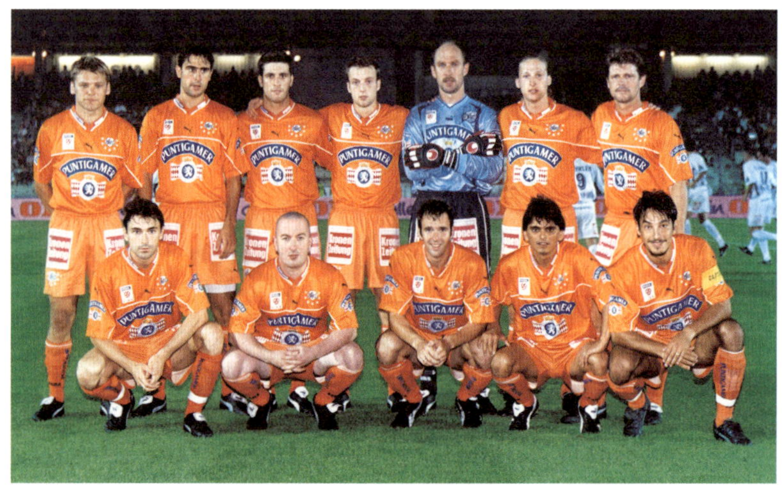

Uroš Djurić, *Populist Project. God Loves the Dreams of Serbian Artists*, 2001

ferences between systems, countries, scenes, community standards, individuals, and the like. By having members of the Central and Eastern European artistic and theoretical community reposition this Pioneer scarf around their necks, I posit that some of them are experiencing significant ideological or theoretical conflict in the face of this Western misunderstanding. It's a gesture of resistance against Western stereotypes of art from the former Eastern Bloc. The idea is to show that this group has already passed through a kind of social nullification once, in the name of equality, and it should not be continued.

In recent years, you took part rather frequently in exhibitions in Austria and Germany; rather often as well "The Balkans" was the theme of these shows. Do you sometimes feel exploited as an exotic by a saturated western art world?

Not all that often. It depends on the context of representation. The nature of my work doesn't belong to the cliché of so-called Eastern European or Balkan art. If the idea is to present a wide range of art practices from a certain region, it's okay with me as long as my work's not misused for some big conclusion that feeds prejudices.

In several projects, you have cooperated with Elke Krystufek. Where do you see parallels and stress fields in the dialogue with the Austrian artist?

She's an impressive personality; her production is enormous, flamboyant. There were lots of parallels, concerning the exploitation of the self, social and political, even cultural aspects of the work, the reception… My main shock was when I discovered that we both started with such similar positions almost at the same time, around 1989… When we met in 2001, it was easy for us to develop a contact that turned into a collaboration entitled *Life as a Narrative*, shown in a couple of exhibitions. I started a series of works named *Elkepop*. I did a ton of self-portraits in the style of Elke Krystufek. It was a replica of what I did with Malevich in '96, but with a living artist this time. It was an exciting experience. When we first exhibited this project in Belgrade, in the *Salon of the Museum of Contemporary Art*, people would ask: "…Okay… but where are your works?"

Are you working on a new project?

I am. It's an ambitious project with the Bosnian artist Šejla Kamerić. She's a brilliant artist, an exceptional woman. The project is called *Parallel Life*, following the forbidden love of two jet-setters, members of post-conflict societies, something like *Dodi & Di*, with a happy end.

Uroš Djurić in conversation with Gerald Matt and Sigrid Mittersteiner in January 2006. The artist took part in the exhibitions *Attack! Kunst und Krieg in den Zeiten der Medien* (2003) and *Go Johnny Go! Die E-Gitarre – Kunst und Mythos* (2003) at Kunsthalle Wien.
Uroš Djurić was born in Belgrade, Serbia, in 1964. He lives and works in Belgrade.

Noritoshi Hirakawa

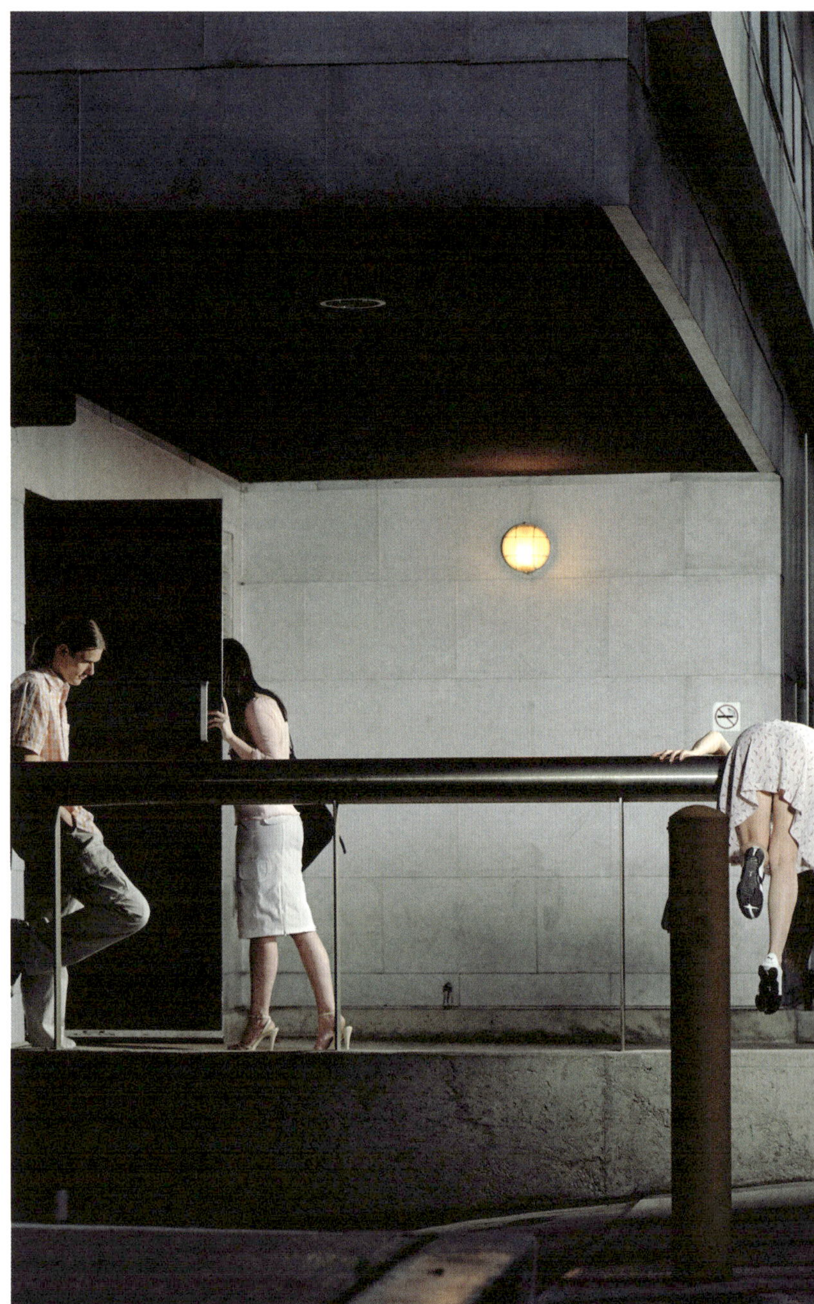

Noritoshi Hirakawa,
Subject - A Project with
Thom Mayne, 2004

In your work you like to confront private, personal, intimate aspects of the individual with the public or else the rules of the game of public self-representation as practiced in the West. In so doing, you appear to enter very deeply into the private lives of individual people. How do you convince people to participate in your projects? Do you explain your artistic intentions? Have you developed a pattern for this preparatory work? Or, does it happen spontaneously, depending on each situation?

I do not know how much I am dealing with intimate and private aspects of individual lives. In my artwork, people often imagine that I managed to disclose the part of an individual's intimacy that normally is kept from public exposure. Perhaps people always desire to know or obtain intimacy from others. I see as a myth the belief that an individual's truth exists outside or away from the public view. In any case, every part of private or intimate life is partially or fully covered by façades (even when looking at some intimacy in the belief it is the truth). Thus, it is not easy to differentiate between an individual's substance and pretensions. What I try to do when working with people is a type of experiment. Each project involves a particular concept developed together with the project participants. When I and my partner or partners begin the experiment, it is unknown for both sides whether the process will reveal intimate and private aspects of our lives. Of course, we sometimes gain a view into the private but that occurs completely spontaneously and as a result of our mutual agreement. Also, these mutual exposures is an important part of the work. And, please get rid of an idea that I am the winner. Perhaps only the viewers of my work have an illusion of me as the winner.

For the exhibition *Desire and Void: Japanese Photography* at Kunsthalle Wien in 1997, you created locally a work as part of the series *A Temptation to be a Man*. It showed a female nude as a slide projection, with the woman's face being whitened out by a spotlight. Alongside this were to be found the dates of the picture's creation and the personal data of the photographed person, though not her name. To be able to produce this work, you had to approach several women in the street, until one finally agreed for you to photograph her in the nude. Does this stage of preparation, including the process of gradual approach, give you pleasure? You were once telling me stories about this, which I found amusing and which, at the same time, demonstrated the diverse, individual reactions in the various cities you worked on this project. Could you recount a few short anecdotes?

First of all, I am not sure that I simply have pleasure because an unknown woman becomes nude by participating in *A Temptation to be a Man*. I am not doing this for seduction or just for the desire of looking at nudity. The offer I proposed to a woman becomes the offer I am obliged to receive in different contexts. Of course, for the viewers, it might be fun to look at the faceless nude image of someone who is residing in the same town. At the same time, by guessing who she is, the viewers are obviously attracted by some linguistic information about a woman. Always what satisfies me in completing the work is appreciating the trust from a woman who truly comprehended the work's structure. This sometimes emerges stronger than the bond of love or a simple relationship between boyfriend and girlfriend. One time, I was in Aachen, Germany trying to find a woman who could participate in the project. I was in a café and there were two men and a woman sitting next to me. Then, I explained the project to the men and asked the best way for finding a woman participant. All of sudden, the woman who was sitting next to one of the men (who was her boyfriend) gave me her telephone number and told me that she was interested in being in the work. The boyfriend was speechless at witnessing what happened just in front of him. And she eventually became the model (participant) and, until the last moment, the boyfriend could not understand why things worked liked that … although from the first moment, she handed me her telephone number, the girlfriend was quite sure how things worked.

In some of your more recent projects the word "string" tends to appear in the titles. Is this a significant metaphor for you? I strongly associate a sense of linearity with "strings", a pre-defined course of events. You are saying though, at the same time, that you are ultimately concerned with the realisation that each phenomenon in the world is connected with every other human being. Does everything dangle by a string?

The word "strings" was used in the title *Strings of Light* and also in *The Homecoming of Navel Strings*. From the macroscopic view, the string means the course of life that is almost predetermined but not fully (this is important). And, the light means the mind that dwells on this string to which everything in this world is tied. Although people are not aware of this very much, they emotionally try to believe that they are creating life themselves by interacting between people and by mentally disconnecting or connecting with a particular person. Perhaps, the desires that form emotional life can be explained by people acting on their past behaviour. Yes, it is a fact that each person has some element that connects with other humans, things and phenomenon. That is why humans have the ability to feel compassion for others. That is why a man can, without an actual relationship, instinctively sense a woman's sexuality. I believe that the basic human perceptions are the same. And furthermore, we are living on the same playing field and having interactions between everyone: each person affects, and is affected by, the others. So, anyway, the string might be marking the route for our passage through this world. And I believe that our challenge is to go beyond the predetermination of our life and simply live our life. This we can do because

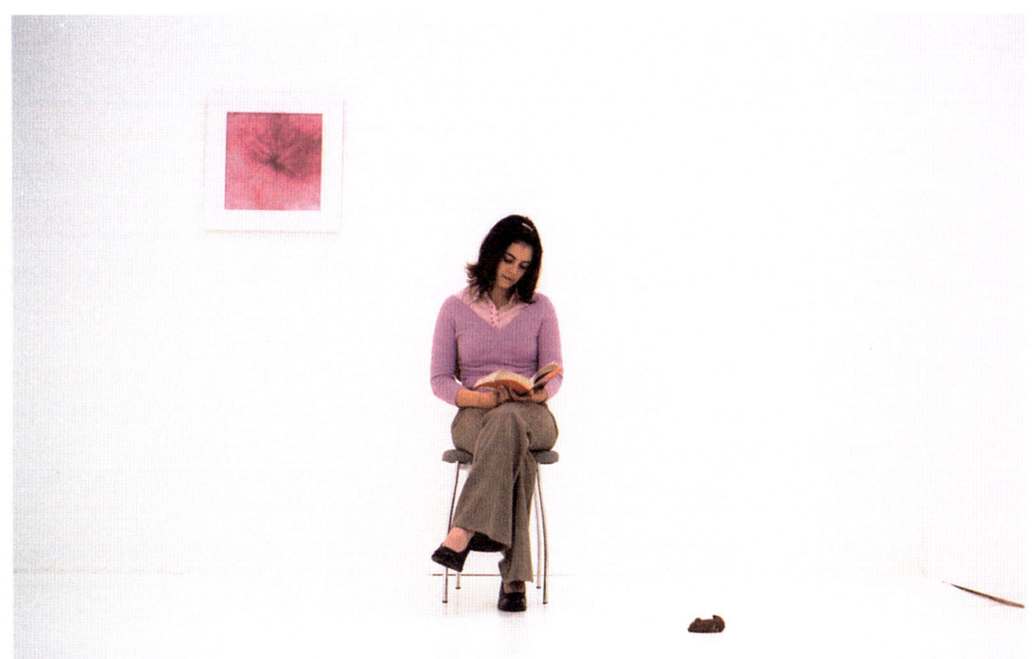

we are connected at each moment with each human being through the "strings".

You like to work in specific local situations and you work with a great variety of media, both static and mobile, ranging from photography to performance work. And there is, in each case, a concept. Does this concept already include the media to be employed or does one develop from the other within the work process?

Yes, when I set up the concept, I speculate on the work while simulating the media and other effects in advance. Obviously, media itself has its own character as a messenger vehicle. So, normally, I spend a long time concentrating on the work matter and I do not start working until speculation is completed. Within the planning or speculation time, sometimes, I experiment by speculating on the concept from different perspectives. Quite frequently, I think over and over again how to shape the logic to be represented, simply but adequately balancing the concept.

Heat Stroke is the title of a work consisting of eighty slides projected one after the other, which you showed at Kunsthalle Wien in Autumn 2003. While the sequence of images does create a kind of narrative, it differs from the usual forms of this genre, in as much as the viewer is not guided in any direction – neither by characters that invite identification nor by any pre-arranged plot. You wrote, at the time, that, "films, literature and the theatre have an enormous influence on how people perceive the world around them. Yet the one-dimensional characters one tends to encounter there are far removed from any reality and scramble the viewers' own thinking. Having been exposed to such characters, one expects real people to act in the same way – which they never do."

Which philosophical, psychological or political ideas have you been focusing on? Are there certain – also, artistic – positions that you view yourself as being closely aligned with? What do you think of programmatically comparable earlier tendencies in classical modernism (Expressionism, The Blue Rider) and their ultimate failure?

Not only film, literature and theatre but also the language itself limits and controls the territory of human behaviour through the framework of mind.

Heat Stroke is one of series of *Streams by the Wind*. On each work, I work with one actor who is very talented, experienced (and well known), the other one who is almost an amateur actor (not really experienced in acting). Then, the scenes become much vivid and tense because you can trace the fragmental element of everyday lives. If you observe human interaction in reality, often what is happening between humans is very complicated and hard to interpret. A life story is not as simple as we think most of the time. Every second and every moment, people are constantly changing their mind and forget what they were saying. Conversation often is not responding to the promise of acts or proof of memory. Instead it is just for a moment of feeling comfort. Immediately after the words spill out, it is eliminated out of human memory. I do not say that life and interaction are emotional and illogical. But many behaviours and changing behaviours are quite difficult to track or put into the patterns. That is why life is not easy as it was taught through films, novels or theatres (as these mediums define the structure of human thoughts, ways of thinking, patterning the configuration of com-munication forms…). But I think it will be more functional to perceive life from daily lives of everyone, if people are aware enough to see what is happening in reality without belief in fictionalised mythology. Concerning the classical modernism you mentioned, perhaps the artists had wanted to seek and present the reality which was not recognizable from the surface of phenomena and revealed something underneath the surface. In other words, they had been creating the notion of substance as a movement to reach the truth. Therefore, the ultimate failure had occurred with focusing only on the truth by detaching themselves from sticking with reality. I am not looking for the truth as the absolute. What is needed is just an adjustment of recog-nition by observing reality. There are various truths that exist all the time from the past to the future. More than we are imagining, humans, if they are not trapped, are always living with much more flexible behaviours.

In the meantime, have you continued to work on the series *Streams by the Wind?*

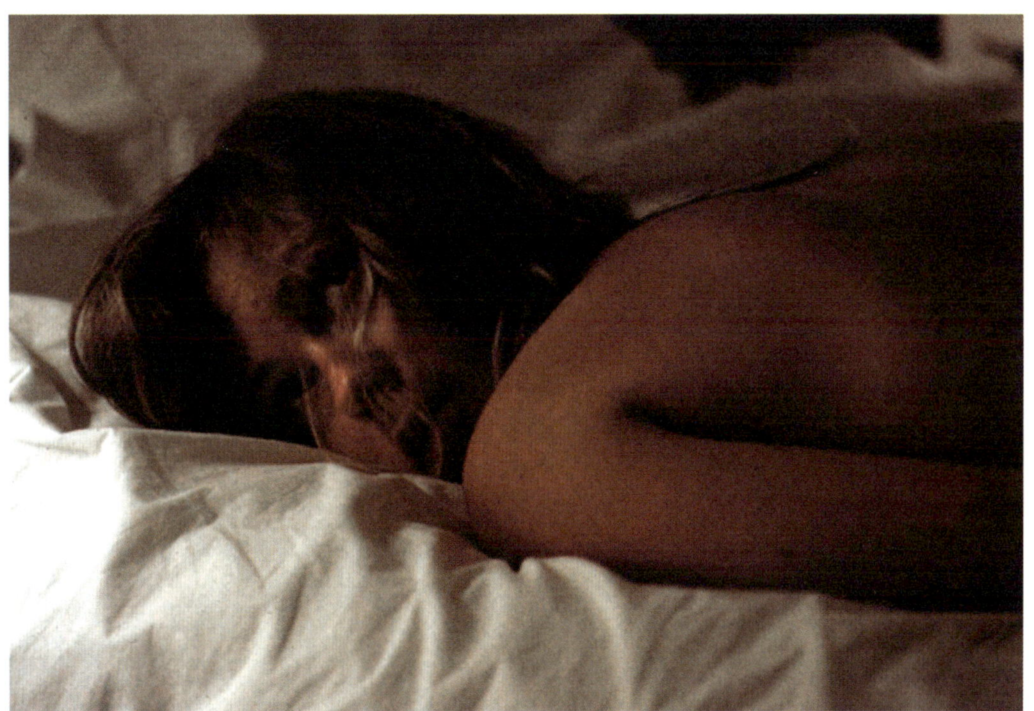

It appears to be a particularly interesting concept of a new genre of the narrative in the intermediate area between photography and cinematography.

I am trying to continue working with this series *Streams by the Wind*. I have already made the new story with particular actors. The story is also inspired by the actor's private life and learning the "American Way of Life" (although I am not making this to affirm American culture – actually it is opposite of that). An important part of this work is the long discussion with the actors in order to give substance to the story.

Subject was the title of a photographic series you collaborated on with Thom Mayne, the American architect and founder of Morphosis (California). One of the principles of Morphosis, after all, is the intuitive and reflexive method – an idea that appears to be similar to your work and which yet manifests itself static forms and structures. How did the collaboration with Thom Mayne work out? Do you see a possibility of a productive combination of architecture and the visual arts in general?

I think art is submitting to the chance of reconsidering the recognition of comprehended world. The *Subject* project was created to change the idea of architecture by using visual art. As an architect that 99 percent of contemporary architects cannot consider, Thom Mayne was radical enough to question the fundamental meaning of architecture. Thom and I were not presenting just aesthetics of art as beauty or variation for securing useless pride with the fragile architectural academic world. The project was made for going back to the stage of rediscovering architecture's reason for existing. Of course, because of the academic establishment and intellectual world's hierarchy, almost no architect and art institutions can tolerate accepting this idea…. The basic reason for architecture has been quite forgotten in this contemporary society for awhile. That was why Thom and I collaborated together to go back to the stage of reconstructing architecture's origin.

Your 1999 photograph entitled *Portrait for a Portrait by Vanessa Beecroft (For the Man as Voyeur)* has a portion of a man viewed from behind who is dropping his pants while in the background a hazy, nebulous indistinct female figure (representing Vanessa Beecroft) walks towards the viewer. Whether an exchange of glances between the two is taking place cannot be determined with any degree of precision. After all, the refusal to lock eyes with her viewers is one of the prime elements in Vanessa Beecroft's performances. How do you view Vanessa Beecroft's handling of the voyeuristic gaze compared to yours?

I think Vanessa's interest is creating sculptures by using humans. Obviously the main focus is rather on the visual, physical or exterior's view; so, nothing to hesitate about when looking at her performances. Models are frozen like statues (reminding me of historical stone statues in Italy). I feel that she wants to control this aesthetics as a centred concept of her work (sometimes, this can be interpreted as masculine.) Also, I perceived some directness of sexual desire from her work or herself. That was why I made these pictures for a magazine to attach to Vanessa's article. Myself? I focus on estimating what is happening in the mind of the model exactly the moment the image was created. Therefore, what you see is not what I am creating for the image, but what you imagine through the image is what I really meant to create.

Some seven years ago you were quoted as saying, "We are all tangled up in a net of behavioural and social patterns of the respective culture we grew up in, whether we know it or not, and sometimes we get caught up in an intense, physically-experienced feeling of frustration about the limitations which these rules seem to impose on us. We may well experience a sense of physical anxiety, when the weight of cultural burdens presses down on us, and yet it is precisely these cultural patterns we find so oppressive that are a subconscious part of the whole package that makes up our selves." You grew up in Japan – with two goats, as you have been quoted as saying, that made up your childhood companions at home, and moved to New York at the age of about 30, where you have now been living for the past 13 years. Which significance do the cultural patterns of your origins retain for you now? And how do you view the changes in the situation inside the US today or at any rate since 2001 – also in relation to the reception given your work?

The statement was made for explaining the more general idea of manipulation of a person's unconscious by cultural patterns and social environments. It can be about Japan, USA or Austria…. Surely enough, my Japanese cultural background gives me a strong belief in the moral principles of human responsibility and respect/compassion to the others. Since 2001, it has been very interesting for me to witness the immediate transition of US society towards intolerant, ill-advised patriotic, emotional, aggressive barbarity. This did not happen because of 9/11 but it has always been like this in the USA since they massacred American Indians with the "Discovery of the New Continent". The aggressors did not recognize American Indians as human – although American Indians treated the aggressors as human. This strong core identity appeared after the 9/11 incidents, when the façade (surface) of an imitated European culture was peeled off the US culture. Even in Los Angeles, Santa Fe or New York, it emerged in almost the same way. American pragmatism does not appreciate culture but values only financial institutions for generating money (in this manner, I can say that believing in money itself becomes religion). And, especially after 2001, the art industry functions with this principle. In this country, there is no art but only art products. However, I am creating art bearing the cultural burden of these pragmatic values and, at the same time, art that transfers to Americans' unconscious mental culture.

As far as the question regarding cultural patterns is concerned, I can still remember a seemingly bizarre work involving the worn undergarments of young Japanese women. Is there anything you can tell us about this – or about the separate approaches to sexuality in Japan and the US?

Unfortunately, that did not involve worn panties of young Japanese women…. The project was called *Garden of Nirvana* and represented, as the metaphorical stage for nirvana, the perception of losing consciousness of existing self by being absorbed by the power of fetishistic purity. When the piece was presented in Paris, New York, Antwerp, Amsterdam and Geneva, the panties were mainly collected at each location. This fetishistic desire has only been permitted to play on women. But I believe it is a very powerful universal desire on both men and women in different countries. Even, I think it has an element of spiritual aspect to it. Yes, I am serious about this. Please notice people's changing faces when they are looking and touching at this fetishistic item: nothing unusual or improper to deal with.

Where do you prefer living, New York or Tokyo? And what are you working on right now, what are your plans for the near future?

An artist like myself does not have a luxury to choose the place to reside. It always depends on the circumstances. Like a slave, I do not have the authority to decide to be in an exhibition (that is always decided by the curator, or other art professionals). I cannot apply for grants without having recommendations and judgements from art professionals. Committee or board members who often do not have the ability to value art control most decisions. Even the art market is established for the people who have extraordinary amounts of money and use art purchases for hiding money, money laundering, or obtaining the illusion of social respect, an expression that provides the social benefit of paying off their past sins (especially in US). Actually, it is very interesting to learn all these things by being in the art world.... However, my plan is to continuously be a slave to just focusing on my creations that propose new perceptions of society to the public.

Noritoshi Hirakawa in conversation with Gerald Matt in the summer of 2004. The artist took part in the exhibitions *Lust und Leere: Japanische Photographie* (1997) at Kunsthalle Wien and *Don Juan alias Don Giovanni oder "zwei und zwei sind vier" oder "Lust ist der einzige Schwindel, dem ich Dauer wünsche"* (2006) at Kunsthalle Wien and Ursula Blickle Foundation, Kraichtal. The exhibition *Noritoshi Hirakawa: Streams by the Wind – Heat Stroke* was shown at Kunsthalle Wien project space. Noritoshi Hirakawa was born in Fukuoka, Japan, in 1960. He lives and works in New York.

Runa Islam

I've always had the desire to know more than one side of the story. Or, have been conscious there is a lot more that is left out (of the main frame) than is included.

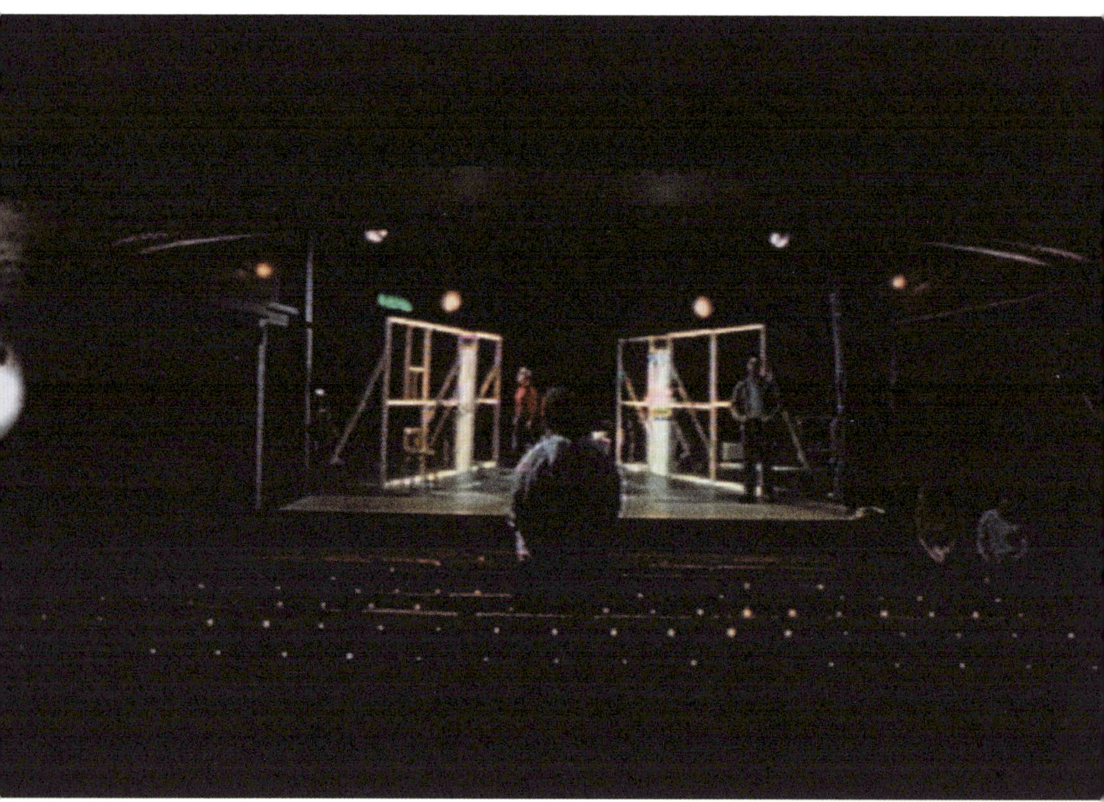

Runa Islam, *Director's Cut (Fool for Love)*, 2001

Just to let you know a little of the background. Initially, when I first had the idea for *Director's Cut (Fool For Love)*, I had wanted to write a script about the relations of authority between a theatre director, the actors and the understudies during a rehearsal process. To write a play within a script became too complex, as I didn't want to predetermine any of the actions and the emotions that could materialise. Instead, I decided to base the film on a pre-existing work. If it would have been possible, I may have just worked with a theatre group during real rehearsals. Instead, I constructed the rehearsal of a play as a staged event from which I extracted loose stories and documentations. The idea was to work somewhere between documentary techniques and fictional narrative. There was an occupation between the authentic and inauthentic from the very start, intensified by the theatrical context. The work exists now as a meta-fiction, a sort of frame within a frame. Finding a play and a playwright to borrow from was actually very difficult. I was very aware that the text would be submerged into my work, and that many of the dramaturgical aspects would be sidelined. Mainly, I didn't know how convincing my "actor characters" would perform, as they were unprofessional actors. (Only my "director" was a trained actor and ultimately I let him do a lot of the guiding and the directing for the stage scenes). I had thought of turning to undramatic plays by Pinter and then Ionesco, but both their works were texts in which the characters were interwoven into very idiosyncratic narratives. Sam Shepard's work *Fool for Love*, stood out for its straightforward dialogue. I felt the roles were based on stereotypical characters that had a "cardboard cut-out" quality. When repeating a couple of lines of a scene in my head, I immediately conjured up the character, context and mood. I felt that I could use isolated passages and lines as perfect vehicles for "play-acting", which was, in part, much of what the artwork was to be based on. It's not to say that the simplicity makes Shepard's *Fool for Love* unaccomplished, it is actually its strength.

It's very true that I've looked back to the period of new wave cinema from the 60s and early 70s. Besides just loving the film works of the auteur directors you mention, I'm drawn to their works because of their provocative approach to filmmaking. Fassbinder's use of the grand narrative as a critical device was an approach where he could employ the thematic and techniques familiar to Hollywood as a way to compel viewers to watch narratives they otherwise wouldn't want to see. I've probably been more influenced by the formalist qualities of Godard and Antonioni, but I have worked with an unprecedented camera technique that Ballhaus, Fassbinder's cinematographer, created. It's a dynamic full circle revolution of the camera around moving subjects. It is an unequivocally vivid and charged scene that epitomises how Fassbinder disguised subject into style and themes. I remade this scene in an early work, *Tuin*, as I wanted to engage the 360-degree perspective of the camera. The full turn was relevant to my work as a motif for looking at all perspectives. This theme of looking over the shoulder of the action into the peripheries and the areas off centre is recurrent in almost all my works. The Ballhaus turn was part of a piece where the construction and theatre of the process was also revealed.

I'm interested in protagonising all aspects of drama, not just the melodrama. In *Director's Cut (Fool For Love)* the camera wanders off into the wings of the stage, away from the action and often ignores the play altogether. What happens off camera, out of frame is another dimension in my looking at the overall. Godard played a lot with this idea of *decadrage*.

Significantly, the two screens (frames) on which the film is shown is a formal device that always splits the audience's attention. It diverges and converges the subject matters like a double helix. The double can contradict and concur in such a way as to shift and destabilise the positions of the subjects. Personally, these themes and forms are important to me. I've always had the desire to know more than one side of the story. Or, have been conscious there is a lot more that is left out (of the main frame) than is included. Whether these experiences come from being a person who moved to an unfamiliar country and always felt both on the outside and inside of a dominant mainstream; or being an artist working in and from the margins; or just being critical, they all feed my practice. Artistically, I find an affinity with Antonioni's work, especially for my interest in non-narrative stories. His unshakable formal aesthetic is probably what he is most influential for, with which he portrayed images as events. I made a work called *Dead Time,* based on Antonioni's *temps mort* technique, where he would ask his cinematographer to continue filming after the action. He felt these were the most poignant moments, which no amount of directing could recreate. My 16mm film both alienates the subject and the audience by using disjunctive and disassociative cuts. The sequences of tableau style scenes promise to build up a story but remain in a plotless, timeless narrative of elongated moments. Though the work is more formally aesthetic and serene than *Director's Cut (Fool For Love)*, the jarring cuts, timing and rhythm have a similar intention. The use of *mise-en-scène* and *mise-en-abyme* come very much from Godard. In fact, the reflexivity in his works like *Le Mépris* or *Pierrot le fou* is something I've carried over into the self-consciousness of the filmmaking process in *Director's Cut (Fool For Love)*. The camera looking back at the camera, or

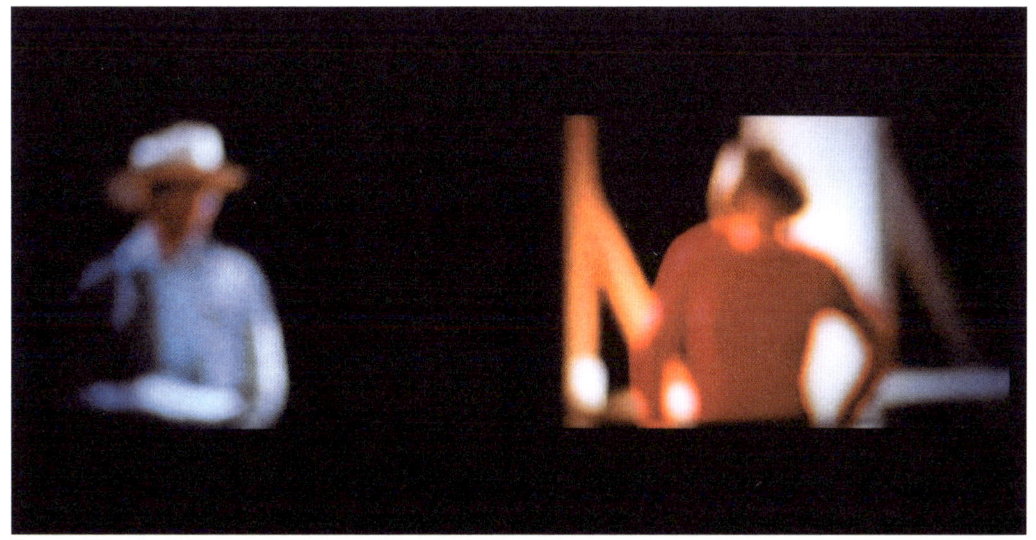

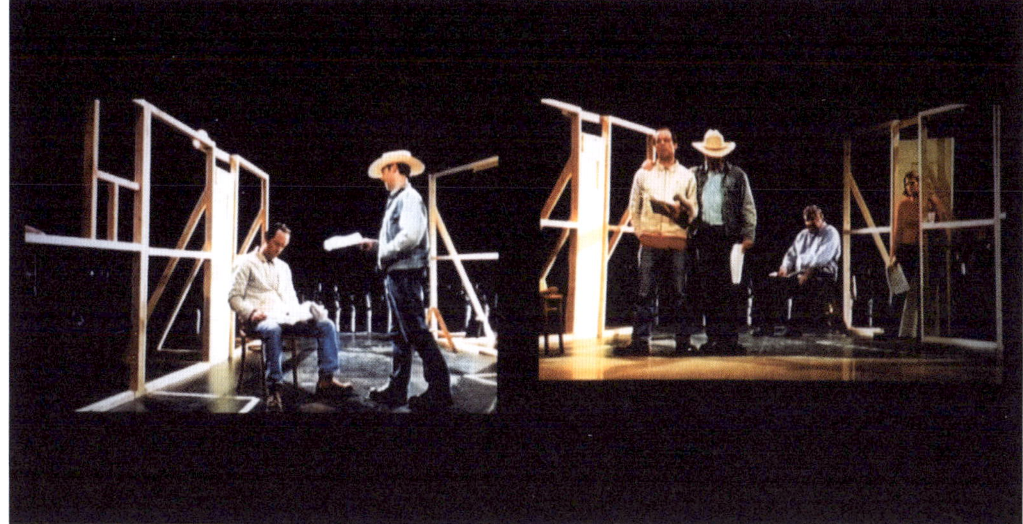

Runa Islam, *Director´s Cut (Fool for Love)*, 2001

the formality that deconstructs as a reconsideration of the medium, only to restore it, is my personal approach. What I find really compelling is the way Godard's iconoclasm for the image, sound and illusion of film heightened what I feel is the pureness of cinema.

In your multimedia installation we see men and women who alternately shout the sentences "I love you" and "I hate you" at each other. The action takes place on the stage of a theatre and is interrupted or controlled by the repeated interventions of a director. Now, in the theatre, or in art in general, the question arises as to whether the authenticity of feelings isn't lost when they are represented. Can feelings be conveyed indirectly, or do feelings have to be reproduced in art because of their directness? To what extent in *Director's Cut (Fool for Love)* are you interested in this aspect between play and reality, authenticity (directness) and production (indirectness), which is especially immanent in theatre?

The "I love you, I hate you" litany at the start of the film is a warm-up exercise. Initially, it was a warm-up for the rehearsal of the filming, but it was so powerful, I wanted to incorporate it into the film work. As an exercise it embodies an irreducible directness that shifts from being inauthentic to strikingly authentic to nonsensical. The shift between the immediate and the interpreted is such a fine line. I suppose it functions on a mimetic stratum, where the expressions are 'real' in a 'make believe' world. The onslaught of the words and self-consciousness of the players reminded me of Brecht's "making strange" theory. I felt that the exercise by its nature, filmed or not, was so alienating that it created an oscillation between "real engagement" and "distance". Seen across the two screens the slinging match is like a ball game of identification and estrangement. The gap between the two screens produced another element of artificiality, in which the antagonising lines tried to bridge. The use of "I love you, I hate you" as a rebounding utterance was introduced by the "director" to distil the core underlying emotions in the *Fool For Love* play. If I'd had more time, I would have filmed it in role reversal with the men and women switching lines so the women could attack/defend with "I hate you" and the men could defend/attack with "I love you". This way the battle of the sexes could inadvertently be equalised. In any case I felt this scene, which is the introduction to the rest of the film, is so emphatic that it goes beyond representation. It is just as the exercise is, a presentation.

Your film, which seems at first sight to be the documentation of a rehearsal, is rather based on its theatrical production. Can you explain, also referring to your other works as examples, how you deal with the extremely ambivalent relationship between documentation and fiction?

The ideas apparent in many of my works of the multi-perspective and the off-centre are features of documentary approach. These combine to form aspects of objectivity. However, the conception of documentary filmmaking as a real, truthful look, is disturbed when you realise that it is a genre, as is fiction. My works appropriate from both styles and slide between the methods. The slippage is actually within the fiction and the meta-fiction.

In *Tuin* the central screen, displaying the Ballhaus remake, is countered by a double screen, where the same scene is portrayed from the actors' point of view, revealing the construction. Both displays are fictional and possibly the experience of it is real. This sense of ambivalence you note is key to my practice as I think the nature of definitions and the language has a weight on the shifting meanings. I don't want to make sly or knowing statements that I am in control of representing these ideas. A work like *Screen Test/Unscript,* where headshots of four "photogenic" people are presented on 16mm film, amongst the lights and the camera proposes to be a documentary, or documentation. When interplayed with the separate soundtrack of montaged music and dialogue from *nouvelle vague* films, an aura and atmosphere form around the "characters". This spell of illusion and fiction is spun from the audience's "re"-interpretation. A sense of stories and evocative narratives is conjured up. The piece is a set-up to allow ambivalent readings and interpretations to develop from the dialogical references. The meanings are read back through the mosaic of quotations and allusions that have absorbed and transformed other meanings. Maybe that's not what you precisely asked about, but I think the "ambivalence" is actually the in-between status that a docu-fiction breeds in. *Director's Cut (Fool For Love)* was partly inspired by the mockumentary films, *Intervista* and *The Orchestra Rehearsal*, both by Fellini; and both very funny takes on directors and composers frustrated at how to train up their progenies. Also, *8 ½ (Otto e Mezzo)* has influenced the work, and other works, by being half complete and half unfinished. Again, such a film exists in the in-between state of looking at the process as subject.

It's in the fracture between the definitions and meanings that my most recent film work *Scale (1/16 inch = 1 foot)* functions. A work dwelling in an architecture that is both actual (a concrete building), artificial (in the form of a maquette) and fictionalised (a film set and actors), the piece slips between single and multiple diegesis. By faceting between the "real", "imaginary" and "model", presented as a two-projections work, it creates what Barthes called "third meanings".

It's probably not possible to escape from narrativity, because it permeates every part of our existence. I like the idea that it is present everywhere but that at the same time it is completely constructed. What I attempt to resist in my work, or else try to work within, is the implied meanings contained in narrative structures.

Many contemporary video and film artists rethink narrative structures, concentrating on themes that circumnavigate action or resolution. In this way, the work becomes more sculptural, positioning the time-based media in the artistic realm. I believe that unless one is creating a feature-length film, it makes sense to work outside the classic narrative codes. In short films the significances found in narrativity can collapse without diverting the viewers' attention for an extended period of time. Some filmmakers, such as Jim Jarmusch or Wim Wenders, do, however, dissolve the narrative element in some of their long feature films by employing slowed-down, intentionally drawn-out picture frequencies.

I really do think in terms of fragments and spaces and find it easy to position the logic or intention of my thoughts outside of a linear arc. Almost all of my more recent film and video works were produced intuitively, working with everything that is cinematic, but getting back to structure and form (the intellectual side of me) only afterwards.

My method has more in common with collage, where thoughts and images always run in different directions, maybe even off into the void. In both *Parallel* and *Scale (1/16 inch = 1 foot)* fragments and strong thought images were transformed into loosely connected stories. There are a lot of narrative counter codes and structures that help to make my scattered approach more understandable.

Eisenstein developed a very complex structure with jump cuts and collisions that is clearly manifest in many contemporary art films. In *Director's Cut (Fool for Love),* various stories revolve around the central axis of the actual story of the theatre rehearsal.

The interruption of the "real" that you were talking about is a further fragment or element that is generated during the process of producing the film. Many filmmakers, in particular also those who create experimental films, employ poetic systems, among other things, to resist the pull of "dominant" stories. The structuralists among filmmakers even invented new types of non-illusory systems for watching films.

I myself started out as a filmmaker with poetical and experimental films, where I would be documenting pictures and events rather than constructing them. My early work *Five Super-8 Portraits* from 1997 consists of a series of open-ended short episodes about people and personalities, who – without intending to do so – become something like thumbnail sketches within a story.

I view myself as an "absent-minded thinker", that is, one who comes across insights accidentally. To me, there's a certain irony in the fact that so much of the chaotic, formative process of my work disappears, in the end, behind these rather formalised presentations. In the dialogue I mentioned earlier, in *Fool for Love,* an atmosphere of absurdity comes into being that is reminiscent of the compulsive incomprehensibility and repetition of the behaviour of the activists in Samuel Beckett's *Comédie.*

What role does the absurd actually play in your own work?

The absurd is a perfect example of a counter narrative. Through the absurd, the formulaic course of events is intercepted. In my work there are a great many references to the absurd, or at any rate, if you view everything that happens outside of linear progressions as being absurd. The endless loop of the music in *Dead Time* evokes a sense of both timelessness and craziness.

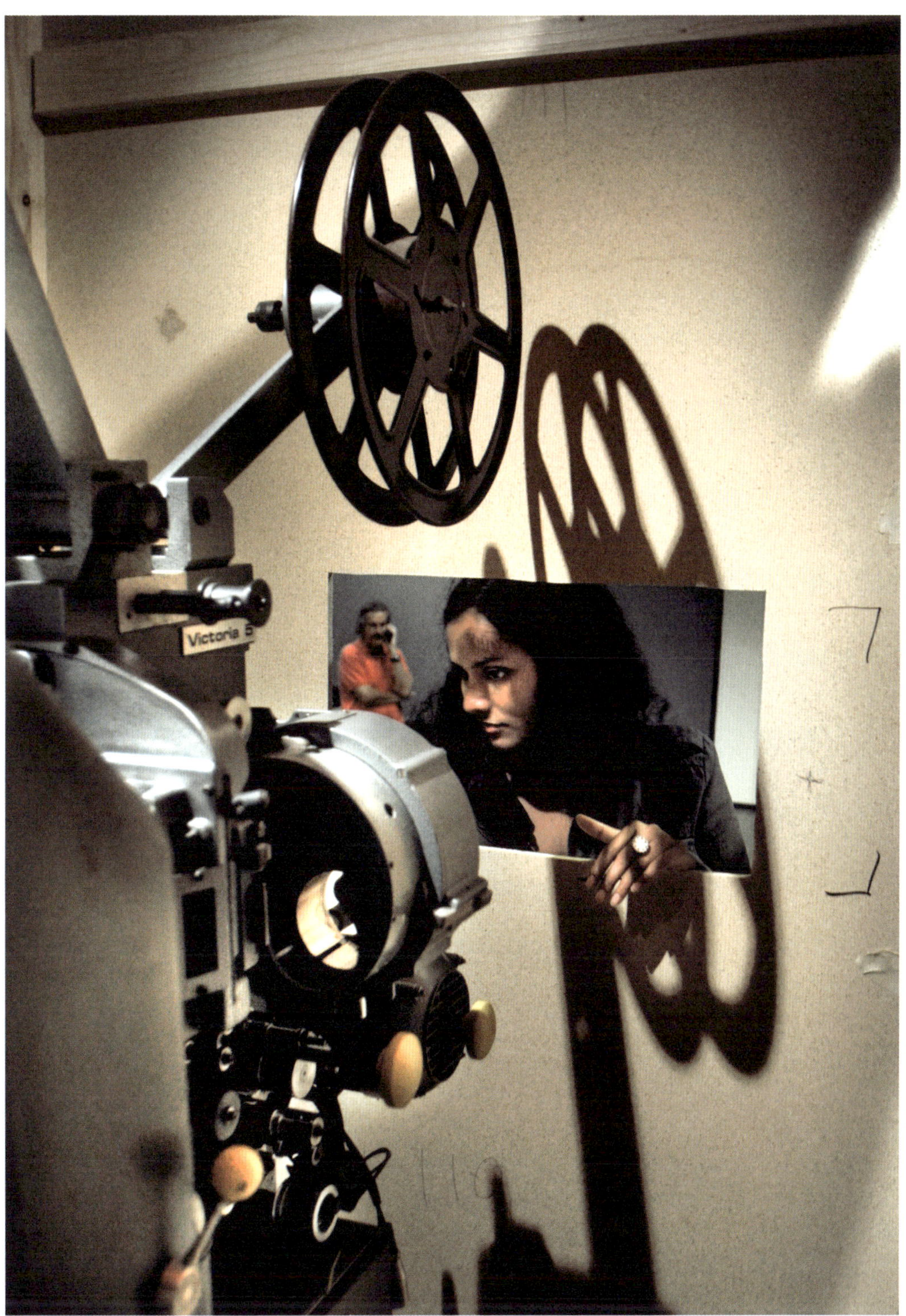

Runa Islam

In my conception of things, anything that is repeated so frequently and with such emphasis quickly transcends the limits of normality. The clock's proverbial thirteenth stroke is erroneous not only in itself but also casts doubt on those that have gone before. If you repeat your name ten times, the statement could well be called into question, or contradicted. It reminds me of the ritual techniques in Artaud's *Theatre of Cruelty*. And if I remember correctly, the gaps between the phrases in Beckett's *Comédie* have been left out, resulting in a wall of voices. It puts me in mind of how a collapse of realism can be achieved through the technical process.

Last year, I finished a film, which depicted discontinuity as a main method for collating pictures. It started out with my renewed interest in Dada and surrealist films. The "absurd" sequences in Buñuel, for example, are associated with images or situations from dreams or the subconscious. But in a technical sense they are unequivocally photographic tricks or manipulations of the cutter's technique.

The short film that I completed was based on the sleep phase known as "Rapid Eye Movement", which is associated with dreaming. My own work of the same name created an analogy between the movement of the film and the shutter of the projector, and the rapid movement of the eyeball and the images during the dream state.

The narrative/non-narrative representation starts with a scene in a train compartment where six people are gathered. The normality of that scene is interrupted when a young woman is told that a wasp has caught itself in her hair. While she is furiously shaking her head, another fellow traveller beats the insect to death and the absurd moment segues back into the common uncommunicative order.

The subsequent scenes grow into ever more absurd and surreal moods, ranging from the imaginary to the hallucinatory, from somnambulism to images of a plain, poetic and clear symbolism.

What is your main objective, as an artist and filmmaker, regarding your audience?

When I reflect on what I am trying to achieve in my role as an artist (although I don't like this question at all, because I do not know how to achieve this outcome in advance), then I guess I would say that I'm trying to steer people's attentions towards things and relationships that would otherwise be overlooked.

Runa Islam in conversation with Gerald Matt in the summer of 2003 on the occasion of the exhibition *Love/Hate: Versuche zum großen Gefühl zwischen Kunst und Theater* at Ursula Blickle Foundation, Kraichtal and the presentation of *Director's Cut (Fool For Love)* at Kunsthalle Wien project space.
Runa Islam, born 1970 in Dhaka, Bangladesh, lives and works in London.

Anna Jermolaewa

I believe that art is by all means capable of producing societal changes.

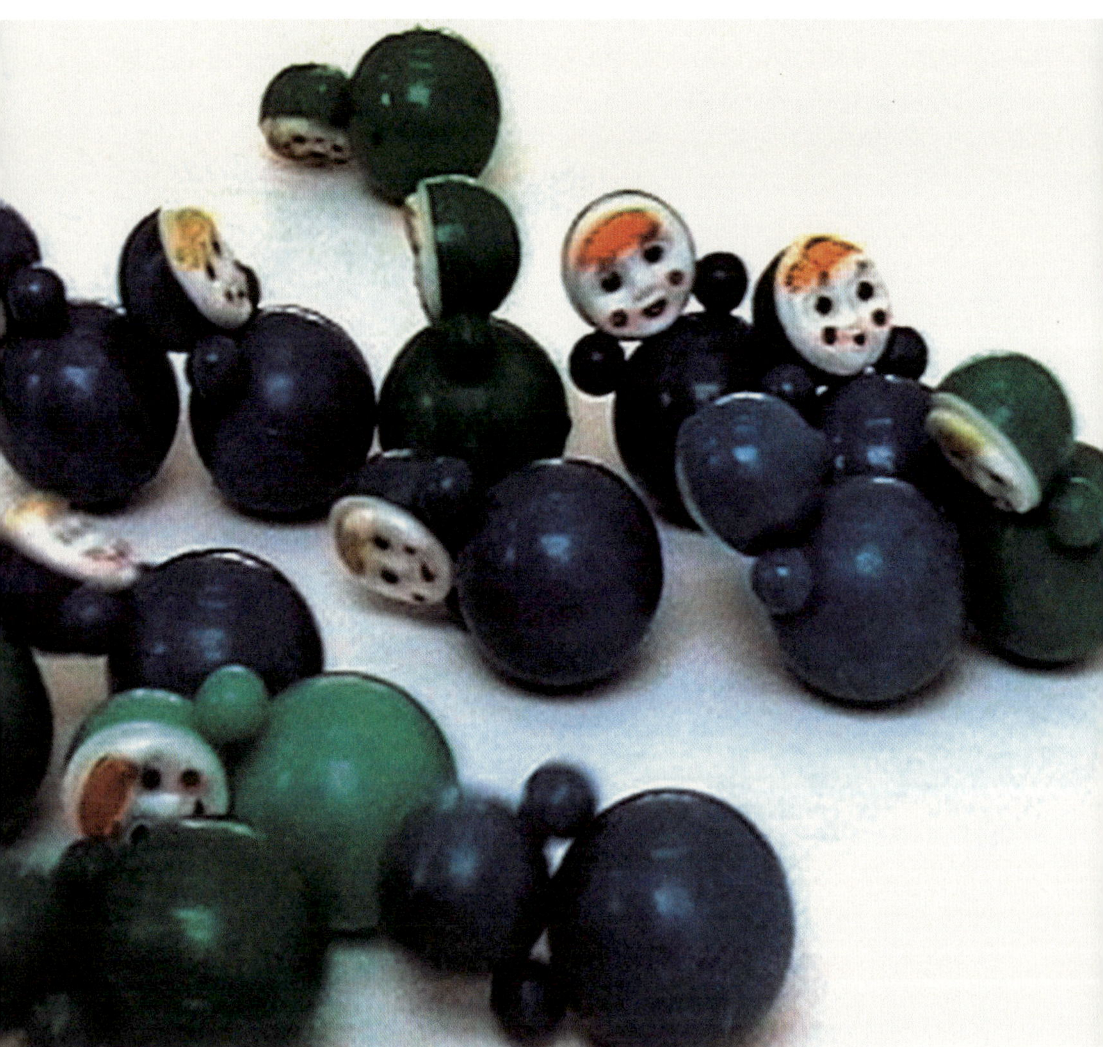

Video still: Anna Jermolaewa,
3 min. Attempts to Survive,
2000

In your double video *Five Year Plan* you choose a specific space: a St. Petersburg subway station. Here you film people riding an escalator. Initially, you shot this in May 1996, and you repeated this process five years later in 2001. In the course of five years, hardly anything has changed, not even the style of dress. The only thing that is different is the product being advertised in the background. The first thing one feels when one sees *Five Year Plan* is resignation, a sense of futility; the five year plan seems to have failed; hopes for a change beyond that of consumerism go unfulfilled. Instead, we are appalled by the monotony of everyday life, because the video suggests that nothing has happened in the past five years except for people riding up and down the escalator. Are you suggesting to the viewer the sense of an existential struggle "in spite of" all odds, the irony of the myth of Sisyphus, or is *Five Year Plan* merely an expression of powerlessness?

"Bounty and Snickers are hanging out at the drug store, and…" It used to be that politics and politicians were the main characters in the jokes and anecdotes people would tell. But now the stories people are telling are about Bounty, Snickers or Mars, and I think this is a pretty good indication of the societal changes taking place in Russia in recent years.

During the Soviet reign, everyday life was swallowed by ideology. The slightest everyday gesture had its ideological interpretation, was considered "pro" or "contra" – absolutely parallel to Orwell's *1984*, where Winston sleeps with Julia and defines this as an "act," as a "blow against the party."

The last ten years have brought with them a radical secularization of social life. The people on the escalator – though their attire may not betray the fact – no longer belong to the species *homo sovieticus* (which continues to be the subject of interpretation in Ilya Kabokov's works). Much has changed above the subway. Keep in mind that St. Petersburg has meanwhile become the ninth most expensive city in the world for tourists, that Moscow is now third in that ranking, and that the greatest number of luxury Mercedes models are exported to Russia. However, most of the people riding the escalators, especially the elderly, are much poorer now and their purchasing power is much less than it was five years ago.

At the same time your double video *Five Year Plan* also reminds us of surveillance camera images: the public realm, a realm under organized state and private control. The perspective of these surveillance cameras is indifferent and unemotional, like a visual vivisection. Both luring and repulsive at once?

One of the principles in my work is to keep every personal flourish that can be read as a trace of the authentic to a minimum whenever possible. What complicated matters in the case of *Five Year Plan* was that it was strictly forbidden to film or photograph in the subway stations in Russia because they were considered military zones – I remember, for example, there was an A-bomb air raid drill at my school and we all had to run to the closest subway station. I was forced, therefore, to use a concealed camera – a camera in my shopping bag with a peephole cut into it. That would explain the indifferent, unemotional impression.

Is *Five Year Plan*, which is your only work that is explicitly situated in Russia, to any extent autobiographical?

It is indeed a very autobiographical work. Especially since it was my very first video (1996). As a child I had to take the subway to school every day and I have always been absolutely fascinated by escalators. You could stare at the other people without having to worry about ever seeing them again. The station I got out at was the lowest station in the city – it took almost eight minutes to ride up or down – so I had more than enough time every day to enjoy my favorite pastime. I guess it makes sense that my very first video work was the escalator video.

You yourself chose *Big Sister* to be the main title of your exhibition. Is this the female counterpart to George Orwell's "Big Brother"? Are you making reference to the questionability of the gender-orientation (male) of this term, which is used as a synonym for our monitoring society?

For us in the Soviet Union, Orwell's *1984* was a very important book back then. We would refer to it constantly and in many senses we could relate to the circumstances in the book. Yes, absolutely, I consciously chose the title *Big Sister* as a female counterpart to Big Brother in order to pose exactly your question to visitors. I do not, however, believe that power is perceived as a female attribute.

In a society in which the media and public observation bodies of the private sector – like *Big Brother* – and pseudo-democratic constellations – like *Taxi Orange* – are becoming ever more prevalent, the individual seems to be reduced to a role that only permits individuality in a thin outer skin of self-representation. In your works, too, the subject becomes entirely secondary, your video protagonists, toys and dolls, are, by virtue of the production method, figures that exist in the masses and in mass. Their movements are mechanical, and they are controlled and manipulated by an exterior force, in this case by you. Anna Jermolaewa as a *déesse cachée*?

Big Brother may be the most well-known representative of this new genre, which first supplanted the talk show, then the game show, and which, as a kind of "reality soap" that combines game show elements and reality TV, has propagated itself, giving rise to "twin brothers" in many different countries.

The rules of the game force candidates – who live in constant fear of being eliminated – to ingratiate themselves not only with the other contestants but with their television audience as well, and these conditions increase the Orwellian vision of a total surveillance state even more, because the surveillance mechanisms are replaced by more subtle models.

The most recent cinematic illustration of this, which I saw not too long ago at the Vienna Filmmuseum, is *Battle Royale* by the Japanese director Kinji Fukasaku. He even outdoes Takeshi Kitano, who incidentally plays a role in *Battle Royale*, in both sheer violence and Takashi Miike. Every year a lottery drawing is held to choose the school class that will be exiled to an island where for three days it must compete in a game with live media coverage. The rules are simple: it's every man for himself and the object is to kill the other contestants until just one winner survives. If more than one player is still left at the end of the game, their collars – each contestant has an identification collar – will be detonated. I sat there shocked while I watched this movie because it reminded me of my own work called *3 min. Attempts to Survive.*

Manipulation, inflexibility, and loss of self-determination, individual disorientation in a society that is becoming ever more convoluted, complex, and confusing, these are aspects that determine today's discussion about the relation between the individual and the modern world. To what extent do you hold our media society accountable for bringing forth subjects that are practically devoid of all subjectivity? What stance do you take as an artist between the poles of observation and change?

I believe that art is by all means capable of producing societal changes. Tatlin, for example, was convinced that the work of his group of artists had "led to the Russian revolution." In much the same way, I hope my artistic work will also effect changes.

Dolls, animals, chickens, toys, male organs, are often the figures in your video films. Their characters remain schematic, their movements mechanical and repetitive. They do not reveal what makes them unique. To what extent do you tie in with the tradition of the *manichino* found in artists from Giorgio de Chirico to George Grosz?

Manichini, those blind, silent, and hollow dolls found in De Chirico's work, immersed in themselves – no, that romantic-mythological, metaphysical camp (he's considered one of the pioneers of Surrealism) is completely foreign to me. When I need dolls, I go to my daughter's toy chest.

In your video *Motherhood* you show a handful of puppies trying desperately to suck at their mother's teats. The mother dog, however, is more interested in being petted by a human hand. The person doing the petting, is seated at a table out of view and anonymous. Superimposed on this scene is an acoustically incoherent conversation. As in some of your other works, you toy with the notion of presence and absence, of invisibility and visibility. The decisive elements seem to take place outside the viewer's field of vision. The relationships between the figures remain vague, the situation unclear. Martin Prinzhorn speaks of a "looking beyond at the whole" (*EIKON* 32). Do you believe that the complexity of life can only be discerned via fragmented – and thus non-ideological – means?

I'd rather not comment on this question.

Then let's change the subject. In the video *On/Off* we see an erect penis turning a light switch on and off. Besides its characteristic monotony this video also reveals an equally characteristic feature of your work: the miniature narration. Paulo Herkenhoff was reminded here of an anecdote about Sigmund Freud: "While she (Martha Freud) nursed Freud's offspring like young puppies, her husband insisted that the light switch only be turned on and off with an erect penis. It's as if the Freuds were acting out Anna Jermolaewa's video." What role does Sigmund Freud or sexual psychology, in fact, play in your work?

In reaction to my work, people sometimes mention "penis envy." Of course, Freud does play a role in my work. However, what I find disturbing about him – like many other feminists – is that he tends to regard the woman as an incomplete man, a castrated male. That's quite a sexist attitude. In this sense, I would say I have been much more influenced by what I know by Michel Foucault and Judith Butler.

The viewer of your work is confronted with a rigid frame that strictly delimits what happens within. The action itself is spartan. There is hardly any narration, or if there is, the narrative is anecdotal. Your video scenarios are not elaborately designed. The reasons for the action are not revealed. The world is confined in the rigid frame of the camera. Do you focus in your films on images of confinement, reduction, and retreat as a reaction to a certain societal form?

You're right, my work is very laconic, I'm not interested in extreme scenarios and elaborate productions, most of the time the production costs for my projects are next to nothing.

Slavoj Žižek addresses the subject of Bond movies in *The Fright of Real Tears* and poses the brilliant question: what actually happens between the idyllic happy ending of the movie – after the mission has been accomplished and we come to the sexual act – and the beginning of the new movie – where Miss Moneypenny calls with the new assignment? According to Žižek, this lapse would be "the ultimate postmodern Bond movie," "a kind of boring existential drama about decay." And it is precisely this that fascinates me: the trivial, quotidian, commonplace, unspectacular, an occurrence that might take place in someone's kitchen or at any given hotdog stand, but which by virtue of being fragmentary suddenly becomes strange and surreal.

In the video *Shooting* the viewer sees you at a shooting gallery firing with live ammunition. Your bullet hits and destroys the camera as it films you. What follows is a brief flickering of the image, which quickly goes blank, accompanied by a noisy roar. The artist destroys her medium; she disappears into her medium. In this first and to date last personal appearance before the camera, is the point you are making a discussion of the role of the artist in the art industry as well as his/her artistic practice, or are you continuing the self-destructive strategies of the feminist position of the 1970s?

As far as self-destructive strategies go, I'd say men have contributed their share. Consider John Fare, who held clandestine sessions during which he had parts of himself amputated, including, finally, his head; or the Japanese artist in the seventies who announced his art event that he called *Life* and then he jumped from a skyscraper, splattering himself on the sidewalk in

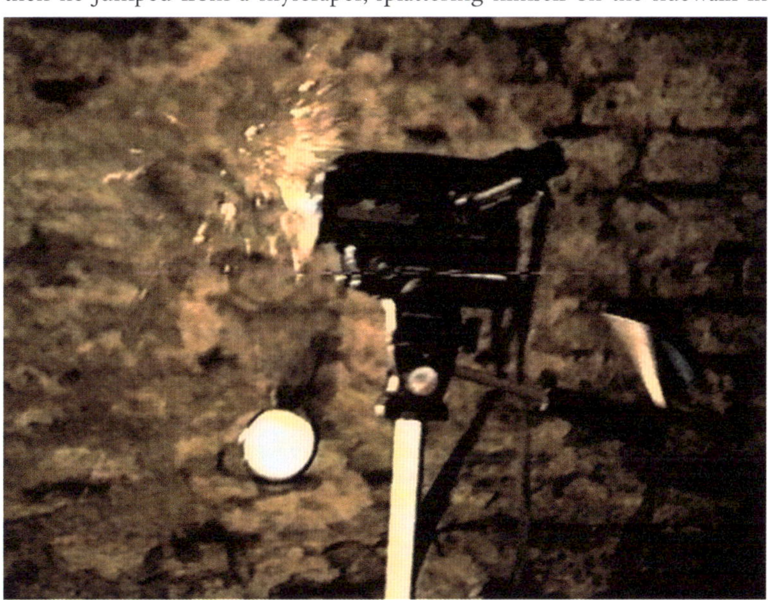

front of the eyes of the audience that had turned out to see him. In the light of these works, I think we can safely consider this chapter closed.

For my part, I am much more interested in questions like "me and the public" and "me and the art industry."

Chris Burden let people fire at him. You shoot at the image of yourself captured by your camera. The artist as "exemplary sufferer" – now and with you: in the age of media society?

You mean this shamanic attitude people attribute to an artist, e.g. Joseph Beuys? No, I'm not interested in that. Maybe I do hurt myself in that I destroy the instruments I've grown attached to, that have become almost a part of me and that I have used to make all my video works up until this point, but I do it for me.

Your three-part series of drawings *3 Monkeys* whose protagonists, upon closer inspection, turn out to be hand puppets, shows marked expressiveness in the monkeys' faces. The progression of intensity starts with the bashful smile of the first monkey and ends with uproarious laughter in the third monkey. The *3 Monkeys* series seems uncharacteristic compared to your other work, not only in terms of the chosen media, i.e. as drawings, but they are your only works that reveal this kind of strong emotionality, something that might even be interpreted as a caricature. Does *3 Monkeys* represent a further perspective of your work, or how would you classify these drawings with regard to your work up until now? Or, let me reword my question by focusing explicitly on the choice of medium. With only a few exceptions, all your art consists of video works. Your photography utilizes almost exclusively frames (or stills) from your videos. What advantages or disadvantages does this media restriction have? Do you juxtapose the moving picture (video) with the still in order to address the dichotomy of this restriction and the potential of these two disparate media in respect of your work?

I graduated from art school in St. Petersburg, where you were expected to work according to strict academic principles. After my arrival in Vienna, I continued to paint, but then there came a moment, when these huge canvases pervaded with a work character that took up so much space in the apartment began to bother me. I wanted to make a clear and radical break, so I cut all my paintings up into small, uniform-sized, puzzle-like pieces that you could toss in the corner in a pile that hardly took up any space and assemble however you pleased. That was an important step for me back then. It was the year I entered the Academy. Peter Kogler told me John Baldessari had already done the same thing, only even more radically: he had burned all his work around 1970.

Many years later, I began to paint and draw again, applying the skills I'd acquired earlier but with a conceptual approach.

As for the medium I choose to work with, I move freely among various media, depending on what I am trying to achieve. The medium itself is never the subject with me. I reject media specificity as a significant value. For me McLuhan's slogan "the medium is the message" is no longer valid today.

In your exhibition *Big Sister/The Five Year Plan* you not only show your own work, but also films that are connected in some way to your work. For example, there's Dziga Vertov, who tried to show the dream of invisibility of the camera's point of

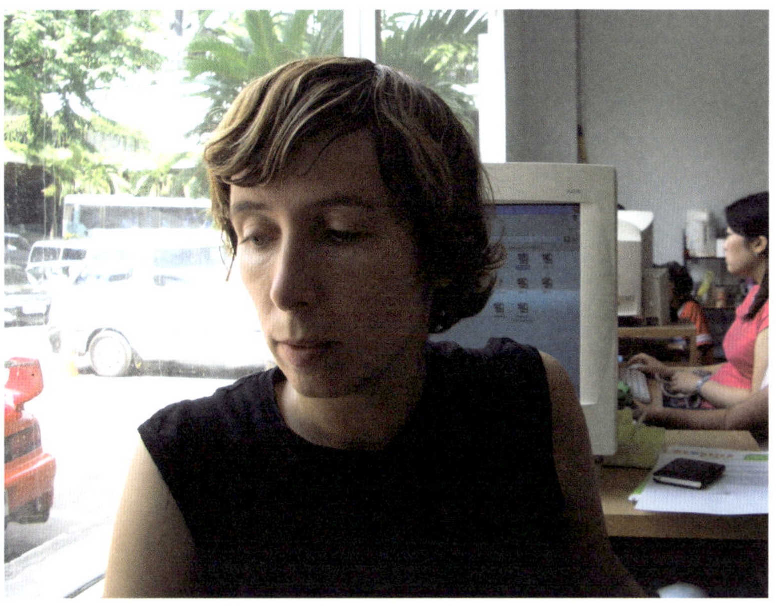

Anna Jermolaewa

view in his films ("the surprise shot – the old combat rule of thumb: wait for the whites of their eyes, don't hesitate, fire"). Do you also see yourself as a discreet voyeur? This calls to mind the film *Peeping Tom* with Karl-Heinz Böhm, where the camera becomes an instrument of murder and the object of observation becomes the victim. How would you position your work between Vertov's warm, documentary view and Michael Powell's cold, enacted view?

You're right, Vertov's camera language and that of *Peeping Tom* – that's about as diametrically opposed as you can get. Vertov's invisible, voyeuristic camera (not to be confused with Hollywood's "invisible camera") and the physically present, aggressive, action-determining camera in Powell's work – I'd say I'm equally interested in both.

Although I have done several "voyeuristic" works, I suppose I currently tend more towards Powell – I'm thinking specifically of my works *Shooting*, *Crashtest*, or *Solo*, in which I deal with the physical presence of the camera.

In the exhibition, you also show films by Gordon Matta-Clark, who makes the invisible perceptible through a perforation of the spatial boundaries. What role does the dialectic between visible and invisible play in your work?

In the seventies, Denis Hollier asked, "Is prison the general term for every product of architecture? … Is it possible to imagine an architecture that doesn't, as with Bataille, induce socially sanctioned behavior?" *(La Prise de la Concorde)*. Gordon Matta-Clark tried to demonstrate the hidden ideological seams in the fabric of political and social life, to bring to light another story. I would say, just as Gordon Matta-Clark was not only talking about architecture, my work with toys is not only about toys either.

In connection with your exhibition, you also present prize-winning Cannes Reel commercials. "Advertising is the sandbox in which we play-act the situations of real life," is the slogan of the exhibition: "Advertising is for everyone." What interests you here? Is it the discrepancy between desires and reality that falls short of fulfilment, or is it the structure, the schema of a commercial that must convey its catchy message in a brief timespan?

Advertising is something that has fascinated me for a long time. I have no qualms about learning from it, despite all the preconceived notions associated with advertising. Just sticking to Russian examples, I can name Wassily Kandinsky, who advertised for a Russian chocolate manufacturer or El Lissitzky who sold his face for the artist paint brand Pelikan. "Tokimeki" is the term used by the Japanese for the desired adrenaline rush that turns people into consumers.

On the other hand, advertising also uses knowledge gleaned from the field of psychology, namely that information conveyed through images is registered and processed much faster than via writing or language. Considering that today only two percent of all available information reaches its audience, sensual appeals are an effective means of getting your message through against the competition of the flood of information and images.

William Wegman's dog films thrive on the element of surprise in which the expectations of the viewer are disrupted. His works are full of irony and humor. You chose to show works by William Wegman in your exhibition. What role does irony play in your work?

What especially interests me about Wegman's videos from the seventies is their undogmatic lightness and irony, particularly because he deals with serious subjects like the performing animal acts and domestication.

Irony is also very important to me. I consider a work to be well done if it addresses important issues without being dogmatic.

You studied under Peter Kogler in the class for computer and video art at the Academy of Fine Arts in Vienna, graduating recently with honors. Were there dialogues with Peter Kogler or with his works that were meaningful to your own work?

I enrolled at the Academy after having studied art history at the University of Vienna for six years, and after all those years of being in an anonymous mass production line I was lucky to end up in a class that was like a surrogate family to me. Moreover, with us, all media was created equal – there were people in my class working with music and performance, others with photography or video. This produced an interesting exchange within the class. There've been many conversations with Peter about my work and about his work and I've learned a great deal from him.

Speaking of *Five Year Plan* – where do you see yourself in five years? What's your plan for the future?

Five years from now? I'll probably be on the escalator with a camera in my modified shopping bag.

Anna Jermolaewa in conversation with Gerald Matt in the summer of 2002 on the occasion of the exhibition *Anna Jermolaewa: Big Sister – The Five Year Plan* at Ursula Blickle Foundation, Kraichtal. The artist was taking part in the exhibition *Lebt und arbeitet in Wien* (2000) at Kunsthalle Wien. Anna Jermolaewa was born in St. Petersburg, Russia in 1970. She lives and works in Vienna, Austria and Karlsruhe, Germany.

German to English translation by Jonathan Quinn.

Isaac Julien

I am interested in avoiding didacticism in my work, but do not want to shy away from making direct statements.

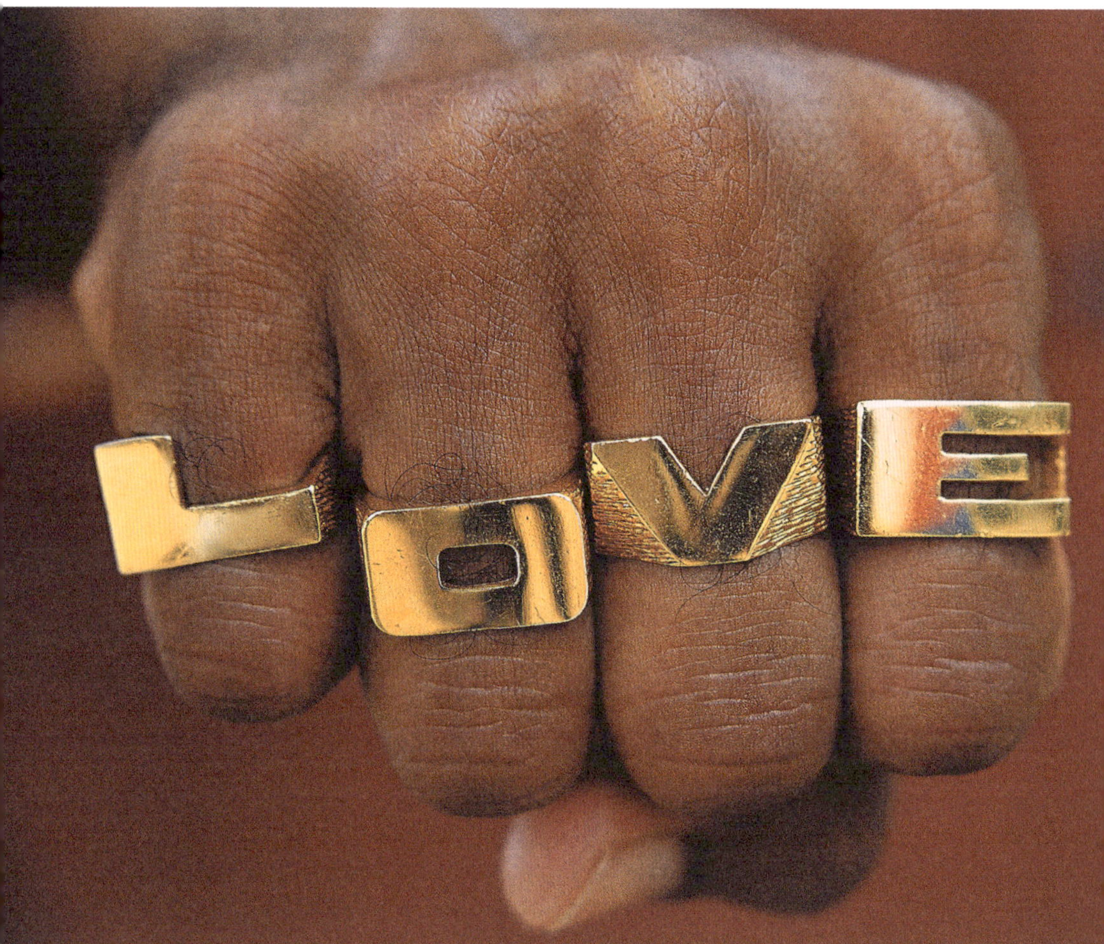

Isaac Julien, *Love*, 2003

At this year's Biennale (2003) you made a poster for the exhibition of Hans Ulrich Obrist, *Utopia Station* relating to Charles Laughton's film *The Night of the Hunter*. What we see is a hand wearing rings, the rings being letters spelling out the word "love". Why did you make only one photo or poster? Why is the word "hate" not shown as in Laughton's film? What interests you so in the Charles Laughton film that you make reference to it?

The photograph is a portrait of the trickster character from *Paradise Omeros*, which is my personal and implicitly political response to the physical dislocation incurred by globalisation. Referencing Robert Mitchum's soliloquoy from the film *Night of the Hunter*, the photograph is one half of a diptych, which alludes to the powerful binary between love and hate, and the complexity of inhabiting the space between the two. It is this uncertain middle ground that the photograph evokes. The (necessarily) ambiguous image encompasses themes of cinema and hip-hop culture (music and fashion) in relation to the unidentifiable body that we are faced with, a body that asserts itself through the authoritative gesture of the fist and the poetic word, love. In this photograph, against a rich crimson background, issues of sexuality and masculinity are raised, and the viewer is encouraged to draw out personal narrative possibilities. I believe that the work would lose some of the ambiguity, which we read into the single "love" image; if the "hate" image was included as well. I am interested in avoiding didacticism in my work, but do not want to shy away from making direct statements.

A basic question that suggests itself in relation to the theme of the exhibition, *Love/Hate. Approaches towards the grand emotion between art and theatre*, is whether emotions can be represented at all. Themes like love and hate have always found their way into both theatre and the visual arts, and for the artist, no doubt, one function of art among others is to be the place where subjective experiences, so strong that they simply have to be ex-pressed, can be processed and sublimated. The question arises as to whether the authenticity of feelings is not lost when they are re-presented in art. Can feelings be conveyed at all from one person to another? Or, doesn't the immediacy of feeling mean that they have to be made separately for the viewer in art?

The question of subjectivity in my works is addressed through the language of cinema. I am interested in what could be termed the "cinematization" of video art, which means that however problematic the ways are in which cinema as an art form grotesquely manipulates spectators, I would say that I am still interested in a critical emotionality for the cause of re-directing empathy with subjects which have been barred from this kind of identification. As a general trend in British Art we can detect a certain "critical emotionality" in the works of Gillian Wearing, Tracey Emin and Steve McQueen. In other words, there is not a separation between intellectual and conceptual endeavours. Making an emotional relation between the spectator and the work of art is perhaps just a British phenomenon, but obviously moving image works will always be contaminated by all the arts, including theatre/performance. So therefore it does not obey to the orthodoxies, which have circulated within the citadels of contemporary art.

In moving image work the sonic/sound component usually has a role to play in con-structing "the grand emotion" between art and theatre. Feelings can be conveyed "en masse", which of course can be problematic, but in most art the immediacy of feelings is always a balancing act between intention and reception, and between sound and image. The spectator usually completes the meaning, but this is always in the unequalness.

Your work *Paradise Omeros* refers among other things to the film *The Night of the Hunter* and deconstructs it. Deconstruction is a typical activity for you, and you use it in a lot of your works. To what extent are deconstructionists like Derrida of theoretical importance for you, and to what extent is their theory echoed in your practice?

You are right to acknowledge what could be seen as the deconstructivist motifs evident in my works, but my main concern has been around the question of translocation, rather than Derridaen deconstructionism. The idea of movement and translocation has been approached in different ways in the works of people such as Deleuze, Virilio and Paul Gilroy. It is not so much that one wants to visualize theoretical concerns but there is always a translation that takes place between these different debates. I see my practice as contributing to these debates where knowledge is formed through the production of art itself rather than it being a mere illustration of someone else's idea. Thinking about my earlier works, for example the museum theme in *Vagabondia*, I feel that dissonance has played an important role in "differencing" space. In *Vagabondia* dissonant rhythms were generated by the movements of the dancer in the space of the John Soane Museum. In a work like *Baltimore* the idea that spaces might be interrupted by "troubling elements" like the introduction of thriller and sci-fi elements into a museum space, is significant.

You originally studied painting at St. Martin's School of Art in London, and then you worked for many years as an independent filmmaker, and you also exhibit these films in museums. A hybridisation of media and genres. In artistic terms you feel at home in several genres, indeed your films are patch-work pieces from author's film, documentary film and feature film.

Interdisciplinary work is of major importance to you. What advantages in terms of media do you find in film, and what ones in visual art? What is the role of theatre in your work?

I have always been interested in an interdisciplinary practice which cuts across different disciplines and transverses and transgresses definitions, and to this effect I see my commitment to this practice as being connected to an interest in how hybridisation can hold a radicality which needs these practices to articulate its being. In this sense, I would like to emphasize my interest in Brecht, where notions of popular culture and high culture intertwine for aesthetic and political effects, which in turn can instil in the spectator a sense of agency and surprise. In his theatre, Brecht always wanted the audience to identify both intellectually and emotionally simultaneously, and I see film as being a medium which can function in this capacity to great effect. Questions of genre and medium are immaterial to me, and subservient to the aestheticisation and political intention. The role of theatre is located in the use of "performance", like in Bresson where the actors are merely models rather than theatre players.

In his video *Violent Incident – Man/ Woman* Bruce Nauman shows a love-hate scene where hate and a quarrel arise within seconds from a situation of deep romance. To what extent do you agree, in your film *Three*, characterised as it is by a marked theatricality, whipped-up emotions, a deliberate staginess and abstract moments generated by the blurred passages from films and the b/w mode you employed, with the idea in the video and in the exhibition, or at least in the title of the exhibition, that love and hate are two sides of the same coin and taken together make up "Grand Emotion"? Is there such a thing as a dialectical inter-relationship of emotions?

I can answer the question in another way by doing a recourse to the sonic aspects of Nauman's work. This relationship to language always carries a degree of emotionality and the powerful sentiments of love and hate are re-rehearsed as the parody of relations between men and women in the theatre of the every-day. The question I think we need to ask, and which I think your exhibition poses, is regarding the relationship between the visceral understandings of subjectivity and their relationship to intellectual and conceptual ideas in contemporary art, and ordinarily these are separated.

This novel approach, therefore, poses the question of the importance of us admitting that the "structures of feeling" (Raymond Williams) are always attached even to the most rationalist/conceptualist aspects of contemporary art.

In an age that democratizes the star principle with TV productions like *Starmania*, *Popstars*, and *Superstars* and has the potential of making the entire world a stage, the relation between theatre in an exclusive aesthetic realm and the self-presentation rituals in the urban space must be redefined and measured with the means of art. How much authenticity and directness is contained in stage design as filtered through the art of theatre, and how much artificiality rules in the rituals of "see and be seen" on the catwalks of the urban stage (disco, hip hangout, cultural event), which themselves follow a predetermined script and define a long-established performative codex?

I think the question of performativity in our celebrity-obsessed culture of the West is significant in the terms that you suggest, and that it plays an iconic role in the British art context, where artists have become very much a part of the publicity game of the media. The languages of mimicry and parody are ironically and sardonically expressed in many works of contemporary art, which perform a commentary on the absurdity of the masquerade, which we find ourselves in. The question is whether or not there is any political authenticity left in a culture which has become so imbued with the languages of what you call "the self-presentation rituals in an urban space". What we are describing here reminds me of Butler's work on "miming". With "miming" there is always the politics of translation between what is gained and what is lost. In this particular moment, I think we are losing a lot, and so therefore perhaps art has a role to play in deconstructing this painful political moment.

Isaac Julien in conversation with Gerald Matt and Angela Stief in the summer of 2003 on the occasion of the exhibition *Love/Hate: Versuche zum großen Gefühl zwischen Kunst und Theater* at Ursula Blickle Foundation, Kraichtal.
Isaac Julien was born in London, Great Britain in 1960. He lives and works in London.

Isaac Julien, 1960 in London, Großbritannien, geboren, lebt und arbeitet in London.

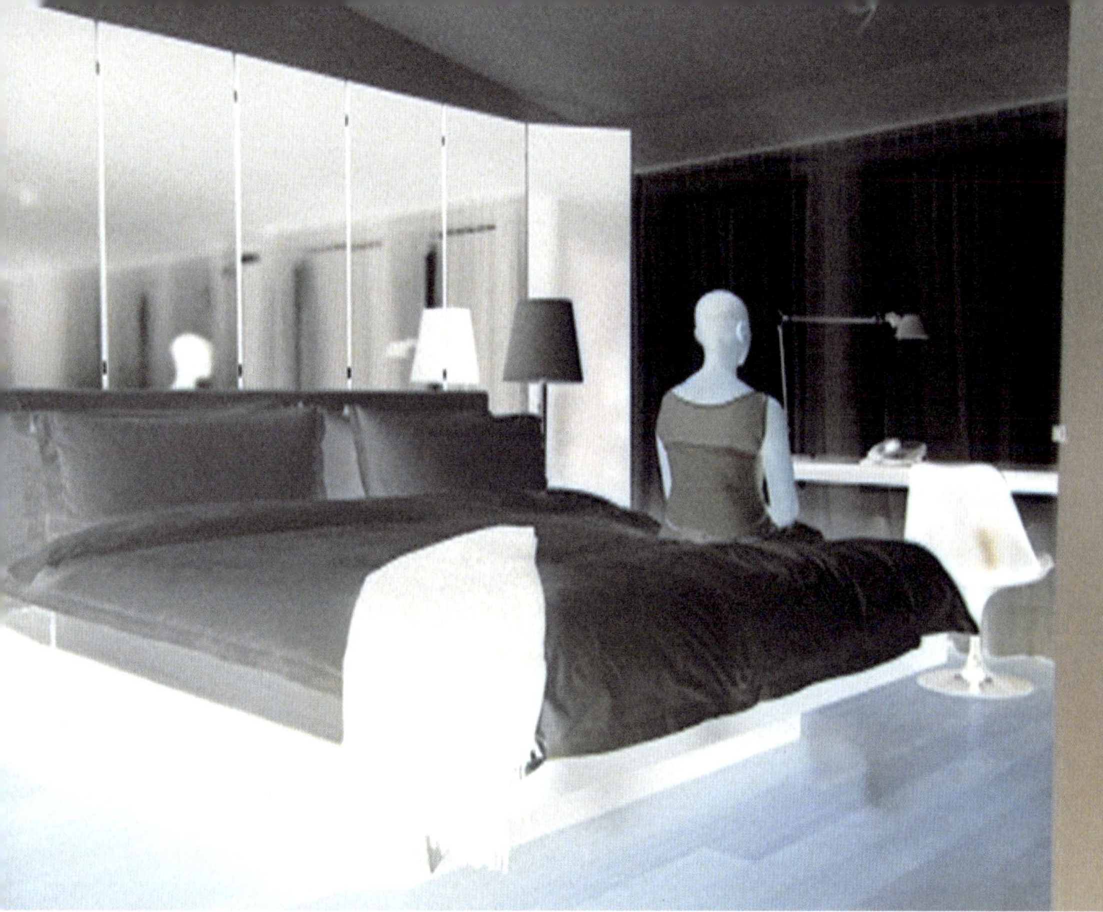

Video still: Isaac Julien,
Encore II: (Radioactive),
2004

Kimsooja

I really wish to disappear at some point by my own decision.

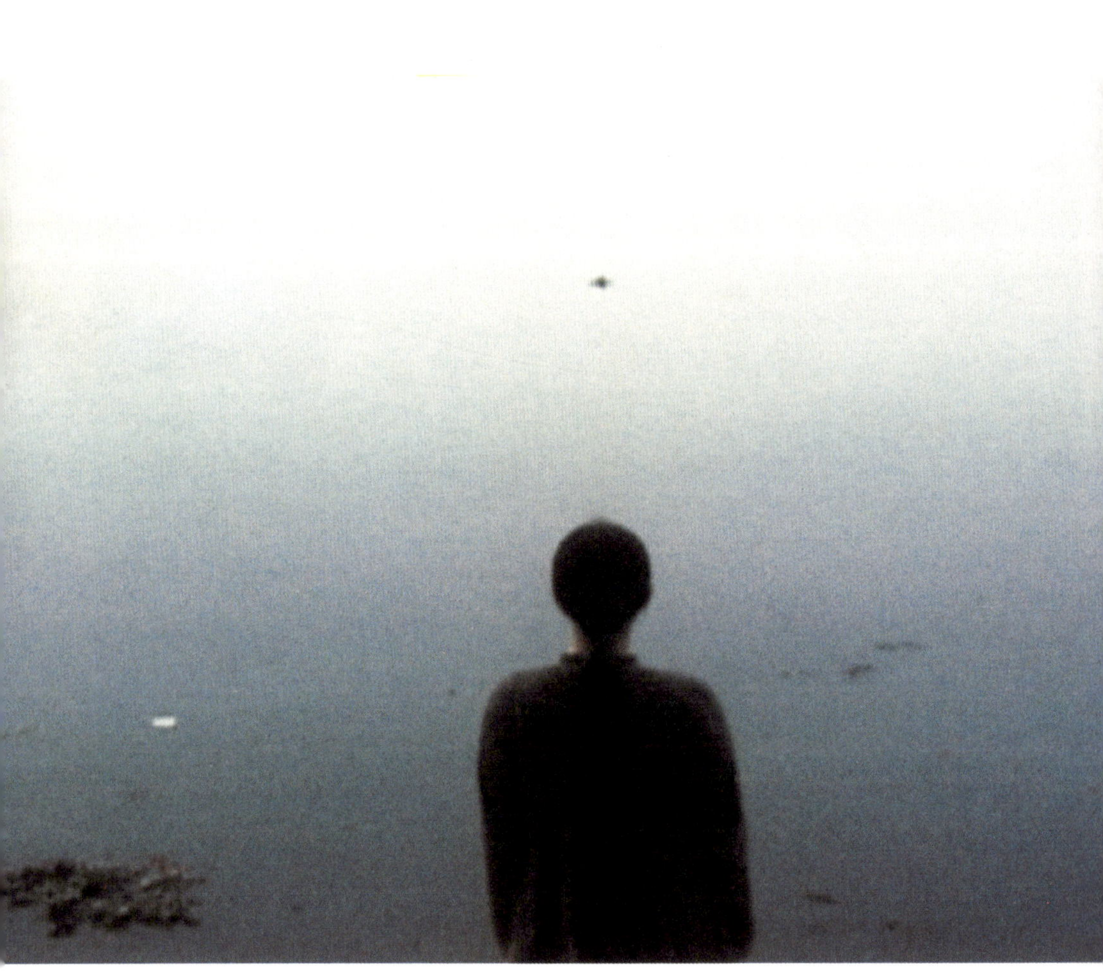

Video still: Kimsooja,
A Laundry Woman,
2000

When I visited you for the first time in your apartment in downtown Manhattan I felt as if I had just been transported into another world; an enclave of contemplation and concentration in a city whose maxim is the acceleration of the pace of life. Have you brought your world from Korea with you and transplanted it into the city context of New York (almost like a Bottari-Bundle) or do you rather see this Korean world as an alternative design/parallel universe to an accelerated existential rhythm which has almost exceeded the human being's biological capacities?

> Whether I live in Korea or in New York, I live in my own world, which is isolated from the outer world, and that's the way I keep my distance, one from the other. In the sense of isolation, New York can be a more isolated place than Korea in a physical way, but I felt much more isolation in Korea in an intellectual and psychological way in a society, which is overwhelmed by mass consumption, which often happens in developing countries. This idea obviously influences, too, the art world in Korea.

Travelling plays a central role in your work. The continually new and changing locations in which you place yourself and your art continue to change the context of your work. (In this respect, one might almost characterise your work as context art.) Would you say that travelling is a sort of means of survival for you – an activity which evokes positive feelings, or do you think what Paul Virilio called "the small death of departure" has a role to play here?

> Travelling for me is not always a voluntary choice but was often a forced one. It's been a part of my life since I was a little girl. My father was in the military service after the Korean War and our family had to move from one village to another, one city to another, almost every two years. We'd been living and moving around near the DMZ area for many years. It was a surprise for me to realise that we had been packing and unpacking bundles all the time, which has been my actual body of work since the early nineties, and how clear and strong the images of the landscape passing by as seen from the train was in my childhood, just as it was presented in my recent videos. Location and dislocation, encounter and separation were always there and I find myself as someone who has a borderline mentality, and I think the fabric I deal with, in a way, is playing that role. I had to carry on a great deal of longing and nostalgia as well as laps of memory and adjustments to the new environment since I was a little girl. When I wasn't travelling somewhere and I stayed in these mountain villages, I was always looking at this black big mountain, which was hulking in front of me just like an obstacle, and I'd be longing to go beyond these mountains to discover another world.

For your work *Cities on the Move - 2727 Kilometers Bottari Truck* you loaded the back of a lorry with bottaris and drove through Korea in 1997, and for the Venice Biennial in 1999 you made a journey from Korea to Venice which was titled *Bottari Truck in Exile* and dedicated to the Kosovo refugees. Which role does the political dimension, or more precisely, political intervention, play in your aesthetics?

In the sense that my interest lies tremendously in the human condition and its reality, I would say it is inevitable to be connected to a political dimension, but basically, I am not so much interested in dealing with demonstrative political issues in any direct way in contemporary art. My work is more related to the dimension of pure humanity and its affection, and contemplation towards mankind, rather than revealing political problems. I always hated the political attitude in human behaviour and this idea made me even stay away from political issues, as I simply don't like people who deal in politics and whom, anyway, I often find dishonest.

You dedicated it to Kosovo refugees.

The Kosovo war was still going on near Venice during the Biennale and I simply couldn't do anything else without mentioning this tragedy and commemorating the victims of that war which never ends in this world, especially the one which was happening right nearby Venice.

The same situation happened to my piece at the 1st Kwangju Biennale which was dedicated to the Kwangju Massacre in the eighties, and again in the case of the piece at Nagoya City Art Museum, when the Sampoong Department store building collapsed in Seoul and killed hundreds of people in my neighbourhood. War was always next to me since I was a little girl, from the time when my family lived near the DMZ. My friends and I used to wander about collecting empty bullets and fragments of mines in the wild fields and we played with them often.

In your work *A Needle Woman* and also in *A Laundry Woman* you present yourself schematically from behind, statue-like and in various milieus and geographical contexts. The global nomad, which generally implies an activism, is rendered immobile, whereas the surrounding alien world continues to move. How do you define this dialectic of motion and immobility? And what role does the Zen-Buddhist concept of the *samandhi* play here - the ideas of contemplation and unity, which are often used in meditation?

Nothing is immobile, and mobility is the fundamental state of existing, of being. Any moment is in a vibration of its own rhythm. It is a relatively fine line, which divides mobility and immobility and this hypothetical standard functions only within a certain perspective. I positioned my body close to the limit of the fine barometer, which distinguishes between immobility and mobility. It is in a way logical that the mobility of my body, which enabled me to place myself in specific streets of the cities of different continents, functions as an example of immobility, while my instant decision of being immobile is made in a brief moment with no reasoning. It is made in the midst of a conflict of energy over the intense mobility happening between two different elements, the one which is my body, and the other which is the outer world.

I always wanted to show the reality of the world more by doing nothing, without making something and showing it as it is, while most performers try to show and create something new by doing or acting.

I've never practiced meditation in my life, but I find every moment for me was a meditation in itself. I reached out to a similar state of Zen–Buddhism through what was completely my own way of meditation on life and art and its practice, without referring to any model or text. I hadn't even read any book for over a decade since I decided not to in the late eighties, but I recently started to read some books again. I had no time to follow others' perceptions and didn't want to be influenced. Now I find extreme similarities between my practice and Zen-Buddhism.

In your video performances you either stand, sit or lie – statue-like – with your back to the audience at the centre of the image – a schematic, faintly delineated presence. You become a template-like form, drawing the gaze of the observer towards the centre of the image and then you confront him with an empty space. Is your intention here to select as a central theme the idea of the "invisible self"; to delineate an area that must first be filled by the vibrations of a feminine *elan vital*?

A critic for the *New York Times* experienced your presence in the videos as mythical and melancholic. He characterises you as a "lost soul in a globalised modernity". Do you find this diagnosis appropriate?

I don't think about my gender while I am performing and my body stays completely in a neutral state during this performance and it only functions as a tool, which witnesses the world. Maybe it is the reason the critic characterises me as a lost soul in a globalised modernity, as I am the only being in the scene who separates my body from the rest of the people on the street and look at the whole world, while the others all relate their gaze to concerns within themselves. I don't doubt it could be seen as a mythical presence, but regarding the critic's perception of my being melancholic, I would say 'yes' only if standing still in the middle of the crowd means to be melancholic. It is a very provocative act and decision.

The installation *A Laundry Woman* will be hanging wash out on a line in Vienna – a common sight in Mediterranean and tropical countries and yet, in Vienna, much less common. Does this concern the demarcation of cultural differences;

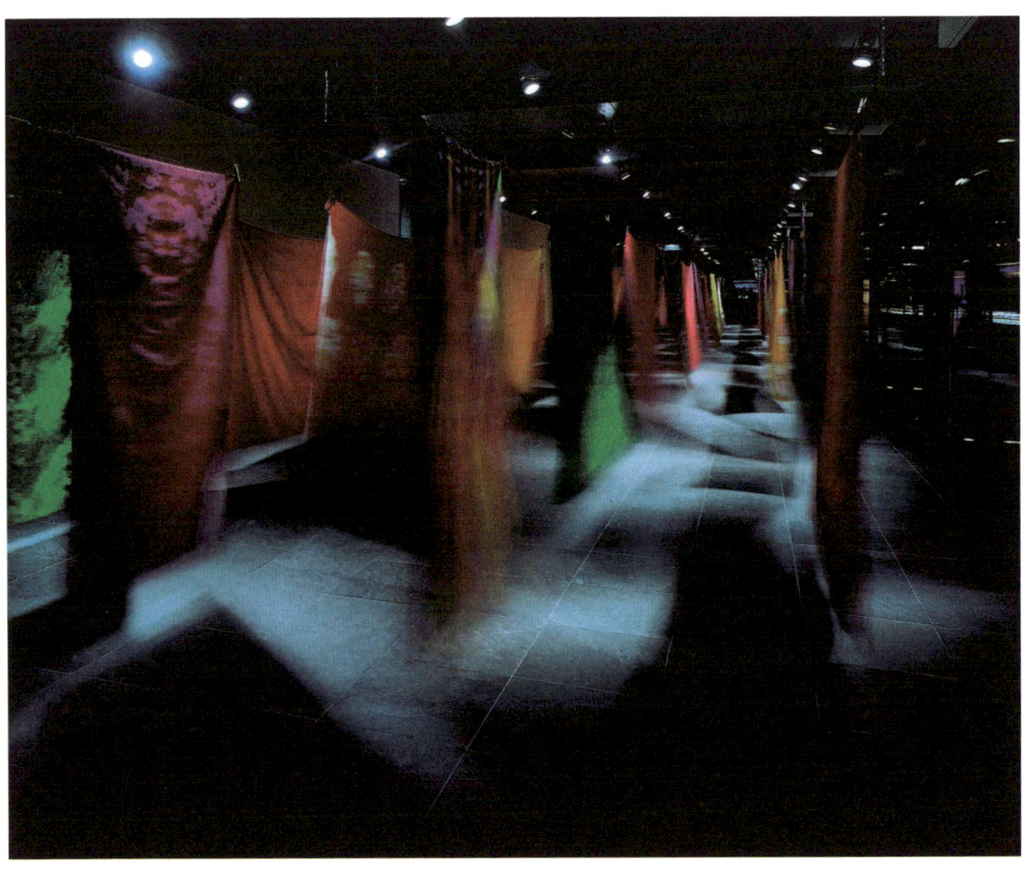

Installation view, Kunsthalle Wien project space 2002: Kimsooja, *A Laundry Woman*

perhaps also the idea of making the public space more intimate by means of the public spectacle of personal pieces of clothing?

Laundry-lines, especially when hung with used bed sheets, can be very much an intimate kind of material, not only because those are personal items but also because the bed sheet itself is about our body and intimacy. I am using this universal way of displaying the laundry (it is disappearing, though) as my own statement, which has been related to the everlasting subject of Life for me. Each piece of laundry hung on the clothes line is a big question for me.

You asked earlier about the reason why I use only Korean bed sheets and whether it is to create a cultural and visual contrast to Western society. The meaning of bed sheets and their fantasy and social contexts is different for Koreans and Westerners. The bed sheets I use are mostly abandoned, used ones, and those are the ones made for newly-wed couples. As you see, these bed sheets have embroideries and patterns with their unique, opposite-colour combinations, which signify Yin and Yang, and they carry the symbols for love, happiness, wealth, long life and many sons, which most Koreans wish for and carry on wishing for, in their lives. Wishing for many sons is a typical wish in Confucian society.

I am using these fabrics, as they are my own reality and my social and aesthetical environment, which has influenced my life so much, but Western bed sheets do not carry such diverse meanings and relationships for me. It is for the same reason that I wrap the bottari with a Korean bed sheet, as it embraces and questions so many different issues and has a private, social, and cultural context to me. The bed sheet, for me, is nothing but a frame of our bodies and lives and it is the most fundamental site of human beings, where we get born, where we love and dream, rest and sleep, suffer and, finally, die.

Could you give us more of an idea about this input of your private life, your biography, in terms of your work or in relation to your work?

I never talk about my private life in my work or in interviews but in fact, my work is all about my private life, its sexual suppression and its liberation, its insight and sympathy, and its contextualisation in contemporary art.

You have been working with decorated, ordinary Korean bed sheets for many years now: the sewn-together and printed fabrics. It is these objects, which in Korea have been allocated to a feminine sphere. Was it important for you, in a male-oriented Confucian society, to place these objects at the center of your art; thereby ascribing to yourself an aura-like presence, which you do not have in an everyday context?

This is true. Sewing, wrapping, hanging laundry, cleaning the house, spreading table cloths, cooking … these are all domestic female activities, which have never been considered as meaningful, important activities, or as high art. I find these activities to be most amazing, fundamental art activities, in terms of their aesthetic, cultural, social, psychological dimension which most people are not paying attention to and which art historians are not mentioning much at all. But please don't misunderstand me by assuming that I am doing this as a feminist artist, as my interest lies in a totality of perception and its realisation.

Women's domestic activities are fully composed of activities of two-dimensional painting, three-dimensional sculpture, installation and performances and we can analyse each activity in terms of a contemporary art context. I am trying to create and expand my own concept of women's and everyday life activities in a contemporary art context, by focusing on mundane, domestic, female activities, as well as on everyday activities. I encountered the methodology of sewing while I was searching for a methodology, which would enable me to express my structural vision of the world in the early eighties (which involved the structures of surfaces and the world and the structure of life), but by practicing this methodology together with this particular view, I was able to extend that and come back again to this vision of the whole world, which is much more broadly based on the mundane activities of human beings. That is how my sewing of clothes transformed itself into the *A Needle Woman* video performance.

The pojagi are commonly made from already used, worn-out pieces of material, which are sewn together. So biographies, personal life histories are written into them. A procedure is thus realised in everyday usage which became dominant in Western art during the nineties, namely, in the form of remix, recycling and sampling. Naturally, although it is not possible to compare the conditions of production and different milieus, it is possible to compare the way of processing the material. Did this similarity play a role in the design of your own types?

First of all, I have to make a clear definition between my wrapping cloth, which was originally a bed sheet, and which was not supposed to be made to wrap things up in, even though people often use it when they move as it is the biggest cloth we can find in any household, yet it is originally made for covering our body to keep warm. The pojagi, which is sewn together mainly from left-over cloths in the household, is called the Korean wrapping cloth and it is made as a means of wrapping and when it is used for cover-ing, it is usually used for covering food. My bed sheet functions as a pojagi, in the broad meaning of a wrapping cloth.

What I sewed together in my earlier career was used traditional Korean clothes from my grandmother, and from my mother, and since the nineties I have also collected used modern clothes from friends and from unknown people. So the most important issue for me was that the people who once used to wear these clothes remained present through this physicality of the cloth, not just the beauty of the materials. The first sewn piece I made in 1983 was from the clothes my grandmother left behind after she passed away and I was so much attached to the texture of the cloth and of the silk woven by herself, which seems to be a kind of skin or a body of hers, keeping in all the memories and the love of her. I expanded my materials later on with unknown people's clothes, which always retained the human smell, so my sewing practice was in a way an invisible networking of human beings and the process of mourning and my aesthetic concerns went always parallel to one another.

When I ask myself, what in the world did I sew and wrap over 20 years, I confess now it was the scars, pain, longing, love, passion, tears, the parts of my psychology and body, as well as my loneliness, which needed to be attached. My sympathy towards others is nothing but a self-love.

In Africa a non-verbal form of communication is unfolded in the pattern, colours and symbols on textiles – a non-idiomatic language competence, so-to-speak.

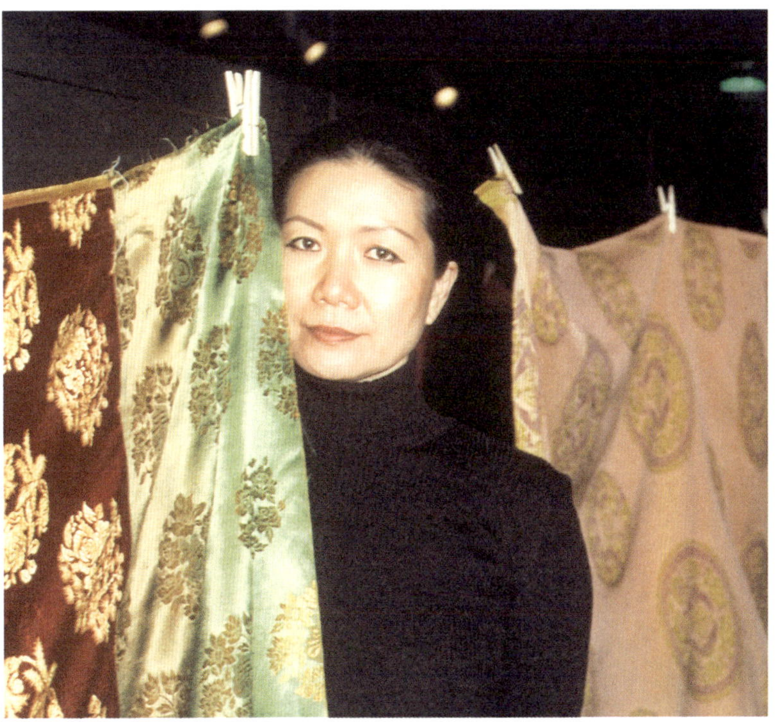

Are such elements of language and segments of communication woven into your pastiches, which include, as they do, completely new combinations of traditional patterns and embroidery?

Absolutely. As I mentioned earlier, these bed sheets have symbolic patterns and rich embroideries – since they are specially made for the newly-wed couples, there are always meaningful signs and wishes for our lives, such as birds (especially a peacock or a Chinese phoenix) and butterflies together with flowers, which signify love, turtles for long life, purses for wealth, deers for many children and family happiness, and there are also written words such as Happiness, Pleasure, Long Life. In fact, the fabrics are full of these wishes we carry with us through out our lives. But the fabrics I find are mostly abandoned ones, which means that the couple have thrown them away or they are not together anymore.

With all these symbols, I always find empty bodies, which used to stay there for a while in their own history and memories.

The body, or more specifically, the disappearance of the body, is among the central themes of contemporary art. In a time of digital production, the physical is often reduced to a trace element of its material presence; think of the online-chats, in which digital shadows communicate with each other. Could your work over the last ten years be understood as an attempt to make conscious and realise the fleeting nature of the physical and visceral in an age where the body is itself disappearing?

> My disappearance and immaterialisation has nothing to do with global digital issues, it is only a part of my own necessity for being light. I've been dealing with so much weight and so many physical bodies, which was a tremendous heaviness on my life. I guess all of the clothes I've been dealing with weighed at least many dozens of tons, and they are basically from millions of anonymous people. I wish I could have payed some amount of my Karma to liberate myself.
>
> I really wish to disappear at some point by my own decision, and I also been planning *A Disappearing Woman* piece since last year, although we all have to disappear someday.

As part of your communication with the public, the visitors may open the bottaris and examine the contents. Is this a conscious attempt to establish the difference to Western reception, where such interventions are interpreted as being damaging to the object or sacrilegious and, as such, are prohibited?

> I didn't particularly allow people to touch the bottaris or any other fabric installations, but people just do it as they are so curious about these colourful Korean tactile materials and about the content, what's inside the bottaris, even though they were installed in the museums. Since it is happening all the time even if there's a guard, I decided to accept the fact and the changes by the public.
>
> In 1995 for the first Kwangju Biennale, which was dedicated to the victims of the Kwangju Massacre, I installed two and a half tons of used clothes on outdoor timber and almost one ton of it disappeared – the show went for two months and during this period people opened the bottaris and took out used clothings – so at the end, with the change of the season from summer into fall, with rain and people's footsteps on the clothes – it looked almost like a ruin. And I thought that was the point, that was why the piece was done.
>
> I find that the perception on used items, in contrast to what you mentioned, is different between Koreans and Westerners, especially as regards used clothes. You say Western people might consider audiences' interventions as something prohibited, but I find that Westerners are more familiar with used items. For example, they buy and wear used clothes worn by unknown people without hesitation (I guess that's why there are so many secondhand markets in Western countries), but Koreans believe that the spirit of the person who used to wear the clothes still remains in it, so they are hesitant about wearing unknown person's clothes. We have a tradition to burn his or her clothes when a person dies and we believe the person's body and soul are sent to heaven.

When did you initially envision yourself to be an artist? When did you first think you wanted to be an artist? Or to study art?

When I was 11 years old, my homeroom teacher at elementary school asked us to write two different occupations we wanted to be in the future. I wrote painter and philosopher. My passion for art was so strong when I was in high school and I was almost trying to quit the school to be just an artist. At the same time, I had a strong conflict between the desire of being an artist and being a religious person, for example, a Catholic sister, or someone who devotes her life to people in need. The time I felt I was already an artist was when I was 13 years old in intermediate school, when I decided not to participate in any art competitions which gave out prizes, which I could win easily and which was a common process for those students who wanted to be artists or go to college in Korean society.

You first began as a painter. You now work exclusively with installations and moving pictures. Does this have anything to do with taking the step from the two-dimensional to the three-dimensional, under the aspect of motion as opposed to immobility? Or was painting simply too far away from the realities of life? Now you are also adding an acoustic dimension to your work.

I have been interested in sound pieces since 1992 and acoustic elements in my videos and installations have been prevalent since 1994, and I used to use popular music and monks' chanting. I've been also making single sound pieces which I want to develop more.

Always changing my vision on space and time has enabled me to open up new horizons but I have only followed the logic of sensibility and my inspiration that lead me to make artistic decisions. The way I developed my idea from the two-dimensional stage into the three-dimensional and then on to video, which has allowed me to deal with time and space, it all originated from my concept of sewing, of wrapping and unwrapping. I think that *Nature of Sewing and Wrapping* already has elements of opening up new dimensions to time, so to speak, it was already there.

If someone were to ask you on commission to do a new work, and give you one million dollars, what would you do?

I would donate the money to support children in famine and pain in this world.

So you would give the money to those children: you wouldn't use it for your work?

That is my work.

Were you – or are you – interested in Western or European philosophy? And are there any philosophers you are especially interested in?

Until around the late eighties, I was interested in structuralism as I was focused on the fundamental structure of the world, so I was interested in Wittgenstein's research on cultural and geographical examples and structures, Freud and Jung, and psychological structure, and I was also interested in Heidegger, related to existential subjects … and now I find how similar their thoughts were in relationship to Zen Buddhism, which I had no concrete idea of around that time. So my interests in Western thought actually stopped at that period as I decided not to read any books anymore and acquire no new information either. From the late eighties onwards, I hadn't read any books for over decade as I didn't want to be influenced by outside information. And, I had also no time to follow other people's thoughts. I recently started reading books again.

So, as you told me, when you were young, you were asked what you wanted to be and you said, a painter or a philosopher – if one were to ask you today what you wanted to be, what would you answer?

A lover, or a monk.

Kimsooja in conversation with Gerald Matt in 2002 on the occasion of the exhibition *Kimsooja* at Kunsthalle Wien project space.
Kimsooja was born in Taegu, Korea in 1957. She lives and works in New York.

Installation view, Kunsthalle Wien project space 2002: Kimsooja, *A Laundry Woman*
→

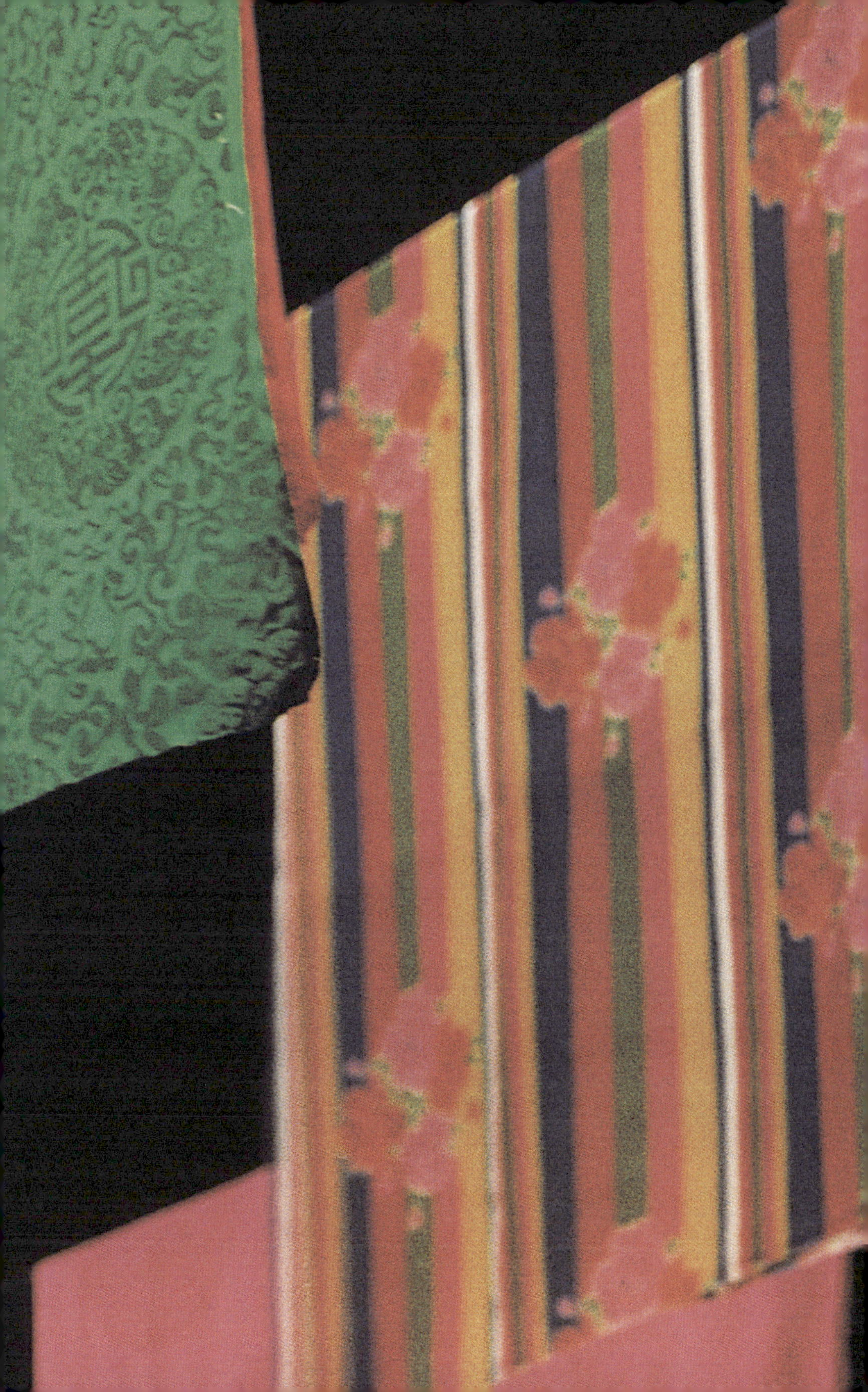

Elke Krystufek

As an artist, one can move over, under and between all existing structures.

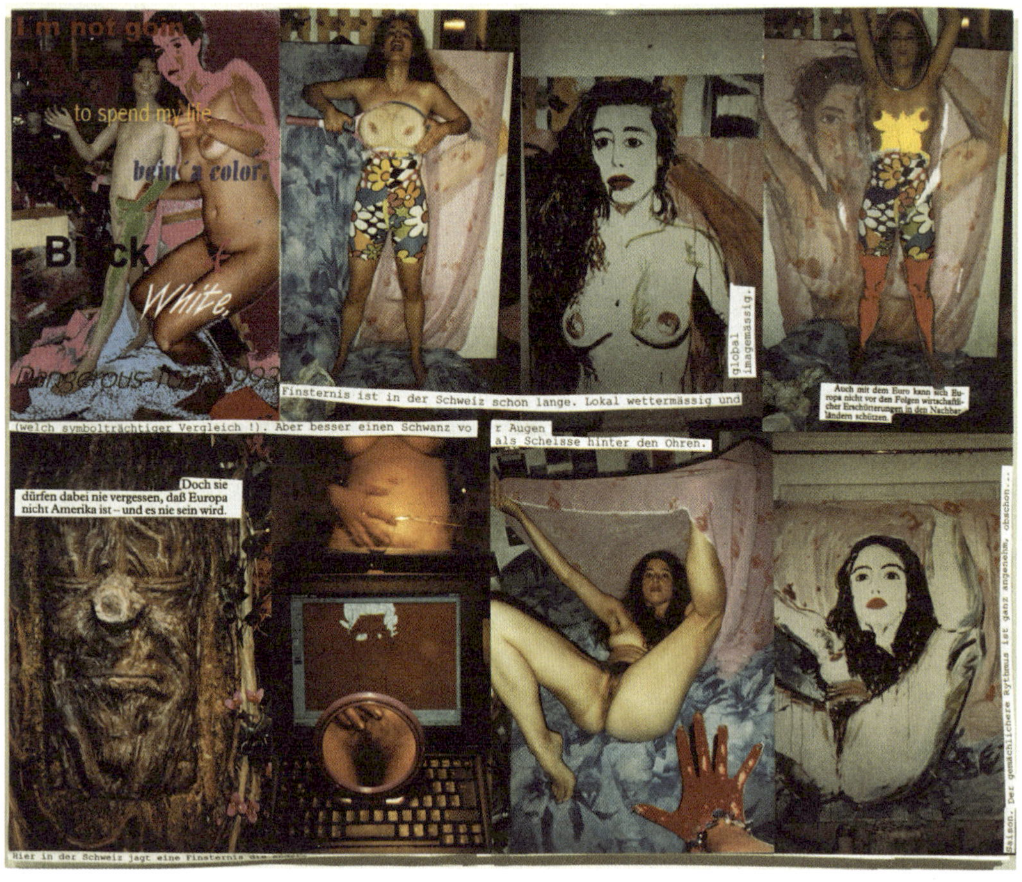

Elke Krystufek,
Migros Collagen, 1999

In your project *we say yes to each other* at the Main Square of Linz in May 2002, you were staging a celebration of a wedding ceremony that was prominently positioned in front of an appeal that read, "you are cordially invited to be our bride/our groom." In your speech on that occasion you were recounting a variant of the story of the "Missing Piece". It seems that it had gone in search of another piece, so that they could fit themselves together and form a circle that could roll perfectly. When the Missing Piece believed it had finally come across the right piece, it was told by the new piece that it was, itself, not in need of the Missing Piece at all and recommended to the disappointed searching piece to try rolling on its own. The story reached its Happy End when the small Missing Piece in fact learned to roll all by itself and both pieces together formed "a perfect example of the 'internal figure eight', or the matrix of the self-perpetuating circulation of the inner drive."

I place this brief summary of that speech at the beginning of our conversation, because this conversation will proceed somewhat differently from the usual interview. We will not in actual fact be encountering one another in person. I will formulate some questions based on my segmental knowledge of your artistic work and reflections upon it (including some by others than myself) and send you these and you may then write something in reply, if you so wish. I will not, therefore, be able to probe more deeply into your answers and you won't be able to plant questions in my mind. Perhaps, though, it could all set something in motion. Would you care to comment on this procedure, so far?

Going by your questions I gather that you also seem to have a special connection with Linz. The performance *we say yes to each other* was a joint project by the students of the Linz Experimental Class, where I was invited to be a visiting professor for a year, and the Frohsinn Institute of Expanded Art in Linz. I had understood my visiting professorship to consist of a specially-conceived performance for this place, Linz, that entailed, among other things, that I would appear for each two-day lecture dressed up in another costume. In this way I was trying to interpret certain characters which I had chosen for myself. These were (1) The Arts and Crafts Teacher, (2) The Art Student from Hell, (3) The Fair-Haired Man, a rather conservative type, (4) The Drag Queen, and (5) The Old Lady. Since these performances occurred in a city where originally nobody really knew me as a person, I was successful in identifying completely with my characters and also to lead an appropriately different life for the duration of my lecturing tenure. My students, whether male or female, did not, for the most part, perceive these character studies of mine as a way of questioning the institutional situation, but saw them as characteristic of the person who was unknown to them. It is possible that my fitness for the role of the registrar/priestess at the wedding performance may have resulted from this actorly conduct. In my view the performance contained some very subtle elements regarding the preservation or reduction of distances within the organisation of the university.

So the people getting married to each other there were largely those who were in a certain way living and working together anyhow, without – to my knowledge – entering into any further combinations than the existing ones as a result of these weddings. In this connection, I found it interesting, for example, that Andrea van der Straeten was the only member of the teaching body who decided to show her solidarity with her students and their activity through her co-marriage, whereas I had, from the beginning, intended for myself the role of a person keeping rather aloof from these worldly things, which really stands in marked contrast to the usual, relatively sexualised perception of my work. For me, then, what emerged from the experience of this performance was the conclusion that the perception of my work, including myself as a person, is bound up, above all else, with my special profession as a freelancing visual artist, whereas in a new profession – in this case, the only other job I have ever had – I was quite capable of generating a completely new external perception of myself. Perhaps I can link up here in a kind of arc to the text you cited at the outset. It was taken from the book *Enjoy Your Symptom!*, subtitled – *Jacques Lacan in Hollywood and out*, Second Edition, by Slavoj Žižek – and the story I recounted, freely translated and slightly modified by myself, is actually one intended to convey the content of Lacan's ideas in a shape that could be grasped by children. The reference back to the story would be, therefore, that rolling and searching is not limited to the struggles surrounding partnership but that they equally apply to the struggle for an appropriate profession or an adequate image of one's profession, which again applies to both the profession of the artist and the questioning of the authority of the teaching professional. I see parallels to my own work in the questioning of authority in this performance. For if the students and instructors were in fact actually married to each other, then all existing hierarchies would be dissolved. Many of my performances to date have circled around such questions as: Who are the viewers and what is their role or function in the performance? Who really are the protagonists and who actually are the spectators? Moreover, what I found interesting was that this action in Linz engendered no consequences like the creation of communes or suchlike, and that therefore it was based on a fundamentally anti-utopian and also a somewhat disillusioned attitude and that thereby it also described something that can be attested to the current art scene, namely, that a good many signals are given out but that they result in ever fewer responses. I would like to reinforce this point by citing here the following quotation from a frieze at the Documenta11: "What do all the libraries, archives, discussions and exhibitions in the world amount to when all this clamour denies the silence with which to reflect them, or the time with which to apply them?"[1] From exactly such a lack of time I move on now to my reply to the next question.

"Attention: This event is not suitable for juveniles. In almost all of the contributions, obscene and partially pornographic scenes will occur. People with good taste, weak nerves and a sensitive mind-set should avoid coming here at this time ." So said, in red on black, the announcement to your event entitled *Video Voyeurs* and staged at the State Gallery of the Upper Austrian State Museum in October of 1999, where you presented your video *Hollywood Cinema*. Even if this "warning" note was tickling the mickey of the bourgeois taste for art, from an advertising point of view, however, it did, ultimately, comply with the slogan that "sex sells". Two years earlier you had been saying, in the role of Marilyn Monroe, "I am simply as sexual as I am, and I don't feel like going out in public to put up with all that social boredom of the art world. My life is more intense than that. ... I'm only fighting for my rights, my physical rights, and I don't care what most people might think or not think of what I do, it is my life and I want to be honest with myself during each minute of it. Why should I send you my biography? You can imagine everything you want for yourselves, because my life was not really that way, anyhow." (Elke Krystufek: *Marilyn Speaking*, 1997.) So, do you reach a point where the interpretations, the categorizations of your work and even of your own person through the art public, exceed the measure that you have allowed for them, and if so, how do you react to this?

After many years of experience in the art world (or should I say the art war) I can state that in this market the "sex sells" tag applies to almost nothing at all. I have surely completely "botched up" many chances for myself of exhibiting or selling something through the element of "sex" in my work. So that's as far as that goes, regarding this misunderstanding. As to your question, there is the example of a problem over a film about me shown recently on ORF [Austrian Television]. Under the strange and more than somewhat inexplicable title of *2001 and 1 Nights – The Embarrassing Fate of the Voyeur*, this was intended to be a portrait of Elke Krystufek. An unknown, still-youngish director had promised me an unrestricted say in the project, but when this cooperation failed the film was subsequently re-titled as *NOT A Portrait of Elke Krystufek*. Documentary material of my performances and openings of exhibitions was snapped up by a money-grubbing Austrian cinematic company, which then proceeded to excise all the elements that might be considered offensive or objectionable. All the blood, violence or explicit sexual imagery as well as all textual elements of my work which might have helped to explain something to the public, and the entire original music from my performances was cut. Finally, the sanitised, safe and squeaky clean version was sold to the ORF so that it could present to its viewing public a portrait of Elke Krystufek that had absolutely nothing at all to do with my reality. The legal mills that were kicked into action as a consequence are still busy grinding …

"Krystufek creates a totally exchangeable body of artworks." Under this title, at the end of November, 2001, an e-mail message identifying you as its sender arrived at the office of the [Linz] City Workshop (Stattwerkstatt), where you had been invited to participate in the event entitled *Under Construction II*. "You could mistake her work for any other easily. There's nothing significant about it. It could be anyone's work. It is also easy to imitate. It looks like it was bought in a supermarket. An expensive super market. Any political remarks in the work are drowned with dripping humour. Therefore it is completely free of any values, provocative exclamations or revolutionary potential. It is everyday work as long as there is no war. Expensive, simple everyday labour. Why do we pay so much for it? Because it is the missing part in our lives. Krystufek is at all times young. Never fashionable but just not ageing – just like old furniture. It's like we have always had her. Sticky like chewing gum."

It does not become clear from the contribution, who may have authored it. Producing bewilderment has surely been a part of the strategies of your artistic work, yet up to this point you had always linked it up to your own identity. Confusion was created, for example, through an unfamiliar self-presentation, or by offering the public a glimpse inside a staged privacy (which most people took to be your authentic private sphere), but not through the employment and/or

Elke Krystufek,
Migros Collagen, 1999

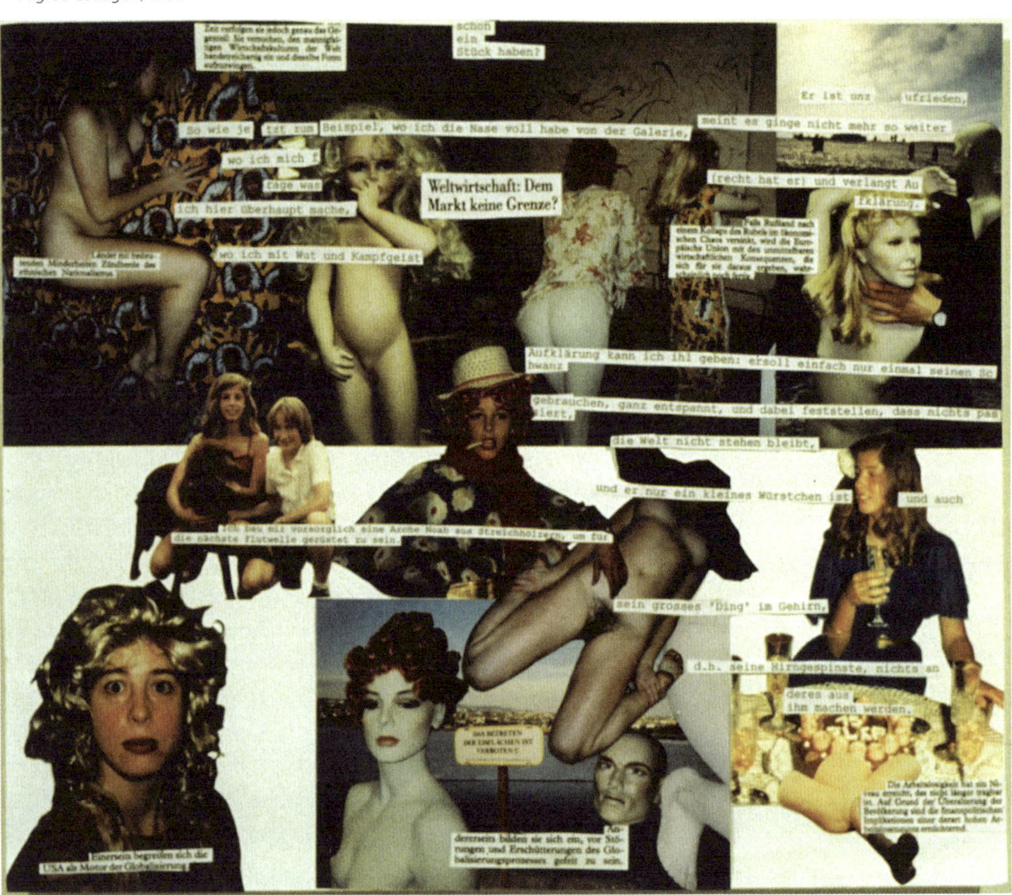

presentation of a "third person", who would speak about you. Will reflections on your work possibly be more of an integral part of your work in the future?

Actually, the reflection on my work had always been a part of my activity already in the past. There was, for example, a project at the Villa Arson in Nice in 1993, where I scripted, together with the American artist David Kelleran, a fictional critique of the exhibition being put on at the time, under the title of *Le principe de réalité*. This was actually a negative appreciation of the 1992 documenta, written by the Italian art critic Giancarlo Politi. David Kelleran and I simply exchanged the names of the curators and artists of the DOCUMENTA IX for those of the exhibition at the Villa Arson and we copied the whole thing in a Felix-Gonzales-Torres-like stack as a poster that we made available to the public at the exhibition, as something to take home with them. Unfortunately, we committed a serious organisational mistake. We asked one of the staff members of the administration of the then director, Christian Bernard, to have the whole thing, for the better understanding of the general public, translated also into French. The administrator had nothing better to do than to report to Christian Bernard on the project, whereupon he, along with his then girl friend and co-curator Francine Stöcklin and the co-curator and artist Axel Huber, convened a conference, at which it was concluded to grant David Kelleran and myself another hour at the Villa Arson, to give us time to pack up our things and to never darken their doorstep again. Further discussions on the text were naturally deemed undesirable. After the announcement of the result of the conference to David Kelleran and myself, as we were on our way to go packing, the artist most heavily criticized, Charles Ledray, pounced on David Kelleran and physically beat him up. That should suffice as an anecdote on the theme of reflection as part of my future work.

Causing bewilderment as a part of the artistic principle contains the risk of misinterpretation, of having connections overlooked that may possibly be important to an understanding of what has been intended. While reading through two interviews with you (that were presumably conducted in person, one with Silvia Eiblmayr, the other with Anja Hasenlechner), it struck me that evidently during your performance of *Satisfaction*, as part of the *Jetztzeit* exhibition at the Kunsthalle Wien (1994), several important references were not being perceived by the members of the public as the concentration was directed at the "scandalously" provocative act of masturbating before an audience. I remind you of your cooperation with Kim Fowley and the production of art as gratification.

Was there a dichotomy between your expectations and the reactions of the public or of the art critics that caused you to re-think or change the concept of your public performances?

The dichotomy was indeed so great that I largely did away with performance work for the following three years, apart from a "performance" of yoga exercises in 1995 on the occasion of a discussion between Catherine David and Austrian artists on the topic of documenta X, where I refrained from giving a verbal reply to a question by Robert Fleck.

At the exhibition *Gefesselt/Entfesselt. Austrian Art of the 20th Century*, at the Galeria Zachęta in Warsaw (2001), you participated with a large multimedia installation. Like all the other invited artists you, too, were requested to name a "reference character" from the older Austrian cultural scene of the 20th century who would then be represented with a work or a document at the exhibition. Solely among the participants you named a younger artist, Katrina Daschner, who then staged a performance at the opening ceremony. You said regarding this choice that you would sooner orient yourself along younger artists than older ones. Still, I would be interested to know how you see your work - internationally - in relationship to the Pop art or also other Pop cultural currents of the past. Pop music is often featured in the sound tracks to your video works. Where do you see the greatest differences between yourself and the older Pop-artists? More specifically, perhaps, also with regard to the artistic strategies of an Andy Warhol?

I am not fascinated by commodity culture. Actually, I wonder, given the poor materials I use and my low budget-principles, why I haven't yet been escorted off into the vicinity of Arte Povera. Or Art Brut, for that matter, on account of the permanent self-reproduction and the contents that refuse to conform to existing contexts. As for Warhol, he was industrious, fast, publicity-greedy, unhappy, lonesome, original and so forth, and willing to sacrifice himself to art and its attendant wheels within wheels.

"Art is a loaded gun that shoots off when you pull the trigger", I was reading, as a quote by Elke Krystufek. On the cover of a catalogue of the Secession you can be seen brandishing a gun. Does this have something to do with the power of art, of the artist as a socially effective potential force, or is it about the danger that art unfolds as a medium if it becomes instrumentalised in a certain way? How do you see the connections between art, power and politics today?

That gun reference was about how one never exactly knows beforehand how things will look once the trigger has been pulled. One may perhaps assume that it will be a mess and that one might have a guilty conscience afterwards, but perhaps one might also finally have silenced a troublesome opponent, yet one can also never be sure, whether the adversary may not survive after all.

Using a loaded weapon, one could of course show up some very different connections between art, power and politics. I would of course quite like, in turn, to put this question to you – although I know that you have answered it many times already – since you are so much more strongly involved in these issues than I am. I'm sure that there would be many interesting details that cannot be found in press interviews or catalogues. One would also have to ask: Which art? For there is art that, for the most divergent reasons, (for example, beautiful irrelevance) is independent of power and politics, and there is the kind that is bound up with the system. I am not unhappy in this regard with my role, which I mentioned to you earlier, of priestess, since the power conflicts really only begin to touch upon the public at much higher levels of the clergy.

With regard to the topic of politics I may quote myself as follows: "I am more above party politics than the acting head of state and I have already existed longer as an artist than did the Third Reich (known to its adherents as the Empire of a Thousand Years)." As an artist, one can move over, under and between all existing structures. That is what is so fascinating about this type of social position. I also believe in slow and nonviolent social changes through art. Like yoga, art can create mental places that people have a chance to relocate themselves to.

In my opinion there are different realities, like in the film *Matrix*, and one can manoeuvre oneself with the help of mental powers into nonviolent realities or worlds, and art is, despite all the bad things that adhere to it, largely a nonviolent place. Even when art becomes instrumentalised (Leni Riefenstahl?) it is not the ruling (?) art (her films can be viewed differently today under a changed political situation), but the ruling (no question mark!) politics, including the politicians, that exercise or abuse power.

In answer to that, let me pop in a question here that you have not yet put to me and that I would like to insert at this point: When am I going to retire? And my answer to that is: This question occupies me daily. I have not yet decided. I could imagine myself, however, being the recipient of a supplementary income.

You have been repeatedly placed in a context with the Viennese Actionists. It has been a classification, however, that you have just as often rejected or at least corrected. Why is that?

I'll give you one example: Hermann Nitsch was still able to say to me in the year 2000, with regard to Valie Export: "That Valie, you know, that girl Valie, she copied everything from us. But you are a dear. Come on, let's have a drink. Cheers." This attitude of one of the Actionists, for example, was a reason for me to disassociate myself from Actionism. Actionism was a rather anti-women and self-hating art form and I would neither like to see myself as perpetrator nor as victim within such a movement nor as a successor to such games of perpetration and victimisation. And besides, as in the Warsaw case, I'd rather approach younger artistic positions, such as the current project, *The Linz Philharmonic*, of the artist Hannes Langeder, under whose direction a group of mostly non-professional musicians and singers are rendering, above all, performances of classical pieces from Austrian musical history. What inspires me about this project is, for example, the relationship that artists and non-artists have with one another, where a nonhierarchical society is being attempted in the shape of an orchestra, a loosely-knit grouping of artists (in contrast also, for example, to the, to my knowledge, comparatively rigid and, at least up to recently, hostile-to-women boygroup gelitin). The orchestra as an artistic project can function also as a social utopia, where somebody may, of course, have to take up a leading function, but only to ensure a harmonious cooperation. This harmony, between the playing instrumentalists themselves and between the orchestra and the public at the moment when the performance emerges from the chaos of the dissonant sounds of this orchestra of dilettantes, is something that I most deeply miss about Actionism.

In another self-categorisation, I place myself gladly alongside the American artist living in Amsterdam, Sands Murray-Wassink, who positions his work in a most complex way within the feminist and anti-racist discourses. The precision of his research as well as the honesty and the enthusiasm with which he takes possession of history and integrates himself with his painterly, graphic, performative and textual works within this history – as may be documented, for instance, in his exhibition- and catalogue-project *Double Trouble: Carolee Schneemann and Sands Murray-Wassink* – which also had an impact on more closely aligning both our works – are a great inspiration to me.

Elke Krystufek in conversation with Gerald Matt in 2002. The artist took part in the exhibitions *Lebt and arbeitet in Wien* (2000) and *Sex in the City* (2003) at Kunsthalle Wien.
Elke Krystufek was born in Vienna, Austria in 1970. She lives and works in Vienna.

German to English translation by Tom Appleton.

1   Dan Fox: *Documenta11*, in: frieze #69, 2002.

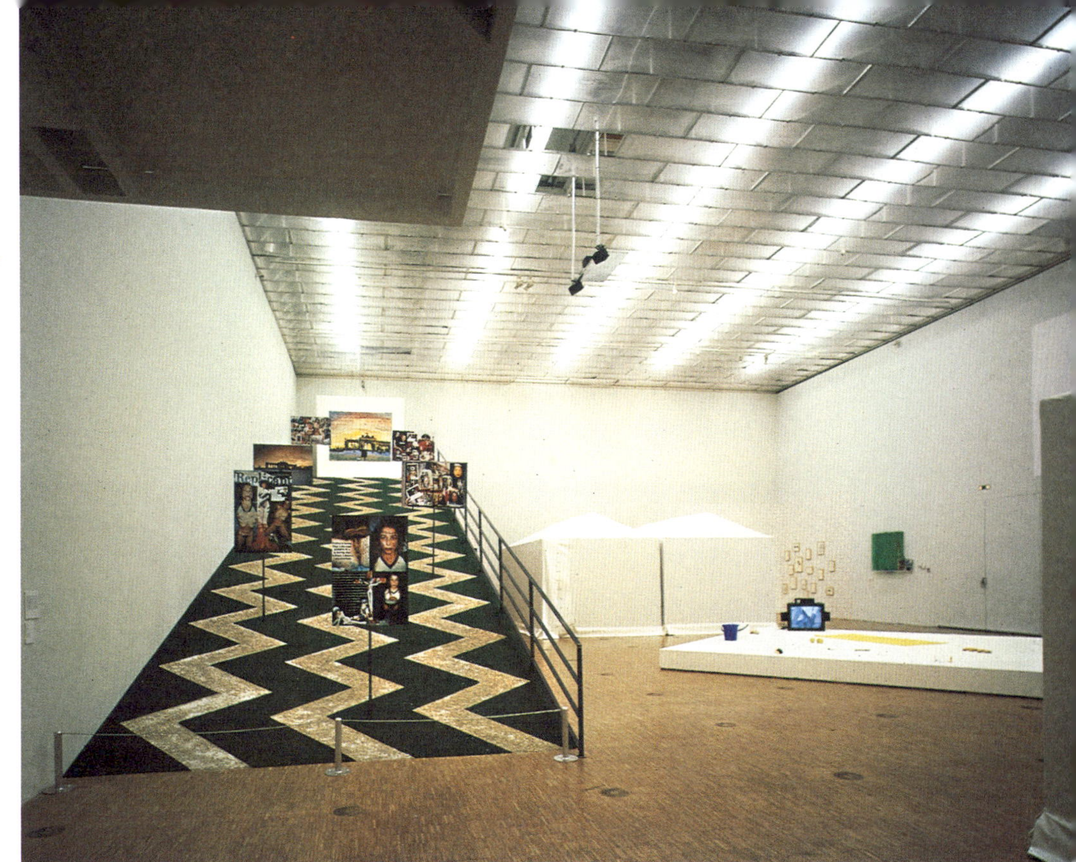

Installation view, Kunsthalle
Wien 2000: Elke Krystufek,
Lebt und Arbeitet in Wien

Surasi Kusolwong

We need to share our experiences together, appreciating a moment in life and potentially forgetting about art for a while.

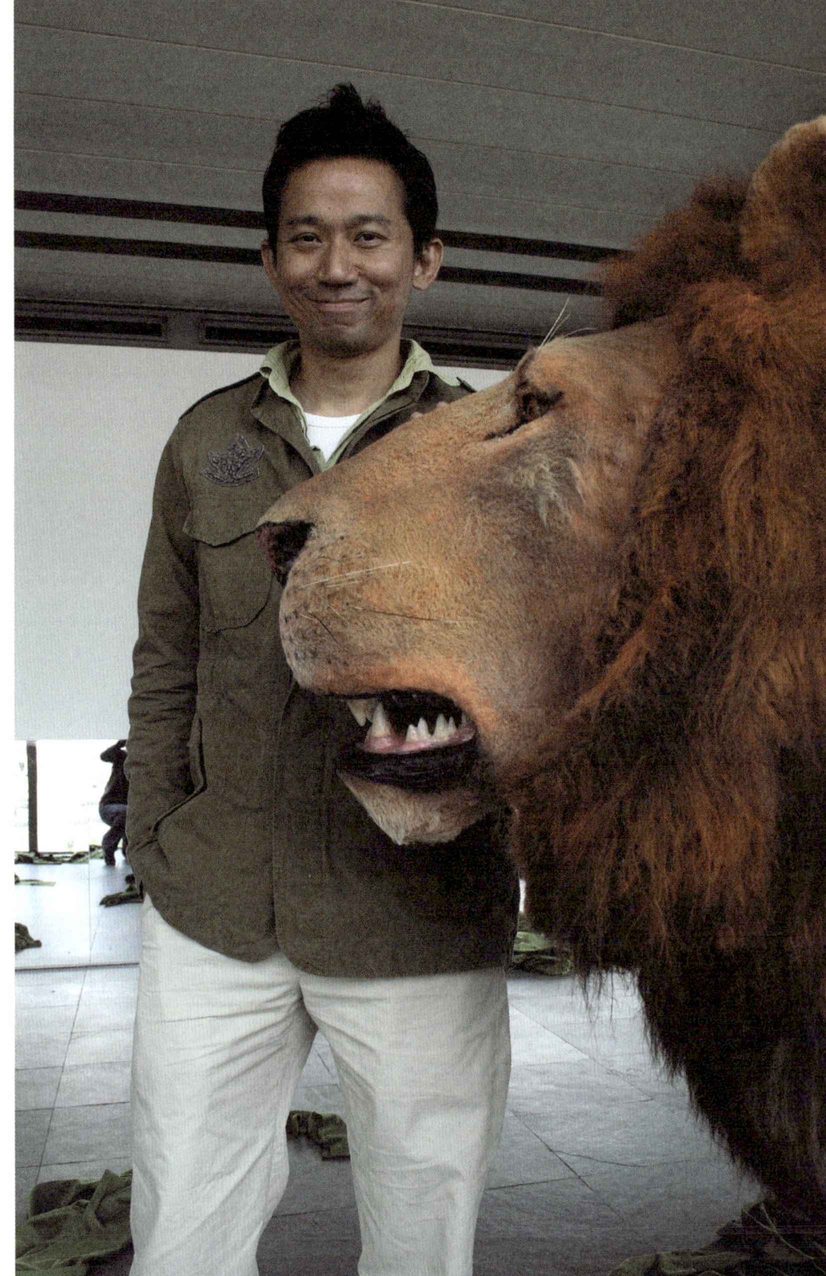

Installation view,
Kunsthalle Wien 2005:
Surasi Kusolwong,
If A Lion Could Talk

In your project *If A Lion Could Talk* for the Kunsthalle Vienna's project space, you are making a lion which is to be placed right in the middle of the glass pavilion by architect Adolf Krischanitz. Visitors can record statements about politics, sex, education, art, philosophy, etc. and they will later be made into the lion's words. Personal views become public words, the donor remains anonymous and invisible. Your work often investigates nuances of linguistic expression and language-related shifts of meaning. Can you tell us some more about the intentions behind this exhibition for the Vienna project space?

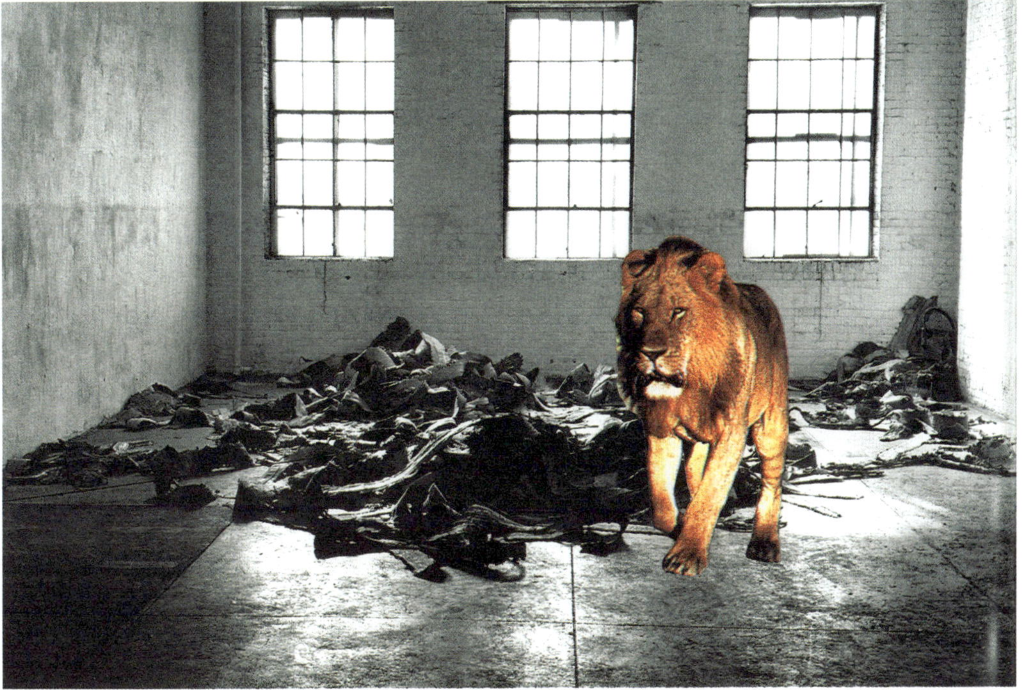

Surasi Kusolwong,
If A Lion Could Talk

My interest in Wittgenstein first started some time ago when I was in Germany. It's quite interesting for me to know how Wittgenstein used his philosophy to explain meaning and to understand language. From my perspective, I may use and relate to his philosophy in a different sense than Europeans, different even from Wittgenstein himself. I want to add more to the idea of 'Language Games' so they shift and react with our ways of life, social behaviour and political issues including urbanism and nature in this century. Private meanings can reflect important statements when made public. I use the lion to express my idea and to relate to everybody's sense. The lion can give unique access to my project for the Kunsthalle project space. It is very open to different readings of oral statements from different cultures and understandings; of how we can express ourselves and understand other people outside language.

As we know, as an animal, the lion is a sign of power. We think we know about it and feel familiar with it when it appears in stories, folktales, mythology or as architectural decoration. But very few people think of its real life and a very, very few have real experience of it in its original habitat in the African landscape. Mostly we have known it from TV productions or from a zoo. A lion is a lion. It has its own life and its own place.

But for this project, the lion is not just a lion. It can be a symbol for an outsider, the public portrait of visitors or a personal portrait of the artist, a sign standing for contradiction/confrontation or even conflict in our modern times and society or it can provoke humans to rethink our processes of thought by doing something like trying to cage and tame nature—and maybe society as well.

Somehow the lion, standing in the midst of glass architecture, does not fit in with the urban cityscape and context at all. It interested me a lot to do this piece, to see how people and passers-by react when they glimpse the lion inside the modern, transparent building in the centre of metropolitan Vienna. The location of the Kunsthalle Wien is a traffic intersection that seems so complicated that the Viennese call it 'traffic hole'.

The traffic is so busy that even if you can see that it's very close, it is in fact difficult to get to. I like this kind of situation. It makes you feel you're losing your orientation, like you are in an invisible trap. It's a specific, dominant space. I think it's really a perfect geographical location for putting a lion and seeing it just stand there.

Inside the space, I make an environment by scattering green velvet all over the floor.

I like to use art history as my own personal language and expression. In this instance, scattering green velvet is as the form using the anti-form of Richard Serra or Robert Morris. Or it could be considered another kind of Viennese action – like Hermann Nitsch… But my action has no blood…

How do you work, how do you approach a new project? How do you work, how do you approach a new project? Can you give an example to describe the work process (also that of the Vienna project)?

I'm interested in the different meanings of culture and otherness. Every place and all cities have their own sound, smell, attitude, history and energy. It depends on how deep you want to dig into the cultural/social background. But I use my own digging tools which, of course, relate to the kind of creative soils which let the same air we breathe flow freely into the soil. So most of my new projects are approached with this attitude, these ways of thinking.

At first, I wanted to show my *Emotional Machine (VW)*, the upside-down VW Beetle, for the Vienna project because it has a double-sided meaning. People in every country love this car. It's been very popular—from the 60s until today. 'VW' translates into English as 'People's Car'. But, on the other hand, that is quite a contradiction in itself. The car was invented on the personal orders of Adolf Hitler for people to use as a uniform. It's another kind of vehicle for the spirit of dictatorship. Whatever the history, VW is part of my family background in a good sense, a beautiful memory and an unbelievably wonderful feeling. The Kunsthalle could have functioned as an upside-down car showroom. Unfortunately, this piece was not able to be shown because the structural limitations of the building do not allow the car to be hung. So I brought forward another idea and decided to make the 'Talking Lion' instead.

You are also planning to have the lion repeat diverse texts such as *Spoken into the Void* by Adolf Loos or excerpts from the *Tractatus logico-philosophicus* by Ludwig Wittgenstein. Is this also to be understood as a homage to Vienna, as site specific, as a project, so to say, in an ideal sense?

Yes, I like and respect them for what they did. But not only those two but many others from your country too. But in any case I also would like to pay homage to everyone, to people's voices… the human voice.

Could the lion as a medium help people to express their own opinion/attitude freely? Perhaps hiding your own personality and making your statement through the lion's mouth instead can give you more freedom and courage to say something you never thought before or never let other people or the public in general know before.

And as a listener: perhaps you can listen and understand other people better and with less prejudice if you don't see them? The glass pavilion of the Kunsthalle, the modern container, shows a very clear view of the inside from outside and vice versa. But the question is: can the clear view of a modernist, architectural, glass box reflect a clearer view of a person's inward-looking gaze, exploring increased understanding of both oneself and other people in the society where we live, sharing the air we breathe? The piece is a kind of self/public/personal reflection, visibility and invisibility, sense and non-sense. It is a social voice to express yourself as well as being a listener.

If A Lion Could Talk is as if everyone could talk. Some might talk about political issues, some might tell a dream or dirty joke or bark like a dog. It's a talking sculpture. Who knows? Maybe my lion can talk in German, English, Italian, Chinese, French, Japanese, Spanish, Thai or whatever… I'm excited to hear the statements, the voices constructing the meaning of the lion himself.

Are the subsidiary titles in parentheses such as *Shop till You Fly* or *La vita continua* to be understood as simply amusing, critical or even cynical?

Yes! I am open for all kinds of readings. The piece related to place/country

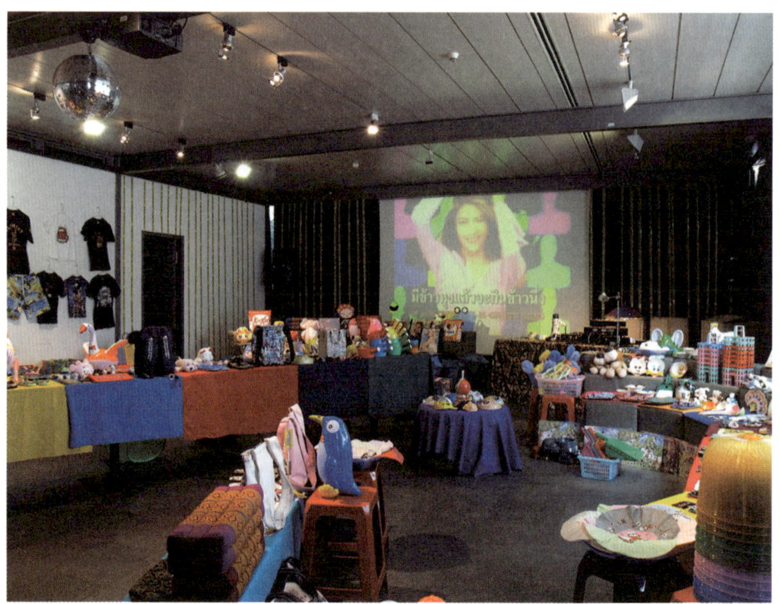

Installation view,
Kunsthalle Wien 2005:
Surasi Kusolwong,
1 Euro Market

intends to balance the attitudes of people in-and-outside the art world. It's about the way you see the world and celebrate your life. The subsidiary titles are more or less about social viewpoints with politics and cultures.

If you buy an object at one of Surasi Kusolwong's markets is one buying art or goods?

You buy art, it is because you have attitude about it. And you buy goods, it's because you have attitude about it. You can buy both art/goods if you have both attitudes. The piece can exist and be used in both ways, like a two-in-one.

Are there objects which you sell to collectors or do you only sell (or give) things to the public without making a profit (since the cost price and cost of transport are more than the income)? What is your opinion of the art market? Are you propagating an altered viewpoint on the consumer world?

I'm not propagating a viewpoint on the consumer world. If you feel that I do, then it's a kind of side effect. I just want to introduce and demonstrate my attitude and points of view to the art world. Of course, the art institution, art collector or art lover can buy or collect the results of my market piece—the money from people when they buy the goods. The money was put into, and preserved in, a minimal, clear Perspex box. It becomes what I call the 'Archaeological Piece'.

I wish and want to sell the money-box at a price that is not the same as the amount of money inside. It's quite interesting to see the cycle of this market piece. Money starts as necessary material to buy goods and then money itself becomes a work of art at the end.

What does the standard pricing, for example 1 Euro for your wares mean? Is it a plea for more democracy in a capitalist society? Are you being ironic about a system of social values or is the standard price an identifying characteristic for it being art?

1 Euro is set up as a symbolic price, it's my own standard. I wanted to make it equal. It's kind of economic democracy. You might even get confused between the true and the real. Your head might still spin like a washing machine when you see various kinds of goods all at the same price, but in fact they don't have the same price/value ratio. And somehow you know that value and price are not the same but you enjoy being part of the market event.

What I like about art is that you can make things expensive or cheap, useless or useful, visible or invisible. Art never touches its real value. And the question is, what is the price of its real value? Who can say what the real value is?

Hilmar Hoffmann once described his ideal museum as a place of cheerful enlightenment. Can art be cheerful, is your art cheerful?

It depends very much on people's minds. If their minds are cheerful, it's cheerful.

Of course, art could help by being like a passage way to another place. In the same way, my lion piece for Vienna could help visitors to say what they want to say or express, perhaps also in a cheerful way.

The colourful hustle and bustle in markets has changed into ubiquitous throngs of people in malls, department stores and pedestrian shopping areas. Shopping has become vicarious satisfaction for a society which has lost its values and is looking for – and finds – ecstasy and meditation in compulsive buying. A collective vice has become a desired drug. Do you see yourself as an observer or more as a critic of object fetishism in an increasingly capitalistically oriented society?

I am practicing and demonstrating the way of happiness. It is more about memories, more about something missing from our society. Unlike the malls or department stores, the street market is the place where people meet their ordinary life. When the sun shines, the colourful sounds, smells and energy spring up full of life. It is quite beautiful when people meet each other in the morning or in the afternoon. They talk to each other, exchange news, information, opinions and so on. The market is one kind of place for life's freedom. I want to perpetuate this kind of freedom. In a way it is very democratic. People come to sell and buy what they need, want or like.

My market project is made with a sense of positive desire and with bright, lively humour. Many people buy a lot of goods for their loved ones, their mothers, children, friends, etc. So it is more about sharing and thinking of the others, not only about oneself… more about relational sentiment with a time-based attitude…

The Thai artist Navin Rawanchaikul with his taxi café or Rirkrit Tiravanija, who cooks for visitors or places everyday activities – such a meeting and discussing – at the centre of his artistic praxis, emphasise everyday life. A coincidence? Are there mutual sources of inspiration or can similar motivating grounds be found in Thai culture?

You are what you are. I think that even when people come from the same social group or culture the way they look, think, analyse and use their experiences can be different or similar…

In your projects the borders between art and life disappear almost completely. The presentation in institutions that are part of the art market still marks your affiliations. For you, is the meta system of art primarily an offer to reflect on everyday culture? Is your art political?

For me, when you think or do something different from what other people do, what you do becomes a political act in some sense.

At first glace your art appears to be the provision of a service almost completely hidden behind everyday life situations. There are projects where visitors get free massages; then there are the markets and you also held a lottery once. A disinterested offer with the intention of doing something nice for people?

My market, free massage or lottery pieces are mediums or techniques just as you would use colours in a painting. It's not about service, it's more about sending and receiving messages between people, a kind of basic human need and a human relationship. We need to share our experiences together, appreciating a moment in life and potentially forgetting about art for a while…

You were born in Ayutthaya, the former capital of Siam and have been living in Bangkok for many years. In your work, are you reproducing the dynamic infrastructural achievements and the currents of energy in a progressive and globalised world?

On one hand, yes. But on the other hand, it's also very local. You have to understand that in the Ayutthaya period the city was the centre of trade in

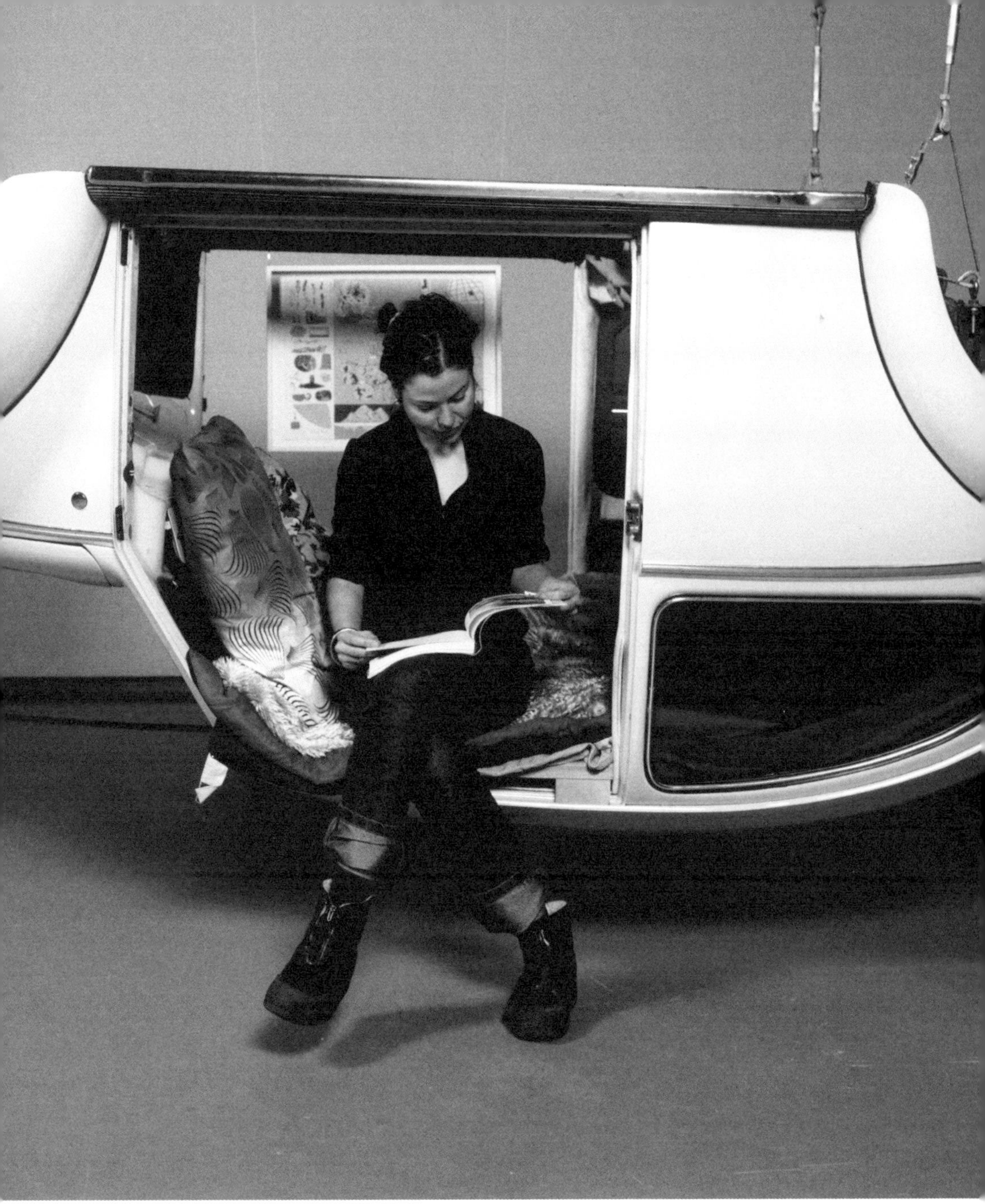

Surasi Kusolwong,
*Emotional Machine (VW
with Fahlström)*,
2001- 2004

Southeast Asia. Sea trade was open to Europeans, Indians, and Chinese, etc. So, in my opinion, there was also globalisation at that time but in a different atmosphere and way of life.

In my work, I am not reproducing but rather reacting to and re-thinking these kinds of dynamic cultural achievements in life. As you saw when you were in Bangkok it is full of energy flows. It is the place where people adapt their own ways of traditional everyday life to the globalization era—like the hundreds of massage salons everywhere in the city waiting to serve and heal people from the stress of the world.

The goods which you sell and give away come from Thailand and are a reference to Surasi Kusolwong's origins. Are they also the mark of a nomadic existence?

Yes, nomadic existence, nomadic culture!

How is it to live as an artist who exhibits all over the world? And the other way round, how important is the art scene in Bangkok/Thailand for you?

It is interesting to move around in different places, to see and experience things in different corners of the world. About the art scene in Thailand: it has different kinds of good energy to anywhere else but it is not really very visible. You can somehow feel it even though there is not much supporting it.

Bangkok is one of the most rapidly modernising cities in Asia. What are the consequences of globalisation on the people and their cultural traditions?

We are good at adapting but sometimes we are too open. However, in general, we are not worried about this kind of globalization, we just flow flexibly and use it in our own way, meaning and understanding. Just like we have and put everything into the department stores. We put in shops, restaurants, banks, passport division, post office, cinema or just move the street markets into the air-conditioned spaces on the ground floor and sell goods in front of the brand name shops. Or even on the top floor: we can go to the zoo and see tigers, lions, bears, etc, etc. It's really great. We create them like a little modern global village!

In the lottery project *My Home Is Yours, Your Home is Mine* visitors could win a trip from Tokyo and Seoul, where the exhibition took place, to Bangkok. Your family made the winners at home there. A contribution to improvements in inter-cultural relationships?

I am interested in human relationship and experience. For the *Lucky* lottery project, I want to extend the physical space of my work between two des-

tinations in two countries; to draw from one point to the other point and
back again. Travelling in and across the blue sky with white clouds floating
all around also expands the duration of this project and makes it more visible, clearer, to the lucky winners.

What are the opportunities and advantages and also the problems and disadvantages of your origins for your artistic career? What was important for your
career?

Francis Picabia once said: "The success of un-success is a success." For me,
likewise: "The advantage of disadvantage is the advantage."

Surasi Kusolwong in conversation with Gerald Matt in the summer of 2005 on the occasion of the
exhibition *Surasi Kusolwong: If A Lion Could Talk* at Kunsthalle Wien project space.
Surasi Kusolwong was born in Ayutthaya, Thailand in 1965. He lives and works in Bangkok, Thailand.

Sigalit Landau

Gravity and decay oppression and cataclysm … monstrously coexist.

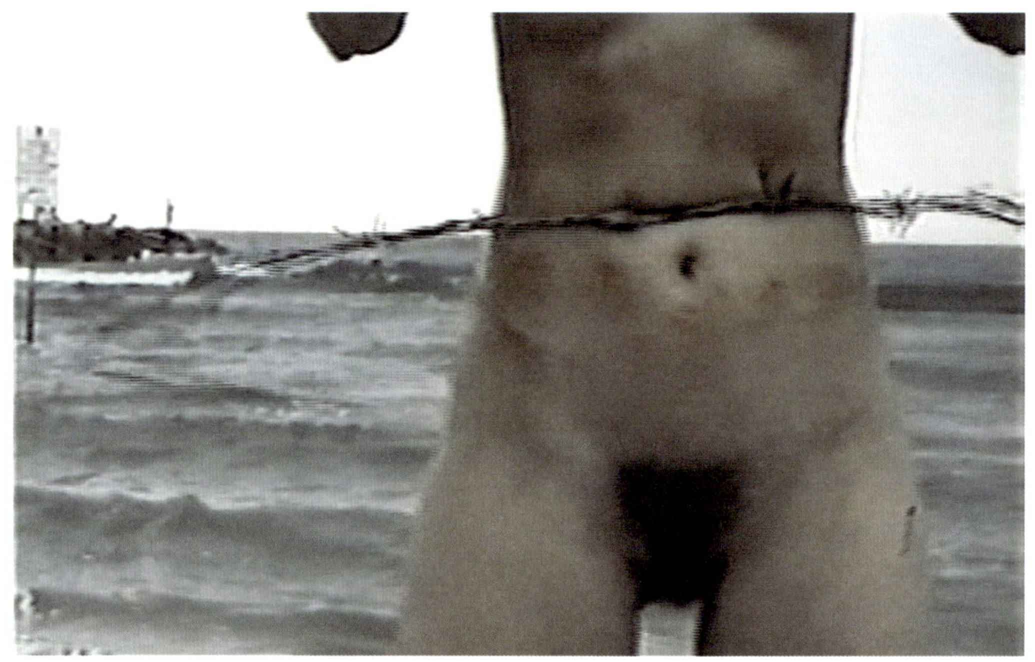

Sigalit Landau,
Barbed Hula, 2000

In an extensive review of your large-scale installation, *The Country,* in the Alon Segev gallery in Tel Aviv at the end of 2002, Philip Leider in *Art in America* described the work as "Israel's *Guernica.*" Picasso's artistic statement against the horrors of Nazi attacks supporting Franco's Fascist forces at the beginning of the Spanish Civil War is considered among the most political works in all of art history. How did you manage to come to terms with this comparison, which is, after all, very high praise?

I see high praise as a moment of "lifting-my-head" but also as an expectation, a trail with glitter … that will not lead to my well … I come from the inside of a local–personal matrix where most perspectives are dynamic with no relation to "the greatness" or "importance" of external ideas and decisions or a tangible result … My unmade works leaves me "praiseless" till the bitter [or sweet] end [cycle of work]. I do enjoy reaching viewers in all channels; I enjoy transmitting my actions … and mixing the tiniest "homeless" moment with chunks of "timeless" time.

You started out, originally, with dancing and sculpture and have since worked with the most diverse materials and media. The human body in motion still plays an important role in some of your performances or video works, such as *Three Man Hula* (1999) or *Barbed Hula* (2000) – a work which was also shown at the Kunsthalle Wien as part of the 2003 exhibition, *Attack!* Both works show, above all, the limits of human freedom of movement and the lust of life within certain systems (barbed wire metaphor) or constellations (groups). Do elements of the dance enter into your work – and, if so, in which form?

I think dance and the "corps de ballet" are somehow in most things I do. I did my growing up on stage, dancing almost professionally, and I think I perform and see myself as a plural; when there is one of me, it equals something "generic", "many". In *Three Man Hula* the performers are in a "knot", they are bound in an allegory, a tribe skidding in opposing directions—but at the same time leaning on each other … In my figurative sculpture, I feel I am very close to the body's ins and outs: core anatomy, choreography, the language of unconscious gestures, – in my installations, I create stories by the way I mould and play with space.

The "limits" of human requirements for liberty in your work are sometimes imposed by nature, as in the case of your video, *Standing On a Watermelon in the Dead Sea* (2004), where you were attempting – as the protagonist, within a visually beguiling, but at the same time, lifelessly dangerous ambience, caught between gravity and buoyancy – to find a balance, an equilibrium. While the laws of physics are unalterable, social rules at least hold a potential for change. What is the relationship, for you, between these two sets of regulations?

Gravity and decay oppression and cataclysm … monstrously coexist, and paralyse me a lot before I move … and "make" something about it…

One of your early installations, *Grrr …/Temple Mount*, which you put up in 1995 at the Israel Museum in Jerusalem, had as its centre a glass cabinet containing a model of the Temple Mount "rock", whose surface was covered with computer mouse pads, on which you were allowing bacterial cultures to fester. Even this early work served up a plethora of possible interpretations. Your language, so rich in metaphors, which in most cases appeals to several of the senses and often expects an educated trans-culturally conversant audience, has since become one of the essential aspects or special characteristics of your art. Is "poetry" versus unambiguousness a better way, for you, to understand social and cultural contexts?

Beauty, play, and poetry are the only concreteness I know in which I can come to terms, and remake the major ties: history, myth, loss of identity, holocaust and sacred pain.

Your installations are often also very complex in terms of the technical and spatial aspects of the materials used. Do you work in conjunction with a staff of helpers and partners or do you manage most things alone?

I collaborate with assistants from slightly different fields whose presence also helps me establish a somewhat coherent and structured labourious routine. There's usually also a component to the process that is a touch "religious" because it is plainly Sisyphus-like and time consuming. This creates a streamline of conversation, and personal exchange, quite different than the normal work, on the one hand; and the personal incubation phase of my projects, on the other hand.

You have repeatedly lived and worked in Europe and the USA, yet Israel appears to be a more significant and content-rich source of inspiration for you. What is it that is so fascinating about a country where, as we would tend to have the impression here, the fronts between the opposing positions are hardening rather than anybody seeking solutions for a less conflict-ridden form of coexistence?

I call it "battleground for found but lost sanity". History is alive and biting, attraction and repulsion meets you while you walk down your street. This mess and mass leaves ZERO alienation between people [… but also ZERO respect]. Living and working in any place is not easy if you are making the kind of art that searches for the seam lines and blind spots … Life in a war zone, post war, pre-terror, keeps you awake, frustrated, exhausted, you have to insist and define your own urgent beliefs – the concept of place is flickering in the air, a feeling there is no place, or not enough place or the place needs to be re-invented … the waves of immigrations, languages, religions, cultures and education.… – everyone is screaming – no one listens … so the noise is not "white noise" of globalisation but a black hole, wound and salt … and guilt. And I now acknowledge that [my] one lifetime may not be enough for anything very different…than THIS.

How do you feel about Vienna as a place to live and work as an artist? After all, you have spent a fair bit of time here by now. Have you been able to establish interesting and useful or fruitful contacts for the future with the Viennese circles of artists?

Vienna for me is one of the most beautiful pulsating intersections of Europe. My family on my mother's side came from Vienna before the war, and I feel it as a tunnel/bridge kingdom. I find it hard to get connected to the scene in Vienna, as my visits are rather short there – could be that in a longer stay I could get a deeper and more contemporary picture on the one hand and also try and detect my ancestry.

In the exhibition, *Heiliger Sebastian* (Saint Sebastian) at the Kunsthalle Wien, you were represented with the sculpture, *Passion Victim* (2003), "…half a peacock with spears instead of feathers. The seductive deadly wheel of sharp weapons raises itself up. An erect blue human penis makes up the body-head-beak of the bird", you wrote, both descriptively and interpretatively, regarding this work. What, from your perspective, is the role of passion, in the dual meaning of suffering and ardour – or possibly suffering *as* an obsession –in the creation of art?

All I can add to your good description and my quotation from back when I made and worshiped my wounded peacock-man (2003) is: Yes, I still suffer. The pain is around the arts of love and the love of art. I need my passion to have a flavour of pain, I need beauty to rise from a current in the gutters … I escape anything which threatens vulnerability, only death and its practices are totally desensitised.

Sigalit Landau, Passion Victim, the Peacock, 2003

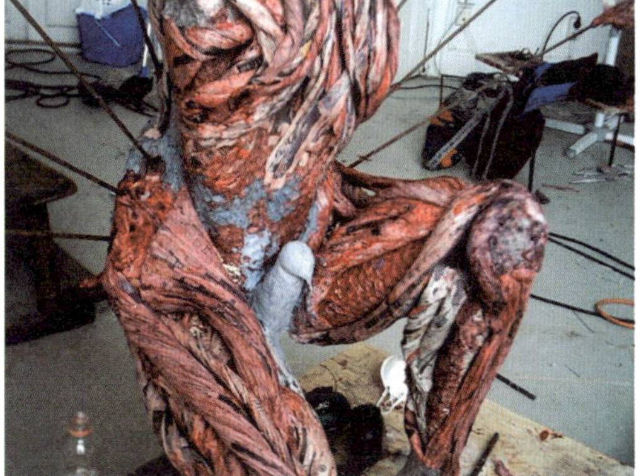

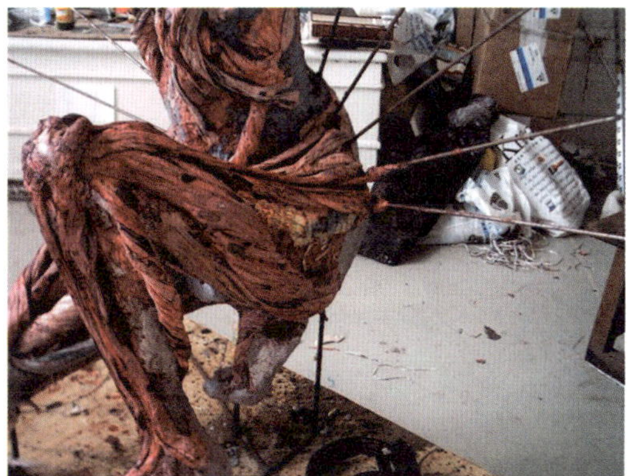

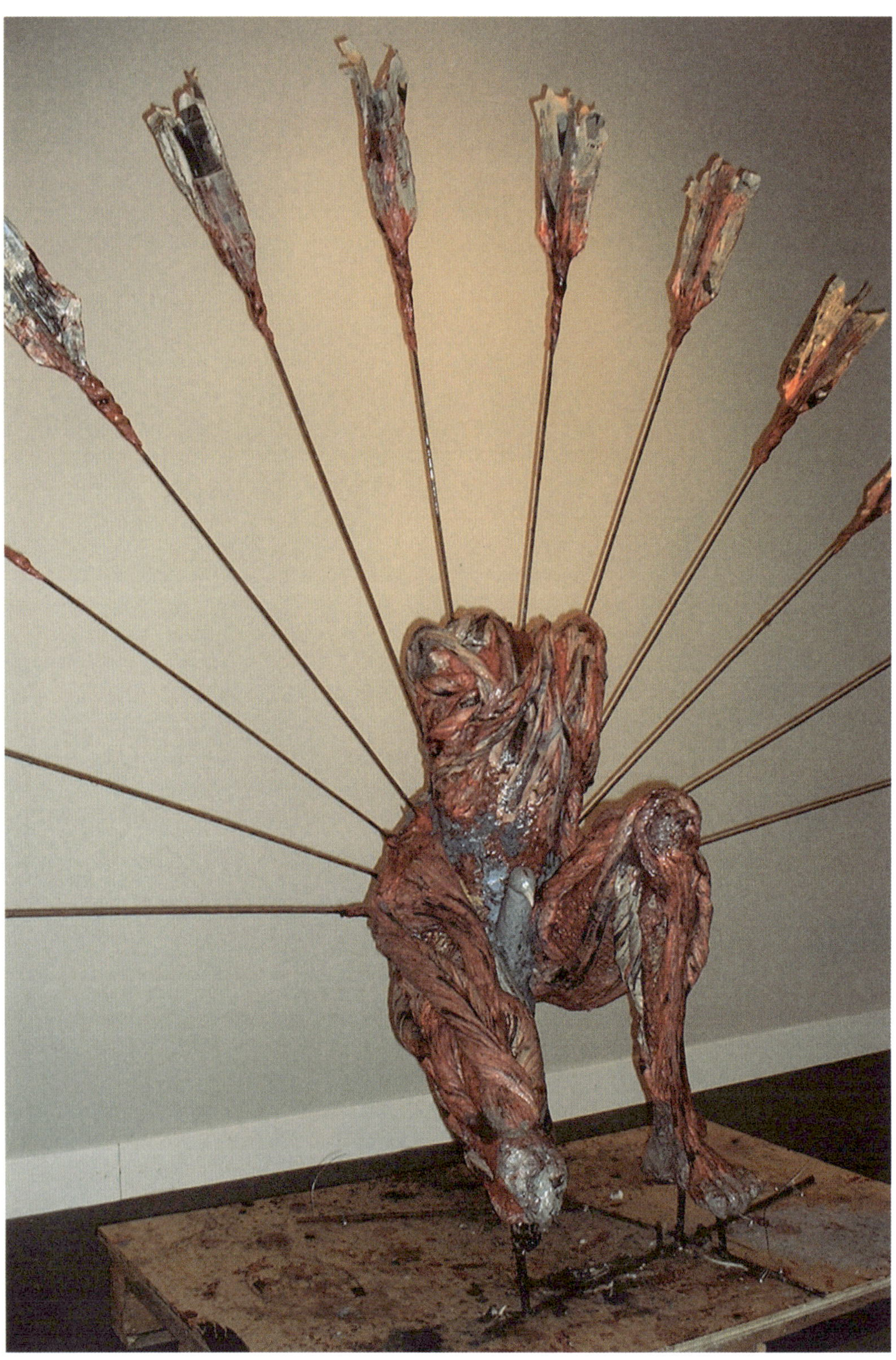

In this above-mentioned work you also clearly refer to male vanity. In your opinion, is vanity, in conjunction with sexuality, a specifically male symptom?

In my opinion male sexuality has a component of "pride in the miracle", the visible miracle is the masculine one – Jewish mothers in particular have something to do with this celebration. Also, look what a festival is thrown when the baby boy is eight days old and the foreskin is removed to free the glans. It is considered to be a connection with god.

Which projects will you be working on in the near future?

I will do something for Kunst-Werke Berlin in 2007.

Sigalit Landau in conversation with Gerald Matt and Lucas Gehrmann in February 2006. The artist took part in the exhibitions *Attack! Kunst und Krieg in den Zeiten der Medien* (2003) and *Heiliger Sebastian: A Splendid Readiness for Death* (2003) at Kunsthalle Wien.
Sigalit Landau was born in 1969 in Tel-Aviv, Israel. She lives and works in Paris and in Tel-Aviv.

Sigalit Landau, *Passion Victim, the Peacock,* 2003
←

Michael Lin

I think that some of the most important works of art are the ones that we live with and that affect our daily lives such as architecture, furniture, and fashion, which can be said to even shape our bodies and minds.

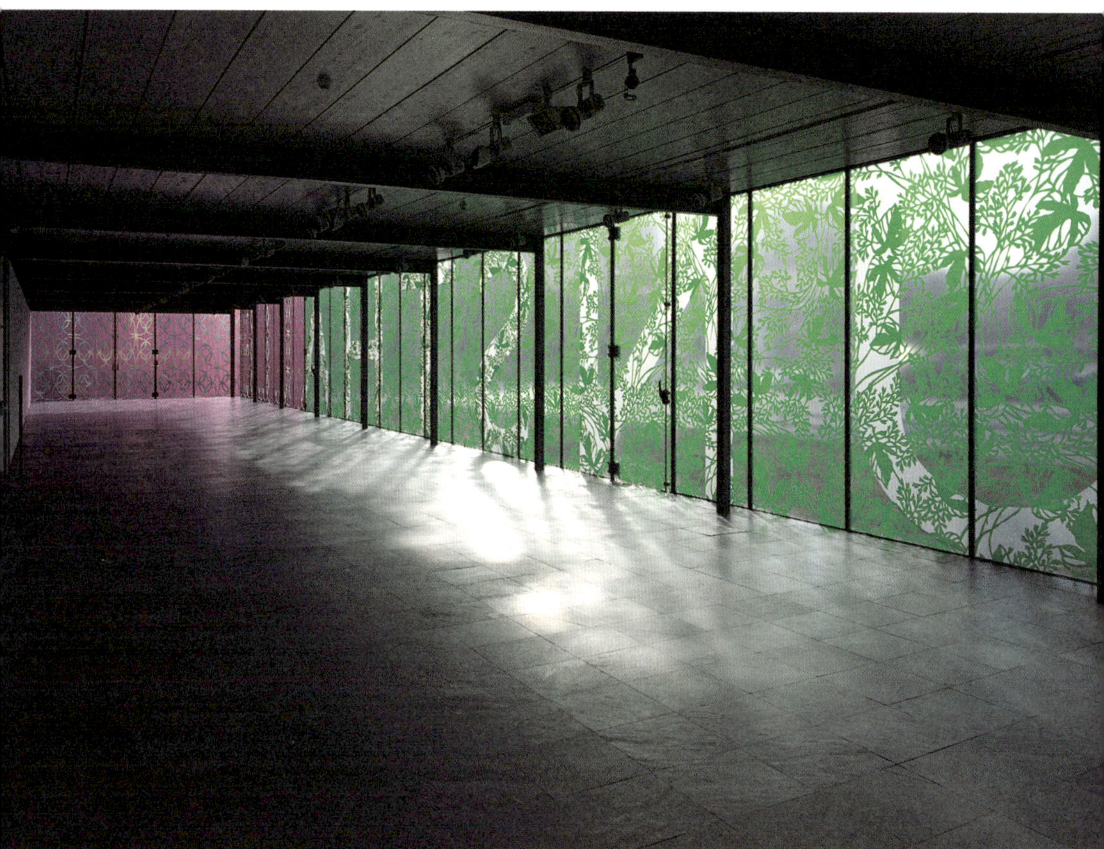

Installation view,
Kunsthalle Wien project
space 2005: *Michael Lin*

Your works are monumental and usually found on floors or walls. Floral patterns inspired by Taiwanese textiles cover the surface of the room. You use many shades of red; the intense coloration escapes from the surface because of its brilliance and creates an extraordinary atmosphere in the room. What is the role of sensuality in your work?

The textiles from which I appropriate my patterns are used in Taiwan as duvet covers that are given as part of the dowry to the groom from the bride's family for the wedding. They are mostly used as the covers of the wedding night bed.

Last week, while I was in Tokyo, I had a very interesting conversation with a young architect. She asked me if I ever considered moisture in relation to my works. She explained to me that, because my works are appropriations of textiles, for her they retain the qualities of textiles in terms of moisture. Unlike paper, which is dry and more rigid, textiles contain a certain amount of moisture that allows them to be soft and moldable to the body.

You were born in Tokyo in 1964, grew up in Taiwan and immigrated to the U.S. with your parents in 1973. You lived in Los Angeles and Paris and after finishing your studies, decided in 1993 to return to Taiwan where you now live. What role does the place where you live play? How much are you influenced by each of the different cultures?

The move from Los Angeles back to Taiwan was the most important for me in regards to my practice. I moved back to Taiwan in 1993, directly after I finished my studies in LA. At the time, the "art system" in Taiwan was very different from the conditions that existed in LA. Contemporary art, or for that matter modern art, in Taiwan were seen as something imported, something that did not develop out of its own tradition. There was, at the time, in the arts and the general society, a conscious struggle to search out and define a vocabulary based on its own cultural parameters. Of course, this condition was a result of the political predicament that is specific to Taiwan since 1949. The precarious and uncertain state of political and cultural identity due to its isolation from the international community, the United Nations, since 1972, gave rise to an identity crisis that provoked a paradoxical retrospective search for a national identity. I identified myself directly with this condition due to both my own past history and my position as an artist. One of the main reasons for my family's immigration to the United States was directly linked to the uncertainties brought about by the United States' transfer of recognition from Taiwan to China. On the other hand, as an artist, I was forced to go back to very fundamental questions in my practice that only came about because of this displaced distance. I posed very fundamental questions, such as the relationship between my practice and the specific contexts that I practiced in, which later led to questions about my practice's relationship to the audience.

Are there things you might term radical breaks in your work?

The most radical break in my work occurred between my first solo show in Taipei in 1994 and my second solo show in 1996. In the 1994 show I was making monochrome paintings on steel. Two years later I was moving my furniture into the gallery for my exhibition. Again, it was this change of context from Southern California to Taipei that changed my concerns in my work.

Which artists or art movements have inspired you?

There are many obviously inspirational artists for me: Daniel Buren, Dan Graham, and Franz West, for example. But what really challenged and provoked me was the very specific circumstance in Taiwan. The Taiwanese New Wave Cinema was something very important for me, the films of Hou Hsiao-Hsien, Edward Yang, and Tsai Ming-Liang. Each of them developed a very specific language in their reflections on the state of contemporary life in Taiwan, Hou with his historical essays, Young's focus on contemporary urban life in Taipei, and Tsai's cinema of the body with almost no dialogue. I, too, at the time, struggled to reconcile my practice with the context of my new environment. At the time I was very influenced by the ideas of Elaine Scarry and how she spoke about culture in the body. The culture that is learned into the body "is more permanently there than those disembodied forms of patriotism that exist in verbal habits or in thoughts about one's national identity." For me, she pointed the way to the body as a site of culture that allowed me to think about cultural identity and its relationship to art practice in a very different way.

Your ornamental patterns are infinitely expandable; they have no center and no composition. The term "all over" structure began with Jackson Pollock's art and deals with surface democratically and on the basis of equality—a structure located between abstraction and figuration. In your case, a natural process of alienation and stylization? Simulacra that cause mood shifts?

I am not sure what you mean by alienation and stylization in regard to my work. For me, the terms "all over," democracy, and equality seem to be linked directly to American cold war politics. My works create temporary places — not a painting surface but a pedestrian, unremarkable place of respite.

I use the term unremarkable for my work, even though they are most of the time monumental in scale, for they recede into the background at the tilt of the head. They are not focal points like a painting or a sculpture.

With your floor works, on which visitors often lie on cushions designed by you, you break with the well-known museum sign "Don't Touch," the Christian "Noli me tangere," and the aura of the artwork. Visitors to the exhibition can sleep on the *Kiasma Day Bed* and recover from the exertion of looking. How do you deal with art becoming functional and applied art?

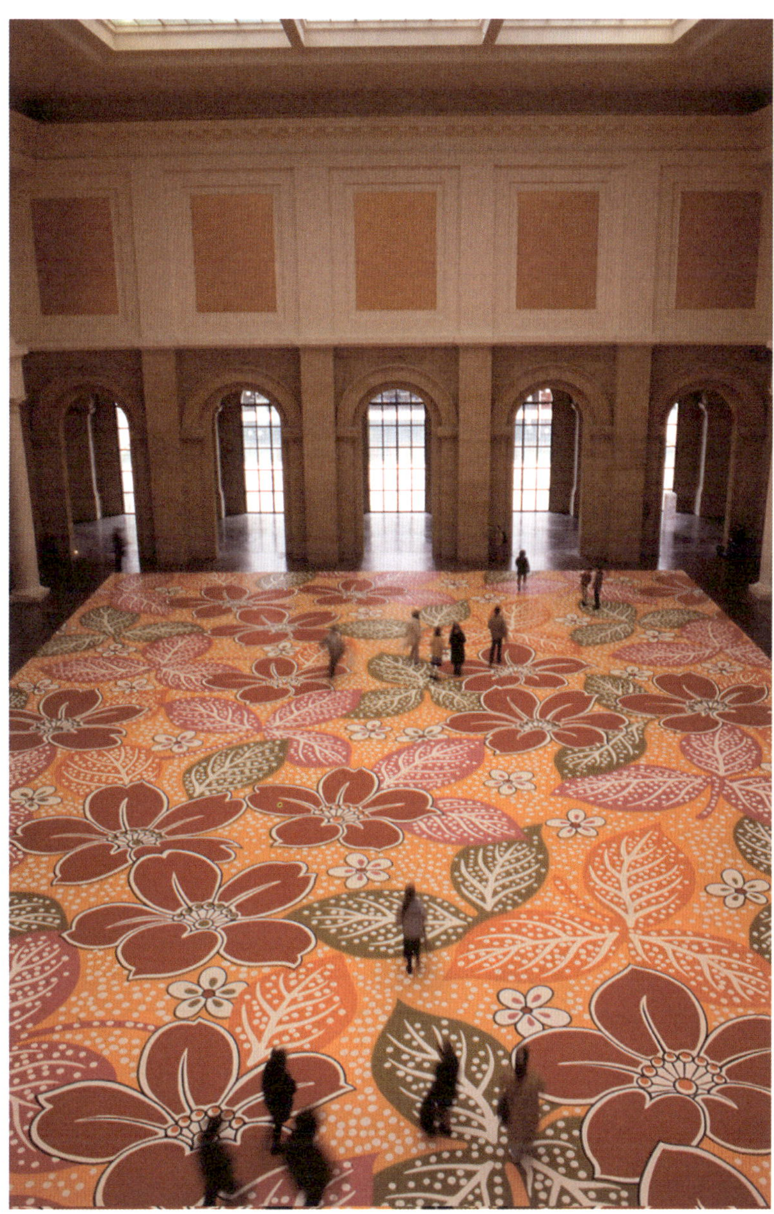

Installation view 2003: Michel Lin, *Palais des Beaux-Arts*

I am not interested in making divisions between fine art and applied art. Art has always been functional. Even if it is a painting on a wall, it is either functioning as contemplative provocation, a decorative object, or as a trophy on a collector's wall. I don't agree with Donald Judd when he said that a chair is not art because when you sit on it you can't see it. I think that some of the most important works of art are the ones that we live with and that affect our daily lives such as architecture, furniture, and fashion, which can be said to even shape our bodies and minds.

You often work together with assistants or students. Even during the production of your works, art becomes a social event. Rirkrit Tiravanija also tries to make possible places and situations where people meet, places where there is communality and communication. How close is your work to this artistic praxis?

I think that they are in some ways fundamentally similar, but I must add that my practice is less utopian then Tiravanija's. All my works are produced by groups of people that we recruit on site because the productions are very laborious. There is communality and communication but in toil. The work is not about my personal expression with paint but more about my proposition for a relationship to a place.

The work *Untitled Cigarette Break* from 1999 appears to be an obvious reference to Andy Warhol and Pop Art. What is your relationship to them?

For *Untitled Cigarette Break* I was thinking much more about the relationship of ornamentation to Modernism. For me, the LC-2-chair of Le Corbusier reflected perfectly the white cube of the gallery space I was showing in. The chairs became a scale model of the room. The paintings on the wall were scaled somewhere between the chairs and the room. I thought of smoking as a more conscious way of breathing. Smoke describing breath. Chairs describing the room. Walls becoming a shirt for our body.

Can you explain the technical aspects of your work? I have heard you refer to yourself as a painter; what do you consider your position in painting to be?

I refer to myself as a painter because I use paint. I am a house painter and perhaps we can say that that is my position in painting. The first large scale painting that I made in 1988 was titled *House*. It was the first time that I painted directly on the architecture with the ornamental patterns that I found in my home.

Sometimes your work appears to me to be film or stage decoration and the visitors are the potential protagonists. Am I mistaken?

No, not at all, even for my first floor painting, I thought of it as a stage for something to take place. The works are places as opposed to spaces. Space is an abstraction while a place has a name, is in time, and necessitates physical experience.

The avant-garde – and above all the neo-avant-garde – had the problem that if their claims for art were realized, namely the combination of art with life, art would then become superfluous and completely assimilated into life. How do your works look against the background of this debate?

This is only a problem if the premise is that art is separate from life. On Kawara once said, "Europeans can't really understand the Japanese. For them, 'one' is the basis of thinking. For the Japanese, 'complements' permeate all thought."

You also show outside the classical exhibition space. Thus art as such is less visible and more difficult to identify. With that, you step outside the pre-existing framework of art, the institution. How do you see the institutional critiques of Michael Asher and Daniel Buren?

Buren's and Asher's critiques of institutions are exactly their limit. I am less interested in the formalized spaces in the institutions for presenting art. These spaces on the margins of the institutional space, the events and social interactions are much more important for me. I am much more interested in the everyday, the general culture. It is in these places that art is not so clearly defined that questions of the function of art come to light. In marginal places like Taiwan, outside of the clear parameters of art as it is defined in the European and American traditions, these traditions are exposed and become more susceptible to being redefined.

In your exhibition project for the Kunsthalle Wien project space you will be making transparent film to be affixed to the inside of the windows. Most of the windows will be covered with a green floral pattern, the rest will show violet, strictly geometrical, interlocked circles. You designed the work especially with the effect it will have in the evening when it is dark and the room brightly lit. Then, the pavilion will take on an almost psychedelic mood reminiscent of Flower Power in the 1970s. Are you playing with these associations and the lightness and hedonism of a lifestyle like that?

I was thinking more of an oriental lamp: this cryptic glass pavilion transformed into a beautiful, banal object.

If someone would call you a decorator who, above all, designs beautiful rooms, what would you answer?

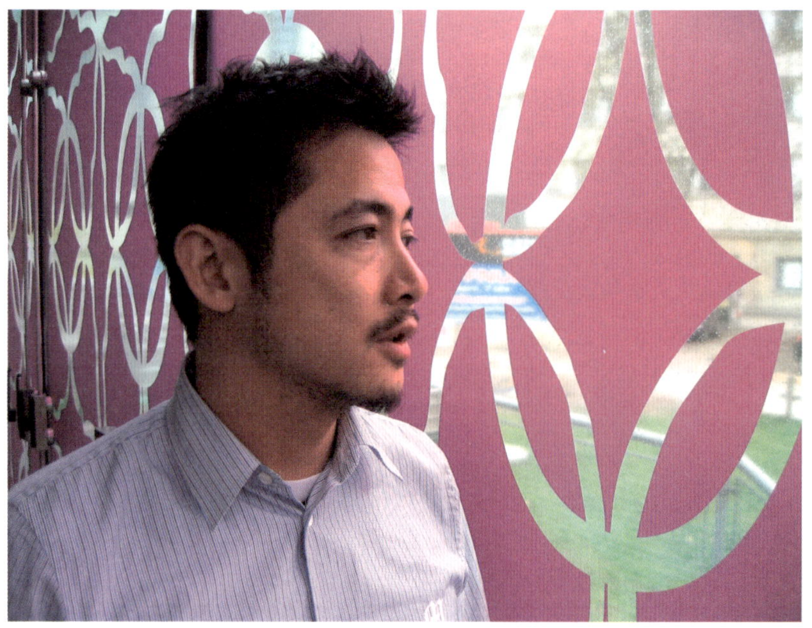

Michael Lin

I would take it as a compliment. Beauty is something I believe to be a quality.

What I notice in the work for the Kunsthalle Wien is the contrast between the irregularities of the plants, which loosely and casually wind their way over the surface, and the strict geometric pattern. Does your use of the oppositions follow Nietzsche's view of art, which confronts the Apollonian with the Dionysian consciousness?

The lattice windows with organic patterns or geometric patterns in traditional Chinese architecture were never seen as being in opposition; quite the contrary, they are seen as being complementary.

The interior of the project space, the museum room, remains empty: a room that could be used or an empty space for the reception of the façade design?

The gallery space becomes a receptacle for the play of light and color dictated by the passage of time and the sun moving across the sky. The glass curtain wall is made more physical and sensual. The gaze is broken by the screen, like a blink, allowing the eyes to see again. Vision becomes more conscious and active.

The music being played in the café will be piped into the exhibition space. What is the role of music in your work? Are you concerned with a synaesthetic experience or are you following another goal with your holistic approach in relation to constructing an atmosphere?

I wanted to normalize the space with the furniture music from the restaurant. To somehow fuse the two spaces with the music: the restaurant as a social space, merging with the exhibition space; one modifying the other, but always returning to the emptiness of the institution.

What was particularly appealing or challenging about the Kunsthalle Wien building? How did you arrive at the artistic solution you are now showing?

The Kunsthalle Wien building is very appropriate for me – one space, one building, one glass pavilion, a very strong symbol of domestic modernism, like the Philip Johnson House. I was very much interested in working directly on the architecture – one work, one space, one building.

Michael Lin in conversation with Gerald Matt in the spring of 2005 on the occasion of the exhibition *Michael Lin* at Kunsthalle Wien project space.
Michael Lin was born in Tokyo, Japan in 1964. He lives and works in Paris, France.

Michèle Magema

My life's journey is based on the principle of construction.

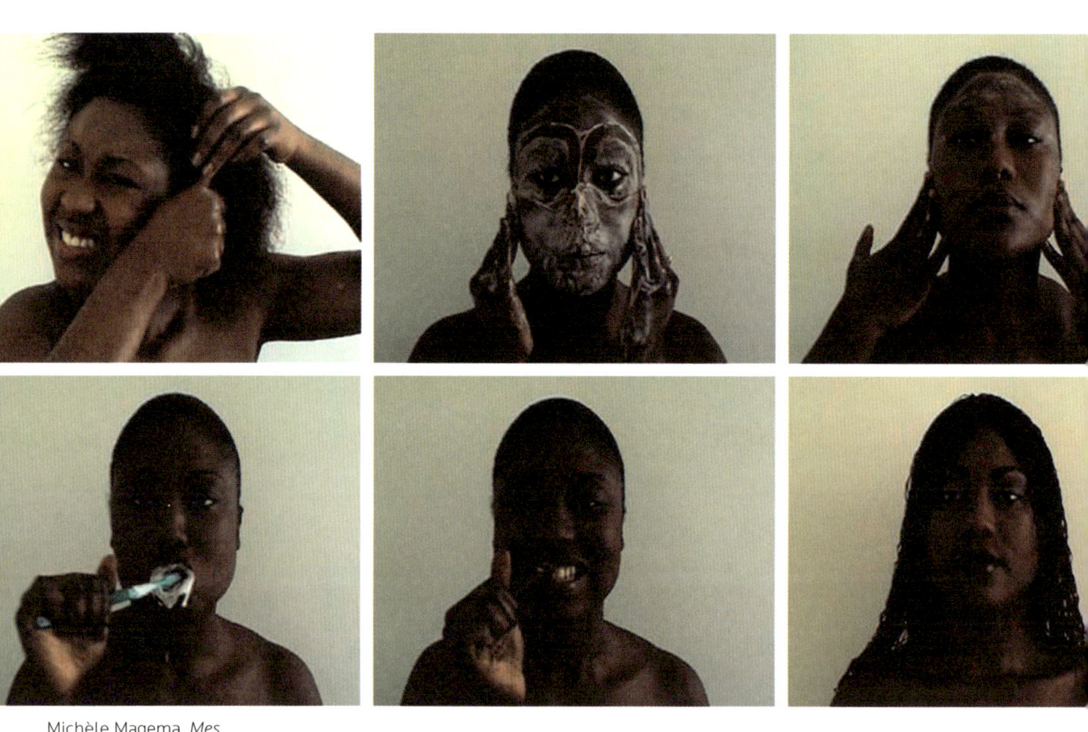

Michèle Magema, *Mes petits rituels*, 2003

Michèle Magema, one of your best-known groups of works depicts, in a series of large format colour pictures, the common everyday ritual of the morning toilette. You once said, "Behind the soap mask I keep hiding my African identity, which I wash off every morning to cover it up with a French cosmetic product." How would you describe this African identity in the diaspora?

You are referring to my video installation, *Rituals*, and specifically to *Ritual #3*. The fact that I wash my face with these products is a trivial and banal gesture, which refers to an element of African unity. The white soap coating one's skin could suggest a French identity. Yet, it is only the surface of the skin and it is only being washed. Once the soap is removed, the character-istic blackness that defines me remains. My African identity has only been superficially touched.

In contrast to that, the crème in *Ritual #4* is actually being soaked up by the skin. The African identity, therefore, quite obviously, absorbs the French one, and accommodates it inside itself. On the basis of this fact, it appears to be trans-formed onto an internalised and intellectual level.

So my work does quite literally inscribe itself into the identity problematic of the diaspora. Born in the Congo and living in France, I pick up what my French surroundings offer me. And I process all of this and incorporate it deeply within myself. In this work, the metaphor expresses the connec-tions between these two identities. Whether this is a genuine African take on occidental means of expression – who can tell? It is, as it happens, the outlook on Africa that I can have. I thus find myself both outside and inside of an African identity.

The problem of identity/alterity has been raised by many African artists, includ-ing, for example, Candice Breitz, who, in one of her works, takes postcards fea-turing portraits of Black African women and whitens out their faces and bodies with Tipp-Ex correction fluid. Is contemporary art, then, realisable only within the parameters of deconstruction and reconstitution of ascribed identities?

Well, whatever the reasons that may have been responsible for the relocation —there is always the option of choice, either to stay or to move somewhere altogether different. In my own case, the French identity was forced upon me by my parents, by their having emigrated. When I was growing up, I made up my mind to make this identity my own, and to accept it fully and wholeheartedly, by remaining in France.

My personal life's journey has been based on the principle of recon-struction. Piece by piece I assembled the diverse aspects of my African and French history. So my work delves into my recollections to reproduce new images, without, however, destroying my African identity in favour of my

European one. I always try to maintain a balance between the two. For me, for this reason, contemporary art is only feasible with due consideration of these parameters of complementarity.

You've lived in France ever since your childhood. How does this affect your relationship with the Congo, your native country? Do you travel there regularly and are you aware of cultural developments over there?

My relationship with the Congo is very complex. I draw my entire inspiration from stories of the past. I utilise Congolese life, its culture and its traditions. Nevertheless, I notice that, increasingly, I am beginning to idealise my memories.

It has been almost 22 years since I was last in the Congo. The longer I stay away from it, the more I keep worrying about my return. The political situation over there is utterly instable. The handful of family members still living in the Congo, I don't even know anymore. At the moment, I am not actively participating in any Congolese cultural affairs. I hope that this will change, and that the times and my projects will one day enable me to return. Of course some local papers have written about my work. But in a place where misery and anarchy dominate all facets of everyday life, what role is there for art to play?

I think that I offer people a chance to dream, because, upon the publication of an article in Anima (an African feminist review) some people wrote to me asking for help. I am aware of the fact that for some people I represent a symbol of success.

The Congo has a particularly gruesome colonial history and has been plagued by internecine strife and power struggles for decades. Has this situation of a permanent state of emergency had any impact on your work at all?

Of course this situation has implications for my work. I cannot remain indifferent towards the situation in the Congo. My video *Oyé Oyé* covers an important part of the country's history: Mobutu and his 30-year-era of dictatorship. I cannot ignore this economically restless context. Art, for that reason, represents a form of commitment on my part towards a curbing of this instability. From beyond the African continent, my work casts a glance from outside at everyday life, inquiring into historical and various other social occurrences and illuminating the social differences.

In Africa, there's a long-standing tradition of studio photography, which has been appreciated in art-related exhibition contexts as well, over the past 15 years or so. This photographic history has created an almost inexhaustible, rigidly stylised reservoir of images of everyday African life.

Specifically, in the Congo, there also exists a tradition of socially critical mural painting, which has, in the meantime, received international recognition, with artists like Chéri Samba or Chéri Chérin. Does an art form like that, which addresses the people, or the majority of an illiterate population, offer any impulses for your own artistic approach?

I don't see myself as an inheritor of traditional African mural painting. I spent all my university years in France, and the study of art has brought me into a rather closer proximity with Afro-American artists, such as David Hammons, Adrian Piper or women artists like Mona Hatoum and Ingrid Mwangi.

Even though I started out as a painter, I don't feel particularly close to the art of Chéri Samba or Chéri Chérin, except for the fact that they cover critical and political areas that come close in content to my own work.

I try to appeal to all visitors, whether they are experienced or not. For that reason, too, it doesn't seem necessary to me to be literate in order to appreciate and enjoy a work of art. I hope to impart to the visitor as much information as possible, so that each person can form their own picture of the situation, independent of their origins or the centre of their lives.

It is a well-known fact that there are few opportunities in Africa for visual artists, both male and female, to develop their creativity. The infrastructure (of museums, galleries and art academies) is extremely low. Is the artistic approach that you pursue realisable only in exile or could you develop similar concepts in Brazzaville as well?

My artistic approach is founded on the consequences of relocation and the resulting acquisition of a pluri-identity. But I don't feel that I'm living in exile. I just cannot imagine living any other way. I think that a few projects could be realised in the Congo, perhaps as part of an artist-in-residence scheme. But, so far, no opportunity of this kind has been offering itself. There are some private initiatives that promote and foster exchanges between artists of the diaspora and those living in the Congo.

What is certain is that my work will change once I return to the Congo. As art, to me, is a place where exchanges take place, as well as a point of intersection, from which to take a different look at the world.

You have won the prize of the Dakar Biennial of 2004. How important is this biennial for African artists? Have you benefited from the prize at all?

Well, I believe that, despite all the difficulties, this biennial is one of the few major art events to benefit contemporary art. It offers younger artists a chance to exhibit their work right next to much more experienced colleagues and, in so doing, to distinguish themselves. It displays a spectrum of not necessarily representative African art, but establishes an opening towards the diaspora, which appears, to me, to be both fundamental and important. As for the benefits I was able to derive from the "Prix du Président de la République" – I was offered an opportunity to exhibit my work at the Kunstraum Innsbruck in 2004. My video, *La Porte* has been mentioned in the book *L'art de la friche: Essai sur l'art africain contemporain* by Jean-Loup Amselle and I still receive inquiries, because my work was seen at the Dakar Biennial.

Michèle Magema in conversation with Gerald Matt in 2005 following Gerald Matt's jury participation at Dak'Art 2004, La Biennale de l'Art Africain Contemporain.
Michèle Magema was born in Kinshasa, Congo, in 1977. She lives and works in Neuilly-sur-Marne and Paris, France.

German to English translation by Tom Appleton.

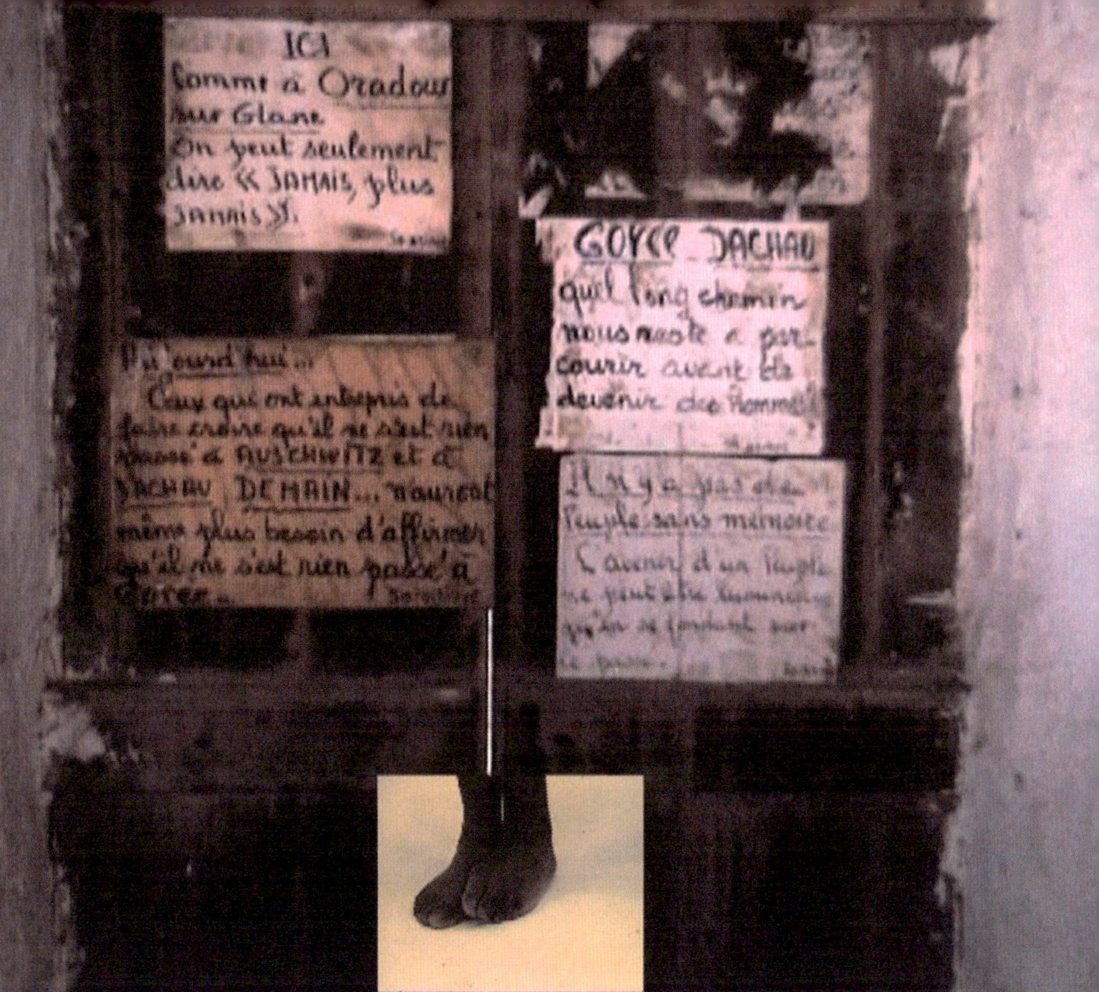

Video still : Michèle
Magema, *La Porte*, 2001

Teresa Margolles

I want to show that death is non-fiction and I don't try to veil the cause of death and what happened. I work with corpses and reality. I investigate who and why…

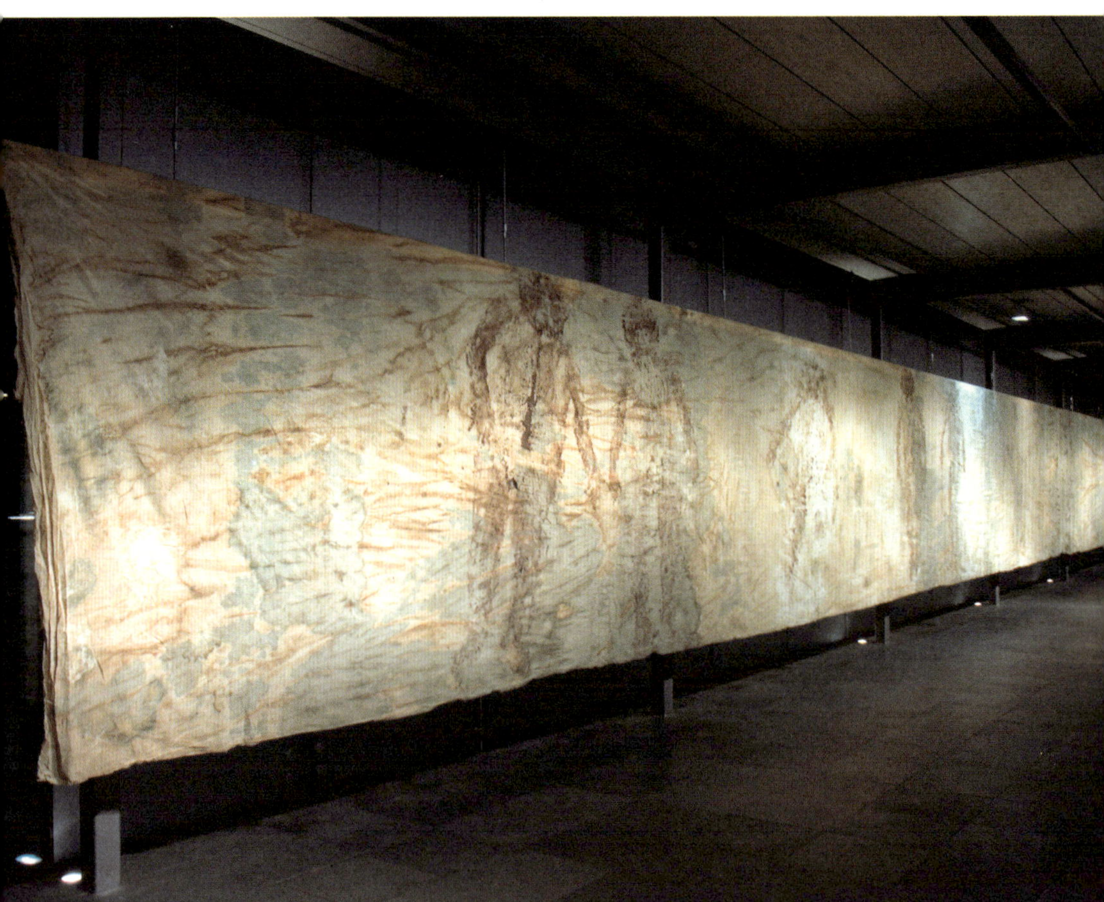

Installation view Kunsthalle
Wien project space 2003:
Teresa Margolles,
Das Leichentuch

As one of the founders of SEMEFO (Servicio Médico Forense / Medical Forensic Service), an artist group well known through their radical performances and installations in the 1990s, from the very beginning your artistic work dealt with death, the dead, and forensic medicine. SEMEFO's "studio" was the city morgue. What is it about death that fascinates you? Does death per se have a certain allure for you?

Since I began doing this work in the 1990s, I have focused on an aesthetics of the corpse, its various states of deterioration, and its many socio-cultural aspects, rather than on death itself. I work with the lifeless body, with the rotting corpse. I always begin with the same question: what has this corpse been through?

There have been several different phases in my work. I began by presenting the corpse in a way that showed the direct violence it had experienced. Then I began using cleansing instruments, which I felt expressed a symbolic value on their own, without any other props.

Because I received my PhD in forensic medicine and not in fine arts, my studio was the autopsy room – a source of social information full of political contradictions. By spending so much time in morgues, I have come to understand how a morgue can symbolize a country's current state.

Your work can be seen as part of performance traditions, particularly of Viennese Actionism and Latin American performance. During your last trip to Vienna in 2002, one of the first places you visited was an exhibition on the Viennese Actionists and a Hermann Nitsch series at the Museum Moderner Kunst. In several interviews, you have emphasized how influential Viennese Actionism has been for your work. Indeed, Viennese Actionism does not only focus on working with the body – even to the point of damaging it (especially in Brus's and Schwarzkogler's work); but a more central role is played by the poignant socio-political critiques (particularly by the Actionists artists such as Export, Weibel, or Mühl, for example in the 1968 action *Kunst und Revolution*), thoughts on religion, and ecclesiastic rituals (prominently in Nitsch's work). Regarding these points, do you see any affinity or great differences between the Viennese Actionists and your work?

The closest point of connection is the intention to radicalize the work and to test its limits using an obsessive and suffocating method. There was one phase when my work more closely resembled some of the Actionists' work, particularly Mühl's work on pain. My more recent pieces have stronger parallels to Nitsch's work on rites and religiousness…, although I am trying to employ as little theatricality as possible by operating with the concept of reality as the work's creator.

I was not really familiar with the pieces shown in the museum or with the quite impressive video footage. But the differences I see here are obviously my background and the era of the work's inception. Unlike the Actionists, I am not appealing to a post-war society that was increasingly becoming more bourgeois, rather I am speaking to a society where violence is almost a national custom and allegory and where the threshold of pain is extremely high (analgesia, desensitization, insensibility), lack of solidarity, and principle of individual struggle are becoming more important social standards.

Vienna is the city of the pomp funèbres. There are more people buried at the main cemetery Zentralfriedhof than actually live in the city. The term *schöne Leich'* [beautiful corpse] is used to describe a beautiful funeral, a concept that could make for an interesting topic of research in relation to your work. What could a *schöne Leich'* mean in regards to your work? What does death signify in society? How is the "culture of the corpse" in Mexico reflected in mass culture?

Unfortunately, most of the bodies I take as my subject of research have no potential of ever becoming (or receiving) a *schöne Leich'*. The majority of the corpses are those of marginalized persons who died a violent death and for whom there is no money available for their burial. In most cases, these bodies land in mass graves, and although their relatives could identify them, they simply do not have the means to cover the costs for even the most modest funeral.

I have been told that the burial/funerals take a long time in Austria and that is why bodies are embalmed. This allows for the dead person to be put on display (which I find fascinating) and gives friends and relatives time to hear the news and say goodbye. Your rituals are laid out, planned, and thoroughly organized. In order to survive in Mexico, people are subjected to the law of the jungle. In places where life is hard, so is death. The corpses mean something to the villages the people come from, but in the city they are only a number in a mass grave that is just waiting for them. It is less about a *schöne Leich'* and more about being forgotten.

Mexico is famous for its cult of the dead and celebrating the *Dia de los Muertos* (Day of the Dead). Does your work seek to forge a counterfactual link to a tradition that goes back many generations or to ironically subvert this tradition?

That is a question I am always asked. I understand why people ask it. It's because I am Mexican, but talking about the little skulls made of sugar and the paper skeleton cut-outs is the most simplified and superficial way of interpreting my work. I try to make my pieces that cannot be read in that way.

I want to show that death is non-fiction and I don't try to veil the cause of death and what happened. Like I said, I work with corpses and reality. I

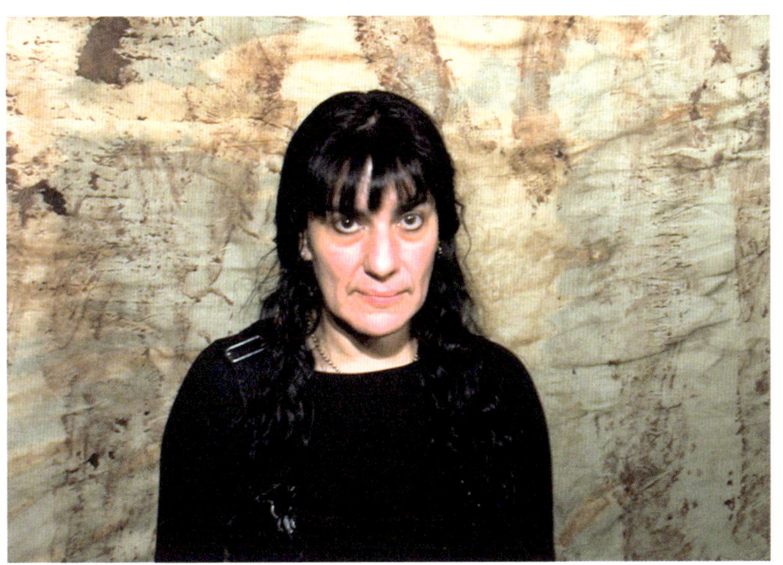

investigate who and why. Death and its traditional symbolic characters are not what interest me.

Your work achieves a certain intensity by shockingly confronting the audience with the epitome of the "other"-death. Do you seek to open up a transitory space or an interstice that disjoins people from their secure systems by also playing on a Baroque idea of the vanitas using contemporary means?

Yes.

Klaus Biesenbach called his exhibition on contemporary Mexican art *An Exhibition About the Exchange Rates of Bodies and Values*. Your work brings political positions and discussions of social problems into the exhibition space. What steps are involved in the encoding process? How do you see the transvaluation of political work through art?

The encoding process actually takes place on an instinctual or even irrational level. The conceptualization comes later.

From Ana Mendieta or Tania Bruguera to Coco Fusco, Latin American performance art is an art form dominated by women. The body is ascribed a central function in their work, but the traditions involving religious rituals and local social rules are even more significant. The object, be it a prop or an artwork, seems to play a more integral part here than it does in European performance art. Yet, several of your pieces draw a sharp line between the performing/representing figure of the artist and the object; for example, steam, bubbles, or the cloth all become "performing" objects. Have you received any inspiration for this from the art world?

Although SEMEFO's actions were largely theatrical in content, I always tried my best to avoid any type of protagonism on stage. I was more interested in observing the whole thing from the spectator's point of view. Now, I perform myself only if it is absolutely necessary. I ask others to perform in the actions and even let objects stand alone to realize a piece.

Your installation *The Shroud* ties together many aspects ranging from "reality" to "virtuality" with elements that are commonly understood as contradictions. On the one hand, there is a real piece of cloth that carries the real story of its function, its real bodily fluids and perspiration, and its seemingly "realistic" impressions and traces; and, on the other, there is the unknown story of a person's life and death, the mortal remains that left these traces, the absence of the body, the seemingly "informal" pictorial-aesthetic aspects of the traces, and the almost magically sacral air of the "vera icon" that evokes associations ....

To an audience unfamiliar with the history of this cloth or with everyday life and death in Mexico (City), this work is highly encoded. Is it possible that the refined sensory quality of your work enables some non-perceptible aspects to be decoded? Would you agree to being called an artist of sensorially loaded artifacts? In other words, are an aesthetics of reality (the real) a way to expand one's view of reality?

For the audience, the origins of the elements I use in my work evoke conflicting feelings. While they may experience disgust when they see the piece, it also evokes a strong sense of morbidity. Although the shroud's origin is horrific, it is still the mortal remains of people who died a violent death, people who are not missed, have not been buried, have continued to secrete pus for months on end, and who were wrapped in cloths drenched with embalming fluid—I render "aesthetically" visible what emerges from these processes.

When I think of *The Shroud*, along with the history behind its function as a holding area for up to fifteen corpses waiting for their autopsies, this work's context is also highly staged, theatrical, and object-based. How do you view this link between the theater/stage and your work? Which art forms other than performance or Actionism are central to your work?

I have tried to stay as far as possible from theatricality, but I do understand why you have mentioned it. In *Vaporización* (P.S.1, New York) I employed water used in morgues to wash corpses after their autopsies. I used this water to fog up the entire exhibition hall. This resulted in a staged piece in which the audience became the dramaturge of their own delusion – everything they needed to complete it was there. The piece I exhibited at the Galerie Peter Kilchmann in Switzerland used the same elements (water from the morgue in Mexico) minus the theatrical aspect (there was no fog). The result was a more convincing piece that is not at all dream-like. It is absolutely real and the audience can still play the part of the dramaturge.

Mexico City is a place that constantly attracts artists to move there. It is a city of immigration. On the one hand, this is a tradition – I am thinking of Wolfgang Pahlen, Juan Francisco Elso, and others – and, on the other, it is still going on today. In recent years, a host of European artists, such as Santiago Sierra, Francis Alys, and Melanie Smith, have moved to Mexico City. This makes for quite a unique art scene comprised of Mexican traditions and émigrés. What do you think it is about Mexico City that attracts so many artists? It has a certain air of "glamour" mixed with criminal pathos, chaos, and unlawfulness. How important is the artistic community for creating your work? How is the art scene structured? What kind of art/ist has been particularly influential for your work?

One of the things that make me want to stay in Mexico City is the city's

Installation view P.S.1, New York 2002: Teresa Margolles, *Vaporización*

ability to continually generate new things for me to address. Although I am not from Mexico City (I come from northern Mexico) I came to understand the true meaning of surrealism there.

Being an immigrant gave me the strength to stay in an extremely tough city. It also offered employment opportunities for me and, most importantly, I had the necessary emotional distance from the city for me to study it. There are elements I would not have been able to decode in my village, because I was too close. Culiacan, where I come from, is the region with the highest homicide rate due to acts of violence, most of which are related to drug trafficking. And, as you said, it has a certain appeal to foreigners, such as the people you mentioned.

The relationship between the art scene in Mexico City and the artists from other countries is quite particular. In the beginning, they are always accepted; but rejection inevitably follows, making most of them go back. Only very few have managed to stay. International criticism tends to pay a great amount of attention to those who stay, thus putting a spotlight on Mexico.

Of all of the artists you mentioned, Santiago Sierra is the only one I am in dialogue with.

What does Mexico City on the whole represent for you? How do you deal with the difficult economical situation and the high crime rate? Do you see your city as a danger, a threat, a challenge, a nightmare, or as a think tank?

The city never fails to present me with situations that push me to my emotional limits. Although I feel like I am under constant threat, there is also room to recuperate. I find the city's multiplicity nourishing. The city has an endless abundance of stories … and an unfathomable reality. Living in Mexico City has made me appreciate and urged me to discover other cities in the world – but I certainly also still view life according to my own parameters.

You use dead bodies as raw material on which there are traces from the subject's life, social status, and often also the cause of death. Are you also interested in life after death, in something beyond the transitoriness and interchangeability of the bodily matter so clearly visible in your work?

No.

Working with death and corpses are certainly social taboos. In a recent exhibition, you displayed a pierced tongue of a young drug addict who had been stabbed to death. You had received the tongue from the boy's family in exchange for financing the coffin for his funeral. Do you think that you could hurt people with this or other pieces? What do you say to charges of disrespecting human integrity and the dignity of the human body – dead or alive?

When I suggested using the boy's tongue for making a piece of art, the first person I felt sorry for was his mother. Her first reaction was to slap me. After she calmed down, she listened to me and understood why I had made that request. She not only agreed to it, but she also came to the exhibition opening with her son's friends. She understood that this would be her only opportunity to speak about the social degeneracy we live in and that maybe even those responsible for her son's death would not go unpunished. I am aware that not everyone can understand or accept my work. That is precisely the catharsis I look for in art.

Your work has definitely gone against the grain of "political correctness" again and again. Because it is so radical, you are often confronted with a lack of understanding or flat out rejection. Has your work been received differently within and outside of Mexico?

I certainly have experienced rejection, criticism, and censorship. All kinds of people, from my closest family members to art journalists, have accused me in several ways using "concretely" aggressive approaches. It is really amazing what kinds of insults art can provoke.

Critics and curators in Mexico have approached SEMEFO's work – particularly the most recently exhibited individual works by some of the group's former members – with a certain caution and distance. However, they have slowly become more convinced by these works and are starting to show an increased interest.

I have also received some notable funding from state institutions, particularly from the Fondo Nacional para la Cultura y las Artes (National Foundation for Culture and Arts), which has been the most important financial source for developing my work. I am often told that particularly in Germany, Austria, and Switzerland my work is seen by a very broad audience. Last October at the Kunst-Werke Berlin, I exhibited a wall that had been painted with liquid fat from human remains. The reviews in the press ranged from "the first artwork of the 21st century" (*Frankfurter Allgemeine Zeitung*) to "the wall of disgust" (*Bildzeitung)*. We'll see what the Viennese critics have to say.

What are your plans for this coming year? Do you have any concrete projects or areas of focus?

I will take part in the Göteborg International Biennial followed by an exhibition in Magazin4 in Bregenz and, in October, I will participate in *Outlook*, a large exhibition in Athens [curated by Christos Joachimides – Ed.]. I'd be interested in getting to know Central Europe better by staying in Zurich or maybe Poland for a while. I would like to do some artwork there in order to become more familiar these societies and their everyday life. And, of course, I'd love to be able to work in the morgues there.

Teresa Margolles in conversation with Gerald Matt in the spring of 2003 on the occasion of the exhibition *Teresa Margolles: Das Leichentuch* at Kunsthalle Wien project space.
Teresa Margolles was born in Culiacán, Sinaloa, Mexico in 1963. She lives and works in Mexico City.

German to English translation by Erika Doucette.

Video still: Teresa Margolles, *Grumo sobre la piel*, 2001
→

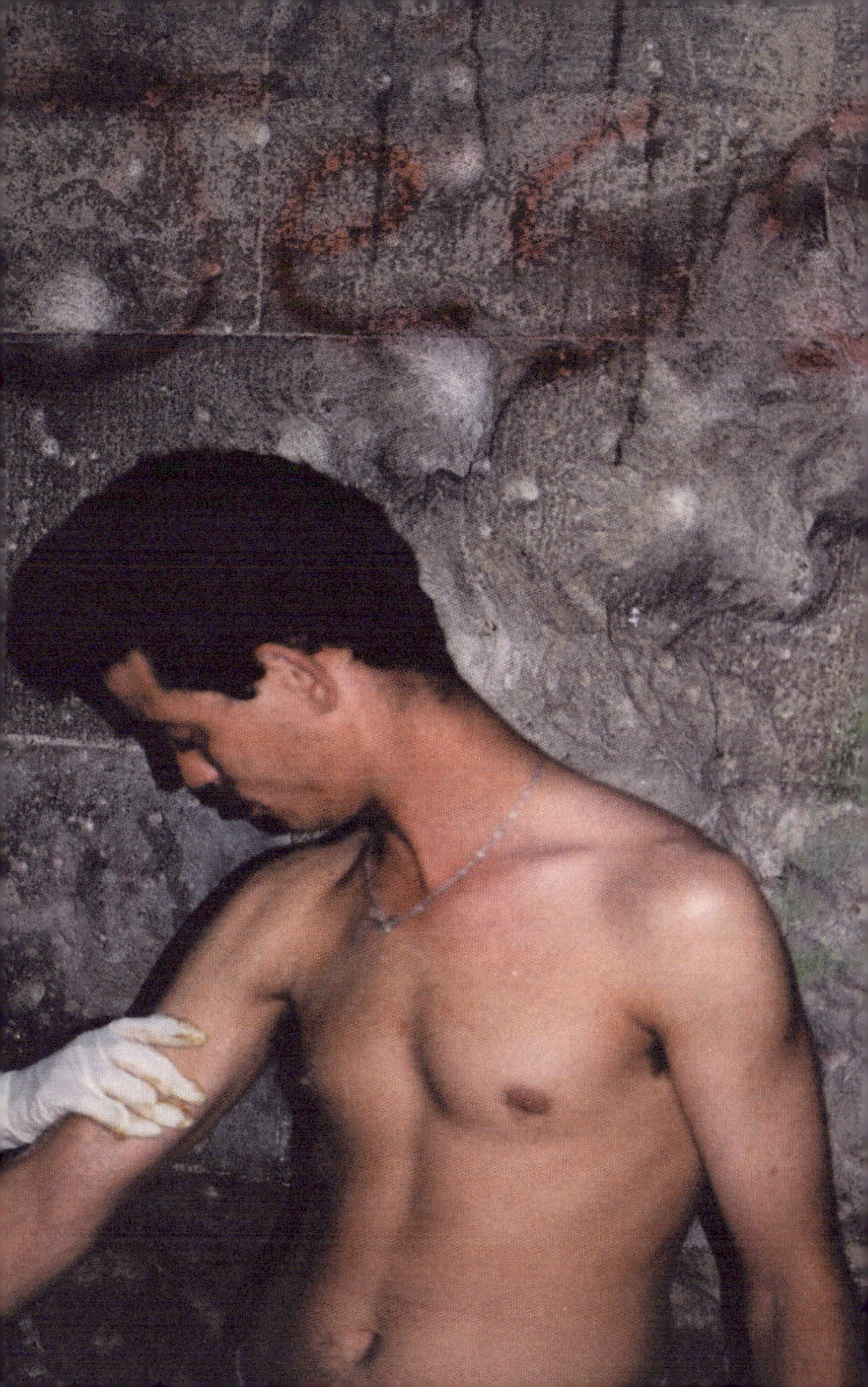

Tony Matelli

There's plenty of dispassionate crap in the world

Installation view, Kunsthalle
Wien project space 2004: Tony
Matelli, *Abandon*

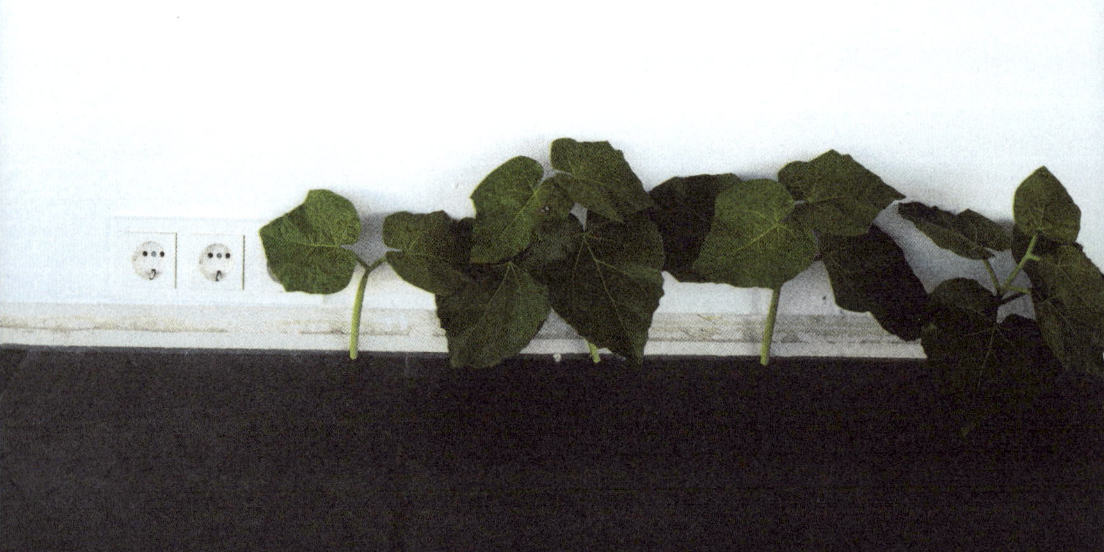

Your installation *Abandon* transforms the project space of the Kunsthalle Wien into an entropic environment. Because of its transparency, the exhibition space somehow encompasses the Karlsplatz area in the center of metropolitan Vienna. You fill the room with carefully mounted hyperreal weeds which seem to subjugate the urban architecture. If man does not continually put nature in its place he will soon be unable to ward it off. Are you fascinated by the tension between culture and nature, or is it back to nature you want?

> No. I'm interested in culture not nature. Nature holds no real meaning for me. I love what people do.

Bad weeds grow tall. On the quiet, almost everybody sympathizes with undesirable plants which, surviving in cracks and gaps despite the most adverse conditions, defy any gardener's planning will and offer resistance by their mere presence.

> Yes, that is exactly the attraction for me, and the idea expands very quickly. Weeds defy not only the efforts of the gardener but they are cultural renegades as well. They have been deemed undesirable, botanical outsiders. It was a matter of selection, and weeds were chosen to be the trash. So they also stand in defiance of or at least in counterpoint to the cultivated plants, orchids, lawns, whatever. They stand in defiance of cultivation itself. They are blemishes, and the more beautiful and quaffed a face the more powerful the blemish upon it is. That's perfect poetry to me.
>
> Weeds initially arose out of a desire to make a sculpture that would be rebellious forever, a sculpture that would question the value and significance of the things around it. I wanted everything to sort of fall apart around these sculptures, to be forced into an existential crisis. Even in an installation like this, when the weeds are alone, they call the room itself into question. A weed's mere presence brings these things up. Weeds are constantly being eradicated because they remain as nagging reminders of our fallibility and vanity. At the same time, they are heroic symbols. They're triumphant, unwanted but very successful. This has intense personal resonance with me. Weeds are the underdog.

Nature is a major classical theme in art history. The care and faithfulness your *Weeds* reveal make us think of Dürer's *Great Piece of Turf*. Yet, in contrast to Dürer, the harmony in your work creates disharmony, establishes a counterpoint. What do you think about Ian Hamilton Finlay's garden *Little Sparta* amidst the Scotch mountains?

> I can't think of anyone more perfectly opposite my interests than Ian Hamilton Finlay. There is no friction in that work at all. I always thought he was making gardens for people to contemplate Plato or Sophocles, the classics. It

is exactly this type of piousness that I hate in art. After all, wasn't he lamenting the fact that contemporary culture has obliterated the harmonious past and that we are living in a fractured and vulgar society? I don't like those sentiments of purity and correctness in art. This direction is ultraconservative; it makes art weak from overbreeding. Finlay's motivations seem aristocratic. Mine are not. This is the sort of fey culture that *Abandon* rejects outright.

Large Piece of Turf, on the other hand, seems kind of radical to me. It is a godless still life. It has none of the requisite symbolism or grandeur expected in art at the time. I'm guessing this was seen as a strange work, kind of below the accepted subject matter. I like the banality of it.

The transformation of order into disorder also characterizes some of your other works, such as *Sleep Walker*, the lifesize figure of a young man in rep underpants wandering through a room, or *Stray Dog*, a lost guide dog irritating the passersby at a corner in Brooklyn.

These pieces are born of self-reflection. They are personal. These kinds of malfunctions are powerful to me because I feel I am constantly breaking down. So *Sleep Walker* was made to capture my mood and what seemed like the mood of my friends at the time. A kind of fatal ambivalence. A denial of reality. This no-man's-land is a dangerous place, anything can happen. There is a kind of power in that social disconnection that I really love – total disregard. This sculpture takes that power everywhere. I love seeing this work in group shows because the sculpture is so unaware of everything around it, it's just going through the motions. It's aggressive to other works in that way.

Stray Dog is a bit more complicated because it was designed as a public sculpture. It needed to address the social world more directly. So I chose something that represents a social and domestic breakdown. Why would pets be wandering the streets unless something bad has happened at home? Stray dogs are emblematic of a kind of urban phenomenon that occurs only in the wrong neighborhoods. They are never in good neighborhoods, only in neighborhoods with serious conflict, domestic conflict.

The dog in this sculpture was not just a normal stray however; I chose the most extreme type of stray animal: a guide dog for the blind, the most responsible type of dog possible. These dogs are considered to be almost human; both beloved pets and depended upon assistants. This was important because the dog becomes a surrogate. It really represents the stray blind master, who is implicated only through his absence. It's a kind of two for one.

It was also important for me that the dog was lovable. So much public art is alienating. There is often no real difference between the glass buildings and the artwork. With *Stray Dog*, I made something that felt vulnerable, not authoritative like everything else.

What can realism achieve in art today? What is behind the deceptive likeness of things?

For me it's just a matter of conceptual clarity. I want my ideas to be seamless and direct. The weeds for example needed to look very real. I didn't want them to feel like sculptures. I didn't want their objecthood to get in the way of the idea. That's why there is no style involved. There is nothing to filter through, no artifice; there's very little art. That's also why there is no display mechanism at all. It is important that they be thought of as weeds before they are regarded as sculpture.

Also with other work that attempts to be, as you say, "deceptively" real, such as *Ideal Woman*, it was just a matter of taking it to the limit and making it as clean as possible. Conceptually, this is a very messy piece so the rendering needs to be very direct. That sculpture is about compressing reality and fantasy and needs to be very convincingly rendered so that the fantasy in a way becomes real. I love when things shed their objecthood in a way that allows for a more direct moral confrontation.

So it is not deception that I'm interested in, it is clarity. Some of my earlier work uses style as a conceptual component, a dialectical component. Maybe this is something I'll shift back to at some time in one way or another.

Many of your works are sculptures, some of them hyperreal, others, as you put it, "just real enough." Every passerby would categorize them as sculptures without hesitating in the least. Do you regard yourself as a sculptor first of all?

I love certain things sculpture can do. I love primarily that it's difficult. It can resist being reckoned as decoration. There is also a direct moral exchange involved because you confront it in your space. It is not just something that you behold. This shit is in your way; it's not always in its place, it's in yours.

I don't, however, have any desire to be thought of as specifically a sculptor. I'm uncomfortable with that type of language. I feel that other things, video, audio, and printmaking, can work for me just as well. I know a lot of artists who are really dedicated to their medium; they have a dialog with the medium. I don't have that sort of faithfulness. It's actually really boring to me.

The installation you realized in the "project space" of the Kunsthalle Wien am Karlsplatz also has a sculptural dimension which does not stand by itself. The *Lecture* is an integral part of the concept. How important is the performative element in your work?

This is the first time I've ever done a performance, and I wouldn't say that it was a very important part of the work. I conceived it as an accompaniment that would fold back upon itself, sort of color the work and push it further.

I have always believed that large ideas can be expressed in really simple ways. I think *Abandon* does this very well. It represents a breakdown, a failure or a refusal to fight the perfunctory battle against entropy. It is a refusal to play by the rules. A protest. One weed is a forgivable blemish, overgrowth is hopeless abandon. This happens with appearances, manners, everything. We have social rules to play by and disregarding them can be aggressive. I always think about this when I'm on the train and there is a homeless guy on board who smells like shit. Like really strong shit. I think, "he wants me to smell his shit," "he wants his shit in my face!" I can understand it that way. It is powerful and political.

Public inebriation is the same to me. It's a kind of erasure, a way of being present and absent simultaneously. It is a form of willful sleepwalking. I am drawn to that type of resistance or protest. I find it moving. You know, "I'll play by the rules but I'll shit my pants while I do." Private resistance. This is totally powerful to me; it appears over and over in my work.

So with the *lecture/performance* I wanted to take the refusal that the weeds represent and act that out in a human dimension, and in doing so implicate myself in this. Become the weed I suppose, or the sleepwalker. So what happens is I give the lecture, I attempt to impart information while being nearly comatose from alcohol, or drugs, or whatever. It culminates with me losing it, just puking on the lectern and myself. I can't contain myself any longer. I spill my guts. Vomiting is obviously a kind of motif in my work. It's simple: what can't be contained comes out. Consumption gone bad. It's my way of saying "NO!", of expressing rejection. Simple. The lecture is just a way of pushing things forward. The beginning of a new body of work.

Reckless Abandon was a performance, actually – a planned systematic booze-up, but it could not be announced as such. Do you still believe in the element of surprise, even in the white cube of the art scene?

My lecture/performance was not really about that. I didn't want anyone to know beforehand because I didn't want any expectations for some big special performance. I wanted to go more like: "I am an artist who tries to give form to my feelings" … CUE vomit. That's it.

Some of your work titles strike me as quite commonplace and descriptive, while others definitely require some explanation. A collection of most ordinary and trite indoor plants bears the title *Fuck the Rich*. How important is provocation as an artistic strategy for you?

I'm interested in provocation, especially when it's seductive. Then it becomes confusing. I also understand that there is a futility to it, that we are in this art space, and things get consumed and understood. That's the cycle of culture.

Bag of Shit on Fire has something of a schoolboy prank cast in synthetic resin. What does the artist want to tell us with this work?

I like pranks because they are ritualized expressions of contempt. I see them as the tip of a huge, insanely misanthropic iceberg. Pranks allow us to misbehave, they sort of function as therapy.

How did you realize the work technically?

Two assistants, a big studio, and hours of back-breaking, soul-deadening, mind-frying labor. It's an extremely boring story.

Steven Shearer describes part of his motivation to become an artist as the urge to be acknowledged by his peer group without having to participate in all events. Would you see yourself rather as the gang's front man?

No. One of my motivations to be an artist was to be useless, of no practical use to the world. You can do that as an artist and still be valuable.

Lost and Sick is one of your best known works. The three boyscouts in their garish colorful uniforms form a sharp contrast to the motto "Ever ready." Puking their guts up, they remind us of our own adolescent carousals – first booze-ups disguised as socially accepted events for the young, contrary to the intentions of the responsible organizations, of course.

I never thought of it as a drunken tableau. That didn't even really occur to me at the time. I was thinking they were puking out of stress and fear. I was trying to make a work that was emphatically about rejection. I wanted to depict a complete rejection of community. I wanted to make an antisocial sculpture.

The sculpture depicts boys who are learning about civic and familial responsibility, adulthood. That is what the Boy Scouts are all about: having good moral character. All these lessons that are to be internalized – responsibility, duty, honor, et cetera – are in this sculpture, being tossed up in total rejection.

It is also a depiction of failure. They are on the proving grounds of adulthood and are failing their first test. This is how I feel – never really up to the task, you know, not quite fit for service.

Formally speaking, Jake and Dinos Chapman's sculptures resemble your figures in a certain way. Do you see any parallels as regards your approach as an artist?

The horror in *Disasters of War* is evident, is manifest, for example. Your pieces have something funny but are profoundly irritating at the same time, they make you smile and give you the creeps.

Yes, I love that work, and superficial connections exist between it and my own things. I don't however see any parallels as far as what we are really up to. I always got the sense that those guys were just kind of fucking around. There's a kind of game playing involved, an equational logic that is directing their work. I don't get the feeling that there is anything personally at stake. You can see it even in their interview strategy, where they are talking only of theory, science and Freud; it's a real project. Their work is totally objective and dispassionate; it's like abstract art. I don't think there is any life left in maintaining that position.

What I'm interested in is something maybe much smaller and more intimate. I am much more concerned with making a personal kind of connection. I want a transparent kind of work. When people look at it I want them to know there is an artist in there, even if it gets a little sloppy. I really am coming from a Romantic position. A kind of skeptical Romanticism. I am trying to create a body of work filled with my own humanity, an artwork that is not so dislocated. This is the real power of art I think, and it has largely been ignored in contemporary art. It is one of the few products in the world that allows for this type of personal connection. I want to look at my work and have it mirror my personality over time; this would be a major success for me. I don't feel weird talking like this. I know it sounds sentimental but that's okay with me. There's plenty of dispassionate crap in the world, and I don't want to contribute to that pile.

Ideal Woman: You have given shape to the sexist joke of the ideal woman as a brainless blowjob machine with your female figure – 1.2 m tall, toothless, flat skull, oversized ears, disproportionately big hands and feet, pale and blotchy skin. She wears nothing but a slip, she is naked – not only in terms of what she wears but also in the sense of being exposed as regards her physical and obviously also her intellectual deficiency. And yet, the hesitating cordial gesture of her spread arms and her bashful and expectant smile have something warm and touching.

How is she brainless or intellectually deficient? I never had that in mind. That never had anything to do with it. We objectify ourselves and others all the time, and it's not because we're stupid but because it's fun or it's a means to an end. This sculpture is about that slippery negotiation of how much is too much. What is acceptable in a loving relationship? How much can it sustain? Maybe everything, maybe not.

The sculpture needed to feel warm and touching because it is not a negative sculpture. It is full of both positive and negative energy. It would

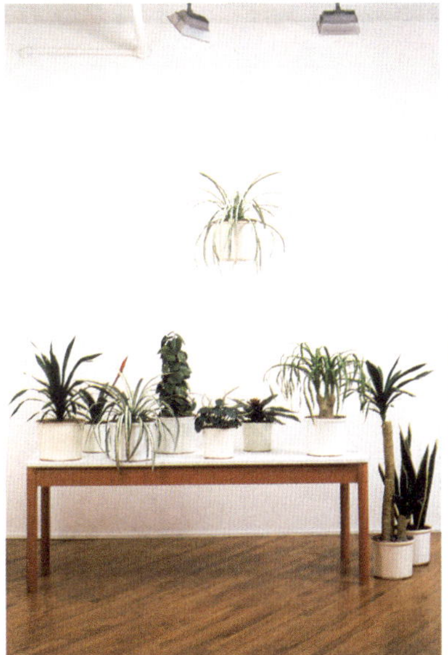
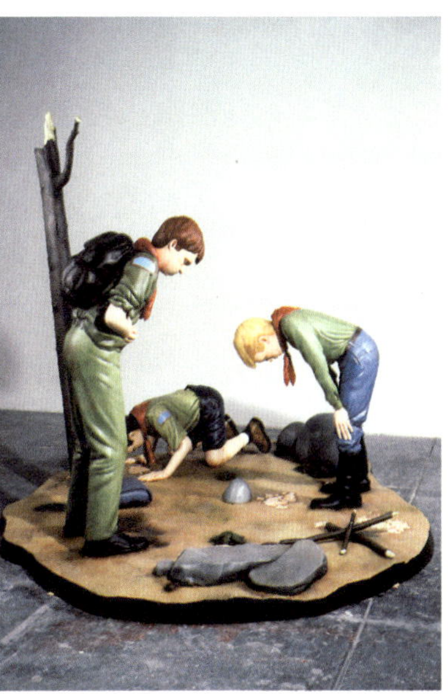

have been too easy if I approached it from the perspective that this perversion was wrong or somehow offensive. I wanted it to be sweet and loving. It's that incongruity that gives this work its potency; a loving depiction of something grotesque. I was trying to bring this piece of folklore to life to see if it could be integrated into my life, ethically. I wanted to see this joke physically rendered in front of me. The only way to make it dangerous and meaningful was to graft my girlfriend's likeness onto it. This way it could have a personal resonance, not just to me but also to the people who knew us. This work was about the capacity of love to sustain lust.

What about the importance of sexuality in your work? Is it a further Jacobean component of order that constitutes tomorrow's disorder?

Our desires shape our reality, sometimes in terrible ways.

In a faked fax to someone organizing an exhibition, which we come upon in the catalogue published by Leo Koenig in 2003, you apologize for your lack of professionalism and describe how disappointed you are about the lack of support. Could you outline your relationship to the art world and its mechanisms?

That fax was real. It was sent to a former dealer, at a time when I was losing my mind preparing for a show and he was calling me every day with questions. That is how it is for me before every show.

I don't think about the art world much. I try just to think about myself. The art world is filled with so much positioning for attention, and so many other artists: if I think too much about it I would be driven so deep into depression that I would never get out of bed. The thing that is great about being an artist is you can be in your own world for long periods of time. I love that. My life contains lots of make-believe.

You worked as an assistant for Jeff Koons, whose contribution to art was, as a critic once said, his uncompromising apotheosis of trite things: there's nothing behind anything, everything is surface. Did Koons's (post)ironical approach have an impact on your understanding of art?

I think most people get Koons wrong, especially Jeff. I see his work as totally subjective, full of longing and disappointment. He would emphatically disagree. He is very clear about the lack of connection the middle-class has to their emotions; they only cling to the emotive signifiers. Well, Jeff too has that problem. It's all over the work: pornography equals love, a puppy equals happiness, and soon it's all fetish and it feels like death. His work had a massive impact on me because of the seductive power he gave his ideas. That's a lesson everyone learned from him: that ideas must be seductive.

In a letter to your Stockholm gallery Andréhn-Schiptjenko, in which you discuss the *Total Torpor* installation, a sculpture that consists of artificial skulls, you mention your profound discontent with everything you have done so far and say that you, being fed up with those always clever ideas, want to leave the Pop shit behind. What is your attitude towards your own work?

I love almost everything I make. What I meant by that letter is that I can now see some of my missteps, and I know how to right them. I've been a little sloppy but now I am in a good position to clarify the ideas. I hope everything will make more sense in 5 or 10 years. The work is getting much better. My real concerns are starting to emerge.

Tony Matelli in conversation with Gerald Matt in January 2004 on the occasion of the exhibition *Tony Matelli: Abandon* at Kunsthalle Wien project space.
Tony Matelli was born in Chicago, Illinois in 1971. He lives and works in New York.

Steve McQueen

I'm interested not so much in what can be seen as in the experimental arrangement, or the axis around which the film will spin.

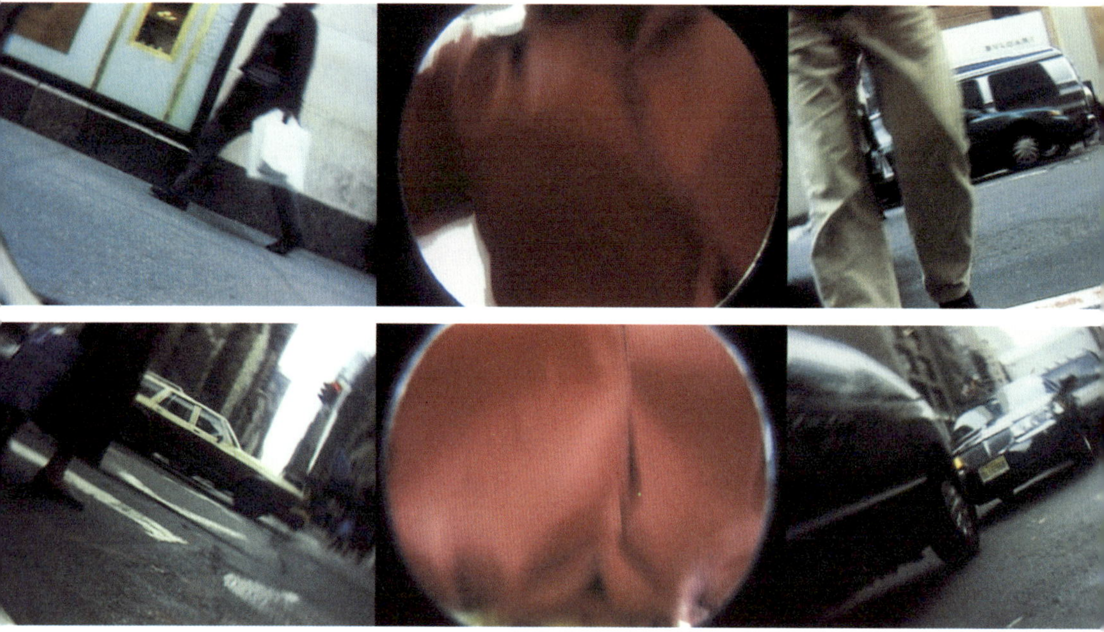

Video stills: Steve McQueen,
Drumroll, 1998

Mr McQueen, in your latest film, *Girls Tricky*, you have documented a recording session featuring the British pop musician Tricky. Jean-Luc Godard did something similar in the sixties. In *One Plus One* the Rolling Stones could be seen recording *Sympathy for the Devil*. Is there some mental connection here?

No, I had been interested in Tricky for some time, in fact, since I'd heard him with Massive Attack, a pop group he'd once collaborated with in the early nineties. After that, he made his famous solo album *Maxinquaye*. I was a fan from the outset. I considered Tricky, and still do, a very exceptional performer, singer and songwriter.

Are you interested in the décor as well, into which this artificial character of Tricky is cast? All those photographs depicting him in female attire, the explicitly sexual lyrics, his image as "the bad boy of music"?

No, I was primarily interested in Tricky as a recording artist. And I mean a radical artist who knows exactly what he wants and realizes what he aims for without reservations. People like this are rare in the pop scene. Of course he has to work within certain limitations – there are always limits. What I wanted to achieve in my film more than anything else was for the images to connect with the music.

Your work is almost an antithesis of the video clip. There are hardly any cuts, no visual exaltations. In a way you just keep watching the artist at work.

My work is certainly no polemical statement against the video clip. I just wanted to get as close to the artist as possible. If you watch ten people walking down the street, and Tricky is among them, he'll certainly be the most interesting of the ten. He has this certain *je ne sais quoi* – just like Marlon Brando or James Dean. Tricky possesses a certain spontaneity, which influenced the film. He is someone who entrusts himself to his own voice. And tries to find out where it may carry him. It's a rare moment that you see an artist so close, gearing himself up for a vocal performance in such a visual way, in effect, a moment not intended for the camera is being captured.

Did you have a specific set-up in the studio? Prepared camera angles, a certain narrative dramaturgy?

Tricky did his thing, and I pursued him with my camera, as closely as possible. Quite frequently he prefers to sing without any lights on, and one night it was in fact completely dark. On that occasion the camera of course was fighting a battle that was already lost.

The manner in which Tricky appears in your film, struggling for sounds, and seemingly losing himself, reminds me of the artist as the exemplary sufferer – a type of contemporary reincarnation of Saint Sebastian.

> I don't see it that way. He is in complete control of his performance – he can always definitely tell which take of a recording was the best one. He knows exactly what he's doing.

Did Tricky actually know you and your work before you approached him with this film project?

> He knew I had won the Turner Prize. That was certainly a starting point.

Do you feel an affinity to British pop music in general, or do you concentrate your interest exclusively on Tricky?

> As I said, to me he is quite an exceptional figure. In particular, also, because of his career decisions. He was so successful, he could have produced U2. Instead, he developed his own music further and allowed himself to drift into ever more arcane areas. He was taking risks.

Wouldn't it be a fascinating concept if your film about Tricky were to be shown on MTV? If you could, as it were, take an artistic work such as this like a Trojan horse and proceed into the heart of commercialism with it?

> We're having discussions with the record company about it. There are some points that still need clearing up, regarding the rights. But it would appeal to me, because this film is in every way the opposite of the MTV-perspective.

I noticed one thing about Tricky who, as an artist, has become known for his ambiquities, among other things. He has himself photographed wearing women's clothes, he explodes conventions of genre in his music and invents counterworlds of sound that oscillate restlessly without ever reaching a point of stasis. When I was watching your film *Bear* I was reminded of these ambivalences. There, one sees two men involved in fisty cuffs. But what never comes out quite clearly is whether they are aggressively fighting with each other or caressing one another or performing some kind of pas-de-deux dance. This hovering upon the cognitive threshold strikes me as something very seductive and at the same time bewildering.

> To me the matter is quite clear. We're dealing with the emotions of two men in a compressed, overheated situation. They may experience emotional charges, but I do not see the element of erotic ambivalence as being relevant to this. It is simply an emotional experiment acted out in front of the cam-

era. The possible discussion, as to whether these two guys are gay or not, did not enter my mind in this context.

How free are the actors in your films? Do you establish some advance choreography, which they have to follow as they move, or is everything created on the spot?

In *Bear* I played the one part myself, while the other part was played by Vernon Douglas, a great actor from the "Old Vic" theatre. We discussed the situation beforehand, and fixed a few movements and possible modes of reaction. But once the camera started rolling, we did exactly the opposite of what we'd agreed upon.

Can we, in looking at *Girls Tricky*, anticipate what direction the artist Steve McQueen will be heading in next? This has been, after all, your first collaboration with an acknowledged star.

I wouldn't think so. My work has not been any too homogeneous in the past.

The public however views you as the artist who makes black-and-white films without any sound. The fact that you are using more colour now serves to disturb this beautiful static image somewhat.

That is a matter of complete indifference to me.

Critics and the public alike tend to search for points of reference, in order to place a work of art into a context, into a system of coordinates, in order to help them with orientation. And, after all, references of this kind are abundantly present in your work. In the film *Deadpan*, you paraphrase a famous Buster Keaton-scene, while in *Five Easy Pieces*, reference is made to a film by director Bob Rafaelson.

These references and choices of title have been quite deliberately employed. The original film, *Five Easy Pieces*, is a kind of foil. It's the story of a man who cuts off his entire past and becomes a blue–collar worker. He hears his father is dying and he has to return to his upper middle class family. His girl friend finally discovers the whole truth about his dual identity. It's all about hiding the past, which is what interested me about it; the fact that things are not what they seem. We always know only as much as the man in the story is prepared to tell us. I wanted to convey something of this in my work, by completely different means. In addition, there's the rather more formal aspect that my film actually consists of five separate pieces.

There is, particularly here in Austria, a strong tradition of the abstract, structural

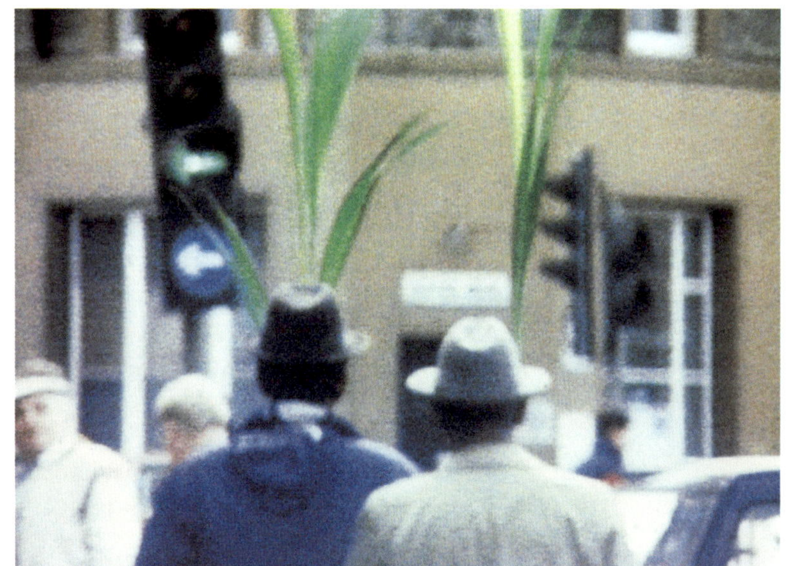

Video still: Steve
McQueen, *Exodus*,
1992/1997

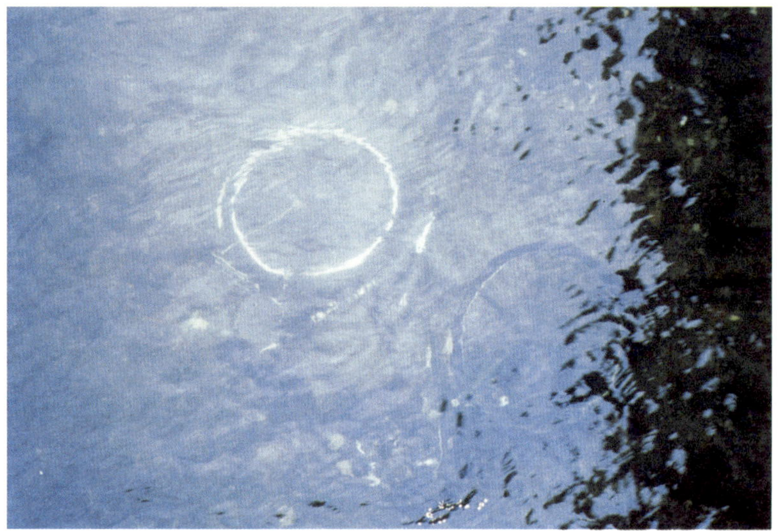

Steve McQueen,
Current, 1999

avant-garde film. These are works that will test different types of material and drive film up to the limits of its own negation. In your works, on the other hand, there are always people at the center. In this way, entirely different emotional registers are pulled when the public views your films. There is always at least some rudimentary narrative, some depiction of somebody's "fate".

It's possible, but to me that's rather a secondary aspect. I'm interested not so much in what can be seen as in the experimental arrangement, or the axis around which the film will spin. In *Drumroll*, for example, the central idea was that three cameras would be rolling through New York City inside some oil drums. This was the best way for me to document a very specific urban situation. Everything was filmed. People in the street, I myself. Everything was perfect, I could do no wrong. I felt almost like a musician. All I had to do was to keep this oil drum rolling almost like keeping a beat. The chaos that was recorded of people, cars, trucks, etc. was almost like improvisation. Everything that slipped into the frame was permitted, it was impossible to make a 'mistake', everything was allowed.

I take it from this description that you like to define a basic situation but then allow yourself to be surprised by your own film. Coincidences, spontaneous decisions seem to play a marked role.

I don't want to be working too close to a schedule. Things simply happen, and these occurrences should be part of the creative act. One has to find a way to handle such a situation.

Do you shoot a lot of footage that doesn't get used in the final version of a film? Do you have, as it were, sizeable material overhangs?

Not really. I like it if my work becomes a kind of tightrope dance. I don't fiddle around much. The first take usually is the best.

One final question. Any idea what your next project will be?

Working with a large crew?

Steve McQueen in conversation with Gerald Matt in 2001 on the occasion of the exhibition *Steve McQueen* at Kunsthalle Wien.
Steve McQueen was born in London, in 1969. He lives and works in London.

Tracey Moffatt

I think all my imagery comes from my subconscious, from dreams.

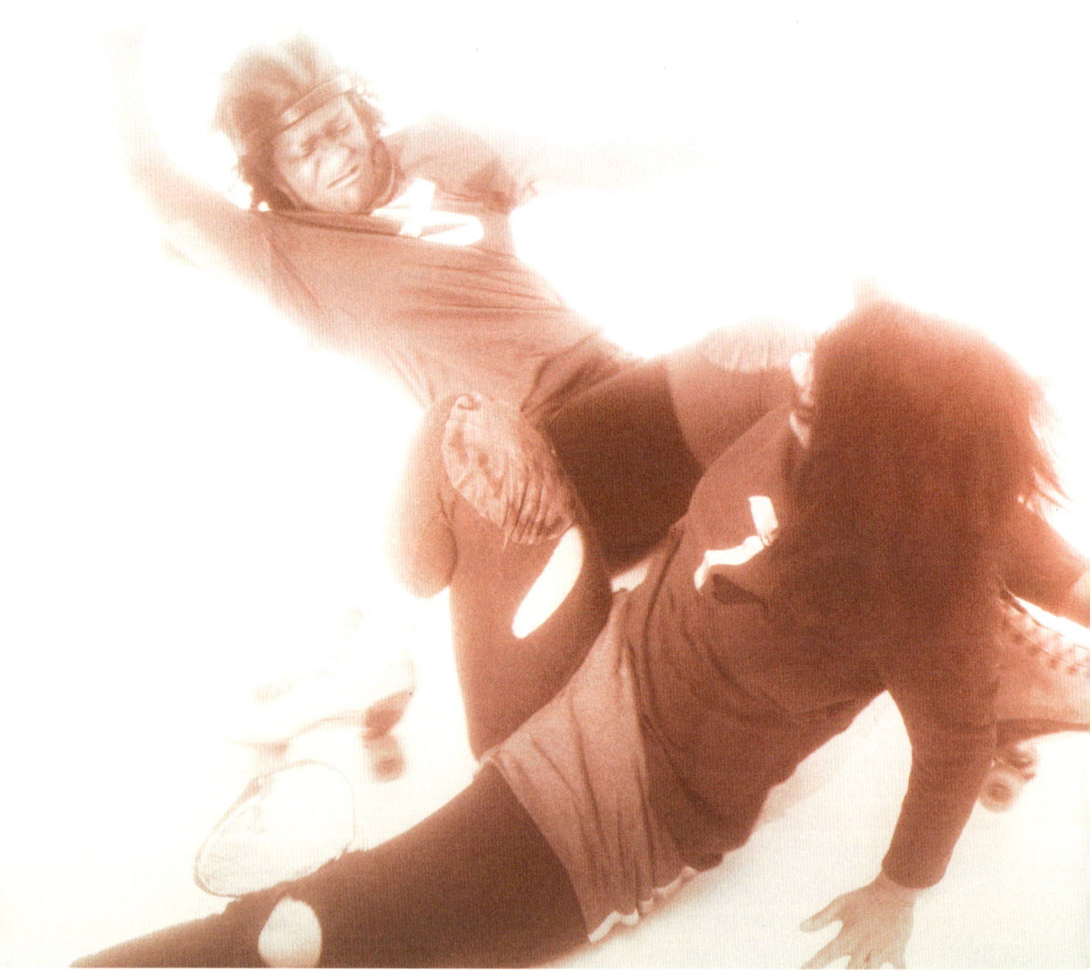

Tracey Moffatt, *GUAPA* (*Goodlooking*) # 6, 1995

Deleuze and Parnet once said: "Empiricists are not theoreticians, they are experimenters: they never interpret."

Do you see yourself as more of an "experimenting artist" – within the meaning of the above quote – even though your works are based on detailed preparations and concepts?

The most interesting artists in history have always been experimenting artists. Most artists I know are such dissatisfied people, dissatisfied with everything, so of course they must constantly be reinventing with their art. Perhaps this dissatisfaction is the reason that they are artists in the first place – I know it is with me.

Although I make careful detailed preparations before I work in my films and photography, one must always be open to elements of surprise that do surface. I can have an original idea for an image and plan it out but the final outcome can be something different. My final image of choice can have a slightly different mood and feel. Most of the time it is better.

In an interview, you called yourself an "image maker". The pictures you make are cinematographic or photographic, using media that reproduce reality. However, your pictures are characterized by an alienation of reality, partly by exaggeration, by surreality. When referring to your representations of nature, you like using the expression "landscape of imagination". In interviews and texts, reference is made to aboriginal art, dreams, some genres of film or painting in this context. What is the relation between realistic and fictitious means, especially when it comes to getting messages across?

I think all my imagery comes from my subconscious, from dreams. I am not talking about when I dream at night (these are far too weird and sick) but the dreams I have when I am awake. We can dream with our eyes open. This is why I have been very hesitant to be written about as a social commentator. I think my work is very dream-like.

The *Up in the Sky* pictures look a little like photo documentary, but there is still a surreal quality. Some of the images are in fact what I saw and photographed but most are staged up, set up. I like that people can't tell which is which, I like that there is an "in-betweenness" about them.

In the *Guapa* pictures the women roller derby queens are obviously shot in a studio. I wanted it to feel like a nowhere space. I like that the images lack a time frame – they're just hanging there.

What are the most significant sources you tap into when creating the fictitious/artificial part of your pictures?

I like to create my version of reality, the work comes from me, what I know. Things I have seen and experienced, and things I think I have seen and experienced. Maybe it's just an exaggerated version of my reality. Sources of inspiration come from everywhere, from the beautiful formal quality of 1960's Japanese cinema – films such as Kabayoshi's *Kwaidan* (1964). This was a film of four ghost stories shot entirely in a studio with artificial sets – Kabayoshi apparently even painted the sky backdrop himself.

But then I can look at trash-TV. This is what I grew up with, I didn't grow up with High-culture, so for me as far as visual went it was television. I am from a working class background, and I was only accessing what was available. But thank god I also read a lot – everything from Charles Dickens and the Brontës to comic books (which I would beat my brother up for) to soft porn (which I would take to school to be popular with).

Were there any more specific films important for your work – e.g. the bizarre Australian cinema classic, Charles Chauvel's *Jedda* from 1955? And what about horror movies?

Jedda was an overblown melodramatic and I think racist Australian film made in the style of a Hollywood western. It was about an Aboriginal girl taken from her tribe and raised by a family as a white girl on a desert cattle property. I cannot bring myself to say that *Jedda* was an "important" film, but I certainly liked the look of it. I recreated the interior set of the cattle property's main house and put it into my own short film *Night Cries*.

Most of all I suppose it is the visual element in certain cinema that is inspiring me. But feel and mood often come from literature, and in particular southern American writers such as Tennessee Williams, Truman Capote and the great Carson McCullers – a woman writer who I believe originally inspired Truman Capote. These writings always remind me of where I come from – the North of Australia, the sub-tropics. In a sense a holiday paradise – the heat, the joy, but also the terrible mood of fear and racism. This mood is evident in my *Something More* photo series.

As for horror film I think nothing has ever matched Hollywood's *The Exorcist*. It's the scariest film ever made.

I like a lot of Hollywood movies, I like the Italian American directors like Martin Scorsese, I like *Terminator II* and the *Mad Max* trilogy – it is the big spectacle that appeals.

But I always have a weakness for anything European – made before 1970 and in black and white like the dream films of Jean Cocteau. What an artist he was! His skill in changing between the different media – he made films, he wrote plays and designed for the theatre and what about his beautiful drawings. One of his famous quotes is: "When the pillow is warm you must turn it over …" For me he is the artist's artist.

What about painting, as an artistic language, also in respect of its flexibility in creation?

You know, when it comes down to it, I wish I was a painter. There isn't anything greater and nothing hypnotises like painting. Nothing fascinates more than what the human hand can do. I think for 99 percent of people, to this day photography and film is a foreign media. It is technical, expensive and most people don't get the chance to try it.

From an early age, all of us in every culture in the world have been handed a pencil, a brush and some paper. From the first day of school we are made to make our mark, but very soon most of us discover to our horror that we can't do it – except for Johnny in the next row. Does Johnny grow up to become an artist? Very rarely.

So for most of us, this must be the first tragic inadequate thing we find out about ourselves – that we can't move paint around. I know that I can't move paint around, you can look at my awful storyboards to see this – so I moved into other areas. Perhaps my work is all about painting – sometimes writers describe my "palette". This delights me.

I would like to mention Georgia O'Keeffe. I first came across her in art school, there was a revival of her in the early eighties. The interesting thing about her was that she was completely American and that she wasn't looking a real lot to Europe for her sources.

Susan Sontag once said: "Only that which narrates can make us understand." Your films and photo series also often have a narrative element. How important is the narrative for your work – e.g. from the angle of linking real and artificial components? Does it serve to enhance understanding, the way Sontag said?

My work is full of emotion and drama, you can get to that drama by using a narrative, and my narratives are usually very simple, but I twist it. In the *Up in the Sky* pictures there is a story line, but the hanging order of the pictures can change it around. There isn't a traditional beginning, middle and end. You can be in the present and shift to the past and come back to the present – it's playing with time and space.

As for Sontag's saying that "only what narrates can make us understand" – unfortunately in the case of what I do and the reactions I've had from a lot of people – my twisted narratives only serve to *baffle*!

Would you link the historically or culturally significant traditions you use in your works (e.g. *ghost stories* of the Aborigines or the cycle of Irish legends in *BeDevil*) with the notion of mythology? How would you define this notion, which you actually do not use yourself as far as I know, and how does it relate to your work?

It is a personal mythology that I use. I wouldn't say that I was drawing on Aboriginal legends, stories because I think that is too easy and I actually think that I don't have a right to do it. My images are so personal that a lot of the time they embarrass me. I'm always saying: "Oh my god, don't make me watch *Night Cries* again!"

For me the film is deep and it probably has something to do with my relationship with my mother – the love, the hate. I made this film at a time when I had these feelings but now I don't have them anymore. Must be a Freudian thing when artists say that their work "repulses them". Look at Woody Allen, he can't stand to look at his films, so don't make me look at mine.

"Multi-cultural" is a buzzword frequently applied to your work. Occasionally, I believe I can detect ironic elements when you deal with ethno-social themes, expressed e.g. in the idea of trading roles or plays on clichés (as in *Nice Colored Girls*). Is there a political intention behind your work? How do the respective ethnic communities react to your way of representation?

Within all my work I want to create a world, a general world. Australia is a very multicultural nation and this has certainly influenced my work. So I don't want to make some grand statement on race – it isn't about wanting to be politically correct, perhaps it's about always striving for an "international" look to my work.

I have made political films. Once in 1983 I worked on a documentary about an Aboriginal land rights protest which was both exhilarating and a nightmare. Some members of the group or rather the "collective" I made it with didn't agree with the film so they destroyed it (literally with scissors – on the night of the film's premier they chopped up nine months of hard work) and it was never seen.

This incident turned me off making political films. But the irony is, and we all know this today, that these important well-made documentaries about issues like indigenous land rights and the nuclear disarmament and the environment really did help to reveal things – educate the public and change the world.

I want to say that if people want to read my art that I'm making now from a political perspective then they are welcome. I just get a little exasperated because this reading usually comes from the "left" and they are most of the time ignoring how I strive for poetry and make statements about the human condition – they can't see that I'm trying to play with form and be inventive.

I think that the fact that I'm trying for a "universal" quality, not just "black Australian" is the reason that my work is getting attention.

But try telling this to some writers … they get stuck on their own trip, their own interests, you know what I mean.

The artificial part of your work also includes the formal aspect of fabrication, staging, choreography in your pictures. This is true of many of your films and

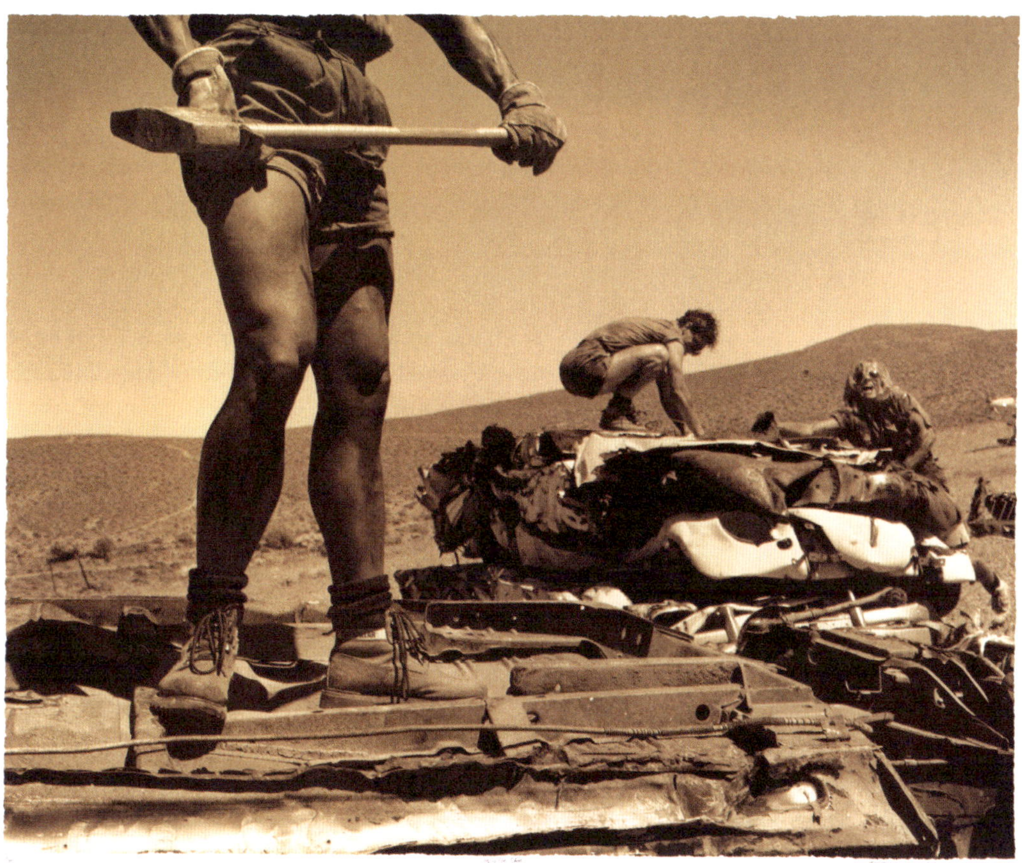

photo series. Moreover, some critics think that your photo series have "still photography" qualities. This is corroborated by a look at your storyboards.

I have never just produced a single photograph and tried to make it stand alone as an artistic statement. Though, of course, art collectors have bought single images from my series – so perhaps certain pictures do appeal by themselves. For me it is always the narrative. It is difficult for me to say anything in one single image.

With working in a photographic serial, I can expand one idea – give it further possibilities. It makes photography close to film in its possibilities.

Every photo series changes completely in look – colour or no colour – glossy or matt – big or small. I don't believe that I have an identifiable style, because I don't do the same thing twice.

I don't think one can readily look at my pictures and say "oh yes this is a Tracey Moffatt". Not in the way you can say this with a Robert Mapplethorpe print. When I first saw a Mapplethorpe picture I couldn't get over the shocking deadly precision in them – they were like ice. Photography never looked liked that, before him – now it is commonplace, it's everywhere – in advertising especially.

With the *Scarred For Life* photo series, I have again changed the format. I have integrated rather ordinary washedout colour compositions with text describing the scene. I was inspired by looking at 1960's American *Life* magazine layouts. A kind of snap shot photography – very everyday moments based on real life, tragic funny childhood stories of my friends and myself.

I felt that this was the only way to keep power in the image – to be ordinary, it does resonate. People remember the little boy giving birth to the doll. I could have shot this in a more clever dramatic way but in the end it had to be like a scene one would see as they passed and glanced in the living room door. In the case of this picture, it is the mean mother's point of view.

Also, as well, at the time I made this work I had no money – it was a purely practical thing to produce something low key and inexpensive.

Now (in 1998) I have more money and I'm making an elaborate photo series based on historical erotic texts. Please don't ask me to say more on this – I believe it is bad luck to talk an idea up too much before you execute it. Just shut the hell up and do it, is my motto – words are cheap!

What are the specific qualities film and photography have for you (e.g. as regards immobility/movement, and reception)? How much leeway is there – for example – for spontaneity in your photographs and films? Where do you place yourself?

I love both film and photography. I don't want to create a division. My relationship to both film and photography has to do with, as I mentioned previously, such things as money. It is a long time in between film projects – film costs so much money and you have to find this money. So in the meantime I'm going crazy – my obsession to create makes me crabby.

Photography is much less expensive – less equipment needed – smaller teams to work with, etc. Photography is always a wonderful challenge, it is all about what one can pull off with a camera, it's the way you use a camera and then how you choose to print the images – so many possibilities it is mind boggling. Of course, now with computer manipulations, the possibilities make you exhausted even thinking about it.

I like the art world as well as opposed to the film world (though both can be just as pretentious. I've just gotten sick of being literally pushed around at those crowded loud international film festivals – although I guess the Venice Biennale is not different!)

I like seeing things on white walls. The contemporary art world is light years ahead in ideas. So often it is much more rewarding intellectually for me to have "exhibitions" as opposed to "film screenings". Let's face it, hardly anything (save a few things) inventive and stimulating and beautiful has been made in cinema past the date of 1977. I have a theory about this but won't go into it now. Don't start me off!

In your works you frequently appear as a performer (*Something More*, *Pet Thang*, *BeDevil*, *Scarred For Life*). What is the part that autobiographical elements play for you, in the context of self-expression on the one hand, and in the engagement with more general social, cultural and political themes on the other?

It is often a technically practical thing to cast myself in my work. Often I can't find anyone else to do it – often as well a money saving thing. It feels as natural for me to be in front of a camera as behind it.

In fact I have never analysed this – as I try not to with most things. When one is too academic it gets in the way of creation. I have no precise plans to appear in my future films or photographs. It's not like I'm Cindy Sherman (I do love her fat ugly wizard series from 1996!).

I like to direct and cast other people, though this is always *the* hardest thing in the creation of my art – to find the right face. I go insane running after people I see on the street and often I get insulted!

Maybe the autobiographical aspects in my work have to do with using myself – probably it is as simple as this.

In an interview you once said that you were a "control freak". You also direct your films, as you told before. For your photo series you recruit professional teams, work in studios, with actors and props, similar to a movie production. You are scriptwriter, performer/actress and director, all rolled into one. The fact that you fulfil such a multiplicity of functions indicates that you, as an avant-garde film-maker, have the greatest possible share in the work, but the massive expenditure involved in the production also points to commercial cinema.

Control freak? Yes! I do want everything my way – to begin with. One has to keep some type of control. But I love teamwork nevertheless. If I didn't like to work with people I would be a painter – like my fantasy – alone in my studio with my brushes and canvases and paint in my hair, with the telephone answering machine on at all times.

But I like communication – I think I can communicate well though I'm demanding (no one has ever told me I'm a bitch to work with – they all come back and work with me again!)

I like to bring the best out in my collaborators. They are always throwing in their ideas – how can they not contribute? They are creative people whom I choose for a reason and I'm lucky to be working with them.

For example, for my film *Night Cries*, I worked with a wonderful theatre designer, Stephen Curtis, who created a very hard artificial desert landscape of the Australian outback. I initially wasn't so sure about it being so hard but I went with his interpretation of my script. Now, of course, I like what he did. When the film premiered at Cannes Film Festival – seven years ago – some critics thought that I was influenced by Robert Wilson, the avant-garde American theatre director. At the time, I was not familiar with Robert Wilson's work.

So I can either take my creative teams' ideas on board or not use them. But initially it is always Ms. Moffatt's ideas and obsessions they are helping to put on the gallery wall or on the big screen. None of them should complain because I always pay them well!

Is the boundary between avant-garde film and mainstream movie of any importance to you? Could you imagine working in something like "mainstream cinema" in the future?

I do want to make a mainstream film. I'm working on a film script now which I cry over because it is so hard to do. It will be as challenging as anything I've ever tried to pull off.

As an artist you must face change. This also has to do with my energy – I always want to move on to the next thing. I think it is fine to switch between worlds like loving both trash and classical and obscure literature and going from Antonioni to Schwarzenegger.

But one of the main reasons as I regretfully rocket towards forty … is that I want to finally make some money.

Tracey Moffatt in conversation with Gerald Matt in 1998 on the occasion of the exhibition *Tracey Moffatt: An Australian View* at Kunsthalle Wien.
Tracey Moffatt was born in Brisbane, Australia in 1960. She lives and works in New York.

Shirin Neshat

The challenge lies in the balance I have to strike between the originality of an idea and the thread of universality.

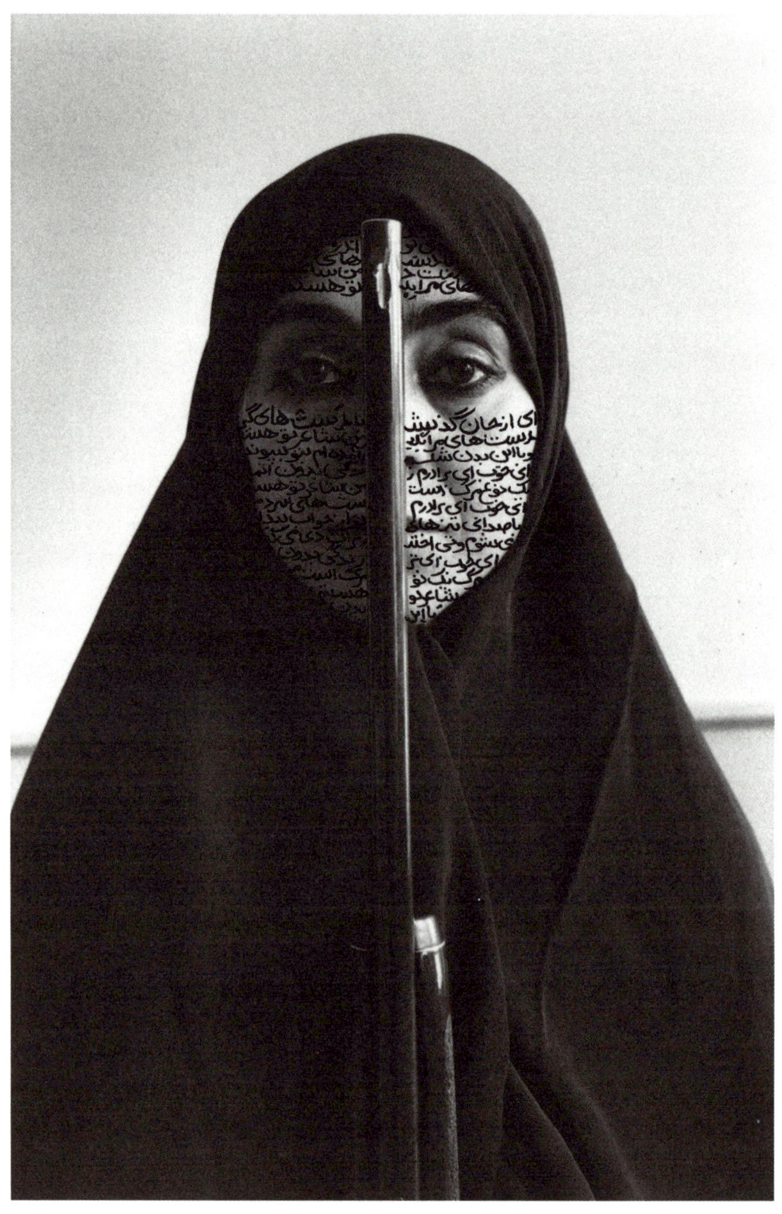

Shirin Neshat,
Rebellious Silence, 1994

Your work is frequently presented in the context of projects or exhibitions concerned with a dialogue between different cultures. Having been raised in Iran and living in the USA, you not only stand between two cultures, but also take your artistic inspirations from these very divergent cultural backgrounds. At the same time, you do not have a certain audience in either of the two cultures, as Hamid Dabashi said. To what extent do you consider a dialogue between the poles of exoticism – which is how your work is perceived in the West – and provocation – which is how your work is seen in Iran – to be at all possible?

When I am in the process of making a work, I try to focus on the importance of the concept within its own cultural context, as opposed to its connections with other cultures or my position as a cross-cultural artist. It is absolutely critical for me to present the subject within its own terms to retain purity and not being bogged down by the pressure of cross-cultural parallels. The point is how to address culturally specific issues, which are heavily based on particular socio-political agendas in a way that is of universal value on an emotional, intuitive level. The challenge lies in the balance I have to strike between the originality of an idea and the thread of universality.

Different cultures impose different boundaries. Referring to Iranian film-makers and censorship in Iran, you once said that the existence of borders enforces a need to get to the core of things. Which are the limitations that you are subject to as an artist, and what is their influence on your work?

When I began to focus on the traditional and philosophical ideas behind Islam, particularly in relation to women, I decided to remain within the framework of the social, cultural and religious codes, to maintain the given boundaries, as I believe to have done otherwise would have been disrespectful and simply reactionary. Once I had established this pattern, I was faced with an incredibly reduced number of elements of representation. This reduction offered me a sense of clarity, of simplicity that seemed to imply the possibility of penetrating more deeply into the subject.

I have often referred to the Iranian cinema after the Islamic Revolution as a major inspiration in how it has created a language that, although remaining within the confines of the social codes, so profoundly expresses the cultural subtleties that would have been otherwise extremely difficult to detect. The approach is simple, concise, poetic, minimalist and powerful as it criticises society without claiming to do so. I think that these filmmakers have discovered a new approach that thrives on the very poverty of the possibilities and creates works of great substance with a universal meaning.

So far, the criticism and reception of your work has focused primarily on the questions you have raised about feminism and fundamentalism. However, the veiled woman wearing a chador is no mere victim. She enters the picture with a direct gaze, as a strong, active personality. Your work highlights the complexities of Islamic womanhood and poses questions ranging from patriarchy to colonialism. Aren't you concerned with putting the system of values and the viewers' conceptions to the test rather than with making political statements?

I see my work as a visual discourse on the subjects of feminism and contemporary Islam – a discourse that puts certain myths and realities to the test, claiming that they are far more complex than most of us have imagined. It is very important to point out however that I don't see myself as an expert on this subject. I rather consider myself as a passionate inquirer. I prefer raising questions as opposed to answering them as I am totally unable to do otherwise, and I am not interested in creating works that simply state my personal political point of view. Some of the questions my works raise with regard to Islamic societies, particularly in Iran, have been addressed in the recent academic discourse. But while academic analysis obviously results in a purely factual and theoretical dialogue, my approach as a visual artist fuses facts and the subliminal. This method in a way universalises the subject and allows a more open interpretation.

You are very involved in architecture and, as co-director of the New York Storefront for Art and Architecture, have collaborated with various architects. How has thinking about defined spaces influenced your conceptualisation of images? You seem to distinguish between male and female spaces in the world of Islam.

My involvement with the Storefront for Art and Architecture, which lasted for about ten years, was pivotal for the development of my personal work. Apart from the fantastic exposure, the Storefront offered me a chance to get to know the latest theoretical and aesthetic developments in architecture. There were several aspects that fascinated me as an artist. While visual art always remains completely independent and unaffected by other fields and even functions on a purely intuitive level, architecture only exists within a complex relation with other fields and issues. As the very premise of architecture is building, it cannot remain neutral to the reality of functionality, community, tradition and cities. The Storefront's programmes concentrated as much on the presentation of architects' research and developmental processes as on the final results. When I began to formulate my own ideas, I eventually leaned towards a similar methodology where information and research became crucial aspects of my work.

What also continues to fascinate me is the integral relation between architecture and cultural studies. Architecture seems to be a reflection of a culture because it embodies its ideological history. As I became increasingly involved with Islamic topics, it seemed only appropriate to explore space and architecture from the ideological point of view. I came upon interest-

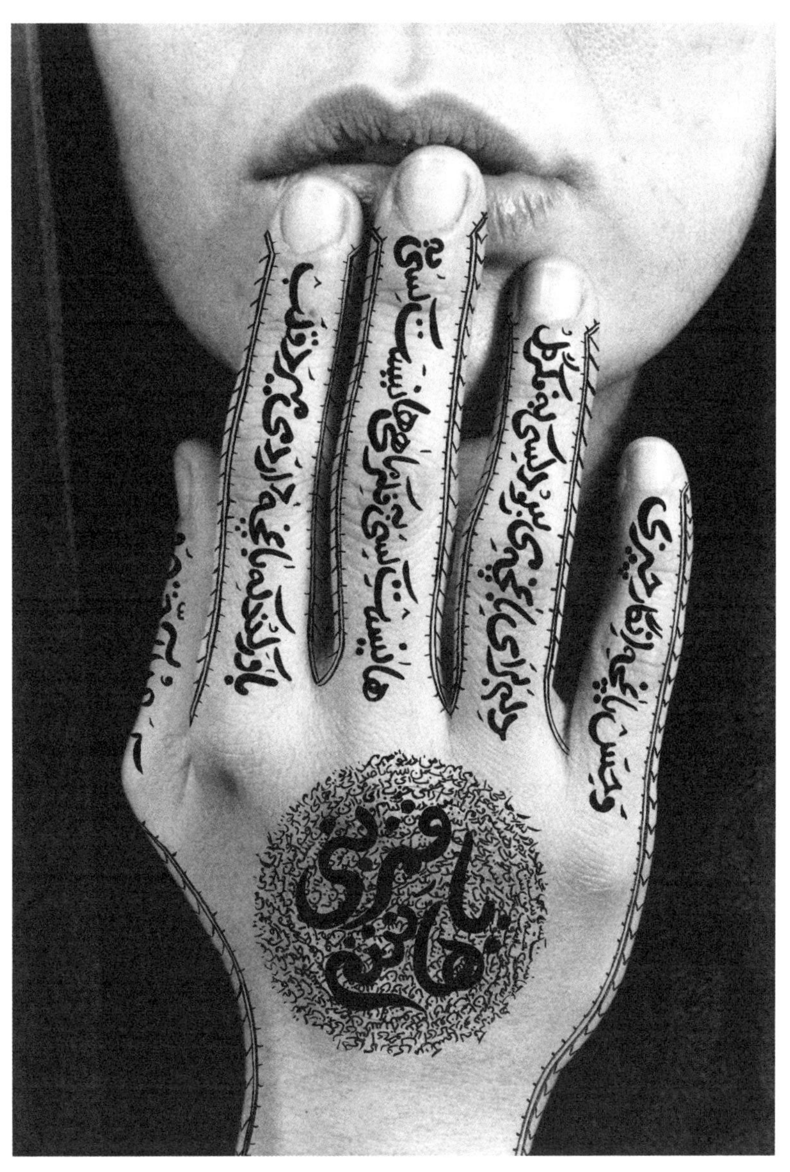

ing parallels concerning the way in which the female body and space are defined, controlled and coded. *The Shadow Under the Web*, made in Istanbul in 1997, is a project that precisely addresses such issues. It reveals how the division of space has been organised ideologically in order to separate the sexes and clarify their roles in societies. For that matter, public space is considered as 'male space', while private space is considered as 'female space'. Since the female body represents ideas of sexuality and individuality, which, distracting men from their duties, are considered problematic in a public domain, women must conceal their bodies by wearing a veil to neutralise their presence. In another film project, *Soliloquy*, which I realised in Turkey and in the United States in 1999, architecture is the core of the narrative since it represents two opposite cultures: the East and the West, the traditional and the modern, the communal and the individual.

You frequently appear in your photographs and films. Is there some pragmatic necessity for this, or is it an artistic strategy?

From the very beginning, performing has been a major aspect of my work. Ironically, I myself have always been uneasy in the presence of a camera. However, when I started with my photographic series *Women of Allah* in 1993, I decided to participate in the work as a performer as the project centred so much on the female body, specifically that of an Iranian woman of my age. Investing my own flesh somehow seemed to guarantee a sense of intimacy that prevented the work from becoming a propaganda or documentary piece. When the production became more complex and the conceptual approach changed, I decided not to appear before the camera anymore and to concentrate instead on directing the photo and film shoots from behind the camera. This distance seemed necessary as I wanted to have more command regarding other aspects of the production. I learned to work closely with models, actors and the crew. Through these experiences I have, of course, expanded my skills and learned a great deal about the processes of collaboration and negotiation. The only recent exception was *Soliloquy*, a film shot in 1999 – aside from writing the script, directing and editing, I also acted in the film because the story is based on my personal experience.

You stage your images like a film director by working with models and photographers and utilising the complex infrastructure of films for your video work. Would you grant us a glimpse into the process?

As you know, my photographic as well as my film and video works are becoming more and more narrative. I no longer seem to try to express my ideas through single images but rather through a choreographed sequence of images that may tell a complete story. This is a major development in my recent work. The narratives in my work are usually based on reality, yet they are fictional as they are slightly exaggerated, abstract and ambiguous in their representation of reality. As regards the process, I first try to identify the general subject I am interested in and then develop a narrative around it. The story line is quite modest as a rule because I do not want to confuse the viewer who sees the piece in two parts. I prefer the work to function as an experience that relies on a combination of images, narrative elements, and music. At the moment, I am experimenting with a fusion of cinema and visual art where I can apply those qualities of the cinema that I am interested in, such as its narrative nature, its entertainment character and most of all its ties to popular culture, yet maintain photographic and sculptural effects. Additionally, unlike the audience of a movie theatre that stays passive while watching a film, people that are confronted with one of my installations have to get physically involved and can hardly remain neutral in the dialogue between the two opposite sides.

Another important aspect regarding the form of production of my film-based work is my collaboration with a team of Iranian filmmakers that started in 1998. They have had a critical impact on the increasing cinematic orientation of my work. This team includes Ghasem Ebrahimian, the director of photography; Shoja Azari, who acted as the male singer in *Turbulent* and has since been helping me translate my ideas into the language of film; Sussan Deyhim, singer and composer of the music in all my films; and Hamid Fardjad, the line producer. We discuss, analyse and develop all ideas together. Due to the unfortunate difficulties of working in Iran, we regularly travel to other Muslim countries to produce films. We negotiate with the local authorities, hire the crew and, of course, audition the cast, which usually consists of locals, sometimes as many as 250. I always find this process exhilarating, as we often encounter amazing experiences when working in a totally new culture. There is also the economic factor: as most locations we travel to are quite remote and impoverished, we are happy to employ local people and businesses.

In your exhibitions, you present films and photographs in tandem. Which specific qualities make these two media so important for you?

As I was mainly concerned with socio-political issues initially, I found photography the most appropriate medium because it offered the sense of 'realism' I needed. I was also attracted to photography because of its accessibility to the general public. I then developed a personal style which incorporated explosive images of Muslim women and calligraphy. These images were minimalist, sculptural and rigid, and resembled carefully carved monuments. Yet, when I began to reformulate my ideas in 1997, I became very conscious of the limitations of photography and its inability to comply with the new orientation of my ideas and started to experiment with film. I was no longer interested in conveying my ideas by constructing a single image, but rather through a collection of images. Though my work remained sociologically inclined as regards its subject matter, my approach became far more philosophical and lyrical, as opposed to directly political. I seemed to have reached out for a new form of language which permitted flexibility, ambiguity and a wide range of possibilities.

Your photographs and your films are characterised by strong contrasts – by black and white, light and shadow, picture and script, male and female, to name just a few. Your language of images sometimes reminds me of Michelangelo Antonioni's early films. Which cinematic references are significant for you?

I have always been mesmerised by some of the most classic Western black and white films like Orson Welles's *The Trial* and by works like Hitchcock's amazing *The Birds*. I find the combination of photography and suspense rather unnerving. Most recently, the Iranian cinema, and especially its great filmmaker Abbas Kiarostami, have had a great influence on me. I appreciate his vision, poetry, visual language and his independence in relation to both his culture and to the world of the cinema.

Susan Sontag once said that only a narrative will allow us to understand. You frequently accentuate your photographs by adding captions, thus expanding or altering the narrative inherent in the picture. What was it that made you increasingly work with video?

I believe that all people have a special relation to all forms of narrative art. We all like to be told stories when we want to be inspired or entertained. Listening to stories is a way of momentarily escaping our own personal reality and entering someone else's. Consequently, the general public gets far more absorbed in films than in any other form of art. This might be partially due to the fact that storytelling, and particularly cinema and television, are a major part of popular culture. I am afraid that visual art is a far more isolated and inaccessible world for the general public. In most cases, it is practically impossible to appreciate any work of art without understanding its relevance to other major concepts and movements in the history of art. I also would like to mention that it has been a great challenge for me to create a type of narrative that is not tied to language, but rather functions purely on a visual and sonic level. Since the narrative is non-literal, abstract and often quite ambiguous, the viewer must rely heavily on her or his own imagination to draw meanings.

Music and sound seem to be very important in your films. In *Turbulent*, the attention focuses on the music and its transcendental power. Does the role of sound in your films resemble the role of script in your photographic work?

Yes, absolutely. The music adds a voice to the image, it brings the picture alive. This is a very similar approach to the inscription of calligraphy in the photographs. But while language requires translation, music becomes universal and transcends all cultural boundaries. Seeing the audience's reaction when watching *Turbulent,* for example, has been a marvellous experience – people become so completely engrossed and emotionally moved by the musical aspects of the piece. Since then, music has become a major aspect of my work. All my films have original scores composed by the Iranian musician and singer Sussan Deyhim. It has been a fantastic experience collaborating with her. She has an extraordinary ability to immediately grasp my concepts at the earliest stage on an intuitive level. Aside from her natural gift as a singer, she is an amazing composer with a deep understanding of traditional indigenous music and an impressive command of highly technological, electronically based music. Her contribution has been essential in creating very experimental work operating both on the primal and the intellectual levels.

You have just finished *Fervor*. One of its main subjects is romantic love.

After *Turbulent* and *Rapture*, which addressed the issue of male and female dynamics in relation to social structures in Islam, and specifically in Iran, this new project focuses on taboos regarding sexuality and desire. Taboos are internalised cultural injunctions that by their very nature allow socio-political structures to exercise their influence on an inner emotional level and that reaffirm themselves through conformity. In Islamic societies, such taboos inhibit the contact between the sexes in public. A simple gaze, for instance, is considered a sin; violations of the code are not tolerated. Men and women face internal and external pressures which forbid any sexual implications in the social sphere. Surprisingly however, this form of control also heightens the level of sexual attraction in the light of the deep sense of guilt and shame that one experiences in public.

The narrative of my new video project centres on an encounter between a man and a woman who first meet in an open and solitary landscape, where their paths cross coincidentally. Here, in passing, an intense sexual tension occurs, but no contact is made, and they go their separate ways. Later, the two meet again by chance, yet the encounter takes place in totally different surroundings, at a crowded public ceremony where men and women are divided by a curtain. The purpose of this ceremony remains ambiguous: while having something of a political event on the one hand, the occasion resembles a theatre performance on the other – there is a bearded man standing on a platform addressing the public. This charismatic character is delivering a speech, a moral lesson about the 'sin' implied by 'desires'. He tells the story of Youssef and Zolikha from the Koran – a story as famous as Romeo and Juliet. Zolikha is overcome by passion and tries to seduce a man named Youssef. The man on the platform emphasises the story's message and appeals to both men and women to restrain themselves and resist such 'evil' forces by all means. As the speech becomes more and more intense and aggressive in tone, the man's and the woman's initial excitement, and modest on-screen flirtation, turn into a deep sense of anxiety, confusion and guilt, eventually leading to the woman's hurried exit. The narrative ends without the protagonists having made direct verbal or physical contact.

Turbulent, Rapture and *Fervor* constitute a trilogy. How are the three related, and did you have a trilogy in mind from the very beginning?

Sexual segregation and the issues of social control and ideology have been an ongoing concern and focus of my work. I never intended the three pieces as a trilogy, but since *Turbulent* each piece has led to the other, raising new questions concerning the relationship between the male and the female in Islam. There are interesting parallels and differences between the three projects. Both in *Turbulent* and in *Rapture*, the issue of male and female in relation to the social structure in Islam is presented through the notion of 'opposites'. In *Turbulent*, for example, where the emphasis is on the issue of gender in relation to music and Iranian women's exclusion from the experience of performing music, image, space and sound are determined by a series of 'opposites': an empty and a full theatre, the rational and the irrational, traditional music and non-traditional music, the communal and the solitary. The crucial idea behind *Rapture* was to describe men's and women's distinct reactions to socio-political pressures, and I presented these different reactions through new sets of 'opposite' elements including nature and culture, rebellion and conformity, the predictable and the non-predictable. *Fervor* no longer focuses on 'opposites', but rather on 'commonalities'. As in my opinion, the notion of 'taboo' in relation to sexuality and romantic love in Islamic societies is equally shared by men and women, although it is often women who are sanctioned. In this project, men and women are therefore no longer presented on two opposite, but on two adjoining screens. Although a curtain separates the sexes, they are near to each other. And while in *Turbulent* and *Rapture* the viewers have to constantly shift their attention back and forth and take sides, here they are invited to distribute their attention equally.

Parallel screens, screens in opposition – what about one screen, what about making a feature film?

I think about it quite often, and my collaborators particularly encourage me to think in that direction. But I could only see myself making feature films if they could be shown on more than one screen. In fact, I prefer New York to Hollywood!

Shirin Neshat in conversation with Gerald Matt in 2000 on the occasion of the exhibition *Shirin Neshat* at Kunsthalle Wien. The artist took part in the exhibition *Some Stories* at Kunsthalle Wien. Shirin Neshat was born in Qazvin, Iran in 1957. She lives and works in New York.

João Onofre

I often implant the actors in a very rigid structure, giving them difficult tasks, to see what happens.

Video still: João Onofre,
*Catriona Shaw sings
Baldessari sings Lewitt,*
2003

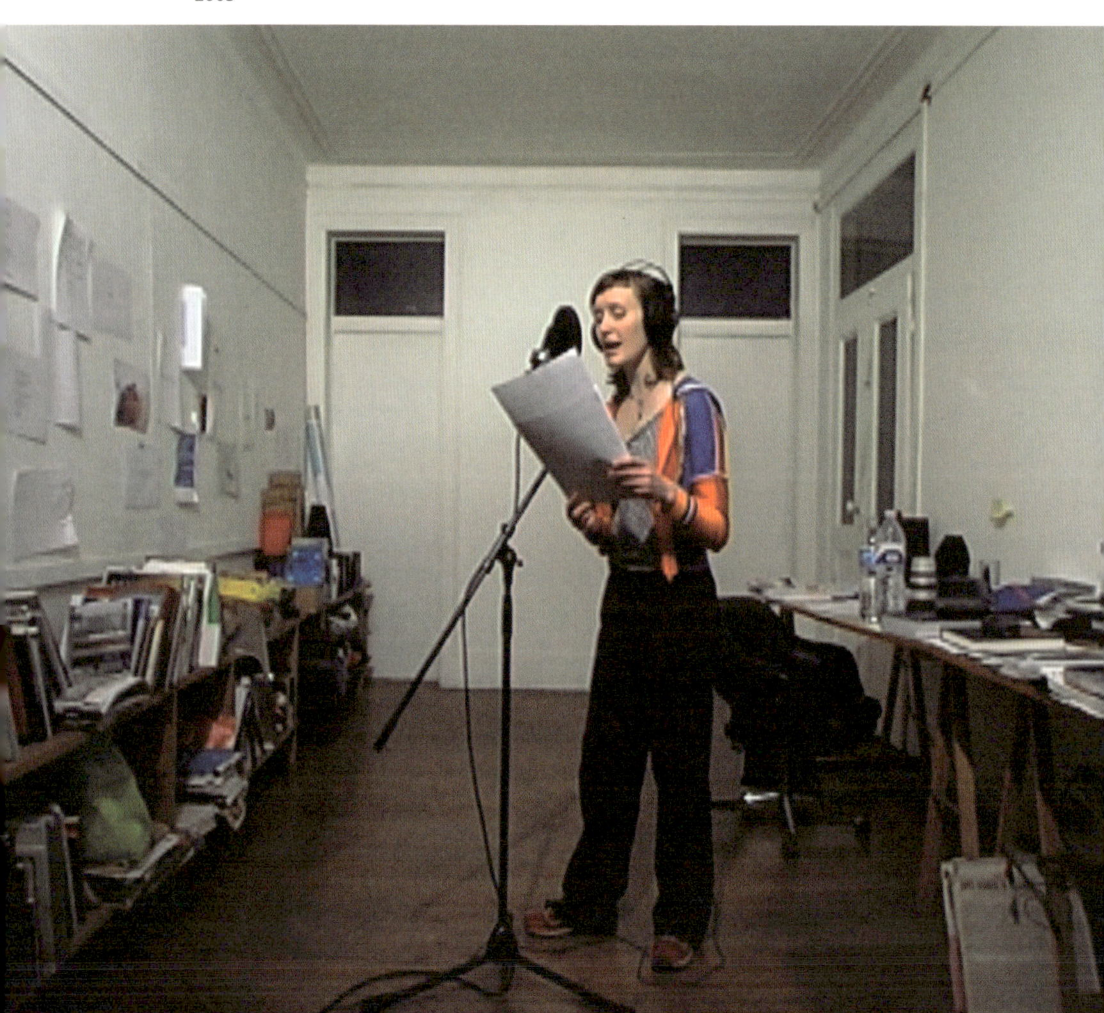

For a start, I would like to highlight some of your artistic positions and your work. As far as I know, you only use video, with a conceptual approach in many of your works going back to the 'Old Masters' of the early 1960s video scene. However, you turn their methodology around: rather than documenting performances, you stage performances for your video works. Does this approach influence the outcome, and how would you generally characterise your work?

> The works *Catriona Shaw sings "Baldessari sings LeWitt" re-edit, "Like a virgin extended version"* from 2003 and *Believe (Levitation in the studio)* from 2002 reference two different works by John Baldessari from the early 1970s, and Bruce Nauman from the late 1960s. My approach does in fact influence the outcome of the work as the performances are made for the video image in its specificity as a medium, with the performers acting for the camera, for the screen.

You studied at the University of Fine Arts in Lisbon and at Goldsmiths College in London. Did you study video art or did you take up this direction later? And where does your relation to performance originate? Have you ever made performances yourself before starting to record them?

> I studied painting in Lisbon, where I started using video – this was before I did my Masters at Goldsmiths. Video seemed more adequate – and I hope it still is – for the things that I wanted to do. But I guess that coming from this background made me more interested in the way artists used this medium than video-makers, who have a different set of questions, a different take on it. Performance is a constitutive element of artists' films and videos, so I believe that working with performance is consequent to using this particular medium. That's mainly where my interest in performance comes from, as well as from my interest in the artworks produced in that particular time in history, and their possible reassessment… But I have never made performances myself, except maybe occasionally, on a dance floor…

Let me be more precise about the references to the 1960s video scene. Many of your videos resemble experimental arrangements: You set up experimental situations, you hire people to carry out the actions, and then you record the outcome on video. This applies to *Casting* (2000), for example, where a group of fashion models were hired to speak out the dramatic last words of Rossellini's seminal film *Stromboli,* as well as in *Pas d'action* (2002), where the whole sequencing of the video is based on the length of time a group of ballet dancers can stay "sur les pointes", on the tip of their toes. It is this performative aspect that draws on many of the characteristics of early video art – Bruce Nauman's works come to mind, amongst others. Of course, you don't carry out experiments on your own body, but you rather seem to put yourself in a more distanced, a mediated position within these arrangements. Would you agree with this reading of your work?

Yes, I would agree with you on that, as some of the early works on video and film made by artists – Nauman and Baldessari amongst others – were influential in the conception of the particular set of works that you mention, but I guess that is reflected in the rest of my work as well. The performative aspect of the works draws precisely from the way artists used video at its early stages. I would say that it is important for me to work with that characteristic, which I see as one of the key constituents of the medium. My take on performance is that I believe it is improbable that performance by itself would not fall in the spectacular domain. For me, the body of the performer is on the same concurrent plane/level as the body of the TV host, and I just have to deal with it I suppose. The image of a person doing something is somehow culturally coded, and that's my departing point regarding performance. Hence, the performances in these works are carried out by professionals, and are always meant to be videos from the start.

So there is no actual 'first' staging of a performance, there is only the video as a work to present. Yet some of the aspects of a 'spectacular' setting remain, such as addressing the viewer directly and using close-ups.

The genesis of the works *Casting* and *Pas d'action* did not comprise the idea of doing, let's say, a live performance with an audience. We can discuss this further but I guess it would be like discussing with a figurative painter if his paintings are not figurative drawings. It might happen that he starts his work with drawings but the form he achieves after the production process is actually a painting – a figurative one. When I speak about 'spectacular' in relation to the performer, I'm talking about the transaction quality of the image of the performance, of its representation value at the time of reception, and not about cinematic effects that might occur in the video – a moving image medium…

What makes your films very different from a purely experimental setting is that their structure is in itself meaningful to the work, independently of the 'result'. For instance, in *Instrumental Version* (2001), watching the models pose while listening to the voices of a choir that sings the Kraftwerk song *The Robots* already makes for a world in itself. Is the experimental feature then more of a mock setting?

Although most of the works are structured, I don't agree with you when you say that, independently of the results, they have a meaning. That would imply evaluating something else than my work. The result after the construction process, the end form, the video – this is what actively constitutes meaning. That's why I think, for example, that the fixed continuous shot brings a lot to the whole. If a normative editing were to intervene in this

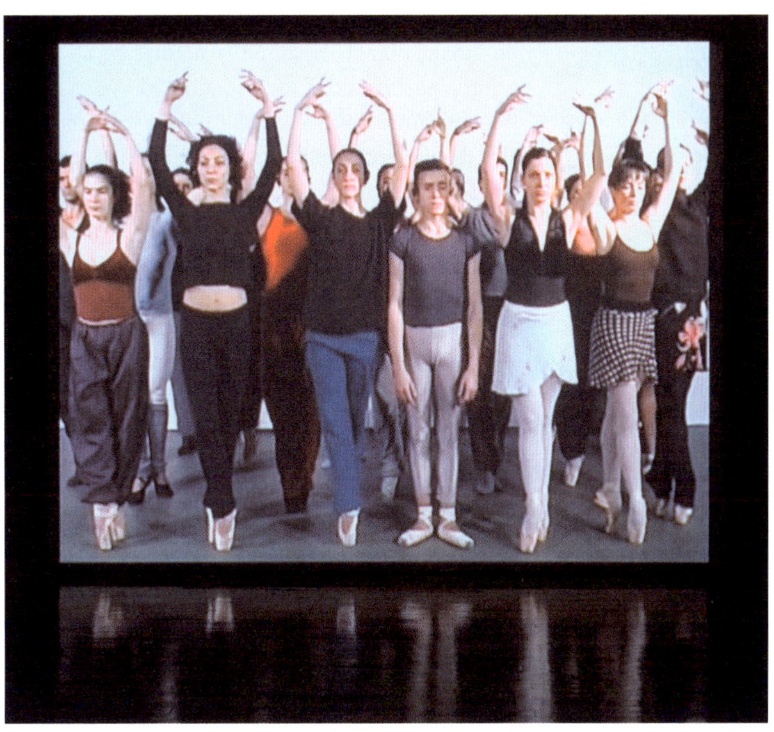

particular set of works, the directness of the shot, its impression of 'realness' would get lost, and, on the whole, it would not function as it does. All the performances are carried out by professionals in their field, so instead of an artist doing his stuff in front of the camera, I have these people doing what they do for a living: singing, acting or something else… This places the performances in a domain different from Nauman's, for example, precisely because the representation of these people is thought of as already being part of a culture of spectacle – rather than pretending that because it is art, it is not.

If you consider *Instrumental Version* like a musical experiment, it appears as a very straightforward and effective work: a computer-assisted musical arrange-ment reverted to the sound of human voices trying to imitate the original compu-ter score; in this case, a Kraftwerk song treated like a classical music score, which is interpreted by a choir. Knowing that the Kraftwerk song was released when you were still a child, and that you have a strong interest in the contemporary elec-tronic music scene, how would you describe your personal relation to this song, and more generally, to this specific era in computer music?

This specific track by Kraftwerk could be considered the mother of all techno tracks as it first introduced techno to a broader public. It actually brought techno into pop culture, and its tremendous success introduced techno into the public domain. Historically speaking, this track, with its dominant digital rhythmic structure, is the matrix for nearly all contemporary pop music. I love this track! You can never quite grasp its weird 'retro-futurism' and meaning unless you take it too seriously, and presumably, Kraftwerk never wanted it to sound campy or kitschy… I first heard the song ten or eleven years after it was made, so although it still sounds good to me, it has this sense of '*passé* futurism' about it.

Getting back to the performative aspect… How much do your performers know of the purpose and the goals of the setting? And to what extent do you know yourself? Do you have a concrete idea of what you would like to see, to record, and to have happening?

It's different in each case, although in terms of the direction of the performers, I prefer to stage them. When working on *Casting*, the models only knew that I was an artist, and that the casting was for an art project. They watched the final scene of *Stromboli* on the set – many of them knew the film already – and they had an Italian teacher to help them with phrasing and pronunciation before the shooting sessions. With the chamber choir for *Instrumental Version*, the process was different. It took a long time to rehearse with three conductors – the one that made the score transcription, the assistant conductor, and the head conductor – and, of course, with the singers one by one because they would propose approximate sounds to the electronic sounds, and all of us would decide which one was more accurate to the original. We went to the set only after a couple of intensive rehearsals, and even then we shot several takes. Everybody wanted to get it really right, so we spent hours shooting, which was really unexpected. In fact I had thought that the choir, being a chamber choir accustomed to singing sacred repertoires, would hate the idea of performing digital sounds, but they didn't – quite on the contrary. They were young students from the University of Lisbon, and loved singing something different from their rehearsals and concerts. I believe everybody got a real kick out of it… In *Pas d'action,* my little crew of three people and the dancers went directly to the set and shot several takes, and it was done. There was not as much backstage rehearsing as with the choir. We shot this work over and over because what happens when you get so many persons to stay close together "sur les pointes" is that they lose balance for a second, and start pushing each other – the domino effect… so they often went out of frame. I have several rushes with them going out of frame against their will, with everybody laughing out loud…

You work mainly with professionals – does this enable you to work without a personal interference with their work?

As they are professionals in their field, the acting direction is somehow out of place here. You can tell an actress or an actor to act like a bus driver, and they will do a perfect performance as bus drivers. But you can't tell a bus driver how to drive a bus…he just drives it. That's why I choose singers to sing, dancers to dance, and so on.

To what extent do you influence the outcome of your films? Do you edit at all? Do you try out several versions before you shoot? Do you shoot more than once, and then pick a version?

Obviously, I make several shots of each work, like most people working with moving images, in order to have more material to choose from for one reason or another. Some of the pieces are quite difficult to perform so the work never finishes with the first video rush. To give you an example, when shooting *Nothing will go wrong* – a one-minute loop of a gymnast doing a headstand on top of a traffic light in Lisbon at night – the gymnast, who perfectly masters headstands, was unable to stretch and tighten his legs because the light post was shaking. So it took two days of shooting before he was pleased with his performance; even so, he had to do it with his legs spread to keep the balance. That's why his legs are in V-shape… There are even some works that I shot but never pulled out of the drawer – they just aren't works, they're merely sketches…Regarding the editing, it is not a diachronic editing where you put time sequences side by side. Here, the editing is operated inside the picture plane, where multiple events happen at the same time. This type of synchronic editing demands careful planning in the shooting. In the case of *Casting,* for example, the diversity of things that happen simultaneously is clear: something is happening in the back, and meanwhile something else is happening in the foreground. That's why the duration of the shot is very important to me, in the sense that the spectator's focus is concentrated on the performance. But more importantly, the duration allows for different times and different things to coincide on the same picture plane…

The set-up of the *Casting* video is itself ironic, quite independently of the resulting work. Isabella Rossellini's lines are overly dramatic, as in an existential drama, but here, spoken by models who usually advertise toothpaste or something similar, they suddenly appear detached from their setting and meaning. On the other hand, there is the experimental structure, which makes one wonder whether this was planned.

I would say that my work does not revolve around the notion of irony…I often implant the actors in a very rigid structure, giving them difficult tasks, to see what happens. To a certain extent, the outcome is unpredictable; when you're working with groups of people there is always something happening that you haven't thought of. The single shot I was talking about earlier is therefore constructed as an integral record that remains open for the accidental. But you shouldn't forget that castings or auditions are a strain on the people who are auditioning: you have spot lights in your face, the camera is recording every move you make, many people are looking at you, and you have to deliver a phrase as best as you can. It's like a job interview… well, in fact it is a job interview. So, in a way, the sentence itself refers to the performer's situation.

Imus in girum et nunquam igne consumemur[1], an outdoor piece with a single performer that you made before *Casting*, is quite different from your later works. Where does the title come from, and what was its main plot?

The title is a word play on the title of Guy Debord's last film. In English it means something like: "We walk in circles and are never consumed by fire." The work shows an actor who pretends to be on fire. A real fire brigade appears, and uses the actor as a dummy, hosing him to extinguish the invisible fire, and treating him for first-degree burn. These actions have no clear ending, as once the actor gets up 'safe' the fire brigade comes in again, hits him with the hose, and so on. This work was actually made before *Nothing will go wrong,* and the repetition in both works – you never know where the loop is at – is somehow essential for me as it echoes their weird actions, which keep on happening over and over again…

One of your recent pieces, *Untitled (Vulture in the studio),* was exhibited at Art Unlimited in Basel, in the Museu do Chiado in Lisbon, and at the Centro Gallego de Arte Contemporaneo in Santiago de Compostela (CGAC). It shows a vulture that flies around in your working space. Is this meant as an allegory of death intruding in your studio?

Well, as I said before, some of my works have been thoroughly planned before the shooting takes place, but here I was interested in something where I couldn't predict the outcome. In other words, how do you write a script of what a wild animal might do in your place? Well, you simply can't! Working with the unpredictable attracted me, as it was in contrast with the more 'rigorous' scripts of my other works. Even the animal's keeper couldn't predict its behaviour, so it was really some sort of an experiment… But I guess all true artworks are. A vulture, as you know, is a large bird that likes dead or rotten meat. That's what it is in reality, and that's what I had in my studio… On the symbolic level you might say it is death. But what I was filming was a big bird with a wingspan of more than three meters, scary to say the least. So, maybe what happens in this the work is a confrontation of the actual creature and its symbolic potential as a representation.

João Onofre in conversation with Gerald Matt in the autumn of 2003 on the occasion of the exhibition *João Onofre* at Kunsthalle Wien project space.
João Onofre was born in Lisbon, Portugal, in 1976. He lives and works in Lisbon.

1   The original Latin phrase "In girum imus nocte et consumimur igni" is a palindrome, a sentence that reads the same backward as forward. In English it is most frequently translated as: "We walk in circles at night and are consumed by fire". It was the title of Guy Debord's sixth and last film (1978). [ed.]

Raymond Pettibon

Whether art is reciprocated or not, it is still worth doing it because it's like a Valentine to people who haven't been born yet, to posterity, to the past, to people you don't know, it's something that may make the receptive audience different, feel elevated, possibly.

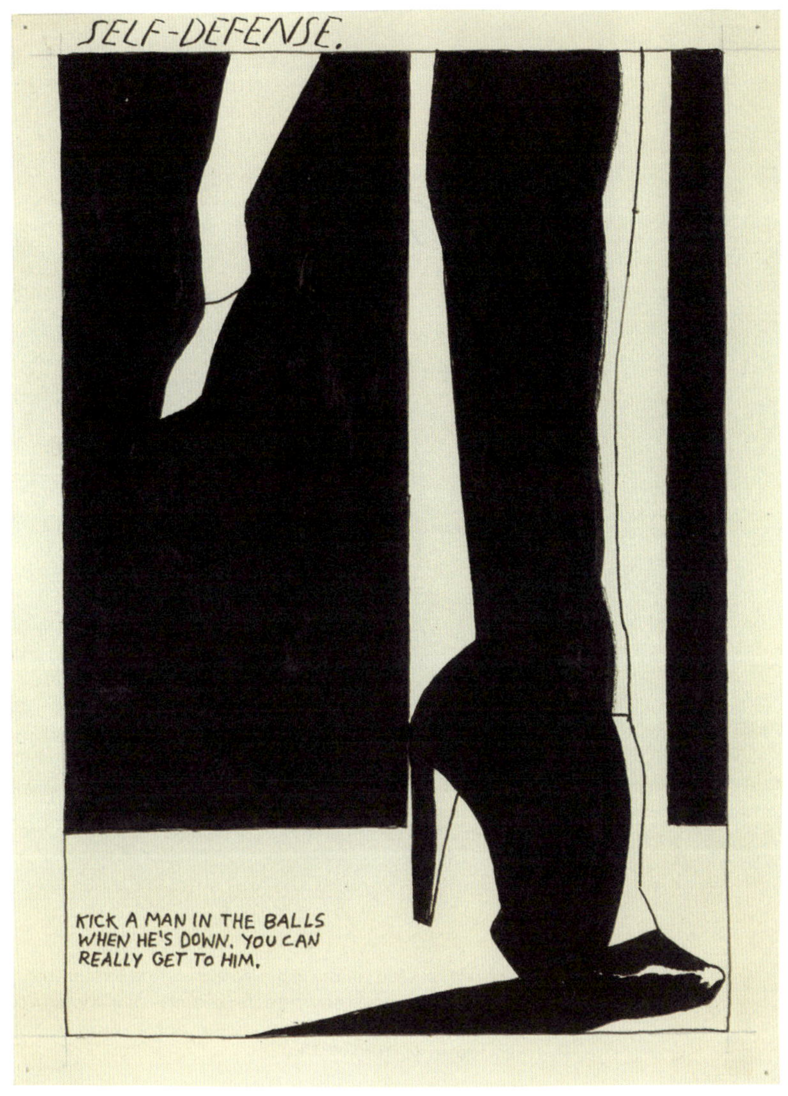

Raymond Pettibon,
Untitled (Self-defense. Kick...), 1984

Well, whatever I do, I should do it fast because whatever window of opportunity opens it opens for a few months, and I deal with all the pressure of
coming up with something new. All those offers you refer to go years back
and we'll see if I can or cannot in the next few months. The pressure is
really overbearing, but I've worked under pressure before a bit, and if I don't
you're obviously going to call off the show and I'll have egg on my face and
be humiliated. I don't know what I'll be able to do – I can't look beyond
and I don't know if there's going to be anything to look beyond after that.
I'm really at a … is it desperation? These are questions you should really ask
yourself! How kind are you, how forgiving? If you can draw something up
from your heart to give someone the benefit of doubt, if he needs to buy
some time, if he doesn't have a sharp mind, a new program, a new direction, something novel … because I know the Austrians expect that – they
should and I'm glad for them – but that only increases the pressure because
I have to fulfill those wishes and expectations and I don't want to apologize
in advance for my lack. I just hate to think of the consequences if I fail. For
an artist, failure is catastrophic, you know, you don't recover from that: you
don't run for a second term, you don't have handlers or excuses. Of course,
the museums, the curators, even the gallerists, they just want whatever is the
hottest, the last, the most happening current artist whose work everyone is
waiting for and that means so much. Yes, I'll do that! No problem, no sweat.
Of course: it's my role. Don't worry, don't worry about that, it's done, I
guarantee that, okay.

But this idea of the new does not seem to be so important for your œuvre. Aren't
all your works related to the past? There are these moments of the forties and
fifties, of the sixties and seventies – an iconography which we connect with our
childhood and all those American TV-series and movies we saw. Your work is not
nostalgic, but it radiates some kind of melancholic feeling.

Well, I don't know. That's a genuine human emotion, nowadays, because all
we have nowadays is looking back at the past. We don't have so much of a
present. Well, here we are in a corner of the Chateau Marmont – odd to be
kickballed from an outdoors table to a corner niche hideaway … Well, the
future is looking even more dire, the future meaning some days in October.
I refuse to go beyond that, I can't see any further into the future than that.

So is it external or internal pressure that keeps you going?

I've always worked best without outside pressure and deadlines. I'm self-motivated, work is something I do anyway, something I have done long before anyone asked me to do the first show. The more constraints on my work, the harder it is for me to work. The most direct way to explain this would be to regard the difference between commercial art and fine art or gallery art and museum art, and even that's not the best comparison because within those fields you can have situations where there's more freedom where you don't expect it. The best gifts are those given unprompted, when you're not asked to do something. The thing about art is that it's almost a miracle when there's a reaction, when something you do is appreciated. It doesn't have to be that direct, I don't have to have laurels thrown on me or reviews, etc. It's not so much a feedback issue, it's not something that is done by demand or fulfilling someone's expectations and obligations, it's more an expression of love. Whether art is reciprocated or not, it is still worth doing it because it's like a Valentine to people who haven't been born yet, to posterity, to the past, to people you don't know, it's something that may make the receptive audience different, feel elevated, possibly.

Frank Zappa once emphasized the conceptual continuity of the work he produced. He said that everything he ever recorded was part of a bigger structure, that everything fitted together in some way or other. Do you see your work as a cohesive body?

I used to buy into that myself until Frank Zappa died and his plan didn't sustain itself. Continuity — I was with Houdini as well, and he promised to give a sign, and I was waiting for that. Zappa — well, I still hear Dweezil and Moon Unit. That's okay though, because … hell, we're all here, and there's no permanence but passing on one's jeans — if they're good jeans like Levis, they last a long time, many generations. — What was it Frank Zappa said exactly?

Zappa said that his work has conceptual continuity, is part of a bigger plan that materializes in the whole body of his recordings. We just wanted to know if you can relate to that regarding to your own work or if you see that completely different.

Frank Zappa's career is very diverse, as are his influences. It comprised many years. While I'm working, it's not like I'm trying to make some coherent package for posterity to look at. While you're doing it, in art much more than in music, everything you do falls into a category — you can't make a dab or a dripper on a canvas or a scratch on a drawing without being self-consciously part of the whole history of art or, at least, as much art as you can cognitively handle at one time, recent art or whatever one's peers are doing or the teacher, the professor is promoting. It's not for me to say, I understand what Zappa aimed at, and he's probably right about himself and possibly everyone else. But every reaction, every thought is atomistic, I think.

What about the exhibition's relation to the public? In which way are you concerned about what happens to your work after it has left the studio? When your works come back into an exhibition, there are works that come together which were not shown together before, which date from very different times … The show in the Kunsthalle Wien may be either hung by you or by us. You will contextualize your work the way you like, of course – but if that is done by curators or other people who have their own ideas, new ways of reading it will show up. What's your feeling about those new contexts?

That's a really good question. I have come to understand that it's not all about me and my feelings and that there's something like a period of grace or distance between my work and the public and the curators and whoever else is involved. The alternative is to be obsessively in control. I assume you've worked with artists and prepared shows where there's variances of one degree or another. Which is okay. On the one hand, hell, I have no hesitation or problem with putting up the show; on the other, I've got to the point where I don't object to other people's participation. Doing a show – okay, this is giving you credit, I'll be appreciative because you probably don't get this all the time, not from artists for Christ's sake anyway – curating a show is, I guess, in a way a collaborative enterprise. That's fine with me. I've always been receptive to your ideas, I think, haven't I? – And that's sincere, and part of the art is not only about making it. Making art in a vacuum, what is that? It would be discovered sometime like the cave drawings, that would be what I'd be counting on. I think even the people who did the cave drawings may have been superstars in their day – but that's an archaeological issue. But again, though I am a very private person basically, just by nature, meaning upbringing and genetics or whatever composes one's personality, art is also communication. I'm not that self-important or blasé and so strictly self-centering, wanting it my way, controlling every little thing and the way it's shown. I think the more one's work is open to everything, the smaller the risk to become reductive. I accept influences from anywhere, really.

In previous interviews, you have talked a lot about literature, about writers you like. We were surprised that you relate to English writers of the 19th century like the essayist and literary critic Walter Pater, for example. You also mentioned Oscar Wilde, John Ruskin, James Joyce, and others – there's a very long list.

What's the list?

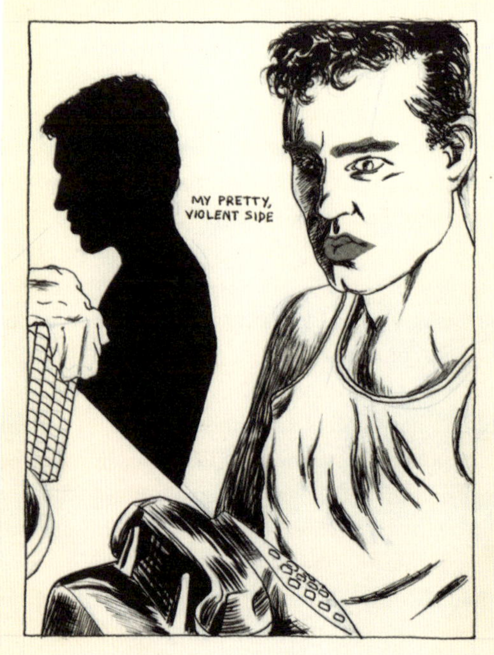

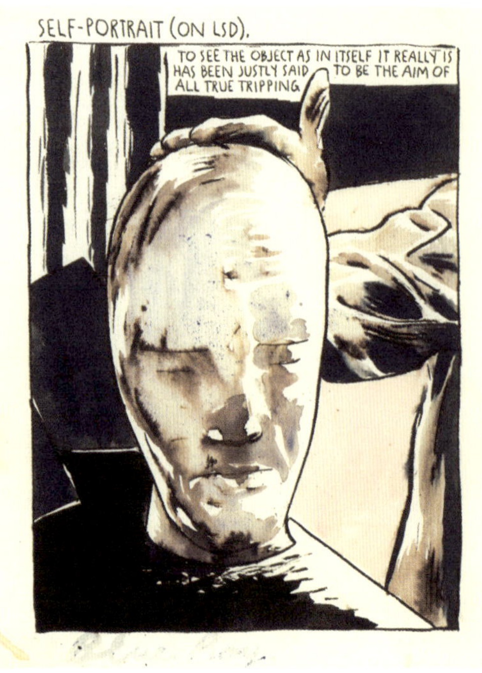

Raymond Pettibon,
*Untitled (My pretty,
violent side)*, 1981

Raymond Pettibon,
*Untitled (Self-portrait
[on LSD]...)*, 1990

The list of people you mentioned in regard to your work. – Do you ever read a book from beginning to end?

[laughs] O yeah, I do; not so often anymore because for one thing it's more practical for me to take pages out of a book … like today: I rip out pages rather than carry the whole thing around.

What pages do you have on you today?

Well [spreads out various pages], this is economics, articles from journals … this is Matthew Arnold's letters, mostly to his family … this is Hart Crane's letters … this is Heinrich Heine's letters … But see, I took the train up from Long Beach to downtown LA and then I took a train to here – so I have something to read on the way. These things are no from-beginning-to-end things actually. I don't read to find out what happens in the end, that's more like what you're thinking of as the plot. The best review you get for a book is one that calls it a page-turner, is to say it keeps you glued to your seat from beginning to end, makes you stay up all night or however long it takes to read it – think of one of those books by Tom Clancy, for example.

The subjects and the iconography of your work we saw in recent years are clearly American or even Californian. Is there something about these stories and the iconography which is really local?

I was impressed by Zidane's head the other day. You know, I would jump him into my gang in LA just from that. If he wants to bang with the big boys in LA he's got an open invitation, okay! – It's local iconography, but not that much. I mean the rest of the world is going to catch on eventually. I don't know about baseball exactly or surfing, it depends on the local conditions … we just need some catching up ourselves because this Iraq thing turned out to be a little bit more than what we're used to. It's not America's fault, it's like considering it a failure that Germany extended itself too far into the Soviet Union. Not everything is so clearly drawn out: one person's invading, one person is being invaded. Sometimes there is a kind of a song-and-dance between people. They could have done a better job with all these beautiful German tanks, but the condition of the Russian roads was just abominable … the mud … they had to cut their own roads … And that's what we have in Iraq. We should have dropped down super highways and freeways first. Then we wouldn't have all this roadside bombing bullshit and stuff because you don't fuck with American highways and freeways. You can leave your piss bottles [accidentally spills a beer over G. Matt; both take a swig and clink cans]. It's just beer, so don't lick it up.

You were on a good thread.

… a good thread …the tank thread … that's what you need to go from one place to another. I think they could have been better hosts or made it more inviting to do something … if they would have taken the resources they had and expended them on the goddamn Potemkin villages and stuff and made some decent roads for those panzers to go across. But now I have completely lost my track. Where were we? Leningrad?

[Raymond Pettibon's Atelier, Long Beach]

All the rooms we have seen here are full of books. You must take books and comics with you wherever you go.

Yeah, it didn't start this way, but they tend to accumulate. I don't have books or whatever else accumulated just for possession or being a pack rat … In fact, there's more books, papers, etc. than there would normally be since I've been working with my father's stuff, with what he had. I don't have that attachment anymore – well, one time when I was younger perhaps I did – for collecting and accumulating. Too much of my works and my possessions were destroyed over the years, and that kind of got me over that. Believe it or not, most of this is just part of the utility, the practical part of how I work. They're useful for what I do in general.

How do you choose a certain book when you want to read something? You have stacks of books piled up – how do you start?

Well, fact is I don't read that much. I haven't for quite a while because I just don't have time.

But isn't it also about covers and titles? Because a lot of the things we see here were designed in the fifties and sixties ... have quite a strong, very evocative graphic design ...

Such things aren't available any longer – well, yeah, everything's available at a certain price. Since I was around 13, I collected that kind of paperbacks, novels from the forties, fifties, sometimes the sixties ... my father had some as well. You used to be able to just pick them up for a dime. It's not easy to categorize or to disdain paperback books because they can reprint anything. They did paperback reprints of authors like Emily Brontë and put some lurid cover on it.

What a fantastic mixture! Look here! Walter Pater's "The Renaissance," then the wonderful title *Love Slave* and *They Died in the Chair* ...

There are also paperback originals ... *Love Slave*, who wrote that?

... Never Kill a Client.

Not all of the tough guy film noir kind of writing is easy to dismiss. Lately, I was reading some of John D. MacDonald's works, which I'd read when I was in my teens. He's one of those writers who are respected, or have been at times, who worked in genre categories. I don't quite know why those categories, there's some good writing and some bad writing.

You once said that you like the idea that Charlie Parker took standard tunes and every time he played them a new melody came up or there were some variations on something that was basically a very well known theme. Would you also regard your own work under the aspect of re-emerging topics in the way a jazz musician might improvise, or is this a complete misconception?

There is an affinity between what bebop musicians did when working with standards and my work: I've never hidden the fact that it can depend on precedence and improvising off of some text. It's not particularly original, a lot of writers do the same thing. Bebop is one of those instances where it was open to more exposure; rap would be the same situation: you have actual sound samples here ... I guess nowadays to sample anyone without their permission is risky. I'm open to anything potentially, and there's more of a collage or an editing nature to my work. That doesn't make such work derivative or less individual. I would argue on the counter.

We've been talking about literature. What about film? You have also been working with film and with cartoons. About fifteen years ago, you did features on topics such as Charles Manson or Patty Hearst. Why did you stop doing such films?

I didn't stop doing such films. I have scripts lingering around for years, and I just haven't got around to doing anything with them. You could say the same thing about the books and fanzines: there are periods when I did quite a few, and I haven't done much of that lately; but I haven't made some conscious decision on that, you know: mapped out what I want to do with it, like I want to deal less or more with it. As for my films and videos, I do almost everything myself. Of course, there are the actors: if I were re-making some Cecil B. DeMille epic, where you have to have all these thousands of extras, I could get some right now, no problem. The hard part is the casting. When I was younger, I could do that, but now it would take me a while to cast a thousand extras. Because you have to do that individually, even if it's a distant crowd scene: you really want well-casted hot girls; as a director, as an auteur, that's what you're going to be judged by. It would be also cheating your fans if you don't go through all that. And I just like to do things right.

What about the cartoons? Will you go on doing them?

I hope I'll do more cartoons. There's much more I could do with that medium than I have done before, I haven't explored it as much as I would like to. But in reality, there are conditions that affect work for any one person: what you're actually able to do, what you finish, publish, the factor of time, energy, expense – that's something that's always been there with my work. I've managed to do a hell of a lot with the means I had at hand. If you look at the animations, the films, the videos – there are so many people who wouldn't even consider doing them themselves in the way that I have. If you have something to say, if you have ideas, a script, or a talent at directing, it's really not so hard to make a goddamn film or video. You don't need the backing of fucking Michael Eisner or the Disney family to be involved; I don't need those motherfuckers to have a role in my animations – I wouldn't want them to in the first place, and they're not going to add anything. I don't need fucking Random House to have their goddamn imprint on the books I do. On the contrary: it would be an embarrassment to do anything with a major publishing company. You know, I'm not easily embarrassed by associations – these are completely necessary. When you see the imprint of some publishing house on a book, well fuck anything this is supposed to be an indication for! Or take fucking Disney, well, okay that's useful, it's like the parent-control thing. In my case, that's something I cannot stand seeing. And this is not out of any of this bullshit do-it-yourself attitude that every corporate thing is bad and establishment and capital are evil. Fact is that in my case – making drawings on paper – I'm not doing fucking Richard Serra, you know – there's nothing that anyone else cannot do to compete with me. It's hard to compete with a phone company, because you have to have all the infrastructure, you have to have billions of dollars just to start up. But to do a goddamn drawing – now, how hard is that? The same thing with music: fuck Warner Brothers! Or going into the studio and spending half a billion dollars on cocaine, producers, engineers, and all the studio musicians who've got to play the parts because one's own band sucks. I gave you some of my CDs, I never even wanted to make those CDs. I feel totally sheepish even handing them over to any motherfuckers – it's like: take this please, apologizing beforehand, and "you don't have to listen to it" … I know they're going to be tossed out, well, you've probably already tossed out my CDs. Understood, that's okay. The same with videos, films – I call them films whilst technically they're videos – but I'm not competing with video art. I make feature-length films, and I don't apologize for anything. Before I make them, I'm writing my own laws – so on their terms compare them to whatever comes out this week from Hollywood! I don't have to apologize for anything. The only difference is: well, they're better! And if they're not, I'll take the heat …

Raymond Pettibon in conversation with Gerald Matt and Thomas Mießgang in the summer of 2006 on the occasion of the exhibition *Raymond Pettibon: Whatever it is you're looking for you won't find it here* at Kunsthalle Wien.
Raymond Pettibon was born in Tucson, Arizona in 1957. He lives and works in Los Angeles, California.

William Pope.L

It's a good idea to keep the smell of decay in one's nostrils. It's much more real than any renown.

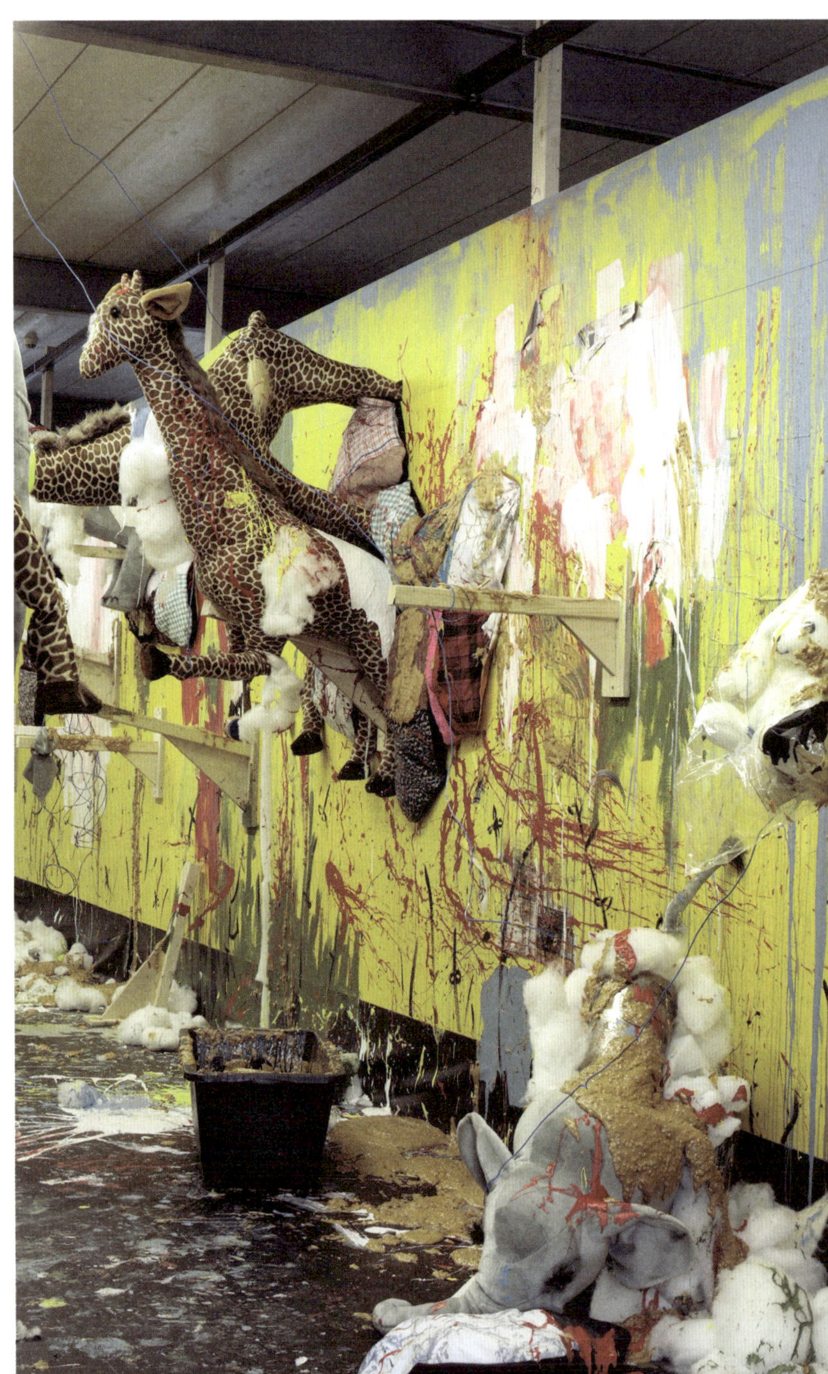

Installation view,
Kunsthalle Wien project
space 2006:
William Pope.L,
Trophy Room

You will have an exhibition in the project space of the Kunsthalle Wien in the fall of 2006. We have been very curious which work you will choose. Why this piece?

I did not choose this work alone. When an artist chooses a project for an institution it is always a negotiation with that institution. In fact, I made two proposals to the Kunsthalle Wien before we settled on a final concept. In the first proposal I suggested we photograph 8,134 people in Austria, superimpose their individual images onto single discs of sausage native to the country and hang them in a vast grid on the wall. The working title of this project was: *As of 2004 there were 8,134 Jews living in Austria*. The second work I proposed was called: *Candy Mountain (vesuvius version)*, which was a truncated volcano of peanut butter (with a hollow center) that theatrically disappeared into and through the ceiling of the Kunsthalle while concert lights flashed and various versions of the American hobo song *Big Rock Candy Mountain* played. The third version I proposed is the child of the previous two. This third work is called: *Trophy Room* and suggests something that is won after a contest, perhaps big game in a safari. A safari of blind people. The physicality and comportment of the work asks the question: what is this work really hunting? What does it want? Maybe the work is hunting for a master piece, yes, that's right; two words, not one: Master Piece. 'Trophies' suggests bodily holocaust like '8,134', but also uses a shit load of peanut butter and symbolically 'effigizes' via pillory, display and vivisection. Another helpful question to ask might be: what is being made into effigy? The toy stuffed beasts in the installation represent animals only found in the third world. The particular herd in this installation was created in Austria and is thoroughly Austrian in look and character though not in type – so what is this work REALLY hunting? Perhaps it is pursuing complicity, a messy interrelatedness that oozes and spills…

The Kunsthalle Wien project space is a glass building that creates transparency between public space and the museum space. Did this architectonic situation influence your decision?

Indeed. The windows of the Kunsthalle Wien reminded me of an automobile show room. I'm hoping some wealthy art collector or institution will want to buy *Trophy Room*. Not because the institution or person would actually want to buy it but because of the conversations that could ensue regarding what constitutes such an oozing work, for example: What does the buyer buy when a work is so open to oxidation? Perhaps the buyer buys an opportunity. Perhaps the buyer obtains, via capital, a means to create possibility for some other person. These days I am thinking a lot about re-granting from sales of art objects to support activist and community organizations that are trying to soften the blow for lesser fortunate peoples concerning everyday tragedies like poverty, health and hunger. If a museum or collector could assist me with this project I'd be very grateful. Selling my soul for this reason makes economical, political and spiritual sense.

Your work hinges on the heritage of dark skin. Your performance *How Much is That Nigger in the Window* (1991) had you sitting largely undressed in the window of Franklin Furnace and spreading mayonnaise on your body. The opaque whitish layer became transparent when it dried, and the Afro-American's dark skin stood out again after some time. Does a nigger remain a nigger even in the enlightened atmosphere of New York?

Provocative and interesting question. Let me try to do it justice. In some ways New York is no more enlightened than Vienna. Unfortunately, to ask this question in this way places the question safely outside the questioner. This strategy places sole responsibility of an answer on the receiver of the question, that is, me the black artist for whom the question was contrived, as if I am more ensnarled in race than my questioner. This sort of question is paradigmatic of the challenges facing whites in attempting to uncynically own and speak of race. Here is a counter-question: Who is the current nigger of Austria and what is Austria, its citizens and yourself doing to better this nigger's status?

Touché. Your work seems to provoke especially black people. For *Tompkins Square Crawl,* a project you also realized in 1991, you crawled along Tompkins Square Park in Manhattan's East Village wearing a dark business suit and having a potted plant in one hand. You paid a white cameraman to assist you and film the performance. A black observer soon felt massively provoked and ridiculed and started to insult your white assistant.

Indeed these things did occur but it also upset white folks who viewed the documentation. Historically, black folk have had a very troubled relationship with issues of disenfranchisement. It is common sense that my work touches black folk in ways that might connect with that history. However, it is important to say that all Americans are foreigners in some way. Some are disenfranchised by lack and some by plenty. Some by guilt and some by anger. All of us are marked by emptiness. The national ethos of the US is a rough, topsy-turvy mix of guilt, arrogance, anger and, of course, emptiness.

You did your first *Crawl Pieces* in the late 1970s. What was your original motivation behind this concept?

Fear. Guilt. Embarrassment. Anger. A willed attempt over time and many versions to become at one with loss.

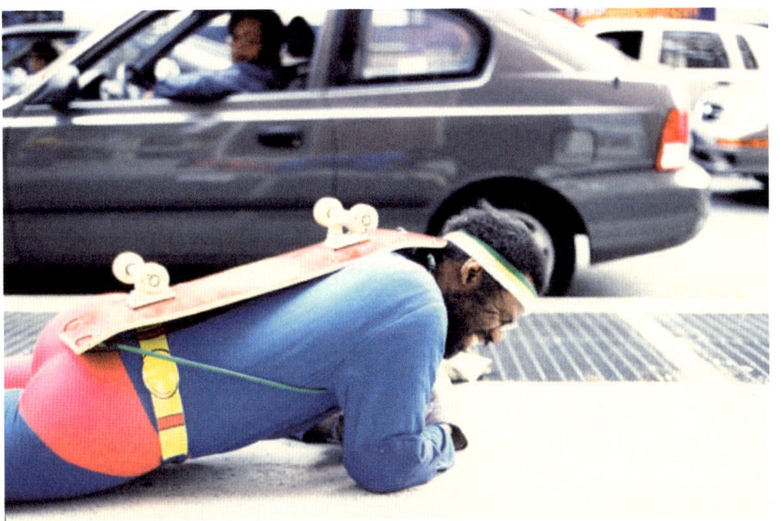

William Pope.L,
*The Great White Way,
22 miles, 7 years,
1 street, Segment: 5,*
2003

You come from Harlem, your family was anything but well-off. How did you come in touch with art?

I did not have to get in touch with art because it is in touch with everything.

Another important subject in your work is waste. Since your time as an art student you have been collecting and using various materials, frequently foodstuffs. You seem to have a special penchant for mayonnaise and peanut butter, don't you?

Actually my real interest is oxidation.

Most artists try to avoid classification. You, however, seem to actually insist on the label "black." You even call yourself "The Friendliest Black Artist in America©." Why friendly? The historiography of racism does not really suggest friendliness.

I think of the word 'friendly' as similar in meaning to how it is used in this sentence: Today the US began friendly relations with North Korea.

Sometimes lyrically, sometimes in absurd texts, *Skin Set Drawings*, which you started in 2001, focuses on myths about skin color: *Black People are the Christmas Tree in the Driveway*; *Black People Are a Falling Star Against a Blue Sky*; *Black People Are Glass*; *White People Are Yellow*; *White People Are Art*; *White People Are Below Freezing*. You started the project with *Black Drawings* and *White Drawings* before you added the skin colors red, yellow, and green.

All the previous is true except I intended from the very beginning to expand my 'palette' but I soon realized: 1) Since racialist policies derive from a set of conventions, I had to build from a set of conventions. 2) Even if I could personally imagine beyond these conventions my audience might need more of a foothold in what is currently acceptable before I could demand that they leap into what might be possible.

You have been a permanent element of the US art scene. In Europe, however, your work has only evoked interest in recent years. What do you think is the reason for this?

The internationally known black artist is a new commodity. My sense is that it is easier for American galleries and museums to export a blackness that is already digested than one that is trying to know itself. Like any product, international black art is provisional and prone to the whim of fad, institution, politics, luck and death. It's a good idea to keep the smell of decay in one's nostrils. It's much more real than any renown.

You are an internationally renowned, highly respected artist today. Are you still confronted with that "nigger moment," with white people's sudden realization that this nigger is a human being with a heart and a mind after all?

Actually [a] nigger moment is not typically understood as belonging to whites, nor does it typically indicate epiphanies of humanity and soul – usually the opposite.

Which project are you working on at the moment?

In my case what I am working on now is what I was working on before. For example, I've been working on a large scale project called *distributingmartin* for about four or five years. Originally its goal was to disperse the historic, cultural and physical body of Martin Luther King across as wide a horizon as possible. The current goals of the project are: 1) To make people good whether they like it or not. 2) To create a biological agent that can do this. 3) To make this agent available to whoever wants it. 4) To create, around this beneficent arrogance, conversations concerning ethical issues, e.g.: Is it ethical to force someone to be good? What is good? What is the best way to get to good and who should make this happen? 5) What sort of artwork would this be and how would it affect the way we make art?

What would be your ideal project if there were no restrictions on your work, no financial limitations, no technical problems, no difficulties with permissions?

If I could do any project, at this point in my life, it would probably be the *distributingmartin*. And I'd like a large government along with a large pharmaceutical company to underwrite the project. But, I must add, if this opportunity was truly at hand, I'd have to reject it altogether and simply work for the good with the best that is in me—but then I can do that anyway!

William Pope.L in conversation with Gerald Matt in the summer of 2006 on the occasion of the exhibition *William Pope.L: Trophy Room* at Kunsthalle Wien project space.
William Pope.L was born in Newark, New Jersey in 1955. He lives and works in Lewiston, Maine.

Antonio Riello

I conduct research into the context of contemporary art and everyday life with the same curiosity and attitude as that of someone doing botanical research in a tropical jungle.

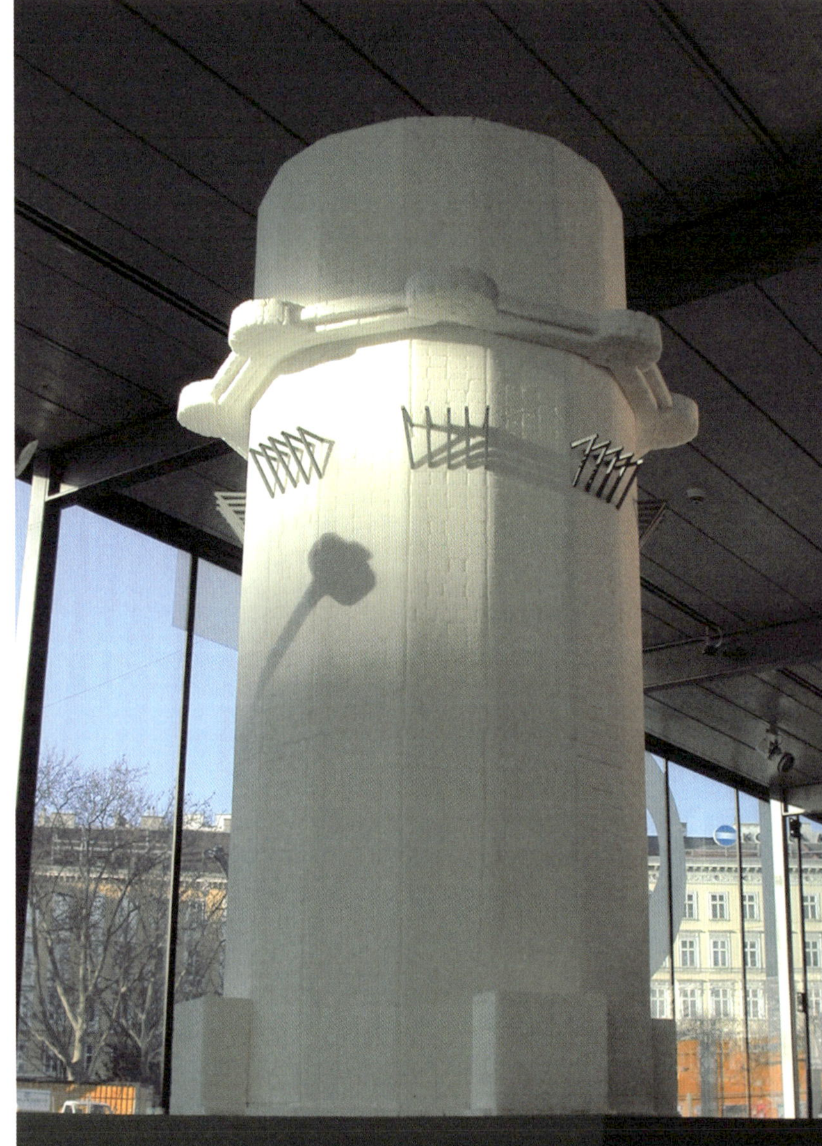

Installation view,
Kunsthalle Wien 2005:
Antonio Riello,
Flaktürme down

I don't think I am, really … I rather think that so-called "contemporary art" makes the mistake of being too boring. However that may be, you could see me as the "updated version" of a particular attitude towards post-war Italian culture, which tried to interpret reality with a certain sense of duty but also with necessary distance and lots of self-irony. You might say that artists like Piero Manzoni, Alighiero Boetti, Pino Pascali and Aldo Mondino are my predecessors in a certain way, and that those like Maurizio Cattelan are sharing my journey. It's not just a matter of irony but rather of intellectual freedom in contrast to a dictatorship that has been defining the rules of contemporary art from the fifties until today, by accepting nothing as a work of art that is not "serious, hard to digest and boring". It works something like the motto of the old pharmacists: "The nastier the medicine tastes, the better it works".

I don't completely agree with that either. I think that these days the best way to be an artist is not to think like an "artist". Tom Friedman is more like a talented model-maker; Wim Delvoye is like a brilliant craftsman who is unusually well informed about decorative techniques; Ron Mueck could be compared to a (very precise) special effects expert. And many other artists (the ones I like best) seem to be working in the same kind of way. Undoubtedly, my experience as a pharmacist and my scientific knowledge have considerably influenced my artistic research. I have always thought my work is like a scientist: I conduct research into the context of contemporary art and everyday life with the same curiosity and attitude as that of someone doing botanical research in a tropical jungle.

And to bring in a Viennese comparison: in my work I feel closer to Alois Riegl than to Gustav Klimt.

This time, I agree with you. As I said earlier, the "heritage of science" has indeed had a powerful influence on my work. Chemical "resonance hybrids" are natural structures so unstable that they seem to be both one thing and another at the same time. Indeed, they are ambivalent structures opposed to any "Aristotelian logic". I'm interested in what is called "Fuzzy Thought Theory", which deals with these kinds of reality in a scientific way. Actually, in my work, I produce pieces that are examples of a "mixed reality": popular aesthetics and art history, the phenomenology of kitsch and Minimalism, fashions like contemporary obsessions and military history, and many other things …

You said in an interview with Michele Robecchi that as an artist you are not interested in evaluations. You see yourself as a disinterested observer, who – beyond any political correctness – uses art as a tool to present the status quo in all its multi-dimensionality.

As we know only too well, various forms of dictatorship misused art on a grand scale for propaganda purposes. What we call "contemporary art" is a small yet important part of the great "Informative Big Game", which is an expression of the global semi-dictatorship that rules the world. This is not a matter of such oppositions as the USA versus Europe, or capitalism versus anti-capitalism; it is rather a kind of location-less, mass-media dictatorship, which no longer needs secret agents because it has merciless observers in the form of television, newspapers and mobile telephones. As an artist, I can change things only under the condition that the media permits me to do so. I have no illusions about that. … What we are talking about is a lobby that can manipulate every artistic act, even against the will of an artist. Even if it sounds paradoxical, it seems to me that it is more difficult to take up a political position in Europe today without being manipulated by this or that organisation. In the USA, on the other hand, experiential activities associated with social or political commitment have better chances of success. Among various experiential activities of this type, I am thinking, for example, of works by Barbara Kruger or the activities of the Guerrilla Girls.

In any case, I think it is easier for my artistic work to interact with society by starting with this position of "neutral observer". And, this degree of freedom permits me to engage with very serious questions, even at a deeper level, without having to relate to banal or outworn positions.…

In the case of your work *Italiani Brava Gente*, whose subject matter is the racism of Italian (and no doubt of non-Italian) society against refugees from eastern Europe, one does not fully accept your standpoint of a neutral observer, even in artistic terms. The video game can still be downloaded free on the Internet, together with a request to donate ten dollars in support of all victims of racist wars.

To begin with, I want to point out that racism in Italy is a social feeling of recent times, and, consequently, racism has not yet been grasped in all its aspects. For me, it was practically a necessity to approach this problem by using a video game. This kind of context (virtual, gaming and aggressive) could – especially in 1997 – really add depth to a topic as discomforting as this one. As you know by now, the only way to draw attention to social abuses is to take on the role of the "naughty boy" ... The players of the artwork or video game, *Italiani Brava Gente,* did certainly not seem like nice, courageous heroes but rather like nasty, ridiculous and neurasthenic, even vulgar beings.

Some of the photographic works of Serrano and Pierre & Gilles are not, as people sometimes naively believed, "propaganda for lust", but rather an intelligent way to direct the attention of the mass media to certain platitudes. The situation of my *Italiani Brava Gente* comes close to this way of approaching things ... as a contribution for the victims among the "boat people", it was also a way of remembering, in spite of everything, that things in an artistic environment still go on having a certain degree of reality....

I also remember some very interesting aspects associated with this work ... The project was hardly online when, on television, I was publicly accused of racism, so that I had to sleep some nights outside my house to avoid the risk of being arrested and also to avoid possible attacks or acts of revenge from people who thought I was a dangerous criminal ... For the Italian media it was hard to find sane, well-balanced words to use when reporting on this work of mine ... Art as an "uncertain borderline" between legality and illegality in society ... This happens sometimes in the world of art, as in the case *Robbery of Space* by Ann Messner in the New York underground or the booby traps and bombs of Gregory Green....

I take pleasure in destroying the myths and the related "dark sides" of the great bastards of history. These include not only the mafia bosses but also the Nazi big-timers, some famous people, general and war leaders – all kinds of people who, from a historical point of view, represent the symbol of evil. In order to destroy them, I take a look at their domestic side and their private lives. For example, I have given reality to Hitler's false teeth, Josef Goebbels' pyjamas (for the series *Original Third Reich Objects*), and Benito Mussolini's underpants... and many personal objects like the broken spectacles of the bloodthirsty and terrible mafia boss, Genco Russo...

How shall I put this, the everyday objects show and demonstrate that myths of this kind, like others, are human in a dramatic and troubling way, and, again like others, grow old and consequently share the fate of physical vulnerability. Their perverse fascination is reduced to wretched relics: a warning and a judgement at the same time.

Your best-known work internationally is probably the series *Ladies' Weapons*, deadly handguns for close combat in a feminine, fashionable style, unique objects with women's names. For example, there is *Lucy*, the US MK2 hand grenade, painted pink, with appliqué hearts in red and gold; or *Betty*, the US CAR 15 heavy-assault carbine, *petit-point* needlework on the barrel and piston, the magazine presented in peaceful green, decorated with pearls. There is also *Maria Theresa*, a 9mm Uzi submachine gun with the modern businesswoman's strict pinstripe of anthracite in a sophisticated combination with violet.

The "Fashion System" has influenced many artists: Lucy Orta, Sylvie Fleury, Pharmacopoeia, Georges Pascal Ricordeau, Erwin Olaf, etc. As an Italian, I live in a country that is weirdly "polluted" by fashion and design. It is almost impossible to escape from that kind of pressure, its actual seductions and permanent obsessions. Much more than fashion in itself, however, I am interested in its instruments and contradictions. And so, I began with my first weapon in 1999, a Russian Kalashnikov, gilded and decorated with diamonds from Swarovski, and I named it Patrizia, after my girlfriend. These weapons became war accessories for "sophisticated ladies". Purely industrial materials, on the far side of every type of styling, manipulated and transformed by the tricks of aesthetic seduction. Can an aesthetic approach transform an ethical value? And how does all this relate to the female and male genders? My *Ladies' Weapons* are merely a simple experiment to find possible (and perhaps controversial) answers to these questions. In 2002, I stopped all that because I couldn't think of any more female first names. Each of these works is also a unique and personal portrait "sui generis" of a woman, a bit like the manner of the portrait painters in the late 19th century....

You recently took up again the topic of war apparatus in the series *Kombat Tiepolo*. This time it was not in association with the gender motif, but with that of classical art history. Motifs from Tiepolo's big ceiling frescos have been painted on big models of military jet aircraft.

I grew up in a Catholic country where the ceilings of churches were often painted completely over with frescos of angels, prophets, saints and classical ruins ... When I think of a heaven, it is easier for me to think of this "artistic and theological heaven" than of the real one. At present, my studio is in the hinterland of Venice, a region where – apart from Venice itself – Tiepolo did most of his work. As a result, the association of this humanist genius loci of art history with a highly technical element – such as a combat aircraft – almost came about by itself, in spite of the obvious incompatibility. Here again, we have ambivalent creations in order to research and document the influence of cultural and artistic experience on ethical values. But there is more of the same: an exercise in "virtual history" – a serious digression it may seem – on the possible appearance of an imagined "Vatican Air Force".

Antonio Riello,
Lucy, 2001

→

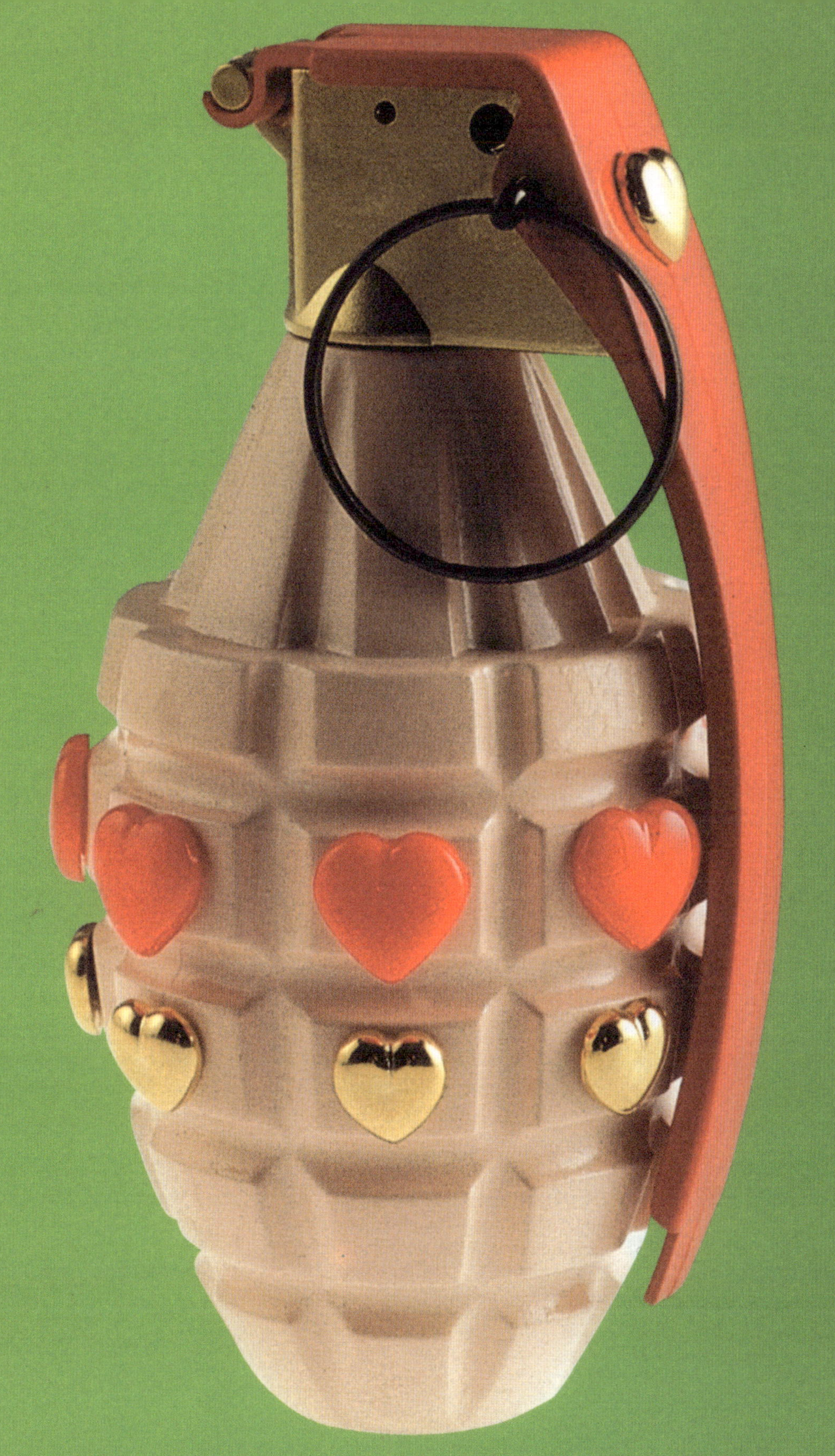

In any case, aircraft seem to have had a strong attraction for many artists: Panamarenko, Fischli & Weiss, Mocchetti, Kiefer, Alighiero Boetti, Pivi and many more. A kind of collective obsession …

Common to all your work is not only the incompatibility of form and content but also the precise and detailed handicraft involved. Are you a perfectionist? Do you make industrial technology? How do you work?

In my opinion, art is purely a matter of intellectual capacity – always under the primacy of ideas. But a work that is technically poor, or in any case carelessly executed, is certainly not a guarantee of intelligent ideas. Don't you think? If I just mention a few artists, who I think of as being most fascinating and rigorous from a conceptual point of view, such as Guillaume Bijl (with his installations from ready-mades) or Meyer Vaisman (with his tapestries and manipulated turkeys) or Heim Steinbach (with his installations) or Elisabeth Wright (with her object in "false" relationships of size), it is easy to see that their works are technically "hyper-perfect" like a handbag from Vuitton … Furthermore, why should an artist create objects whose quality is any less than that of objects from industrial production? Of course we know that there is also the rather quirky skill of deliberately taking "artistic licence". But that's another story …

Just one more point: I like thinking, perhaps a bit naively, of artistic production as a job requiring time, patience and sacrifice: something that seems absurdly anti-economical, but which transforms art into something absolutely necessary. On the far side of economic logic and countable necessity, where the existence of us Europeans seems to be suffering a melancholic shipwreck …

Mr. Riello, where were you born?

That's my secret. But I can let you know that I was perhaps born, like one of my "resonance hybrids" at more than one place at the same time. My parents were obviously Italians … But as you can see in some of my bios, the places of birth change from time to time. In reality, that is part of an ambitious art project that will continue throughout my life and will be complete only after my death …

Antonio Riello in conversation with Gerald Matt in 2005 on the occasion of the exhibition *Antonio Riello: Flaktürme down* at Kunsthalle Wien project space.
Antonio Riello was born 1958. He lives and works in Milan und Amsterdam.

German to English translation by Tom Appleton.

Anri Sala

Existence without Resistance is like living without feeling it.

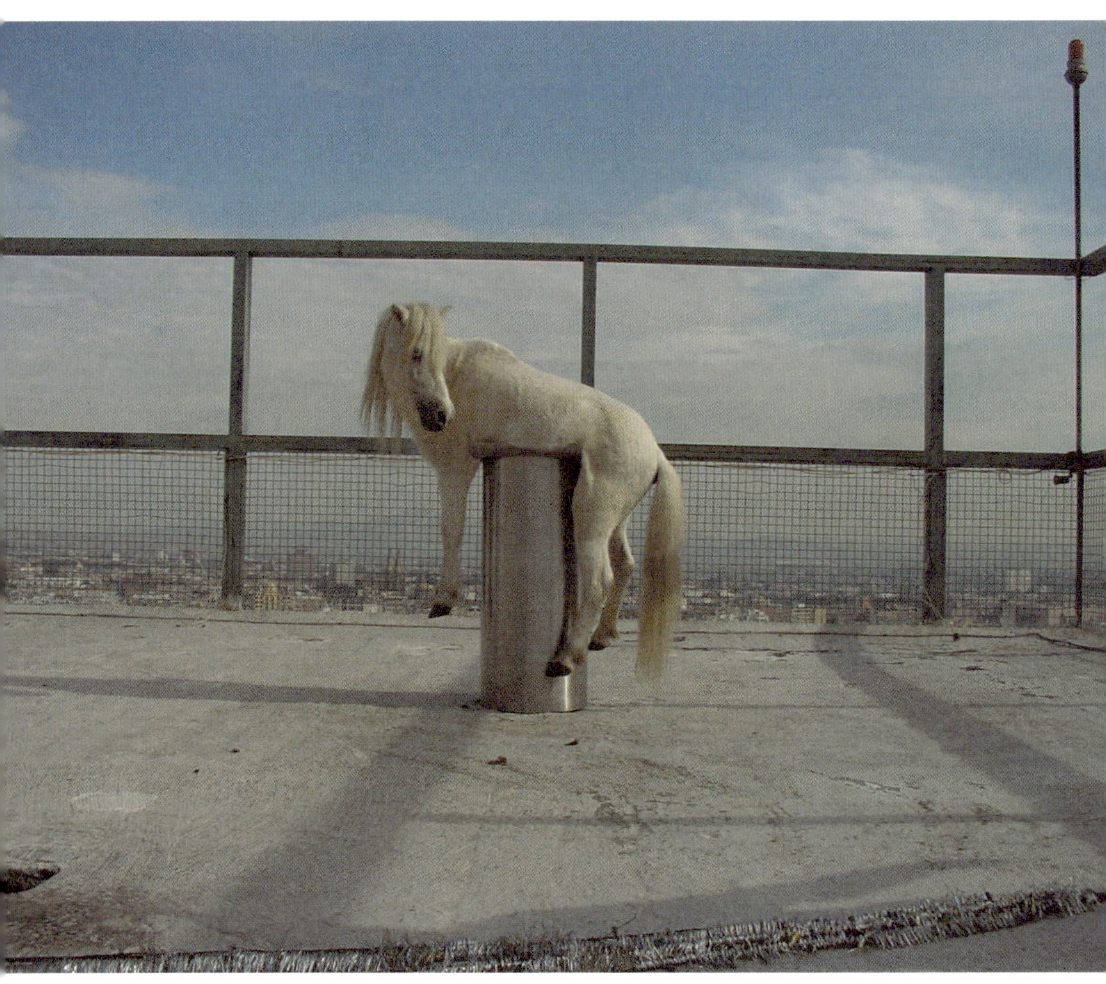

Anri Sala,
No Barragán No Cry, 2002

Anri, let's start by talking about your video works. Your early films are very close in style to documentaries; you record in a simple, quite lapidary way. Very often, not much actually "happens". What makes these films an artist's work then? Where would you draw the boundaries between an artist and a documentary filmmaker? And is this difference important to you?

I like to work my films until, as you said, "often not much actually happens". Concerning boundaries between an artist and a filmmaker, or documentary and fiction, I personally do not feel the need to draw a line, to categorize or make things fit. How to approach something comes first.

This carefulness with images, and a certain "stop-and-go" use of the camera in a process of constant acceleration and slowdown, are significant features in your work. Sometimes there are these very short kinds of introduction, for example as you take an image, which you then put into its visual context.

For example, this could be found in the case of *Arena* or also in the case of *Missing Landscape*. It is about a missing landscape; the one you cannot see but feel its presence. It is the threatening backstage, where the village, the parents and the relatives are, an environment that will be decisive for the kids when they will no longer be in the playground kicking the ball. The missing landscape will maybe swallow them as it sips on the ball. When the ball is away, the goalkeeper is left alone, unoccupied, wondering. These short moments, when his eyes wander and his feet kick the air, this *waiting*, this "in-between" time is the reference for the title *Missing Landscape*.

There are places, I think of the zoo in *Arena*, where anxiety and mutation is in the air. These places have something meaningful, not because they are videogenic but because they are condensations of time, like time-clouds.

I would like to speak about two other important aspects in your work: one I will call a moment of fear, because one often gets the feeling that there is a lack of time, and a lack of place in your films; a feeling of timelessness, and lack of a known place. There are people in an interview, but you don't really see where they are, they could be from anywhere, they could be not of this world. And this creates a feeling of a void, of disorientation. The other thing I would like to talk about is a moment of surreality in your works, of rendering the depiction of reality fictional.

The surreality thing … all these odd, weird, strange, other realities. Maybe we love thinking that there is *one* reality and we live in it, it's a comfortable and reassuring sensation. And if somewhere else is different or weird, then it is because it's wrong or abnormal.

Also in the sideline countries, increasingly people start using the words "absurd" and "surrealist"; they are becoming part of middle-class language.

But the difference between there and here is that *there*, people call their own everyday reality unreal and absurd, because they are aspiring to join "a normal world", they are already in touch with this "normal world" via media or emigration or, rarely, travel agencies. People start considering their own reality as surreal because it's different from the standards they wish to join. Their wish for "normal" or, let's say, "European" reality is so strong that their present reality is qualified as surreal. This constant judgment between "there" and "here" creates a kind of comical geopolitical depression. But what they call "surreal reality" is the reality they produce themselves everyday. I find myself in the middle of this consideration of one's own or the others' reality as absurd or surreal.

These moments of fear you mentioned, for example, I have experienced myself when I was preparing *Nocturnes* or filming *Uomoduomo*. Watching the man fall while sleeping, I couldn't explain what his condition was and how far it was from me. I guess the feeling of void and disorientation comes because suddenly we are unable to situate someone else's story or condition somewhere away from ours, far enough away to be able to feel safe, to be entertained without being concerned. That's interesting, because disorientation, timelessness, and lack of a known place make it universal, too.

I think the perspectives in which we stop believing, become unreal in a hurry. So maybe it's a sort of resistance to the future for me. I'm often interested in things that don't function or have failed. The future judges failed things or societies as having had inefficient goals, through the specs of the ones whose goals were more reachable. Of course there are those who failed and those who didn't, but I dislike it when efficiency becomes the priority, when *efficiency is the winner*. Technocrats are a very helpful and constructive brand of people so badly needed in the underdeveloped countries; they make infrastructures and the whole system function better and maybe people will live better due to their improvements. But unfortunately, when it comes to reality building or tracking the future …

I also think that you are in many ways a storyteller, but in a way of being somebody who helps people tell their stories. So would you say your function as an artist is to choose people to tell their stories or to look for interesting situations?

In everyday life … I realize that I don't know how to tell a good story. I mean, I'm not a good joke-teller. I don't think I'm a chooser either. Maybe a catalyst, as a starting point … but not always! I find extreme importance in details. I serve them, because in my point of view these details are so consequential. I try to reveal in them an emotional dimension, unveil their potential.

In Vienna, you will also document and do a public sound project, *No Formula*

One, No Cry, which you have previously done in Birmingham and in Frankfurt, a sound installation in taxis worldwide, which includes a soundtrack of racing cars and barking dogs. Could you just tell me more about how this idea evolved and what you want to do with that?

> Vienna will be the sixth station of the *No Formula, One No Cry* taxi network, which is or will become functional by then in Frankfurt, Birmingham, Miami, Kitakyushu and Paris. When you get in the cab, the driver will play the *No Formula One, No Cry* CD. The soundtrack is conceived to be listened to when one is driving. You experience different speeds; the real driving speed with the view of the city around, the racing car sound speed, plus a third layer, which could be linked to the notion of speed, the presence of the stray dogs barking, who introduce another world. So it is like coupling together different realities, different physical and psychological speeds.

And what about the dogs? – because I find that this is a kind of recurring theme. There are these animals which are alone, you hear sounds of animals, I have found this sound myself in many Eastern cities ...

> It's pretty much the same experience. I know this experience because there are plenty of stray dogs in Tirana and you find them also in …

... Belgrade, and Bucharest, especially in *Arena*, but also here with these dogs, there is a moment, in my opinion, when you look at what happens when a society breaks down, rules disappear, and then there are the animals which seem, in a way, to be mirrors of this disorganised society. What is the relationship between animals and human society in your work?

> I think they are not a metaphor good for a fairytale; they are there, along with the humans, part of the society. Sometimes they even replace us in places where we are supposed to be, like the dogs occupying the visitors' area in the zoo, in *Arena*. They are there where the public is supposed to be, the public being absent. They do not come as a metaphor; they are not a representation of something else.
>
> Have you ever seen a dead body of a dog? It's full of worms, until only living worms and dead skin are left, but it always looks like a dog. I always wondered if it's a dog or worms?
>
> It's interesting; in Paris the presence of the dogs is discernible by the dog shit on the streets rather than the dogs themselves. In shifting cities like Eastern capitals, you see the dogs and not the dog shit. While in Paris or Vienna, you don´t actually see them. Why is there no dog shit on the streets of Bucharest, Belgrade or Tirana? Once walking in the streets of Paris with a friend from Belgrade, trying not to step on dog shit and apparently having it in mind, we thought that maybe it is because back in the countries of our

origins, there are more unfinished spaces, not yet developed or finalized, where you have mixed areas of park, garbage, mud, grass, flowers, ruin, pulverization and construction leftovers that swallow the dog shit.

Do you think this moment of presence and absence is important in your work?

Yes, it is, because, like my life, it is continuously shaped, inspired or constrained by things like rupture, transitory or intermediate stations. Maybe I am insisting in making visible things that I find meaningful, which in our rush, we fail to appreciate, forget and let disappear or go invisible.

There is a general question about exhibition context I would like to ask you about: contemporary art from Eastern Europe, also from the Southeastern European countries, is more often shown that it was before, both in the West and then also in the East itself. For example, on the occasion of the Tirana Biennale one could see that it is also coming back to the East itself – maybe this is even more important, that it is shown now in Tirana, in Warsaw and other places. Do you feel at home in the context of a presentation such as "Eastern Art"? How would you like to have your work be contextualised geographically? Or shouldn't it be geographically?

The fact that Eastern and Southeastern European contemporary art is increasingly shown in the West is a very good thing for the public and especially for the artists. What is great is that through exhibitions on Eastern art (prior) or Balkan art (now) artists from these areas can show their work and it could be their last chances and hopes. I know a few good artists in Tirana that can intellectually survive as artists to a certain extent thanks to these exhibitions. On the other hand, I don't believe that "Eastern art" or "Balkan art" are very pertinent categories. Exhibitions on Eastern art no longer make sense, also because differences between Russia and the Balkans, East Germany and Macedonia, have grown more significant. What they probably have in common is 50 years of ideological past, but in terms of habits, attitudes, culture or problems of religion....

So it's not the ideological difference anymore, it's now more the specific problems that hold regions together.

I think specific differences have always been there, but were previously shadowed by the international character of our common past ideology, and more recently by contemporary art positions, which being of an occidental nature, often go through the same interrogation points that occidental policy does. In the 1990s, "Eastern" was the keyword, now it becomes "the Balkans".

But there were things like "Eastern art" even before that, which concerned positions such as Irwin or Laibach and so on. But not works, which are now in the focus, such as works from Milica Tomić from Belgrade, or your work. I think you're right with this idea of "Balkan art", and so you don't feel comfortable with this term either?

No, I don't. But that's okay, I can't give a better version either, but maybe we don't need to.

So you think it will just disappear, and nobody will care anymore.

I wish life would care for the artists. Let's put it this way, if you choose artists for a show that concerns Balkan or Balkan identity, often these artists no longer live in the countries where they were born.

Like you.

They live in new relationships, new vulnerabilities, and new identities in-between the countries they live in, travel to and come from. So if you just want to see them as artists from the Balkans, then sometimes it will not bring justice to the complexity of their work and engagement, it's not fair. What I mean is that often when people try to question and ask you to perform your identity, there is a risk that the public will see in you only where you come from and not what has become of you. I don't know how far we can be considered loyal mirrors of the context we came from. But maybe there is a generational occurrence too, maybe what I'm saying could be untrue if we think of artists of an older age or generation, even when they live abroad.

You have grown up in Tirana, left for Paris in 1996, and have been, it seems, travelling the globe ever since then. Your work deals with many questions related to themes of travelling and cultural identity. Which place now would you really define as your home? If you're not an Albanian artist, do you see yourself as a French one? Or do you rather try to avoid these schemes?

If in Albania people saw me as a French artist, and in France they considered me as Albanian artist then I would feel very lonely. If I had to give a recognized answer then I would check my passport and read that Anri is an Albanian living in France with a "profession liberale" visa. That counts because it's real! I would avoid the rest. I cherish travelling and not belonging. When I was living in Albania I was trying hard to get out of the country as often as I could. After arriving in Paris, during my studies I travelled less than before, but I found other ways of travelling like watching hours of movies or meeting people. In the last years I've been travelling more … I feel closer to some places than to others. I feel closer to cities than to countries, I feel closer to Paris, Tirana or a few other cities, rather than France or Albania. I feel closer to a street than to a whole city, and by consequence, because of travelling I feel sometimes close to terminal 2F of Charles de Gaulle. Yesterday in the tube station I saw a man begging on his knees with a piece of paper on which was written: "Je suis un réfugié, je n'ai pas de maison". I wondered why it didn't say: "I'm a refugee, I have no country"?

What's the relation between plan/will/decision and, on the other hand, chance and circumstance, for your work? Let's take an example such as *Ghostgames*. If you take this relation and try to explain how a work like *Ghostgames* comes into existence – what is the relationship between "I want to do it, I know exactly what I'm doing, I have a plan, I have a script", and, on the other hand, the chances, the things to pick up and integrate into the work?

I look for continuous change in my work, going from one step to another. I got the first impulse for *Ghostgames* when I was in Brazil. The nature of some of my recent works is also related to the possibility of having a more intimate relationship to a larger world. One night, walking along the beach with a friend, we were trying not to walk on the crabs, because there were plenty of them. We made our way with the help of flashlights, and when we noticed the impact the light had on the crabs, we started to use it and play with them. A strong image remained in my head and often visited me later, maybe because of its density, strangeness and ambiguity. So I decided to come back, rewind and go further, draw a structure and formulate rules, invent the game. I researched in order to find out which crabs those were, and see where and when the shooting could take place. I contacted many experts and researchers in Brazil, Chile, Taiwan, Cape Verde, Australia, United States, before I continued the project with Dan Rittschof, a brilliant researcher from Duke University in North Carolina, who helped me with the filming on a small East Coast island in the U.S. It was fascinating to work on a "game" with people with scientific approaches. There is an immense sense of playfulness, freedom, generosity, curiosity and risk. Sometimes I was freaking too, I was investing time in this idea, convincing people and making it happen with them … and then the ghost crabs, oh my god … their walkabouts are so much related to the environmental degradation, urbanisation and human impacts on the one hand, and on the other their movements also depend on the new moon, temperature, high and low tides. All these circumstances created a big difference to my previous experiences. The difference between *Ghostgames* and previous works is that with *Ghostgames* I envisioned the whole thing, thinking it up from the beginning, in terms of inventing the game and its rules, and finding an ideal place to do it.

Ghostgames has many aggressive, fight-like elements; the title "games" seems ironic in many ways. You film the animals trying to escape, and being irritated by

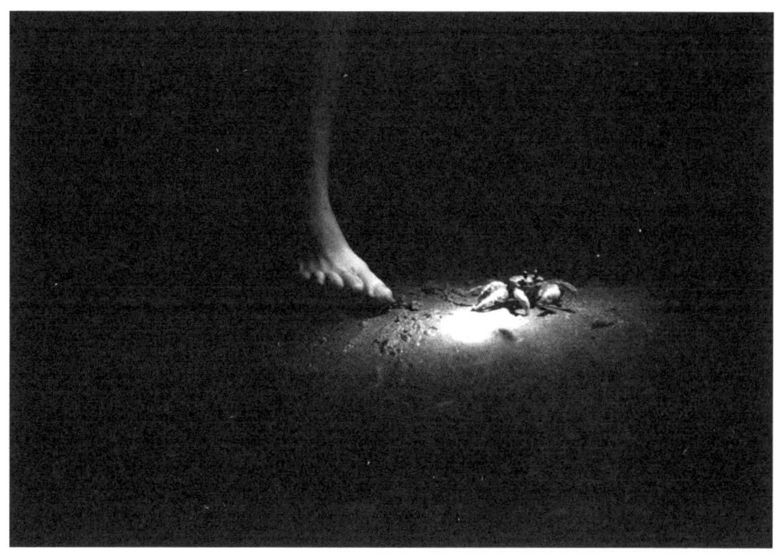

the light and directed in circles by the players. Do you think of this also in terms of a metaphor of aggression or war? And if so, what would then be the structural function of the players?

> I'm very thrilled that *Ghostgames* enacts such questions. At some point I would fear that the final result would carry no hints, and would look like a sort of *National Geographic* tape. This playfully aggressive, chasing and ominous situation … I was hoping that these questions could break the surface. I was working for it. But the thing is that I feel more at ease doing work that backs questioning rather than answering them myself in an interview.

We didn't get to speak about Edi Muka and what he said about fatality, the fatalistic artist. There was an imaginary interview he did, so it was not really done with you, but what would you have answered?

> I don't know what I would have answered, but no … I don't think at all that I'm a fatalist. But I find it witty. And he too, he does, I think.

He also said that, in one of your works, I think it was *Nocturnes*, but maybe you could also talk about this in *Arena*, maybe even in *Promises*, he said that "the smell of death is present". What is there about this smell of death? Has this something to do with your work, do you feel comfortable with this idea of death?

> I think it's more about dead moments rather than dead people. More precisely these are moments that play the dead, moments that hide rebirth potentials.

We've touched upon the moment of truth in your work, when we were speaking about truth in documentary, and that you act like a catalyst.

Are we closer to the truth in a documentary? I think of [Werner] Herzog when he says that in cinema, "there is such a thing as poetic, ecstatic truth … it is mysterious and elusive, and can be reached only through fabrication and imagination and stylisation." When you cut and edit documentary rushes, at best you can create new moments of *truth* or *truths*. You show something and consciously leave out something else, as if it had never existed. Where there is a moment of choice there is a moment of manipulation. The "truth", I would say, doesn't interest me as a fact. I'm interested in what's missing, forgotten or left over. I'm interested in the truths that originate from our needs and the hopes and wishes or the things we don't need or we don't wish.

In an interview with Hans-Ulrich Obrist, you spoke about "resistance – existence", in connection with the exhibition *Les Immateriaux* on the Internet and the media by Lyotard – he had an unrealised plan to do an exhibition about resistance. What would you say if someone asked you or told you, you are a political artist, you deal with political issues, with war? Could you place this context of "resistance – existence" somewhere? What is political about your work?

I am interested in politics without being a political artist or a social worker. It's very difficult or maybe impossible to play such a role, when you grow up during the capitulation of a society with social ideals and come out of its wreckage. Where people start saying again "sir" instead of "comrade" and enjoy it so much as a sign of freedom. I totally understand it, because I'm aware of the context, and anyway, many words lose their meaning.

I think I'm interested in politics through my work, in terms of existence and survival and continuation. So at that point it depends on how somebody asks me this question and on the context. There are an increasing number of works that are straightforwardly related to politics, but in a way I don't feel familiar with.

And what about this "resistance – existence", what did you mean by that?

Maybe something like … Existence without Resistance is like living without feeling it.

Anri Sala in conversation with Gerald Matt in the spring of 2003 on the occasion of the exhibition *Anri Sala* at Kunsthalle Wien.
Anri Sala was born in Tirana, Albania in 1974. He lives and works in Paris, France.

Markus Schinwald

I'm so much opposed to expressive art that it doesn't even play a role as an opponent.

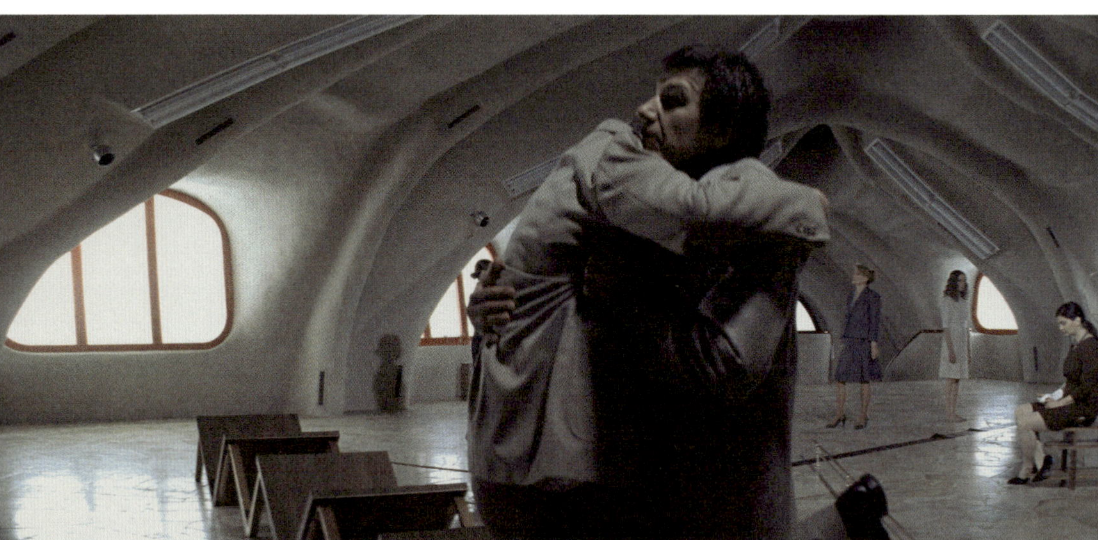

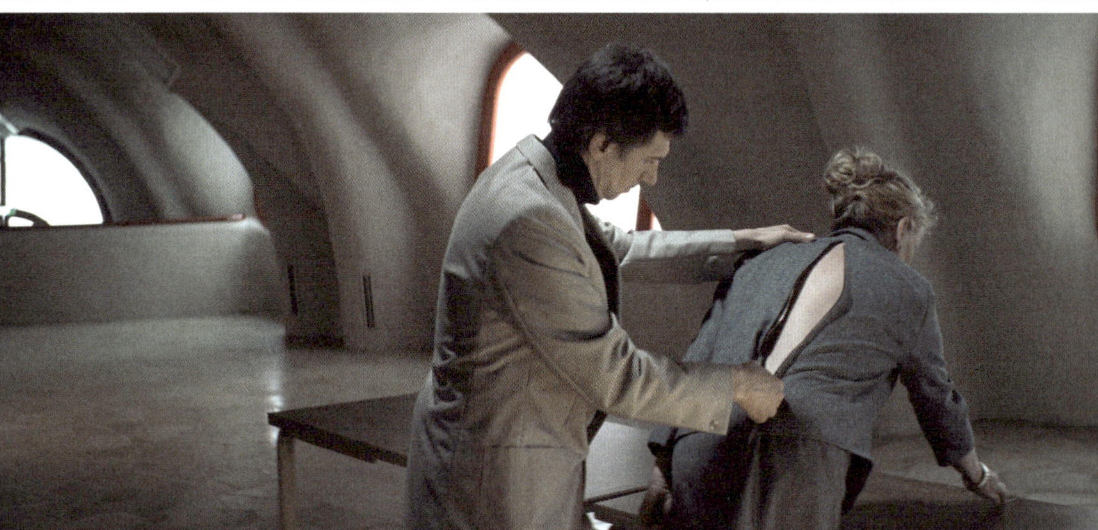

Video stills: Markus Schinwald,
Ten in Love, 2006

Your work *Stage* is positioned in the area outside the exhibition *Love/Hate: Approaches Towards the Grand Emotion Between Art and Theatre*. It is in the outside area because, from a curator's point of view, a tense relationship should be produced between it and the overheated, stark and passionate emotions, which play a role in works exhibited inside and which represent "Great Emotion" in all its diverse variants. In contrast to this, and in contrast to the illustrated red curtain, which actually leads one to expect expressiveness and theatrical feelings, *Stage* shows unrelatedness and undercooled emotions. Are you criticizing expressive art in this way?

> I am so much opposed to expressive art that it doesn't even play a role as an opponent.

The subject on the poster does, of course, have something to do with unrelatedness, but on the other hand there are some features in common, especially since all three persons are situated in a room where not much else is going on – and don't similarities create such a thing as relatedness?

> The woman in front of the curtain is, by the way, a kind of inversion of a Hitchcock-style character – we, who are not in the poster, watch the watcher watching.

The exhibition's theme suggests the question as to whether emotions can be represented at all. Themes like love and hate have always found their way into both theatre and the visual arts, and for the artist, no doubt, one function of art among others is to be the place where subjective experiences, so strong that they simply have to be expressed, can be processed and sublimated. The question arises as to whether the authenticity of feelings is not lost when they are represented in art. Can feelings be conveyed at all from one person to another? Or, doesn't the immediacy of feeling mean that they have to be made separately for the viewer in art?

> Presumably the latter, if we view sublimation not as the translation of a feeling from the production into that of reception, but as a necessary exchange of feelings into something similar, the painting of wild images, for example.
>
> But of course it doesn't have to be art. Freud speaks in a much more general way, if you think, for example, of his wonderful "Comments on Faces and Men"[1], where he writes about coarse effects of sublimation in the portraits of famous men and says that the most lively faces were those of men in whom sublimation had the slightest effect.
>
> But, in spite of the beautiful texts, I don't want to believe completely in the idea of sublimation. Making art, for me, has more social or political reasons than psychological ones. Even without art, I would not go mad.

In his video *Violent Incident – Man/Woman*, Bruce Nauman shows a love-hate scene where hate and a quarrel arise within seconds from a situation of deep romance. To what extent do you agree with the idea in the video and in the exhibition, or at least in the title of the exhibition, that love and hate are two sides of the same coin and taken together make up "Grand Emotion"? Is there such a thing as a dialectical interrelationship of emotions?

> The same coin would mean the absolutely identical object, and I don't believe that. Perhaps hate is the negative dimension of love, but that doesn't make it the same thing. What is true is that feelings can be translated more easily into feelings of similar intensity; for example, hate is closer to a "great" feeling such as love than indifference would be, which may be closer on the scale of feelings but would need a much greater effort.

You work both in the field of contemporary dance and performance and also in the various media of visual art. You once said that you yourself can really practice no craft to perfection, which is why you always work together with people who can provide the technical know-how. Then you are the one in the background who pulls the strings. That gives you enormous flexibility in the medium and supports your mental access to art. Why is the variability in the medium so important for you? What different opportunities do you get, for example, from the stage, the customary exhibition area or from billboard walls?[2]

> Since I came into contact with other forms of cultural production before art, the decision to limit myself to only one medium and one audience is less natural to me than to work with forms which have specific qualities in both production and reception (anyone who has ever played in a band or shot a goal knows what I mean). Books have no sounds, films have no breaks, etc.
>
> When I work with specialists, then, it is not always in the form of a commission, but a request for complicity. In other words it's not just a matter of technically carrying out a commission, but of bearing at least part of the decision-making process. In this way, I also don't have to spend so much time in the same medium; that is practical, because I didn't get into art to end up doing the same thing every day.

As in many other of your works, in *Stage* as well, the protagonist's room for action is limited by a suit in which both sleeves have been sewn together, and, in other places, bodies, objects and fashion are manipulated so that original functional processes are interrupted and the things or parts of the body are practically no longer able to fulfil their purpose. For example, the person wearing the *Rejoicing Shirt* cannot stop rejoicing; the sleeves of the shirt are raised up stiffly – from rejoicing to a straightjacket. You make the human dependency on the body painful, and conscious of their everyday use: how sadistic are you?

Not at all. Basically I mean well. I never work with pain, although people might sometimes look silly or make a poor impression; but, in the end, I am more concerned with a kind of story about coping with the body, in which functions, dysfunctions, solecisms, rituals and utopias had a role to play. The *Rejoicing Shirt*, for example, evokes celebration and capitulation simultaneously – but from a technical point of view, I have merely exaggerated a piece of cultural history and done what is always done in any case by conductors' suits; namely, I sewed the sleeves on with a slight twist. So, I'm a maker of prostheses for indeterminate cases.

In an age that democratises the star principle with TV productions like *Starmania*, *Popstars*, and *Superstars* and has the potential of making the entire world a stage, the relation between theatre in an exclusive aesthetic realm and the self-presentation rituals in the urban space must be redefined and measured with the means of art. How much authenticity and directness is contained in stage design as filtered through the art of theatre? And, how much artificiality rules in the rituals of "see and be seen" on the catwalks of the urban stage (disco, hip hangout, cultural event), which themselves follow a predetermined script and

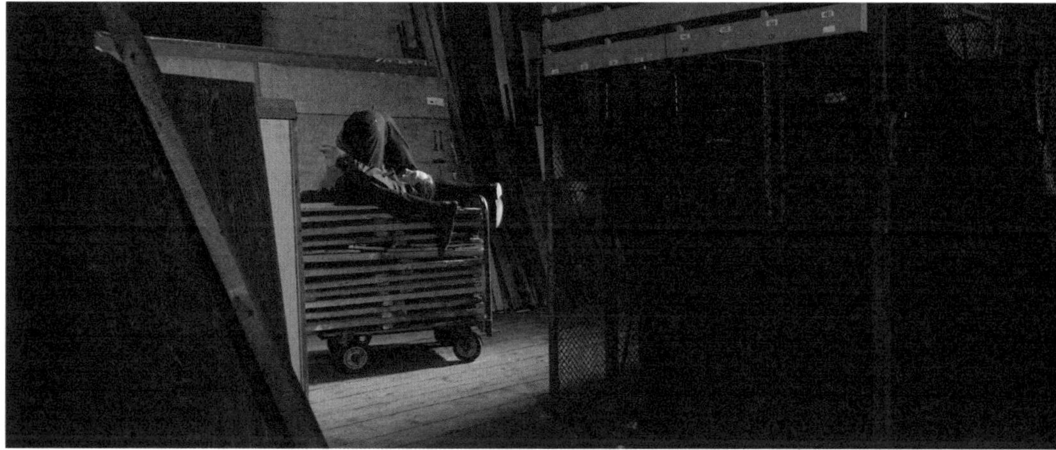

Video still:
Markus Schinwald,
Contortionist (Hait),
2006

define a long-established performative codex?

None. Authenticity is corrupt, which is why we have buried it. Theatrical or artistic productions of all kinds are not to be measured by the yardstick of authenticity but according to how good they are, what they achieve, what they leave out and how they are consumed.

Star-shows, which have become the in-thing, not only in music, don't work because of their authenticity, but because they create opportunities. In times of worldwide unemployment and lack of opportunity, it is only human to be happy about the few opportunities that exist, even when they are not completely honest. Unfortunately there is still no quality version of such things, but perhaps this is only a question of time.

Subject-object relations are frequently reversed in your art. Artefacts and constructions are very nearly auraticised and fetishised, machines and rooms are given a life of their own and people are almost naturally made dependent on prostheses and their own creations …

 Just as in normal life, really, because we tend to bestow an independent existence upon things to become emotionally attached to them. Whether it makes sense or not is not even a relevant category. Many things, possibly even the nicest things in life, dodge any rational purpose. And as long as we can choose which things we wish to become dependant on, I've got no problem with it. However it stops being funny when this dependency is prescribed. So what I do in these works isn't all that different from the way that Tamagotchis, or high heels or tuned cars function, with the slight difference that the things and objects people get attached to in the films don't have an immediate parallel in everyday life

Last weekend, the Styrian Autumn exhibition was opened. The project you realised together with Oleg Soulimenko for the Kunsthaus is structured as a performance at the exhibition hall. You are once again employing a very much reduced stylistic vocabulary, positioning a wall with a kind of double casing inside this room, a sort of trick chest or strange apparatus with which the performer occupies himself, tirelessly exploring it and using it to entertain the audience. Is the absurdity of this wall and the action that accompanies it a metaphor for the navel-gazing of the individual in a society where people no longer find a way to make contact with one another?

That's actually not how I would see it. I don't believe in any collective increase in loneliness, though it may happen in individual cases. Mankind is not lonelier now than it was 200 years ago just because we have the Internet. What has most certainly changed, though, are the forms of intimacy

Markus Schinwald,
Children's Crusade,
2004

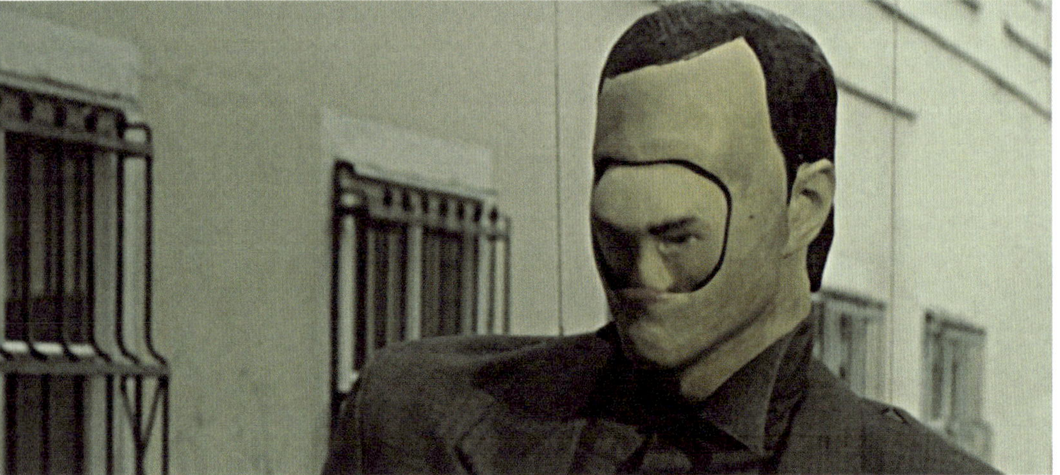

and public sphere. Today, the private and public sectors are barely separated and there ought really to be a much broader vocabulary to describe these changes, situations and hybrids. In the project I did for Styrian Autumn, I picked a situation where the attempt was made (given that public occurrence of the intimate often appears absurd) to use intimately absurd means to anaesthetise a kind of public feeling.

Ritualised acts, children who, in *Children's Crusade*, follow a masked leader as if they had been hypnotised, automatic motion processes, blindly steering protagonists who, it would seem, can no longer feel their own bodies and carry out their activities movements like robots or puppets on remote control. Pure art objects? Or, a philosophical allusion to the determinedness of man's fate or perhaps his socio-cultural dependency on authoritarian structures?

A song against authority.

Film is one of the main media in which you have been working. Could you perhaps name some of the films that have particularly interested you and have they also had an influence on your work?

I always follow quite a few films, though I have acquired the habit of seeing films in fragmented form. More and more, I keep watching for details and subtexts rather than the storyline. An entire story interests me little and my tolerance threshold for predictable ends is quite high. Hollywood cinema is a factory manufacturing details and for that reason closer to my heart than European film, which tends to function very hermetically and is difficult to "skim read" – it's no accident that very little good slapstick has come out of Europe and that science fiction film is underdeveloped.

But it's difficult to pick your influences; it's a hand you are either dealt or denied. To give you one example – when the time came for me to get to like Fassbinder, suddenly the most unappearing people all around me started to worship him, so of course it was impossible for me to do the same. Had there been different concomitant circumstances I would most likely find the stuff quite good today …

In the usually discursive context surrounding your work, terms like hysteria, the uncanny, shibboleth, obsessive-compulsive symptoms, etc. keep reappearing. What has been the role of psychoanalysis and its theory or its theoreticians for your work, in actual fact?

Well, if you work with your body or its perception by others, you cannot escape psychoanalysis at all. It's hardly possible to do anything that hasn't been commented on at some point or other by psychoanalysis. So it does play nothing but a major role.

Diarios (to you) is a strongly appealing and atmospheric film work in black-and-white, likely to be the most poetic among your works. It is a combination of text / poetry and moving picture with, among other things, landscape shots and the play of light. Is it a screen romance?

Absolutely.

What are your next steps, any definite plans? What are your dream projects?

I don't get a real chance to really wish for anything – a lot has happened recently. At the moment there are a few wishes that seem to fulfil themselves even before I´ve had a chance to wish for them.

For one, there's a "disguised exhibition" taking place in conjunction with the Museo d'Arte Moderna of Bologna in Italy, where I'm having an exhibition at the Palazzo Poggi, a science museum, dating back to the 18th century, a time when the division line between art and the sciences wasn't as strictly drawn as it is now.

For the exhibition I will be removing objects from the collection, commenting on some or replacing them with works of my own. Next, I have an exhibition at the Aspen Art Museum, in Colorado, which I'm very much looking forward to. And then, next year, another project, which will be a completely new departure for me – I'll be doing a sitcom series.

Markus Schinwald in conversation with Gerald Matt and Angela Stief on the occasion of the exhibition *Love/Hate. Versuche zum großen Gefühl zwischen Kunst und Theater* (2003) at Ursula Blickle Foundation, Kraichtal and in 2006. The artist took part in the exhibition *Lebt und arbeitet in Wien II* (2005) at Kunsthalle Wien.
Markus Schinwald, born 1973 in Salzburg, Austria, lives and works in Vienna and Los Angeles, California.

German to English translation by Tom Appleton.

1   Sigmund Freud: "Notes on Faces and Men" written after a visit to the National Portrait
     Gallery in London, published in: *Unser Herz zeigt nach dem Süden. Reisebriefe 1895 – 1923*, ed.
     Christfried Tögel, Berlin, Aufbau Verlag 2002

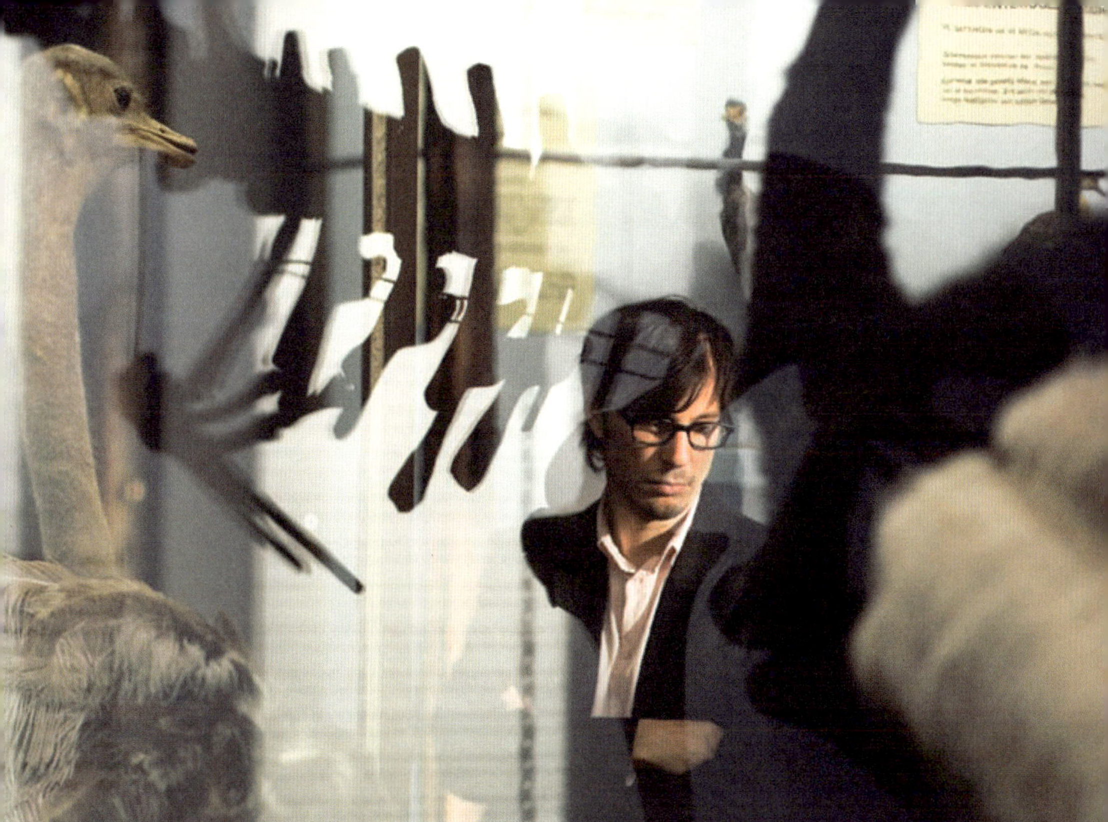

Markus Schinwald

Bouna Medoune Seye

One cannot lock djinns up.

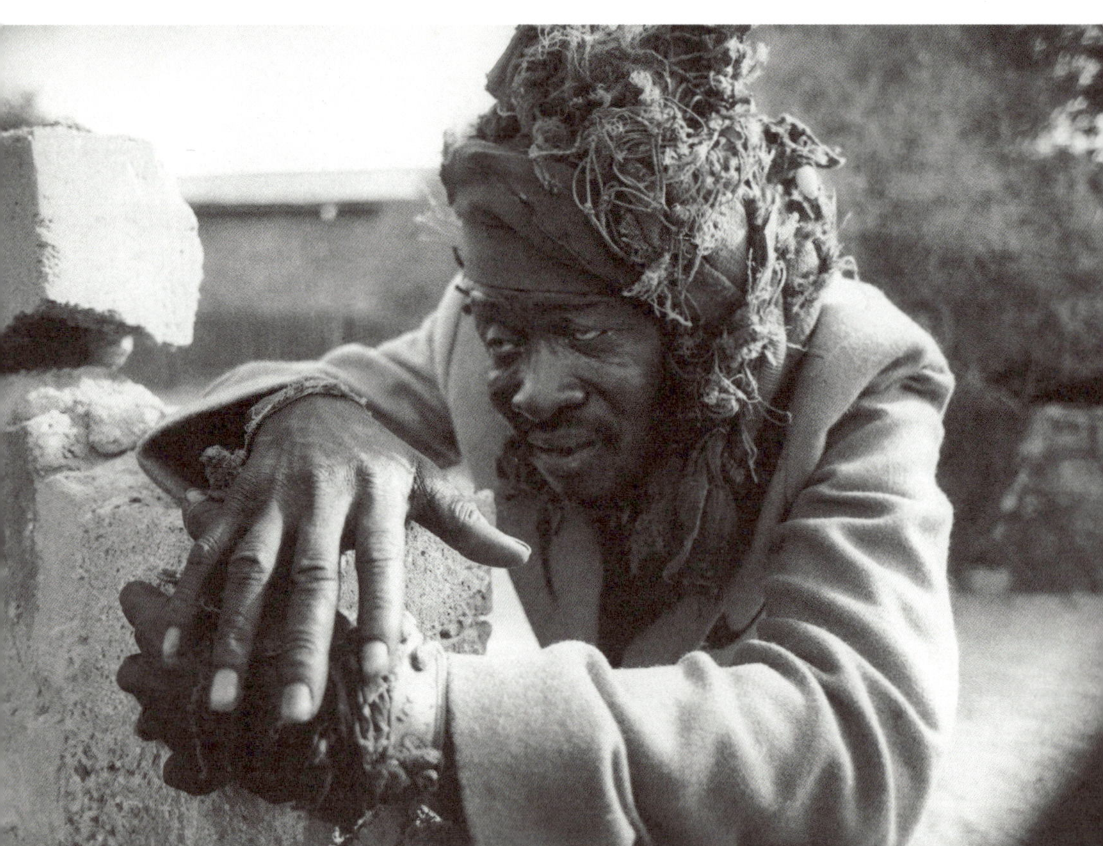

Bouna Medoune Seye,
Les trottoirs de Dakar

Monsieur Seye, you are a photographer and a film producer. Among your most impressive works are *Zone Rap*, a documentation on Senegalese Hip-Hop, and the photographic cycle, *Les Trottoirs de Dakar* (The Sidewalks of Dakar). Can you tell us how this work came about, and how long it took you to complete it?

I now reside in Paris. However, I was born in Dakar and have also lived there for a long time. With us in West Africa, families have the option of leaving mad relatives outside to live in freedom. They have the alternative to either undergo a traditional or a modern form of therapy – but they are not locked up. I wanted to make this photographic cycle above all, because I have a feeling that I am like these people, footloose and fancy-free. Before the book *Les Trottoirs de Dakar* was published, I had spent ten years working with the mad people who roam the streets of the city. I worked with them and I lived with them.

Are there many of these "fous" in Dakar?

Yes, very many. Generally, a great liberality prevails towards these mad people in Dakar, yes even in all of Senegal. The fact that they are not hospitalised is for them almost like a kind of therapy. They can move about freely in the streets, feeding from rubbish bins.

Does the permissive attitude towards these mad people have anything to do with the strength of the family units in Senegal? Or is it simply that the people are too poor to afford a proper therapy for their relatives?

No, no, this has nothing to do with poverty at all. The mad people were always free in this country. Usually they get group therapy and, of course, there are also hospitals in Dakar that specialise in treating them. But many of these people simply prefer to remain in the streets, and their families accept that.

And how does society react?

Society doesn't discriminate against the mad people either. Do you know, for us the "fous" are not merely mentally benighted, they are also illuminates. The mad person remains an individual like everybody else; with the only difference that he or she is, as we say, possessed. Sometimes we also express it in this way: the mad person has too much spirit and his or her consciousness is not human. If the spirit of a person lives with the djinns, then one must also accept that the djinns are free. One cannot lock them up.

Do the mad people come from certain environments or from all areas of the population?

They come from all ethnic groups and from all social classes. In former times a kind of therapy existed for the violent ones. They were tied up from morning till night and that made them calmer and less aggressive. There are mad people from very large and affluent families; but they are not locked up, because one simply doesn't want to restrict the djinns' freedom of movement.

Were the people you worked with just total strangers that you approached in the streets?

Often it was like that, and in the course of our work together we became better acquainted with each other. But it is not easy to establish contact with these people. They are usually very reserved and do not like to speak with people. It took me ten years to get to know them really well. I will never be done with this work, because I am actually quite mad myself, but then again not as mad as to want to become like these homeless people. When I'd already been working on this project for some five years, my family suddenly panicked. They said, "You will end up like these mad people some day."

Are there also people who were virtually driven to madness by their ever-deteriorating living conditions?

Yes, there is such a thing as madness brought on by economic duress. Usually they are people, who moved from the country to Dakar on account of their financial problems. Then they live here and no longer wish to return.

How did the public in Senegal react to *Les Trottoirs de Dakar*?

Well, the mayor, for example, said to me: "Now you're exaggerating." And I replied: "Was it I who brought the mad people to Dakar?" There are people, you know, who do not show much sympathy for art, or are even downright aggressive towards it. But that is all part of the game, even part of its intention. One needs to force people to take a look at the things they see every day, but which they do not wish to see.

Are the family structures we talked about earlier still a concern in Africa, or are they slowly being eroded by globalisation and the neo-absolutism of the post-independence era?

I believe one would need to look at Senegal and the other African countries separately in this regard. Here, the families are not being destroyed. It's all the same, whether you are rich or poor. Family members do not leave each other in the rut. Individualisation has its limits as far as we are concerned.

Normally the people always remain within the context of their families and their village communities. If they come into the city, they only do so, because things have come to a head. During the dry seasons of the Sahel it would be pointless for a Senegalese peasant farmer to remain in the country. There is often no rain, and agriculture is then no longer possible. That is why Dakar continues to grow and become ever more densely populated.

How did you begin working as a photographer and what was your family's attitude to this profession?

My parents never understood it. I started out by studying law, but soon gave it up and devoted myself entirely to photography. I told my parents that this was my destiny and at some point, they finally accepted it. In my own self-estimation, I was always a photographer ever since my childhood. When I was still quite small, I sought out all the photographic studios in the neighbourhood and took much delight in the fact that my mother quite happily and frequently had herself photographed. I also played with a kind of puppet theatre with figures I had cut out of cardboard. That was my first access to an artistic form of expression. It is not easy being an artist here in Dakar because the politicians generally have no awareness of how creative people can contribute to the nation's economic prosperity. We are a country where peanuts are cultivated, but in truth art contributes substantially more to the gross national product. In Senegal, however, artists are pushed right out to the edges of society, particularly if they originate from less affluent families. There have been people, who were driven to suicide by this situation. On the one hand, they were obstructed in practising their art, while on the other, they were regarded as sluggards by their families.

Can you tell us how photography in Senegal has developed in the 20th century?

In actual fact, everything started with Mama Casset. This man was the first major photographer in Senegal. Before him, there was Meissa Gueye, who was already taking pictures in the early years of the previous century. Mama was born in 1908, and he took up his photographic apprenticeship in 1920. He was an NCO and a photographer in the French army and took pictures during colonial times throughout Africa. I even met and became personally acquainted with Mama Casset and quite consciously followed the tradition that he had created. In this way, I wanted to expressly point out that Senegal has a history of photography, which dates back at least a hundred years. In the past I would often tell acquaintances, "I have a Senegalese photograph that is 80 years old," but nobody would believe me.

Monsieur Seye, you have not only taken photographs, but have also made films and videos …

Yes, I wanted to watch my photographs starting to walk. I wanted to see the continuity of movement, and to observe how the negatives came in motion. I had returned from France to Dakar in 1986 and was given the opportunity by one particular producer to take my first steps in the field of cinema.

We were particularly impressed by your documentary work, *Zone Rap*, introducing a Senegalese subculture that is hardly known here at all.

Now, they always told me: don't ever allow the rappers to get a word in, because they have nothing to say anyway. But that is not true at all. I have known the Rap movement for the past 15 years. I am a part of it, myself. I know most of the groups, no, I actually know them all. And I shot the film, because I wanted to help them find their own language and a means of expressing it. They should be able to say what they think. My camera was only a witness of their expressive intention. The Hip-Hop people explain very well what is awry in Senegal and also on the Ivory Coast. They point a finger at the errors of the public administration, they speak of the young people who are sacrificed by the politicians for their own personal aims, of those politicians who led our country into misery. To give you just one example: if a government minister embezzles cash that was intended for inoculations against polio, to buy a Mercedes for himself, then three or four thousand young people will end up in the streets as cripples. The rappers state it clearly: there must be an end to the suppression of public funds, the people in government must stop thinking about themselves only, they must find a way to think of the common weal.

Your film is made very cleverly. There are scenes, which are swayed by a strong groove. Then again, one only hears the voices of the rappers, inventing a rhythm of their own without any drum accompaniment.

I don't know. I have a quite elementary style of guiding the camera. But I do not leave anything to chance in my art. If I cannot master a subject, then I won't touch it. For me it would be dangerous to show a work, which I could not explain. It would be dangerous for my own mind.

Is it true that the rappers in Dakar are a kind of Voice of Youth, a kind of oral CNN for the many illiterates that live in the city?

The rappers, in any case, are no informers for the authorities, they inform the people. In Senegal the educational system, which was called the "système claque", was a failure. This system involved instructing the pupils by means of televised courses. What they learned in this way was only to repeat things but they still could not read. Now the rappers are helping them to be informed about social and political events in our country. This they do by stating in a very straightforward way just what is what. The politicians do not like them, that is quite clear, because the rappers come out with the things that they would rather see concealed.

Monsieur Seye, in Francophone Africa, the arts are strongly linked with French institutions. Is this a helpful link, or does it just build up a renewed relationship of dependency?

I do not understand the concept of "assistance" in the cultural area at all. These cultural centres to some degree represent a real danger for the artists. If they take a big name artist under contract, then in the long run it's the cultural centre that becomes the star and not the artist. All of these biennials, which were created in Africa – what was the outcome for the artists themselves? Next to nothing. And in most cases, they are also very poorly organised. If the artists dash off to the biennials in Dakar or Bamako and buzz about with their invitation cards from one idiotic reception at a gallery to the next, then that doesn't do anything for anybody. At best the organisers themselves stand to gain: France doles out some cash, the European union pays for it, but only those people are promoted who had been favoured from the very outset.

Is there an alternative to these conditions, in the shape of some idea of an all-African form of art or do the artists in each country work along by and for themselves?

I believe that art is in any case a personal effort to begin with. The pan-African vision was primarily a political and economic concept and only at a secondary level did it also have something to do with culture. I respect the creators of pan-Africanism, but I am convinced that if one had placed artists at the head of this movement, then we would not be in the situation we are in today.

Bouna Medoune Seye in conversation with Gerald Matt and Thomas Mießgang in 2001 on the occasion of the exhibition *Flash Afrique: Fotografie aus Westafrika* (2001) at Kunsthalle Wien.
Bouna Medoune Seye was born in Dakar, Senegal, in 1956. He lives and works in Dakar.

French to English translation by Christoph Winder.

Santiago Sierra

I do not caricature capitalism for I consider it a kind of "eternal damnation" inflicted on humankind.

Santiago Sierra, *Banner Suspended in Front of a Cove,* Cala San Vincente, Mallorca, 2001

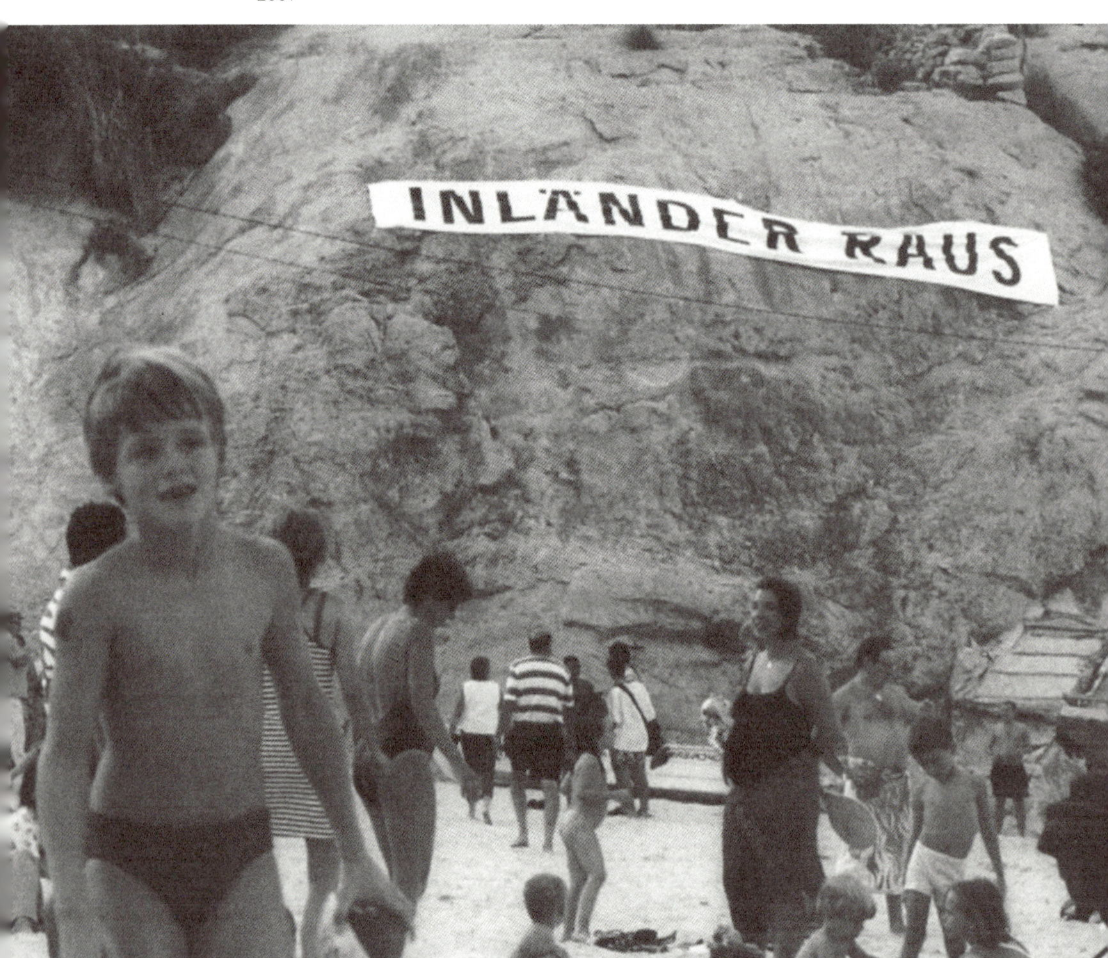

Central to your work are seemingly pointless tasks performed by persons who are paid for participating in your art projects. In one of your pieces people supported the wall of a gallery at an angle of 60 degrees during four hours over a period of five days; or for another work – *250 cm Line Tattooed on Six Remunerated People* – you paid people to have a line tattooed across their backs who are now branded for life in exchange for hardly more than a little pocket money.

Unlike any other artist, you dramatise the well-known, and often heard, dictum "time is money" for art shows. You take this saying literally although the type of remuneration offered is not necessarily money but can even be a shot of heroin. In fact, how cynical is Santiago Sierra?

> We call somebody "cynical" who is a shameless liar or we use the term in the sense of "impudent". This question tells me a lot about you. You are of the opinion that it is wrong to say that people work for money and sell their time and that somebody who says so is a great liar, and this in fact suggests some priggishness in dealing with these issues. I think that your question reflects attitudes quite common in the art scene from which I would actually like to dissociate myself.

You use people – to put it in your own words – as material and objects. In your projects you are concerned with the social structures of work and pay in the capitalist system as well as the consequences of modernism. By using different methods, you try to depict capitalism as a caricature of itself. Isn't this a strategy at the expense of the deprived and underprivileged who are exposed in your works and who are already "victims" of the system?

> As, to the introduction of your question, I do not use any methods distinct from capitalism, since there is no such alternative methodology and I do not caricature capitalism for I consider it a kind of "eternal damnation" inflicted on humankind. As far as the rest is concerned, this is a statement rather than a question, to which one can add only "yes" or "no". Yes. When we hire people we do so with a view to their usefulness for our own purposes – and this is always profit. Of course it would be impossible to speak of "the privileged of the system" in this context and I agree with you when you define them as those "who are already victims".

You know that the strength of capitalism lies in its capacity to market everything it wants to, even the criticism about capitalism. As a radical critic of capitalism, you yourself are caught in a network of an art industry that is an integral part – sometimes maybe even a critical part – of society and of capitalism. Aren't you afraid of being swallowed up by the system?

> I am not qualified to act as a critic of capitalism, this would be very optimis-

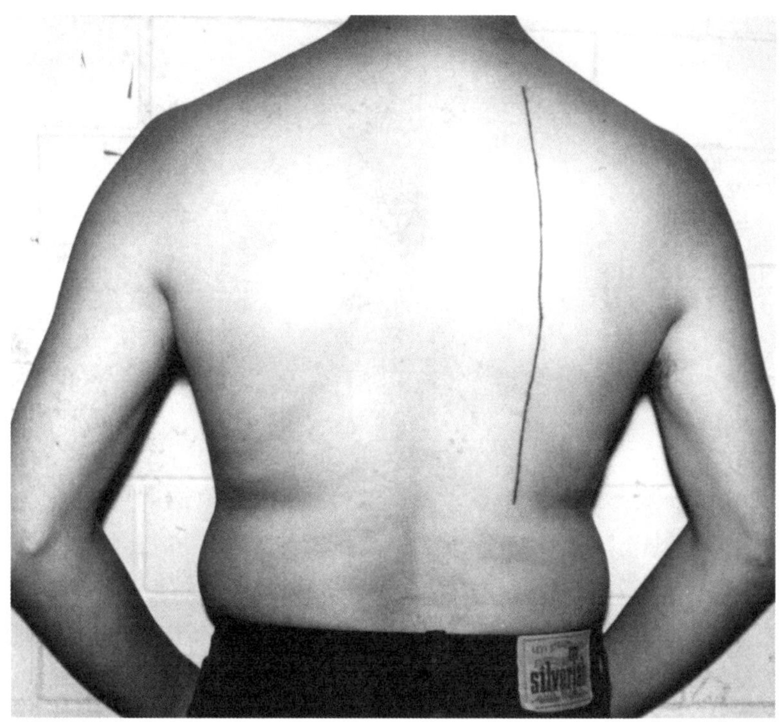

Santiago Sierra,
*Person Paid to Have 30
cm Line Tattooed on
Them*, Calle Regina,
Mexico City, 1998

tic on my part. And this is exactly why I am not afraid of being swallowed up by the system. I was already swallowed up by it when I was born.

For your work at the Project Space of Kunsthalle Wien, you arranged 30 people from Vienna into a palette of skin colours ranging from the lightest to the darkest. Why did you choose this work for Vienna? What connection does this project have with previous ones? For the P.S.1 Contemporary Art Center in New York you planned a project that would have consisted in arranging people by hierarchical order. This project was not realised. Can you tell me more about it?

Race is a factor that does not have anything to do with formal education but rather with genetics and is generally used as a criterion to select staff. This practice is more widespread in multi-ethnic environments than in places with little ethnic diversity. I tried to arrange the entire staff of the P.S.1 in a line reflecting their position in the hierarchy – from the director to the lowest-ranking employee – but not based on their colours. In fact, we could have used the colour of their skin as the criterion – the result would still have been the same. The lower echelons of the hierarchy quite liked the idea but the executives found it intolerable. In Vienna, just like in the rest of the European Union, a strange discussion is going on that is all about race but without ever using the term. But they are only getting adjusted to something that is a common practice in places such as New York.

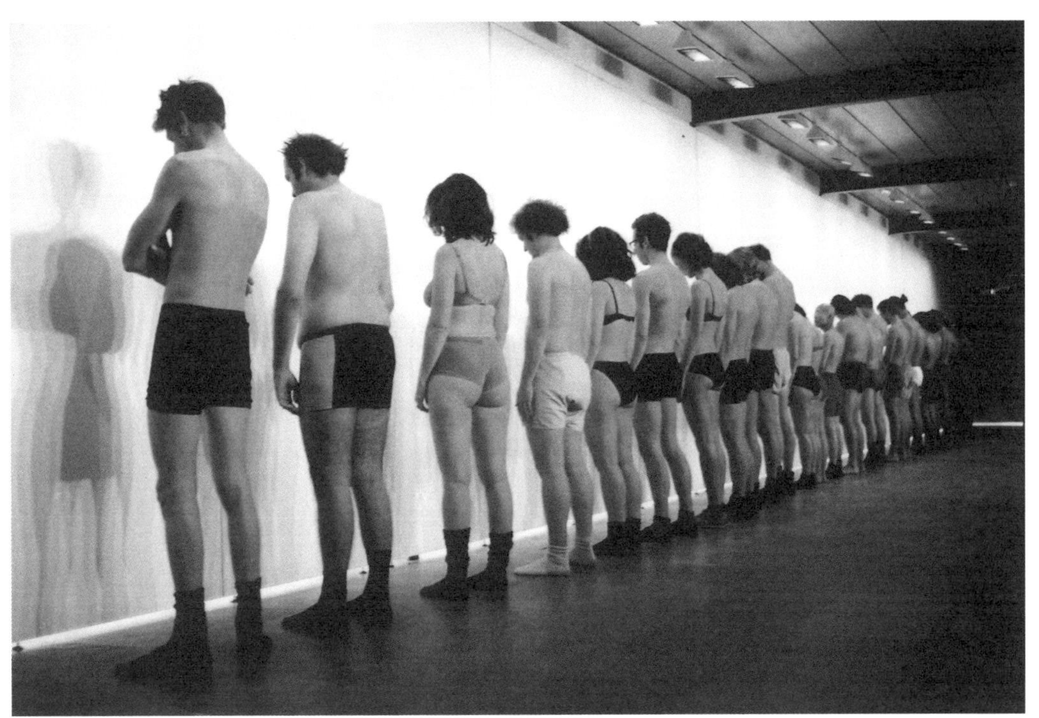

What do you think about the socio-political concept of "civic work" formulated by the sociologist Ulrich Beck in 1997? Beck proposed that in nations with mass unemployment the jobless should do voluntary social work under the supervision of welfare officers. They would be rewarded but not paid for their work.

I think this was formulated by Groucho Marx: This seems hilariously stupid to me.

The expectation of provoking action or reaction by participation of the audience can be considered quite important in contemporary art. If so, this would also apply to the break with the traditional and static relationship between the work and the onlooker. Your pieces spotlight one form of participation, i.e. remunerated people. Usually it is the onlooker who participates, whereas in your projects the onlooker is confronted almost exclusively with the traditional photographic and documentary work. Which role is the onlooker/audience/recipient expected to play in your art?

The onlooker is an integral part of the work in the visual arts, Velázquez was well aware of this fact in his work *Las Meninas*. I distinguish only between people with different intentions who share a common space. It is wrong to think that the semantic meaning can be found only where the work is to be found. When the work consists of a group of persons and the audience as well, these people can exchange their roles without a problem since, from my point of view, both constitute the piece in equal parts.

For your project *Obstruction of a Freeway with a Trailer Truck* you chose a road with a heavy traffic load in Mexico City. I think this is a very typical work of yours as it symbolically stands for the interruption of dynamic structures frequently found in your pieces. You use stylistic methods of negation. Moreover, your work reflects confrontation, futility, bulkiness, doing-nothing, tautology, fatalism and even hate. Is that your way of pleading for more resistance and "conflict culture"? Or is it simply resignation in view of reality?

Rather the second but one should not forget that resignation is close to hate, as Machiavelli said: fear and hope weaken the heart.

Why did you go to Mexico City? How did Mexico City change your attitude towards art and your strategies in art? How important is your artistic environment in Mexico City? What is the link between you and the work of Teresa Margolles?

I went to Mexico for various reasons, maybe the most important was that I was losing interest in what was happening in my surroundings, and Mexico offered me a lot. Above all it offered me the immersion in a different – and unbearable – political reality, and this changes something in the conception of your work and the perception of your own attitude. When I was still in Europe, I thought Mexico would not offer me integration into like-minded groups of artists, not even the usual art scene, but it promised to be a way of distancing myself from all that and making a more independent art. However, when I arrived in Mexico I was confronted with extraordinary artists and a vitality inconceivable in Europe. This and the fact that Mexico City alone and at the socio-political level is almost as complex as all the other cities together made me extend my stay to date, although I do have my doubts that it is really a free choice.

With Teresa Margolles I have had a close relationship from the very beginning, and artistically we have grown a lot. She has not been afraid of going to extremes with the density and urgency of her work, and this has always impressed me.

Your work reflects the influences of minimal art, happening, concept art, site specific art and intervention art. You are a professional sculptor. Could one speak of a wider concept of sculpture with regard to your work and how do you define contemporary art? Which artistic traditions do you feel attached to? What or who has influenced you most?

Broadly speaking, the direct and convincing approach of the American anti-form sculpture and of the Italian Arte Povera or the radicalism of the German

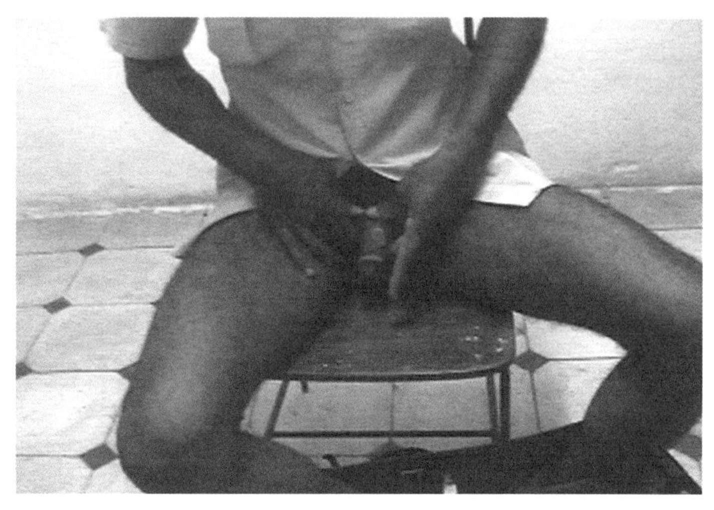

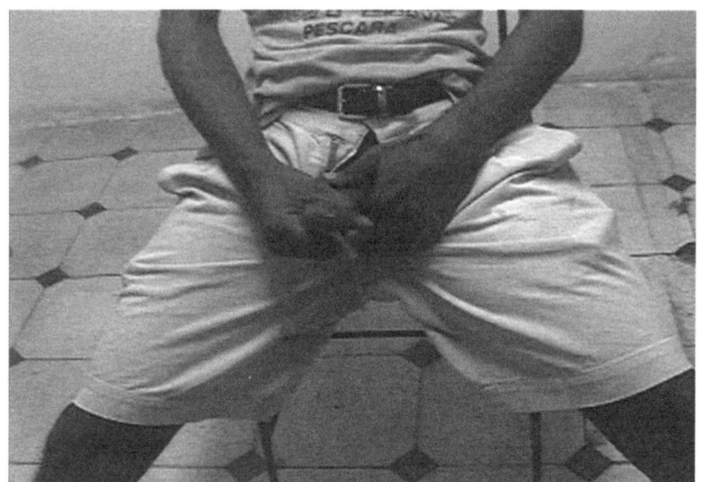

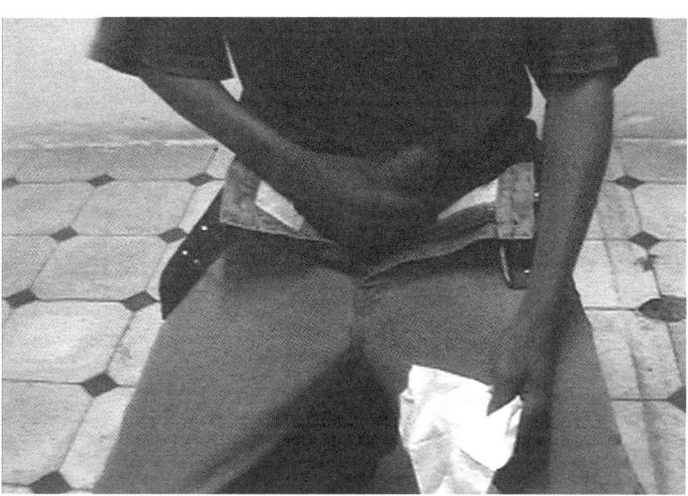

Installation view, Calle
Tejadillo, Havana, Kuba
2000: Santiago Sierra,
*Ten People Paid to
Masturbate*

authors of the seventies are always at the back of my mind. On the other hand, minimalism is the best training as far as syntax is concerned. This is why I use it as a formal "basis". But also direct contacts with artists of great integrity such as Stanley Brown and Isidoro Valcarcel Medina have been very rewarding. An influence outside art is the arrangement of elements in a building that is visible, practical and well done at the same time. Mexico contributed a chaotic formal repertoire mirroring the violence generated by its social conflict.

In Vienna you have shown great interest in the work of the representatives of Viennese Actionism. Unlike them, you stay out of your work. What aspects of Viennese Actionism are relevant to your work?

It is relevant as a methodology. We can engage in a discourse about instinct or the "counterconscious", if I may say so, but this is not possible unless we have a strict method and clearly defined systematics.

You told me that you loved the freedom you had in your artistic work at the beginning of your career. Closely linked to your career is, as you said, a biography that is increasingly putting your work in the background and yourself in the foreground. How are you going to react to this?

If you work from the underground, nobody exerts pressure on you and nobody really cares what you say and do but this changes as soon as a museum puts your work on show. This institution provides you with a greater feedback for your projects and as a compensation it gives you a name. And now it is no longer the work that is speaking but I, the one of whom we know this and that. As far as I am concerned, that is Santiago Sierra, I cannot be anything other than a reactionary, somebody who is concerned with his convenience, his career and other profane matters. This clashes with the power of a work that does not say anything about me and that is not interested in who I am. If you see Mr. X in a museum and then in another one, you will stop to pay attention to what he said and sometimes even to Mr. X himself. The only possible reaction for me is to continue working as before.

Santiago Sierra in conversation with Gerald Matt in the autumn of 2002 on the occasion of the exhibition *Santiago Sierra: Anheuern and Anordnen von 30 Arbeitern nach ihrer Hautfarbe* at Kunsthalle Wien project space.
Santiago Sierra was born in Madrid, Spain, in 1966. He lives and works in Mexico City.

Spanish to English translation by Heidemarie Markhardt.

Milica Tomić

> *I move within the areas of auto-analysis, of the personal, although in my works I always speak of myself in the third person and I experience it that way, as well.*

Video still: Milica Tomić,
I am Milica Tomić, 1998

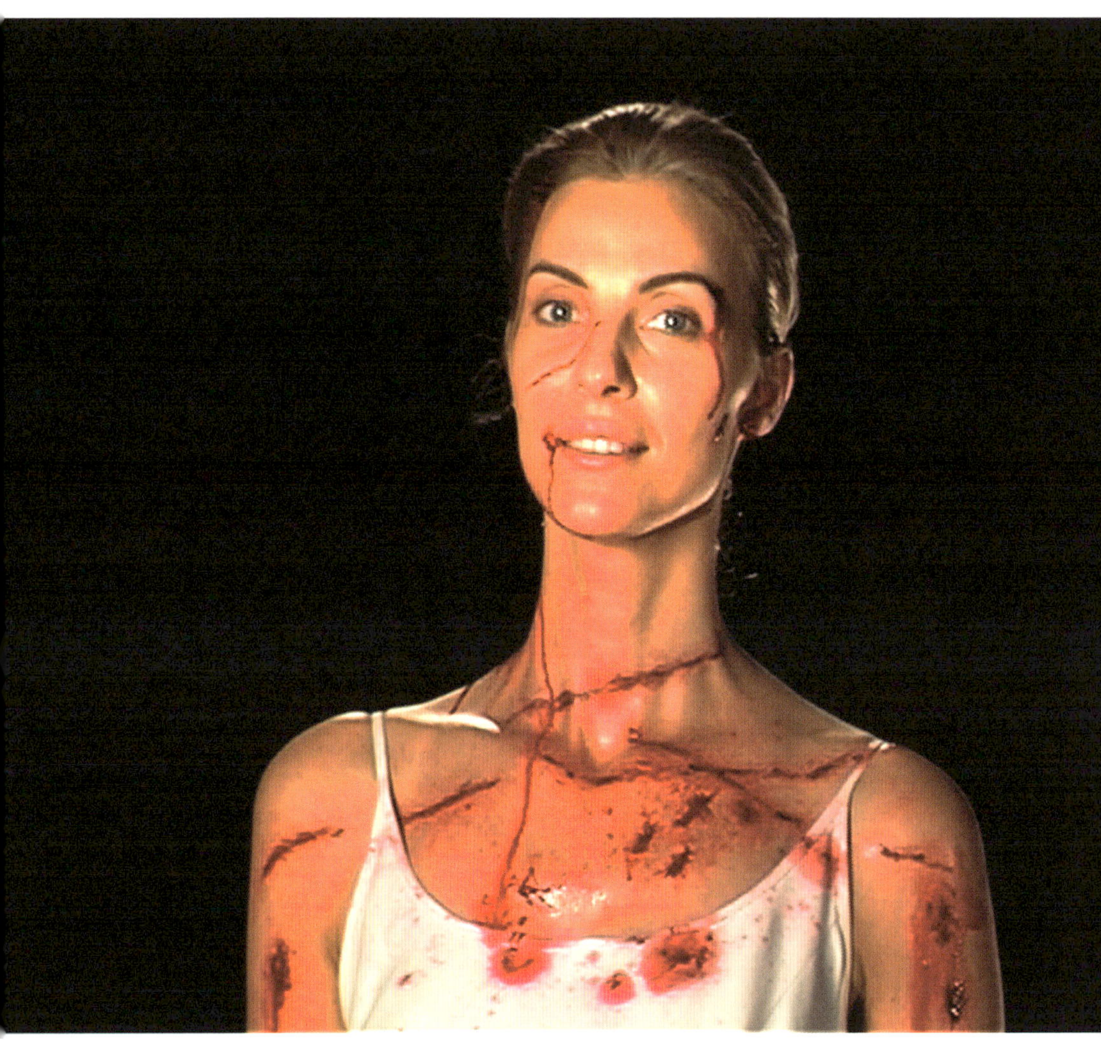

In the exhibition *Unstable Narratives* at the Dortmund Museum am Ostwall in April 2002 you were showing a work entitled *Dortmund remembers* .... What there was to be seen was a large-scale print of a contemporary membership card of the German Communists Party, onto which you had projected your face. The employment of your own picture or an image of yourself together with political contents or symbols is found almost throughout your artistic work, while the relevant political and historical context is usually expressed in concrete form in the course of a narrative event (as for example, in *Portrait of My Mother*) or at any rate in the shape of an image fashioned in a cinematically narrative manner (for example, in *Milica Tomić and Roza El-Hassan driving a Porsche and thinking about overpopulation*). In the work for Dortmund the "remembrance", pragmatically considered, only comes to light in the title – what we see is the present time, and the viewers are brought to an awareness of the historical and also the supra-national dimension of the statement solely through their own historical knowledge. One could almost speak here of a "visual" or "concrete" poetry. Does this work mark a possible path in the direction of a reduction of narrative processes?

Each narrative, as you well know, is an attempt to escape or evade something traumatic. In other words, the narrative presents a certain view of a trauma, or more accurately, its framework. A trauma is not immediately accessible to us, it has to be relayed through a narrative that envelopes it and that paradoxically both obscures and reveals it. *Dortmund remembers* … is a response to one of the most monumental narratives of the 20th century. This is the liberal narrative, a part of the liberal ideology, its mystical and secretive core, a narrative which commands us to live in a society that is at an equal distance from both the left- and right-wing totalitarianisms. The Dortmund project has been put into practice in Germany because this is the only country in Europe that has instituted legal sanctions to outlaw both the Communist and the National-Socialist parties. In this way, Communism and National-Socialism have been equated. The project intervenes in this liberal taboo and breaks up this equation. In other words, it points out that Communism is fundamentally different from National-Socialism and that the production of terror under a left-wing totalitarianism is different from that in a right-wing one. Terror in leftist totalitarianism is inherent in the attempt to create a new world that calls for a radical break with the existing world which is, from the left-wing ideological perspective, a dead one. National-Socialist terror is the attempt to preserve the old order. In that sense my project is not a narrative one, because it reveals this trauma that is being obfuscated by the liberal narrative.

In your video work *I am Milica Tomić*, which has been much shown since 1997, you not only permanently change your identity, in that you say in one language or another, who you are or what your name is, but also it expresses your state of being in an ambivalent way. So, while your facial expression retains an unchangingly friendly, in fact almost beatific smile, with each change of language new bleeding wounds appear on your body. The contradiction between emotional immobility and furious physical reactions causes one to think of pictures of Christian martyrs, who maintained their blissful smiles even under the greatest physical torments up to the bitter end. Admittedly, those legends were meant to show us how the right belief and sacrificing one's own life would lead to moral steadfastness and just wages in the hereafter.

Even if your video work is interpreted primarily politically, you do, however, also declare yourself as a Serbian Orthodox Christian. What is, in your view, the relationship towards each other of religious belief and a powerlessness kindled by political arbitrariness?

This smile of my heroine's is not the smile of a blissed-out, religious person, who sacrifices herself, who suffers in hopes of being rewarded for it in the afterlife. It is rather the smile of a person who believes unconditionally that we are totally identical with what we identify with.

It is actually a matter of that certain phantasmatic space defined by de Sade and the position of the victim within that space. The victim in de Sade's *Phantasma* succeeds, despite everything that happens, in preserving a sublime inner beauty – and even beyond that: the more the victim is being tortured, tormented, destroyed, the more beautiful and radiant does she re-emerge.

And now my answer to the last part of your question. In the statement, which refers to the work *I am Milica Tomić*, the protagonist Milica Tomić declares herself to be an Orthodox Christian and a Serb. This statement fulfils a function within the work. Your question, however, no longer refers to that Milica Tomić, who acts as the protagonist of my work, but rather to Milica Tomić, the private person.

Your route right across Belgrade in the video installation *Portrait of My Mother* proceeds visually with a quasi-monotonous look of indifference at everything in the way of buildings and passer-by that your camera encounters – the concentration is directed towards the recollection of a conversation between yourself, your mother and a friend of hers. However, now and then there are short interruptions, or transmission failures, if you like. And then again there are those moments, where from the general stream of passers-by a single person emerges, who for a brief moment transforms the flow of pictures into slow motion. These moments are for me the most disturbing, as one does not know what is going to happen next (even disregarding the fact, perhaps, that one simply expects to see something happening in a film). It has something to do, in this case, with a second type of memory, which is not stored as a verbal exchange that can be intellectually reconstructed and so is also cognitively verifiable, but which surprisingly appears through the recognition of a visual signal, so to speak, and then triggers off a

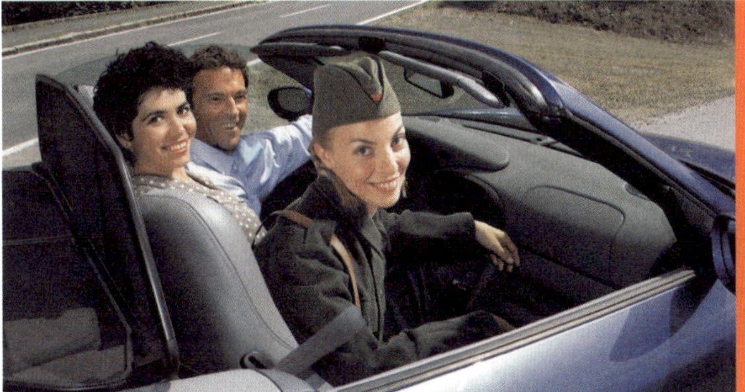

Milica Tomić, *Milica Tomić and Róza El-Hassan driving in the Porsche and thinking about overpopulation*, 2000

hardly verifiable reaction. I would be interested to know how you came to employ such different "stylistic means" and whether these might indicate two levels of reality, where, between them – and if so, how? – a chasm opens up, which leaves us stranded on shaky grounds.

What the subjective camera takes in on its way through Belgrade appears at first glance to be a documentary stroll. But that is by no means the case. Among the individuals who walk past my camera, there are some people who, when viewed from my perspective, were very important people in my mother's life. My intention was to have these people just filing past us like all the other passer-by. It was also necessary, however, to draw attention to them, yet in a discreet way, so that they could carry on being only people in the streets. I decided on another means of drawing attention to them, one to which we would react subjectively and also quite physically. That is to say, I have attempted to produce this reaction through a change in the frames per second of film and through the sound.

There are, in this video- and slide-installation, several parallel channels that run simultaneously side by side, yet which appear sometimes to be completely separate: dialogues, picture sequences, noises, individual frames. It is through the noises, the sounds, that the dialogues are joined to the pictures. Superimposed on the dialogues, these sounds transport us out of the conversation and on to the street, directing our attention, emphasising the importance of those events that visually belong to the second or third tier. The sounds lead us into spaces beyond the pictures and the dialogues. During the in-set black passages, or "black outs", the sounds become abstract and move about independently, and only after a certain point in time are we brought back again to the dialogues.

The distance from my house up to my mother's house in the video corresponds almost exactly to the actual time it takes to cover the route: 64 minutes, without the cuts. The only clearly perceptible interruption or "disturbance" of this real-time situation, then, is produced by these "black outs", which are accompanied in each case by another noise, which, being attached to no visual recognition point, it is difficult or even impossible to identify. That is to say, there is at these moments no picture that would correspond to the perceptible noise.

A second element confusing the flux of real-time occurs at those moments when the camera encounters certain passers-by who are important to us. It was my intention to reconstruct the manner in which we function if we repeatedly pass along a certain way, without being conscious of the usual run of this course of events. We tend to be rather absent-minded or concentrated on our own thoughts, only, through the movement of any passers-by or through an ordinary noise in the street, to be suddenly brought back again into the immediate presence of the street. Something similar happens, if a person we encounter in the street calls forth a wave of memories in us.

As a visual artist you are used to working with visual codes, as an author you avail yourself of language. Which medium would you prefer to use if you wanted to evoke in the recipient of your work feelings of uncertainty, of giddiness?

Which medium I would settle on would depend on what it was that brought about this giddiness. It is the concrete analysis of concrete situations, which alone decides the question in such cases.

In your works you appear almost without exception as your own chief protagonist, both in the videos and in your performances. Do you see yourself as an object of identification for the recipients of your work or do you see the share of your own subjectivity as being of major significance as a counter-weight, so to speak, to other, more objectifiable elements (like language, props taken from actual realities, etc.) in order to produce, in this way, something like a mirror-image of the human interior world? Which significance does the element of the theatrical have for you in all of this?

I have tried repeatedly to let other main actors take the lead. In the beginning I did not think that it would be necessary, or, as it turned out later, unavoidable, to employ myself as the protagonist in my own works.

I move within the areas of auto-analysis, of the personal, although in my works I always speak of myself in the third person and I experience it that way, as well.

The friend of my mother's who participated in *Portrait of My Mother*, felt deeply insulted after seeing my work, by some of the statements that my mother had made about her, and she openly reproached my mother about them. She did not want to face the truth, which was that these "insulting" dialogue had been cut and edited by me in reference to a certain picture, and that it was solely an art product, which basically bore no relevance to our lives. She felt personally insulted even though, like my mother, she is an actress herself and one might expect her to have a certain experience

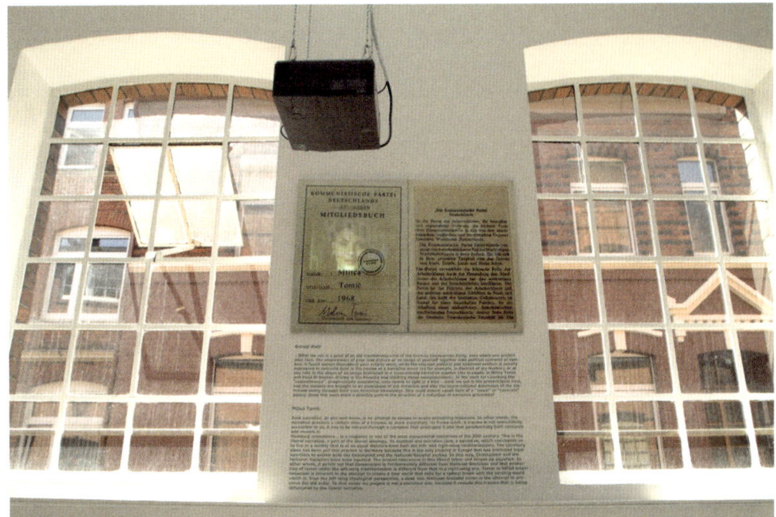

Installation view, Halle
für Kunst Lüneburg
2004: Milica Tomić,
Hamburg Remembers

in being able more easily to see the distinction between an idea, a picture and real life. This is a good example of my position as the protagonist in the medium of video.

With each attempt of presenting myself personally and directly, the video as medium succeeds in converting me completely into a fictional character. And conversely, when I try to construct a fictional character, the video as a medium transforms her back into me as an actual person.

All of this is somewhat akin to the Moebius loop, which has neither an inner nor an outer side. The more I try to present myself as another, the faster do I return to the immediacy of my own everyday life; the more I try to present myself, personally, and my life, the further do I move away from my life; and so on.

As far as the theatrical element is concerned, this is the only thing, which has no place within the genre that my work covers.

Milica Tomić in conversation with Gerald Matt in 2001 on the occasion of the exhibition *Vertigo* at Ursula Blickle Foundation Kraichtal.. The exhibition *Milica Tomić: Ich bin Milica Tomić* (2000) was shown at Kunsthalle Wien project space.
Milica Tomić was born in Belgrade, Serbia in 1960. She lives and works in Belgrade.

German to English translation by Tom Appleton.

Francesco Vezzoli

Apparently my work is about celebration but in the end it is all about deconstruction.

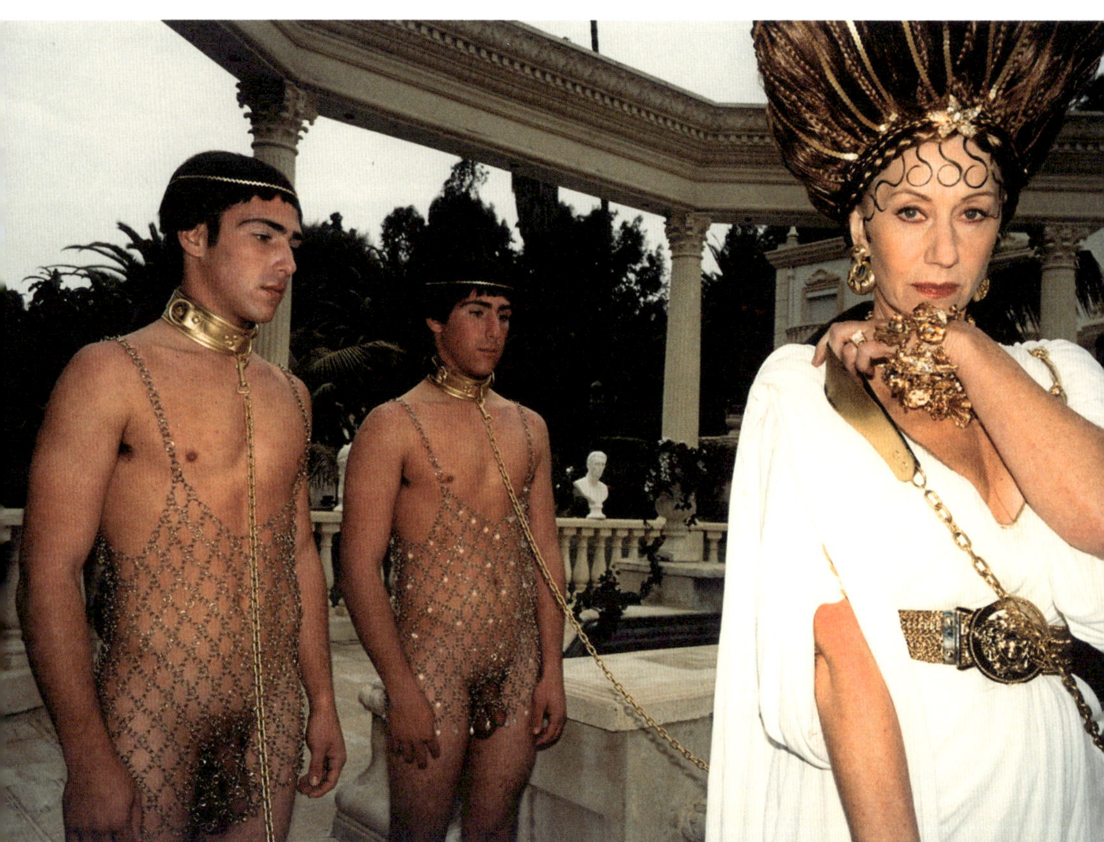

Video still: Francesco Vezzoli,
Caligula, 2005

Andy Warhol's Factory with its set of no-name participants elevated to ad hoc, would-be superstardom has often been likened to a counter-strike on the Hollywood system. Warhol's films offered the absolute opposite of mass popular appeal in terms of theatricality, action and glamour. But, in terms of fame, the small-scale New York production outfit did not do too badly compared to the multi-million-dollar Californian turnover-machine.

The illustrious names from film history and contemporary cinema are almost always a component, or the source or subject of your film, video and sculptural works. In comparison to Andy Warhol, how do you instrumentalise stars?

> Warhol used to hang out with stars and then he loved having rather unknown people in his films, while I engage stars for my projects, but I love to hang out with my friends.
>
> I don't feel like I instrumentalise stars at all. I just involve them in my projects.

In contrast to the frenetic speed with which you ran through, for example, the lavishly decadent orgies of the Roman emperor Caligula (as seen in the 1979 scandal flick produced by Penthouse chief Bob Guccione), there stands, for me, in your *Trailer for a Remake of Gore Vidal's Caligula*, (2005) your deployment of a high-carat cast for this mere teaser: with stars who, between the rapid sequences of shots, and samples of old and new material, and pockets of text, are practically able only to flash up for mere moments, thus barely offering any fodder to feed our yearning for their immortality. Is your concern, then, the deconstruction of a possibly outdated star principle?

> Yes, the act of "renting" their star image and put it in a different context allows me to take a distance, to frame their role and power in a twisted perspective. Apparently, my work is about celebration, but in the end it is all about deconstruction.

Slowness versus the high-speed rush has been an ongoing component of your work, especially when you combine moving pictures with embroidery, as for example in your *Trilogía della Morte* for the Fondazione Prada, shown in Venice in 2005. In this complex work, which takes its cue from one of Pier Paolo Pasolini's very first films (*Comizi d'amore*, 1964), which you have transformed into a kind of reality show, the "end" is marked by an installation which references the concluding scene from Pasolini's final film (*Salò o le 120 giornate di Gomorra*, 1975) – one hundred and twenty chairs (of C. R. Mackintosh's1904 *Argyle* model), placed before a wall rug, with images of actors from the director's films embroidered onto it. To mention just a very few out of a possible very many questions:

Embroidery is associated not only with (traditional) female handicraft; it also stands for labour-extensive burden, possibly also consuming leisure time, and in any case it also involves patience and usually also reproduction.

Regarding the question of time, have you introduced slowness and constancy to counteract the demon of "a society reaching the limits of acceleration" (Paul Virilio)?

Yes, absolutely. I chose embroidery as my form of expression as a way to conceptually dilate time. Needlework is very slow; fame comes and goes very fast.

The embroidered images of the stars lead us back to the question of "immortality."
However, their faces are not covered in blood red tears. Do you mourn Pasolini or the end of your own role?

I mourn the loss and the lack of a challenging intellectual figure like, for example, Pasolini: a homosexual who was questioned by homosexuals; a Catholic who was hated by Catholics; and a communist who was disapproved by communists.

Regarding reproduction: even, if here, it is not "industrial" reproduction, as with Warhol, the person depicted is distributed more widely, and, as a piece of embroidery, almost in the style of a classic icon: iconisation with Warhol – iconisation with Vezzoli?

Iconisation is a word that works better for Warhol's time and work. On the contrary, my projects are more about de-iconisation.

Do you have a vision of how the relationship between a traditional constitution of reality or a sense of identity and the construction of realities will continue to develop? Is your work based more on an observation and analysis of the status quo of the (media) society or more on dreams and visions?

Definitely more on analysis and criticism of the world we live in and the structures of power that rule it.

The cinema seems to be highly fascinating for you. Your works have repeatedly seemed like paraphrases of great cinema moments. Does Francesco Vezzoli himself hold plans for making a grand film someday?

Not really. I think the contemporary art world is what suits best my desires and visions. And it's the only field that allows me to act with such creative freedom.

Your work consists to a large extent of communications and facilitation efforts.

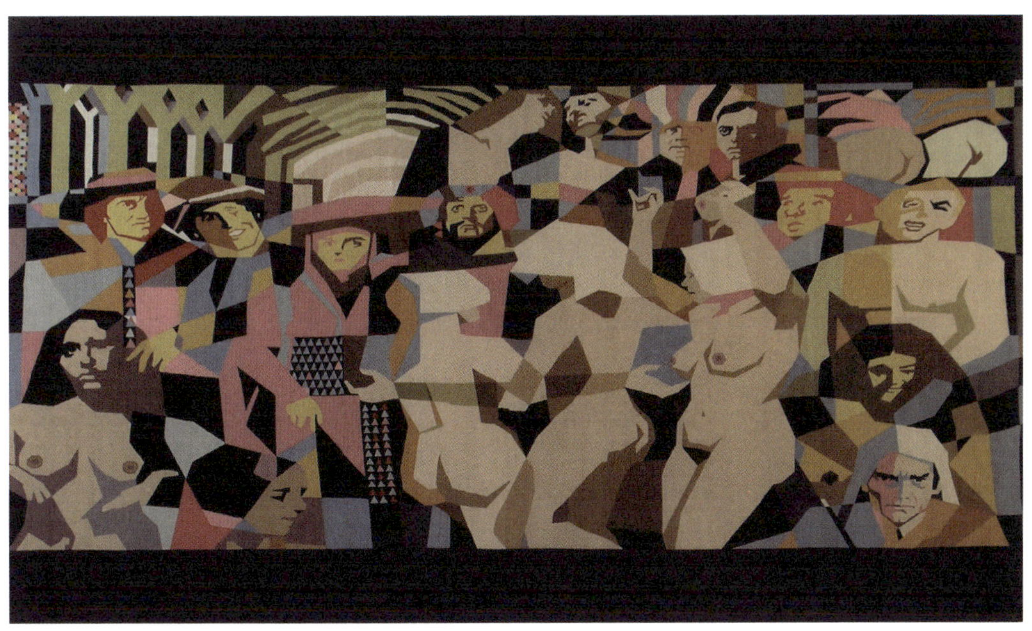

Francesco Vezzoli,
La fine di Canterburry,
2005

How do you succeed in winning over so many stars, with whom you want to work, to take part in your projects? Is Francesco Vezzoli a charmer and enchanter?

I would say I am a corruptor. I just convince them to do something they would never do, I hope, for anyone else.

And what are your upcoming projects?

My intention is to remake Maximilian Schell's documentary "Marlene", which is very special to me. In fact, in the same movie, you can see the most important German diva, Marlene Dietrich, and the queen of Bauhaus, Anni Albers.
I would like to conceive it as a sensational fake TV show – a sort of E! True Hollywood Story– about art, fame, self-representation and that deep sense of failure that I presume haunts every artist.

Francesco Vezzoli in conversation with Gerald Matt in February 2006 on the occasion of his presentation at the ursula blickle videolounge in Kunsthalle Wien.
Francesco Vezzoli was born in Brescia, Italy, in 1971. He lives and works in Milan.

Wong Hoy Cheong

I enjoy destroying what we believe to be texts with authority, such as dictionaries, video documentaries, and novels; and anything that suggests that there was only one true way to do things.

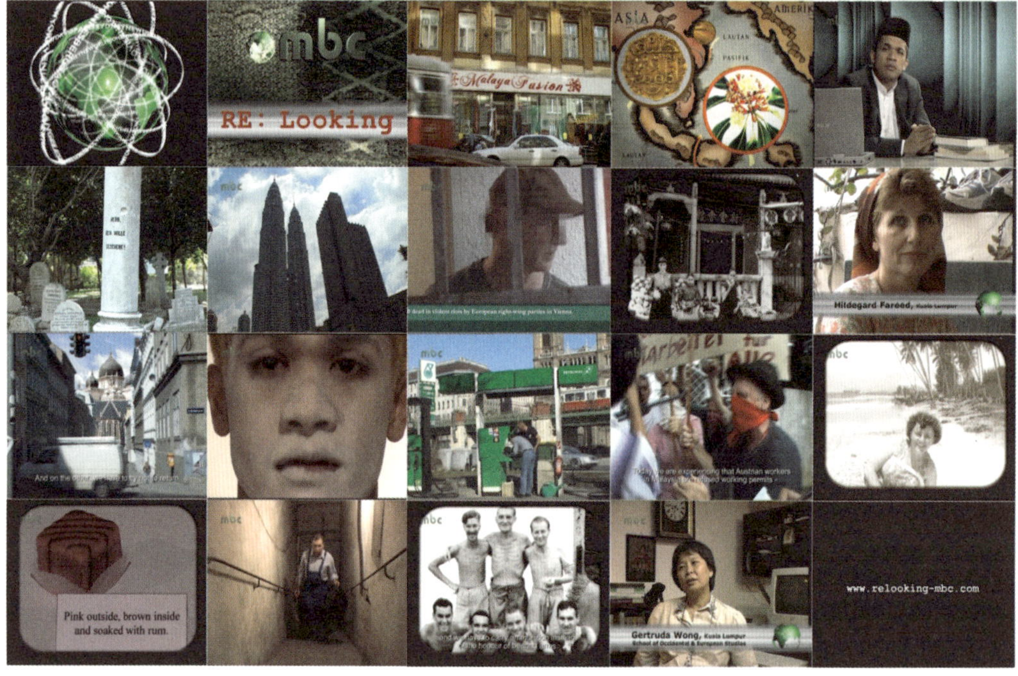

Video stills: Wong Hoy Cheong,
Re:Looking, 2002/2003

Your video *Re: Looking,* a fictitious documentary that plays with reversing Austrian history, was created as part of the theater production *Marco Polo Wunderwelt* at Schauspielhaus Vienna. Could you tell us more about the role of video in this play, and also generally about your artistic position that seems to oscillate between visual arts and theater? You produced *Re: Looking* in collaboration with Malayan performer Mohamad Arifwaran. How did this collaboration come about? Had you worked together previously? Is this why you are now working in theater?

Well, it all started last year when I was contacted by Martina Winkel from Theater ohne Grenzen and Airan Berg from Schauspielhaus Vienna, who had seen my video *Sook Ching* in Singapore ten years ago. They asked if I would be interested in collaborating with them on a new project. I can't remember how we came up with the idea for this documentary, but I do remember waking up one morning and thinking it would be an interesting thing to do, because they were working on Marco Polo. It was about the West setting out to discover the East, so I thought: if discoverers from the East came and explored the West? What would happen if discoverers from Asia would have came and colonized the West? What would have been the result? Then I started to read up on Austrian history and found lots of information on the first and second Turkish sieges of Vienna. The work I did for the play consisted of making this documentary. It was the director and her creative team who selected parts from the video and worked them into the play. It was planned that the full-length video documentary would also run in the theater. I have always been very interested in theater, because you work together with a group of people…

How important is theater in Malaysian culture?

It is very important, because historically the performing arts have had a greater significance than visual arts. There are far more Asian art forms in the area of performing arts such as, puppet theater or music and dance performances, than there are in the field of more static, visual arts. The interesting thing is that the performing arts here are very visual—there are lots of props, backdrops, costumes, and music. Most of it is music-based. The performers tell the story in song: there are dancers, narratives, theatrical elements, and pantomime. In Asia, performing arts is a mixed field, and differs from the West where music as well as dance, theater, and realism have their own genre. So, in comparison to the West, the performing arts have, historically, been more significant in Malaysia.

Didn't Modernism also cause a rupture in traditional art forms including theater and dance in Malaysia too? Is there such a thing as modern Malaysian theater or dance theater? How does this relate to traditions and history?

Many people who work in the visual arts draw from traditional forms, including movement and language use, in their work…

In their stories as well?

Yes. For instance, about seven years ago, I participated in a theater production, which was a new version of the mythological story *Ramayana*, an Indian epos that also plays an important role in Malaysian culture. The director worked with young adults and reworked the story to tell a more contemporary version of *Ramayana*. Here, Rama and Sita were lawyers who fell in love over the Internet. In the historical version of the myth, the evil king Ravana abducts Sita—and in this version it happens in a discotheque and Ravana is a post-industrial shape–shifter, who even changes into Brad Pitt to kidnap the girl. So, this version draws from contemporary culture, but was still based on the historical myth, even in its dance and music. There are many productions that experiment in this way, taking traditional material and combining it with today's issues or contemporary movements…

This way the audience can easily understand what's going on in the piece, because it is already familiar with the story line.

That's right. It can be very funny, but it can also cause problems. For example, when we put on the production, several religious Hindu traditionalists strongly spoke out against it. There was even a demonstration because we had dressed the goddess Sita, who stands for purity and beauty, in a miniskirt and had her dance in the disco. I like the fact that it is provocative and that it really touches on what is going on today. It resonates with a young audience. And it's funny too.

There is also some of this humor in *Re: Looking*, because when you turn the story around, the influences are also reversed. The West appears to have been ruled by the East for centuries, and you cite examples to make this point. The crescent shape of the Viennese croissant is derived from the Turkish crescent moon. When you speak about humor and filling in the historical details with contemporary images, the question arises of how you can address these issues with such ease, because they are quite serious matters are really part of today's reality. You turn the tables on the history of immigration as well. In your piece, people from the West try to come to Malaysia to find work and make a living. Where do you find the humor you use to address these issues with such ease?

I like humor, black humor. We are talking about fact and fiction here. And if you take a good look at *Re: Looking* you can see that I play with questions of media manipulation. Because all the technological advances of today, we know that each and every fact can be fictionalized and that we can also fabricate facts from each and every fiction. I was quite interested in seeing "what if…" and some of the things we tried worked really well. Although taking turn-of-the-century Austrian workers such as farmers, produce merchants, or people selling milk, and putting them in Malaysian pictures looked somewhat convincing, it also looked extremely ridiculous. It is, however, common knowledge that the media manipulates things like that all the time. So, I like to be naughty and manipulate, too.

So, *Re: Looking* is a humorous analysis of Western and Eastern clichés that contributes to shaping one's perception and identity, but also can be very problematic. In your pieces, such as in *Exile Islands*, you also investigate the effect that clichés of others have on the identity of a certain culture. The models of the Malaysian islands are made from the leaves of spice plants. Could you tell us more about this piece?

In certain respects, *Exile Islands* is a far more personal piece than *Re: Looking*. I wanted to do a piece on memories, childhood, and the things we learned in school. I remember when I was a child we still read the books the British colonial powers had left for us: Robinson Crusoe, Enid Blyton, Agatha Christie, *Treasure Island*, *The Swiss Family Robinson* by Johann David Wyss, and adventure novels about discovery and people from the West who would come to a tropical island paradise and live a good life while discovering and experiencing a new place. I always saw myself as Robinson Crusoe. Now I know that I am not Robinson Crusoe. I am Friday [laughs].

In *Re: Looking*, you are Robinson Crusoe, the discoverer.

Yes. It's fun to slip into this role, because I think there are a Robinson Crusoe and a Friday in all of us. This is especially true of people from former colonies, because colonialism has transformed the way we think. I love Robinson Crusoe; he had an impact on my childhood, a time when I was growing up on Penang, an island in Malaysia. There I was Robinson Crusoe … But, to come back to *Exile Islands*, the aspect that interested me the most was: Who am I? How did the colonial era affect me? How much of the colonizer/colonized is in me? I took texts as well as plants associated with colonial trade or plantations and slavery: rubber, bananas, and tobacco. I found all these "exile islands" in Southeast Asia, mainly in Malaysia and Singapore. They are tropical islands that at one time had been beautiful places, which the government had now made into prison camps or leper islands as a means to exile and isolate people. I was interested in playing with both of these faces of the tropical islands. When you reflect on your childhood you begin to realize that the islands were not just these exotic places you thought they were.

One of the main issues in *Marco Polo Wunderwelt* is that Marco Polo's view and accounts of his discovery voyages and all of the things he encounters are a fictive: he saw and found what he had expected; i.e. what he was supposed to find. You are also always traveling—to what extent are the Western projections on the East and vice versa are still valid? If you were to put yourself in Marco Polo or Robinson Crusoe's shoes, what kind of stories would you take home with you?

Well, I think that many of the clichés and stereotypes that come up in Eastern and Western societies are a figment of written history and the media, particularly of television. I think that is an interesting point, because how we see things has changed. If I had come here from Malaysia for the first time now, I would be surprised by many of the things I see here, and going back to Malaysia… It's as if you are constantly putting on new glasses and seeing thing differently each time. I like that, because it is very refreshing. You can see that there are so many similarities, that there are so many differences too. Racism, ignorance, cynicism, enthusiasm, along with a bit of naiveté, exist there too. What particularly interests me in the fine arts and theater is this whole idea of being in transit or living a nomadic life. I think that lots of artists these days can only exist as nomads. They move from one country to the next where they work on their projects. And I also notice that the travel itself shapes the way you think and not necessarily the place. Recently, my dreams have taken place in London, Vienna, or Malaysia, but all of them have been at the airport. I meet friends and have conversations at the airport, which are interesting, because airports are transitory spaces or way stations. When you travel this much, the airport becomes an important place in your life.

Malaysia is a hybrid culture that has been strongly influenced by both the West and the East. In view of this, where do you see yourself situated in Malaysia?

Malaysia has to be one of the most hybrid cultures. There are historical reasons that have to do with Malaysia's particular location, with Malaka, and with its position as a gateway between East and West. When I talk to non-Westerners, particularly with people from former colonies, they frequently have a very strong anti-Western, anti-colonialist attitude. That is not true for me. While I acknowledge my anger, I also enjoy the Western culture I grew up with. For instance, I grew up in Georgetown, the first seat of the British colonial powers outside of India before it was moved to Singapore. I grew up in a heavily British-influenced environment, which was strongly visible in the structures, layout, and streets. We even have a Downing Street in Penang – I also did a piece on it – which is where the administrative headquarters are. So, to me, the first Downing Street – the "real" one – was located in Penang. Only in my late teens did I discover that another Downing Street existed. So, which is the real Downing Street? The one I grew up with for eighteen years or the one I found out about when I went to London for the first time?

The British had already left by the time you were born. What cultural remnants of British rule were still there? Were there movies or television?

I think the greatest influence of "westernized" culture was in my schooling. My school was the oldest British school in the East. It was founded in 1816, and some of our teachers even spoke a gentlemen's English and still wore khakis and knee-highs. We read things like *Robin Crusoe*, Shakespeare, Oscar Wilde and George Orwell. The strange thing was that we were taught to culturally identify with the long-standing tradition of British colonial culture, which is quite twisted, and outright ludicrous. For example, every year in my school there was a spring concert. There is no spring in Malaysia, but the concert took place every March to welcome the spring.

Unlike many of your colleagues who had the chance to study in the West you decided to return to live and work in Malaysia after your studies. And now Kuala Lumpur, a rapidly growing, young city, has become your home. You travel a lot, and live and work in different cities all around the globe. Is there a difference between working in the West, especially in a city like Vienna that strongly harks back to its tradition, and Kuala Lumpur, which is presumably a more future-oriented city? How is this reflected in your work? Why did you decide to stay there?

I decided to go back to Malaysia even though I had an opportunity to stay in America where I studied. I would go home for the vacations, and I also went and took a look at Kuala Lumpur in the 1980s. I found the city fascinating. Although I had only been away for eight years and did not want to move back there, when I went back and saw that so many exciting things were happening there in art and theater, I decided to go back for two years and see if I liked it. I also wanted to get back into Malaysia's political and cultural spheres. When I finally got there, I thought to myself, "this isn't bad at all." Kuala Lumpur is a rapidly developing city and the world is rapidly developing too, so going back to Kuala Lumpur doesn't give you the feeling that you're stuck there for the rest of your life—which is what it's often like for artists from the South. So I made Malaysia my home base, and I am glad I did so. I also continue to benefit from this decision. I travel abroad a lot too and have noticed my work has changed significantly. Before I began traveling so much my work had stronger roots in Malaysia and were seen as subversive, as critiques of Malaysia, or what have you. After spending more time abroad, there were several reasons that made me want to not only address Malaysian issues. First of all, there is the cliché of the artist from the East, from third world or developing countries. This cliché says that we either revert back to working with traditional art forms and thus maintain an exotic air, or that we live within such a repressive political system that our work can only ever be about human rights and oppression. The sheer fact that I continue to work in this very culturally coded Malaysian environment; my work is constantly rendered either exotic or politically subversive—and, as a matter of fact, I do come from an oppressed country. I was confronted with this cliché for the first time at an exhibition I had in Australia in the 1990s. The people only asked two sets of questions about the exotic aspects of my culture or the oppression of the people in Malaysia. Then I began to rethink my work, and about how to express these things in Malaysia and still make a statement in other contexts while addressing people there in a way they can understand. Then I started to make pieces like *Exile Islands*. People in Malaysia said, "Oh, that's about the leper island" or "that's the refugee island," because there is an awareness of it there. Using texts specifically related to Asia and Malaysia evokes different responses in each context. For example, people in England said, "Oh, that's by Enid Blyton," and identified with it in that way; and the text they see is *The Secret Island*, a story they know. I am trying to present the issue on another – aesthetic – level that people will understand. These pieces aim to arouse interest and evoke curious questions like: "Is that sugar? Are those leaves? Is that fiberglass?" It also makes a statement about the society in which the work is shown. *Re: Looking* is about Malaysia but it is also about Austria. In Malaysia people watch it and think it's funny and in Austria people watch it and think it is bizarre and pretty funny. So I try to create a balance between the piece's inner workings – it has to have some sort of relationship to my background – and its outward relation to the international context.

I wanted to ask you about your artistic training. In an interview you once said that you studied painting with people who had been exposed to Hans Hofmann's style of painting. This is an interesting point, because of the artwork you have come to develop. What teachers or artists have influenced your art? Where would you situate yourself as an artist?

Well, I always say I became an artist because I was a very scholarly. I say that in jest, but there also is some truth to it. My first academic degree was not in art; it was in literature and critical theory. I studied German philosophy, particularly the Frankfurt School, and read loads of English literature. My second degree was in education. I studied the complex nature of pedagogy, particularly education in third world countries, the colonization of the mind, and the development of ideas. Afterwards – all through my studies I had also taken courses in art – I thought about which field I would focus on. Should I go into art or into Islamic studies, which was my other main interest? I thought Islamic studies would help me to deepen my understanding of Malaysia as a non-Muslim. I applied to a program for Islamic studies in

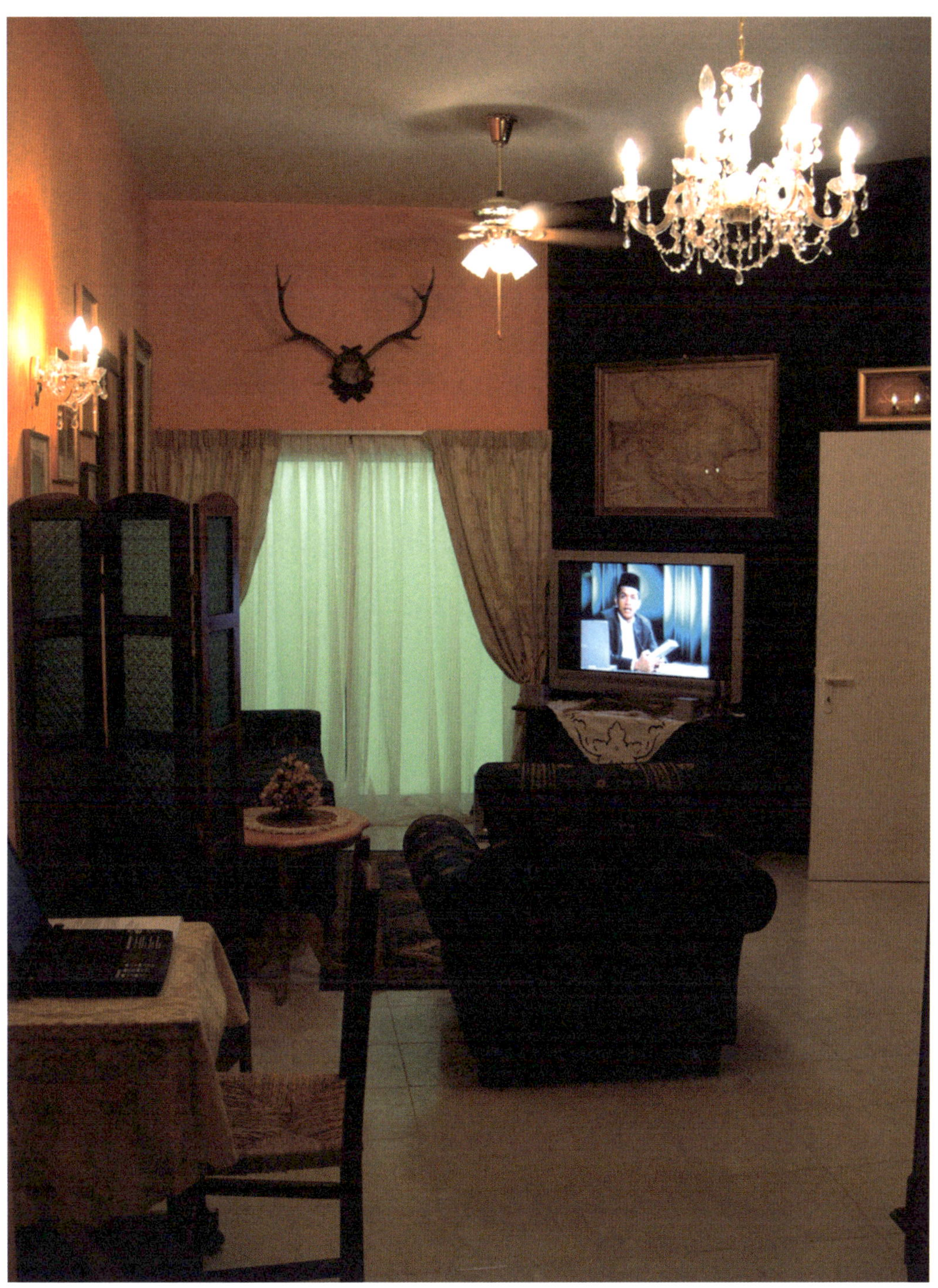

Installation view:
Wong Hoy Cheong, *Re:Looking*,
2002/2003

Cairo and one for art in the States. I received a scholarship to go to America and study art. I didn't get one for Cairo. So I became an artist. It was by chance. But, to come back to your question on Hans Hofmann, I had many professors who had received their training in the 1930s and 1940s, and at the time I studied art in America, art education was still very conservative. Abstract expressionism was still seen as the ideal approach to art. Many of my teachers conveyed the principle of pure art and the idea of a qualitatively supreme work of art. I received quite rigorous training: I learned about sculpture, "push and pull," and all of Hans Hofmann's approaches. I did abstract painting, but after a while I realized I couldn't keep it up. I thought about what to do. Although I loved abstract painting – Hans Hofmann happens to be one of my favorite painters along with Pollock and the others – but I knew I was never going to be able to do that kind of work.

You once stated in an interview, "you can address and show sociopolitical issues in visual art, but it will never mobilize the masses. It will never stir them up and get them to change their convictions. It can only function as a reminder." You also have quite a critical view on the political involvement of visual artists. Where would you politically situate visual artists, such as yourself?

When I said that – the interview you quoted – I meant that, from Diego Rivera to Grosz and Goya, there have been so many visual artists who have done critical work or political satires. To what effect? Have they really been able to bring about cultural, political, or historical changes? They have not had that effect, but instilled the idea that something is wrong. I think the visual arts function in a completely different way than literature, text-based work, performances, or real-time art forms, such as theater. Words can change the world—we already know that. For instance, we will never be able see the world as it was before Freud. Freud changed our view of the world, just as Marx and Hitler have. These are three figures from German-speaking culture who have each significantly changed the way we think in their own ways…

The latter was not really a great writer. He was more a man of actions than of words…

Yes, he was a man of actions and a man of words—he used speeches to influence or mobilize people. Words can do things like that. I have seen performances in Asia that have done so as well. For example, the demise of the Marcos regime is strongly linked to street theater. It is used in South America and in parts of Asia, such as Thailand, Indonesia, and the Philippines. Street theater can stir up the people and incite them to take action. Visual arts, however, do not have this effect and we should simply acknowledge the fact that they have not – historically – had this effect. I meant what

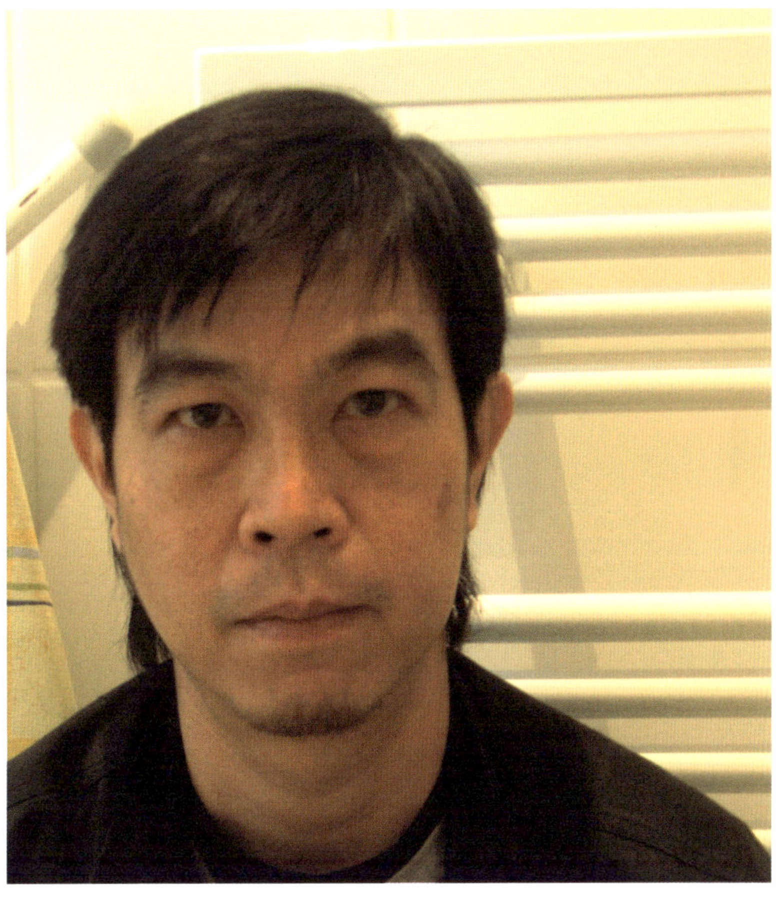

Wong Hoy Cheong

I said. That is my relationship to it. I show these issues because I am really concerned about them, but the audience can think whatever they want about them. It will not change the world. Things that remain on an exclusively political level are merely one-dimensional. That is why I also pay close attention to the role of beauty in my work. You are somehow attracted to it because of its beauty, but then you notice that it is actually about something else. For instance, the tiles I made for the Gwangju Biennale stand out as pretty tiles, but when you get up close you see a story of its own laid out in little pieces and burned on the tiles.

Which ideas have most strongly influenced you when you looking back on your early work as an artist as a painter, i.e. in your later developments? What has been the greatest change for you, say over the past decade or fifteen years?

The most significant changes were realizing that after I returned to Malaysia my concept of it had nothing to do with the reality there and, secondly, that non-traditional art forms are really exciting to work with. That is why I also went from using traditional media to trying all sorts of new things.

But what has captured my interest the most in the last ten years is working with documents. I began to forge documents, make false documents. I have made fake books, fake documentary films, and fake maps. There is something about documents that just makes me want to destroy them. I love to destroy books, I destroy the documentary film format, and I enjoy destroying what we believe to be texts with authority, such as dictionaries, video documentaries, and novels; and anything that suggests that there was only one true way to do things. I like to play with things like that. I think that is a very important to change and develop in my work.

Wong Hoy Cheong in conversation with Gerald Matt and Eva Kernbauer in January 2003 on the occasion of the exhibition *Wong Hoy Cheong: fact - fiction* at Kunsthalle Wien project space.
Wong Hoy Cheong was born in 1960 in Penang, Malaysia. He lives and works in Kuala Lumpur, Malaysia.

Yang Fudong

The ideal, utopia, and paradise are like the moon in the sky. Some people let it hang up there in the sky; some pull it down and hold it in their hands.

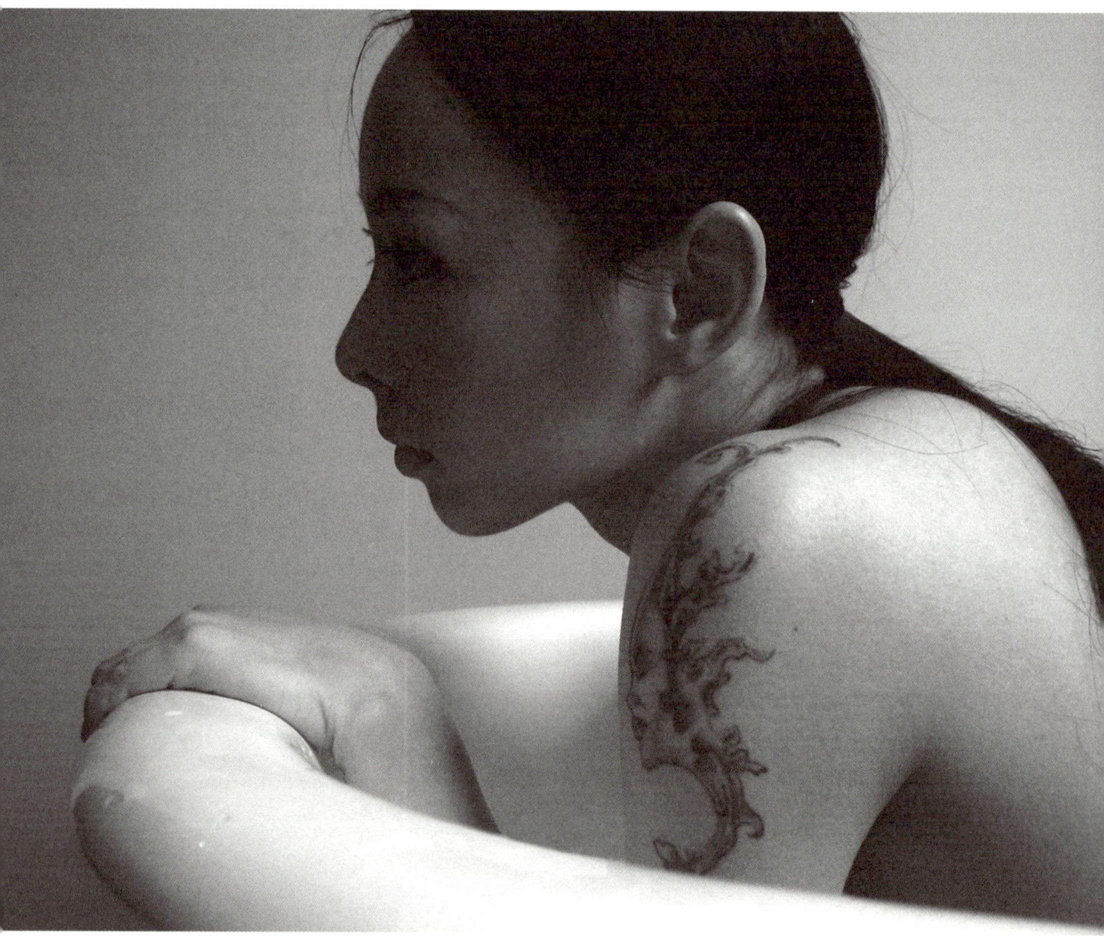

Video still: Yang Fudong, *Seven Intellectuals in Bamboo Forest,* 2004

How does one live as an artist in Shanghai? Were you able to realize all of your plans up to now?

Actually, living as an artist in a city is just like living as a normal citizen. You live quietly in a city that is either familiar or unfamiliar to you. In time, you get used to a place. It might not be your hometown, but it is, in fact, already your home. For me, to realize my works is a process that takes a great deal of time thinking. One by one, I try to realize them, to complete them.

How do you finance your works? Are your films low-budget productions?

Yes my films are all low-budget productions. At the very beginning I got help from my friends. First of all, my friends participated in the films for free and sometimes I even got money from them. I produced *An Estranged Paradise* with minimal funding and I couldn't finish the project due to financial problems. Five years later I was able to get funds from the Documenta at Kassel and then I could finish the film. To earn some money I also worked on other film projects.

What are you working on right now?

I would like to finish all five parts of *Seven Intellectuals in Bamboo Forest* and after this I have another project related to both video and film, which I would like to realize in the next two years. This project is about where the spirit of a person comes from.

What is the art scene like in Shanghai?

Shanghai is a city that is becoming more and more open, more and more international. Meanwhile, it possesses the typical Chinese features in the course of growth and transformation. In terms of film production, I believe that I need my friends very much. For a long time they have been helping and supporting me in a selfless fashion to better my works. Sometimes, this feeling is beyond language. I just feel I should further my efforts in my work.

Do you have a strong network with local or international contemporary artists, film makers, and curators?

In ancient China, Confucius once said, "Among any three people walking by, there must be a teacher for me." I learn a lot from local and international artists, including some excellent curators. They are not only my teachers but also my friends.

Could you briefly talk about the working environment in China, a country, which in the point of view of many Westerners, is still between economic liberty and political repression.

> I can only say that the working environment is getting better and better in China. Also, it is becoming more and more liberal. As long as an artist tries their best; that's most important.

Gao Xingjian is interested in his ideal of the so called "Cold Literature," a "writing of one own." He says art is neither about the market nor about political propaganda, real literature is born of a deep inner and subjective need. In the end, the author only writes for him or herself. "Cold literature" is beyond all "isms" and beyond ideology. Do you feel close to this attitude ("Cold Literature")?

> I haven't read his works and I don't know the theory of Gao Xingjian. But from my perspective, the films I create have to be close to myself.

As early as 1964, Marshall McLuhan had already created the concept of the "global village." Since then, the trend towards globalization has become stronger and stronger. On the one hand, you make films which are anchored in local tradition and are made exclusively with Chinese protagonists. On the other hand, you live the life of a global citizen, an international artist, who exhibits in the world's major cities. Do you get the impression that Shanghai has lost its meaning as the source for your art because of this, and that global topics are too obtrusive? Or is it the other way around?

> For me, it's difficult to say what is internationalized and what is localized. I come from my experiences of growth and perceptual knowledge, very much influenced by my education. I am learning gradually how to think and be aware independently, to deal with my works sincerely. The audience senses that.

Could you imagine making a film abroad?

> If a good opportunity arises, why not?

The subtitle of your exhibition sounds like one of your photo series: *Don't worry, It will be better...* How should we interpret this title, which appears as being either cynical or naive?

> It may be something I'm confident about, a belief. The beautiful life is not necessarily a luxury. Sometimes I think that reality is very cold. People are very cold. It seems that one can hardly recall childhood dreams. But if

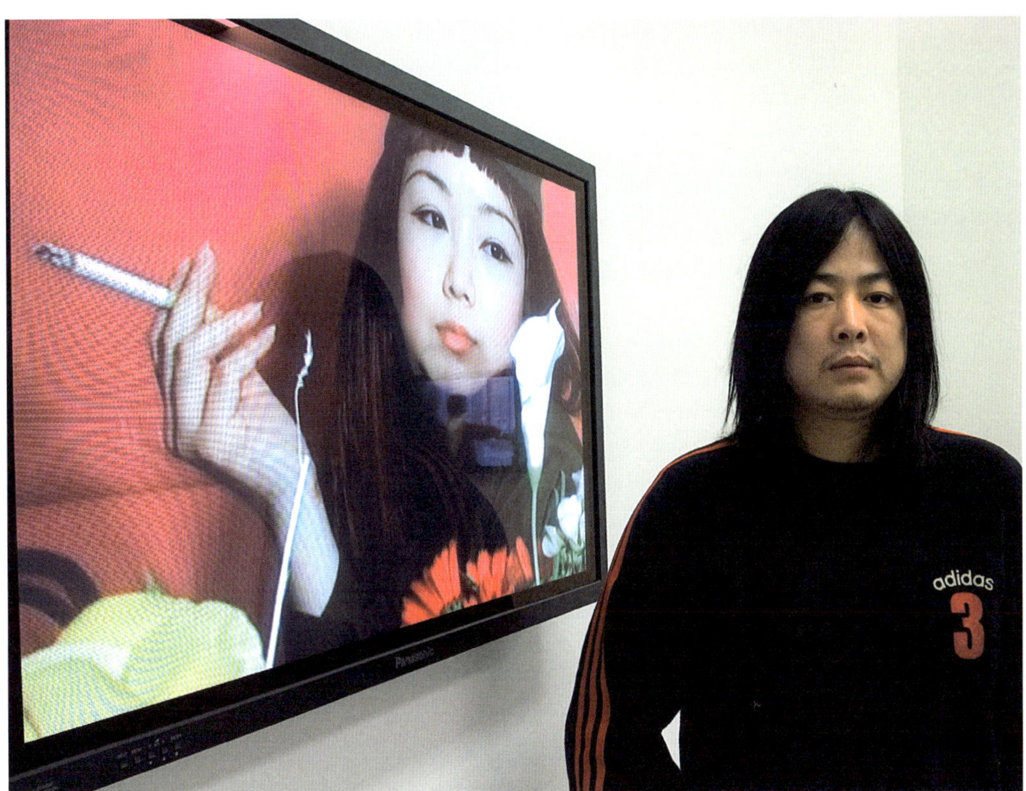

Yang Fudong

dreams are still in your heart, in the end you might discover that life is actually quite beautiful.

Your major media was painting. You quit painting for the sake of film. Your films such as *Liu Lan* have a strong painterly quality. Is it that the camera replaced the brush?

I think all roads lead to Rome. With camera or with painting; one seeks the same effect with different media. People are not immutable. Perhaps one day I'll pick up a brush again.

Nature is a frequent theme in your works. The creation of your works is associated with high technical costs. *Tonight Moon*, in which the landscapes and lakes of the Imperial Gardens are seen through many small screens, for example, is, technologically, a costly installation. You let nature arise in its splendor as a media representation. Is this a metaphor to say that today's world is no more than an illusion and the authentic is gradually disappearing?

Sometimes I believe only in feeling. I don't worship technology. It only offers some kind of help. As for nature, when you are surrounded by it, you don't necessarily understand it. If you want to catch it, it will blow away like the wind. You can only feel its freshness in your breath.

What advantages do your media such as photography, film, and installation offer? What content is best transported by which media?

For me, I use feeling to tell which work or which plan of mine is most suitable to which media. Then I go for it.

In some of your works such as in the film *Tonight Moon*, *Jiaer's Livestock* or *Close to the Sea*, you distanced yourself from the classical film media and turned your interest toward installation settings. Are you interested in using installation as a possibility for expansion, in the sense of the keyword "expanded cinema." Do you think the forthcoming spatial and sculpture aspects will prove more meaningful?

A spatial image installation differs from traditional ways of viewing films. I prefer to explain it as the image of the heart, the image of perception. When the viewer stands in the middle of the exhibition space, I would hope that their mind sees a beautiful building based on a group of invisible images.

The color film *City Light* deals with a look-alike in its real sense. A game of identity begins: two men in suits stand or lie towards each other, and are captured by the camera in strict profile positions so that one is only visible when he leaves the "shadow" of the other. Actions such as holding an umbrella or shooting are done by one and imitated by the other. I hope the association with slapstick has not gone too far. Do you prefer Buster Keaton or Laurel and Hardy?

The original intention of the film *City Light* is based on my feelings of living in Shanghai. Shanghai is a big city. I wasn't living here before. Now I live and work here in order to earn money. Everyday life is like a routine. Sometimes I feel I'm two persons. The me during the day and the me at night. The me during the day works all the time while the me at night constantly thinks. I was working at a software company. And I think especially for middle class people there is the problem that you go to work and later you are at home and feel like another person, there is a juxtaposition of identities, this is also shown in *City Light*. *City Light* is about a person's split identity. The comical aspects in the film are not necessarily humorous. Behind the comical there is cruelty.

In *City Light* the dance by the two men – also the dance by a woman and a man – has the effect of self duplication. One figure appears to be the mirror of the other. It has nothing to do with a relationship, but maybe with the relationship with oneself independently from one's own gender identity. In western thinking, one might interpret it as a solipsistic reproach. The "I" as the creator of one's self-world?

> Life presents everyone with a mask. Underneath the mask, one even loses the difference of sex. Only a self is left, and its constantly bouncing nerves.

As for *Flutter, Flutter … Jasmine, Jasmine*, one might understand it as a love story on the city roofs. Scenes of tolerable lightness of being – singing, swinging and looking into the distance – illustrate moments of contemplation and luck without succumbing to kitsch. The recurring motif of swinging up to the house's fire ladder seems completely symbolic. How did you deploy these gestures, allusions, and symbols?

> As for *Flutter, Flutter … Jasmine, Jasmine*, the original idea comes from the antiphony of love songs. As a kid, I saw these remote villages in films with young people standing on two mountains, singing to each other. They are so moving! In a city, there are scenes everywhere that show love directly. This popular way of expressing love is also very passionate. I made the young man and young woman stand on the top of a huge building, telling each other about their feelings and whispering loving words into each others' ears. They face the pleasant view of blue sky and white clouds while happily singing love songs to one other. The title of the work is exactly the title of the love song that I created.

Your films are typically built up in the Asian/ Buddhist tradition. To us, due to our western experience, which is shaped by the drama of Greek tragedy, it seems quite unfamiliar. Your films know no development of suspense, no climax, no solution, and no drama. The end comes quite indirectly. Is the plot comparable to a Chinese scroll painting?

> Film is like life. Sometimes it's like rain on the water, very beautiful and very quiet, the waves not necessarily very violent. I'd like to advocate a kind of abstract film, author film, without regular rules. The artist offers it a limit.

In *Backyard – Hey, Sun is Rising!*, we see people in Mao suits, the Chinese working uniform, at their morning rituals. They massage each other and do exercises with swords. Their activities are military, not very believable and often strange. The actions turn out to be empty and make no sense. Boredom rules. People just stare blankly. The protagonists are empty-minded and appear to be at a loss as to what to do. Is this Marxist alienation, Nietzsche's nihilism or Eastern philosophy? Is it an allusion to empty-minded political rituals?

> No matter what kind of life, there will always be some ambiguity in it. It's like experiencing a lot of the four seasons. No clear memory of them any

more. Sometimes life is contradictory in one's heart. The heart goes forward, yet the body itself goes in another direction, further and further away, like a piece of cloud, one feels nothing by going through it. But it does flow beautifully there in the sky.

In your first photo-series *The First Intellectual* one sees a young crazed man with a bloody face going through Shanghai. He has a brick in his hand and doesn't know at whom or what to throw it. In the new world of quick money and mushrooming skyscrapers, he seems to have lost all possible orientation.

Sometimes life is just like this: when you find no way to get out, you gradually learn to adapt to society and change yourself.

In one of the central works of your exhibition in the Kunsthalle Vienna, namely, the first two parts of *Seven Intellectuals in Bamboo Forest*, you come back to the topic of intellectuals again. The film is based upon the Chinese story of *Seven Sages in the Bamboo Grove*, who were a group of Chinese scholars and poets. In the middle of the third century B.C., they fled the turmoil caused by the change of dynasties and retreated to pursue an ideal life. Which role do you assign to the intellectual in today's China, and accordingly, in today's society and art?

I think intellectuals should be people with a good education and an independent spirit. No matter from which society or which country, most important is self-respect.

The individual in society, the human being who does not feel good about him or herself and does not receive recognition in the community. Part one of *Seven Intellectuals in Bamboo Forest* is set in a natural setting of almost dreamlike beauty. Part two of the work, however, takes place in an urban environment. You once talked about intellectuals, saying that they do not know if their problems are derived from themselves or from society. Could you talk about this contradictory condition in *Seven Intellectuals in Bamboo Forest*?

Seven Intellectuals in Bamboo Forest represents, to a certain extent, open-mindedness among the ancient intellectuals, freedom and bravery. I'm trying to make such a film composed of five parts and it is a trial for me. I guess I need five years to finish it gradually. Since my thoughts might change during the coming five years, this film is still uncertain. I can't say concretely yet. But I like this plan very much. This film is divided into five parts: 1. Travel Diary of Huangshan 2. The closed-up Life in the Metropolis 3. Another Kind of Life (Go to the countryside.) 4. The Island in Belief (Because people always regard the life on an island as a utopian life.) 5. Back to the City Life in Reality. What I shoot is the life of today's youth and the life which is aloof from the true life. It is abstract, existing in one's heart. It

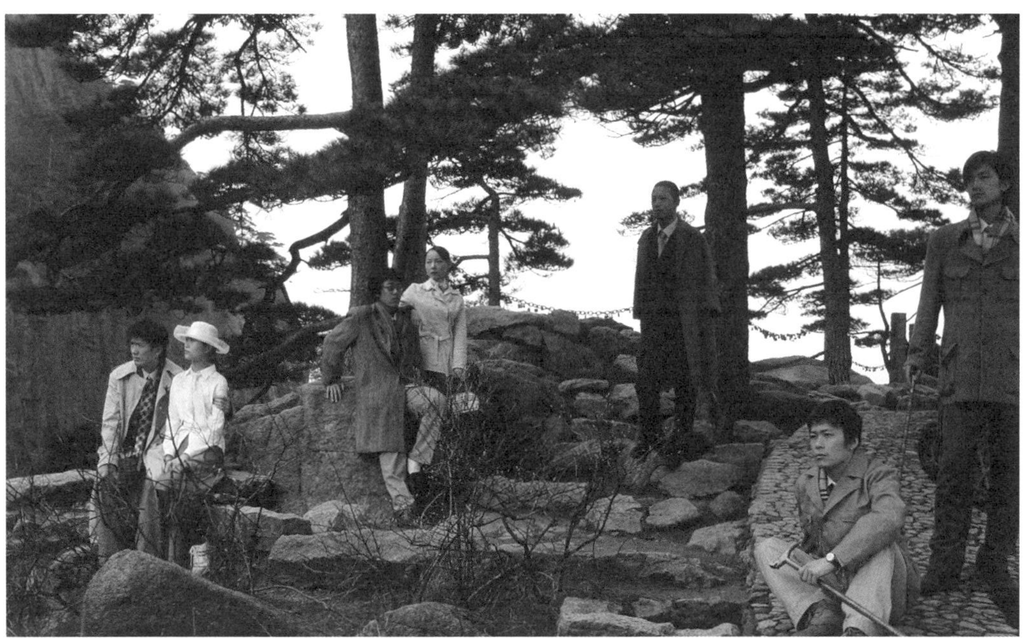

Video still:
Yang Fudong, *Seven Intellectuals in Bamboo Forest*, 2003

doesn't have a concrete concept of time. Sometimes I think that life today is changing more and more. Many people seem to have become nonbelievers. They have lost belief in everything.

Your works have to do with people's relationships and non-relationships, with attraction, indifference, speech, and speechlessness. Your works are often dominated by a certain melancholy, but also display idyllic situations, paradise and utopia. Yin and Yang?

The ideal, utopia, and paradise are like the moon in the sky. Some people let it hang up there in the sky; some pull it down and hold it in their hands.

The French philosopher and China Scholar Francois Jullien, who wrote a book about Chinese painting, *La grande image n'a pas de forme*, assumes that Chinese painting is neither abstract nor concrete. Abstraction is only possible when there is an art that has existed earlier from which abstraction is made. Is this the reason why western abstraction and Chinese abstraction are not comparable?

Chinese painting stresses very much the content, the idea, using an object to express one's feelings. A person draws a plum flower in the winter. We see the plum flower. But the flower is not necessarily the painter's real intention.

Your films are principally shown at exhibitions and in the context of artworks: necessity or merit?

If the form of exhibition is different, the feelings of the spectators will be also different.

What impact do the booming TV- and filmproductions have on your work? Are you interested in an expansion of your distributing and financing possibilities?

Since I'm doing more and more movies, I am also becoming more concerned about the quality of my films. No, I don't see a link between the outside developments and the process of my work.

Your works, the visual and narrative vocabulary of your films, closely follow Chinese, but also international tradition. Could you tell us more about this? Do you like to go to the movies? What kind of films do you like? What kind of films can't you stand?

I'll definitely go to the cinema to watch the films I like, as long as possible, since these films are not prepared for TV. I like all kinds of films, never telling myself what I should see. Sometimes I don't think there is a difference between traditional art and vanguard art. There is only what you like or dislike. The most unbearable films are those with a lot of advertisements in between.

Could you explicitly mention 3 or 4 films which you like very much regardless of their relevance for your work?

Huang Tudi (Yellow Earth) directed by Chen Kaige from about 1985, it's about a soldier going to the countryside to collect folk dances. It's a love story between him and a girl from the countryside. Then *Xiao Cheng Zhi Chun* (Spring in a Small Town) directed by Fei Mu from about 1948, it's a love story between two men and a young woman during the war. And then *Qing Chun Ji* from the late 1970s/early 1980s, it's about a young woman's life in the provinces during the cultural revolution. I also like very much the black and white films from Jim Jarmusch like *Dead Man* and *Stranger than Paradise*.

Your films are often in black and white, I get some kind of nostalgic feeling while seeing your films. Is this nostalgic feeling of black and white film intentional?

Although the images are directly in front of you, the black and white movies create a distance. A distance between you and what you see. But these films are in fact very close to your heart. And this closeness to the heart creates this nostalgic impression.

Hollywood calls. Will Yang Fudong follow?

Just like when you are walking, you will only look for the road which is
yours.

Yang Fudong in conversation with Gerald Matt in the beginning of 2005 on the occasion of the exhibition *Yang Fudong: Don't worry, it will be better...* at Kunsthalle Wien.
Yang Fudong was born in Beijing, China in 1971. He lives and works in Shanghai.

Chinese to English translation by Hui Chang.

p.111: Deutschbauer/Spring, *Interview Machine, Austria at ARCO*, 2006; Photo: Kristina Kranz, © Deutschbauer/Spring

p.111: Poster: Deutschbauer/Spring, *Flirt Maschine Don Juan*; Photo: Kristina Kranz, © Deutschbauer/Spring

p.112: Poster: Deutschbauer/Spring, *Österreich ist Matt*, 2005, © Kunsthalle Wien

p.114: Uroš Djurić, *Untitled (Black Star)*, 1999; Photo: Uroš Djurić

p.117: Uroš Djurić, *Non-objective Autonomism. Murder or 2 Greatest Serbian Painters Subdued by Their Own Greatness*, 1997; Photo: Uroš Djurić

p.121: Installation view, Kunsthalle Wien 2003: Uroš Djurić, *Populist Project Hometown Boys*, 1999-2000; Photo: Hertha Hurnaus

p.122: Uroš Djurić, *Populist Project. God Loves the Dreams of Serbian Artists*, 2001; Photo: Uroš Djurić

p.124: Noritoshi Hirakawa, *Subject - A Project with Thom Mayne*, 2004, © VBK Wien 2006

p.127: Installation view, Wrong Gallery booth Frieze Art Fair, London 2004: Noritoshi Hirakawa, *The Homecoming of Navel Strings*, © VBK Wien 2006

p.129: Noritoshi Hirakawa, Streams by the Wind - Heat Stroke, 2002, © VBK Wien 2006

p.134: Runa Islam, *Director´s Cut (Fool for Love)*, 2001, Courtesy Jay Jopling / White Cube, London

p.137: Runa Islam, *Director´s Cut (Fool for Love)*, 2001, Courtesy Jay Jopling / White Cube, London

p.141: Runa Islam (portrait); Photo: Lisa Thanner

p.144: Anna Jermolaewa, *3 min. Attempts to Survive*, 2000, © Anna Jermolaewa, © VBK Wien

p.149: Video still: Anna Jermolaewa, *Shooting*, 2001, Courtesy Galerie mezzanin, Wien; Produktionsaufnahmen: Marlene Haring

p.151: Anna Jermolaewa (portrait)

p.154: Video still: Isaac Julien, *Love*, 2003, Courtesy Isaac Julien

p.159: Video still: Isaac Julien, *Encore II: (Radioactive)*, 2004, Courtesy Isaac Julien / Victoria Miro Gallery

p.160: Video still: Kimsooja, *A Laundry Woman*, 2000; Photo: Monica Narula

p.164: Installation view, Kunsthalle Wien project space 2002: Kimsooja, *A Laundry Woman*; Photo: Christian Wachter

p.167: Kimsooja (portrait); Photo: Christian Wachter

p.171: Installation view, Kunsthalle Wien project space 2002: Kimsooja, *A Laundry Woman*; Photo: Christian Wachter

p.172: Elke Krystufek, *Migros Collagen*, 1999, Courtesy Elke Krystufek / Georg Kargl, Wien

p.176: Elke Krystufek, *Migros Collagen*, 1999, Courtesy Elke Krystufek / Georg Kargl, Wien

p.181: Installation view, Kunsthalle Wien 2000: Elke Krystufek, *Lebt und arbeitet in Wien*; Photo: Margherita Spilluttini

p.182: Installation view, Kunsthalle Wien 2005: Surasi Kusolwong, *If A Lion Could Talk*; Photo: Ellie Wyckoff

p.183: Kunsthalle Wien 2005: Surasi Kusolwong, *If A Lion Could Talk*; Photo: Ellie Wyckoff

p.186: Installation view, Kunsthalle Wien 2005: Surasi Kusolwong, *1 Euro Market*; Photo: Christian Wachter

p.189: Surasi Kusolwong, *Emotional Machine (VW with Fahlström)*, 2001- 2004, Courtesy Rooseum Center of Contemporary Art, Malmö; Photo: Vegar Moen

p.192: Sigalit Landau, *Barbed Hula*, 2000, Courtesy Sigalit Landau

p.195: Sigalit Landau, *Passion Victim, the Peacock*, 2003, Courtesy Galerie Frank, Paris

p.196: Sigalit Landau, *Passion Victim, the Peacock*, 2003, Courtesy Galerie Frank, Paris

p.198: Installation view, Kunsthalle Wien project space 2005: *Michael Lin;* Photo: Christian Wachter, © Kunsthalle Wien, 2005

p.201: Installation view 2003: Michael Lin, *Palais des Beaux- Arts*; Photo: Michael Lin

p.204: Michael Lin (portrait), © Kunsthalle Wien 2005; Photo: Ellie Wyckoff

p.206: Michèle Magema, *Mes petits rituels*, 2003

p.211: Video still: Michèle Magema, *La Porte*, 2001

p.212: Installation view, Kunsthalle Wien project space 2003: Teresa Margolles, *Das Leichentuch*, 2002; Photo: Christian Wachter

p.215: Teresa Margolles (portrait); Photo: Christian Wachter 2003

p.217: Teresa Margolles, *Vaporización*, 2002, Courtesy Galeria Enrique Guerreo, Mexico City / Galerie Peter Kilchmann, Zürich

Colophon

INTERVIEWS
Editor: Gerald Matt / Kunsthalle Wien
Project Manager: Angela Stief
Editing: Angela Stief, Lucas Gehrmann, Sigrid Mittersteiner
Proof-reading (English): Harold Otto
Proof-reading (German): Theresa Haigermoser
Translation: Tom Appleton, Erika Doucette, Elisabeth Frank-Großebner, Christoph Hollender, Hui Chang, Kimi Lum, Heidemarie Markhardt, Justin Morris, Jonathan Quinn, Nick Somers, Nelson Wattie, Jennifer Wen Ma, Christoph Winder
Intern: Anna Schwarzenberger, Michael Miess
Grafic design: Dieter Auracher
Print: Holzhausen

© for the texts with the authors
© for the images see credits, VBK Wien 2007
© for the book KUNSTHALLE Wien, 2007

Verlag der Buchhandlung Walther König, Köln
Ehrenstr. 4, 50672 Köln
Tel. +49 (0) 221 / 20 59 6-53
Email: verlag@buchhandlung-walther-koenig.de

Die Deutsche Bibliothek – CIP-Einheitsaufnahme
Ein Titelsatz für diese Publikation ist bei
Der Deutschen Bibliothek erhältlich

Printed in Austria

Switzerland
AVA, Verlagsauslieferungen AG
Centralweg 16, Postfach 27,
CH-8910 Affoltern a.A.
TEL. +41 (0) 1 762 42 00
FAX +41 (0) 1 762 42 10
a.koll@ava.ch

UK & Eire
Cornerhouse Publications
70 Oxford Street
GB-Manchester M1 5NH
FON +44 (0) 161 200 15 03
FAX +44 (0) 161 200 15 04
publications@cornerhouse.org

Outside Europe
D.A.P. / Distributed Art Publishers, Inc.
155 6th Avenue, 2nd Floor
New York, NY 10013
Tel: 212-627-1999
Fax: 212-627-9484
www.artbook.com

ISBN 10: 3-86560-188-X
ISBN 13: 978-3-86560-188-9

In case that the Kunsthalle Wien has not been able to contact all copyright holders despite strenuous efforts to do so, claims will be happily settled upon request.

Kunsthalle Wien is the institution of the City of Vienna devoted to modern and contemporary art and is supported by the Departement for Cultural Affairs MA7.

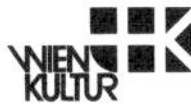

Director: Gerald Matt
Personal assistant curator to the director: Angela Stief
General Manager: Bettina Leidl
Head of Exhibitions: Sabine Folie